Grassroots Unity
in the Charismatic Renewal

Grassroots Unity
in the Charismatic Renewal

Connie Ho Yan Au

WIPF & STOCK · Eugene, Oregon

Dedicated to the late Fr. Michael C. Harper, with heartfelt gratitude

Contents

List of Illustration and Table ix
Foreword xi
Acknowledgments xiii
Abbreviations xv

Introduction 1

1   The History of the Fountain Trust 19

2   The Five International Conferences 57

3   The Grassroots Unity of the Five International Conferences 98

4   An Analysis of the Grassroots Unity at the Five
      International Conferences 141

5   In Search of Complementarity in the Charismatic Context 183

6   Complementarity, Convergence and Continuity 223

Conclusion 247
*Appendix: Numbers of Non-British Attendants
      of the International Conferences 251*
Bibliography 253
Subject/Name Index 277

List of Illustration and Table

Growth of Fountain Trust's publication
and expenditures in 1971–72 page 31

Ecumenical Stream page 258

Foreword

It is with great pleasure that I write the Foreword to this book written by Dr Connie Ho Yan Au. I first met Dr Au when I came for interview for my current post at the University of Birmingham and then when I was appointed she was assigned to me to supervise. Although I had successfully supervised other research students at the University of Wales, Lampeter, Dr Au was my first doctoral student to complete at Birmingham. I am delighted that Wipf and Stock have decided to publisher her doctoral thesis, which makes an original contribution to knowledge in at least three important ways.

First, there are not that many research projects that have considered the nature of the British Charismatic Renewal movement at the level of detail found in this book. Dr Au spent many long hours visiting archives and unearthing new material in order to understand the nature of the movement from the inside, so to speak. She personally became acquainted with many of the figures associated with the early days of the movement, including becoming very fond of Michael Harper, who sadly passed away in 2010. Therefore, oral history informs and supports written and audio sources. She took seriously the need to ground theological reflection in the testimonies of the key figures in the movement as well as the historical documents. Together they form an important witness to the events and understandings of the past.

Second, this is the very first detailed analysis of the Fountain Trust international conferences. In most of the discussions of the British Charismatic Renewal movement, they are often mentioned in passing. At last, in this book we have a clear and detailed analysis of these five conferences and their significance not only for Charismatic Renewal but also for ecumenism. The connection between these two features is important and needs to be more fully appreciated. Dr Au's work enables us to understand this connection in much greater depth than ever before. This unique contribution to scholarship cannot be underestimated.

Third, Dr Au ably moves the discussion from analysis of the grass-roots unity so evident in the movement and demonstrated in the conferences to a proper theological analysis and proposal based on a recovery of pneumatology for ecumenical theology. In other words, this is not just a historical discussion but also a constructive theological proposal. She argues for an approach to ecumenical theology that takes seriously the grassroots nature of theological convergence and uses this to articulate a model for Pentecostal and Charismatic engagement with other Christian traditions. It may surprise some readers that her main sources for this reflection are Roman Catholic (especially Vatican II, Dulles, Küng, Rahner, and Suenens), and initially this came as a surprise to Dr Au, but given the nature of the grassroots experience of unity between Protestant and Roman Catholic participants it became a natural research development. Of course, this discussion is also placed within a broader ecumenical and theological conversation, which is also fitting given the book's thesis. Complementarity (institution and charism, Christology and Pneumatology), convergence (of different ecumenical streams), and continuity (with modern ecumenical history) are key features of the proposal and together suggest a way of not only understanding the past but also envisioning future ecumenical engagement.

This book makes a significant contribution to both Pentecostal and Charismatic theology and ecumenical theology. Dr Au is someone who is passionate about the unity of the Christian church, as well as being someone who is committed to Pentecostal and Charismatic studies. I regard this study as a gift both to the cause of ecumenism and to the cause of academic theology. It is hoped that it will be understood and appreciated for what it represents as well as its visionary quality. Now, I hope that Dr Au is working on her next book, and I look forward to reading it with the greatest of interest. May the Lord of the one, holy, catholic and apostolic Church bless her richly in the years to come!

Mark J. Cartledge
University of Birmingham
27 September 2010

Acknowledgments

THIS STUDY ON GRASSROOTS unity in the charismatic renewal started in 2004 when I was doing the doctoral programme in Pentecostal and Charismatic Studies at the University of Birmingham, UK. I am indebted to my first supervisor, Prof. Allan Anderson, for kindling my interest in the British charismatic renewal and drawing my attention to its ecumenical significance in the 1970s. My research was then supervised by Dr. Mark Cartledge, who had been working on the theology of the British charismatic renewal at that time. His critical theological thinking and personal concerns as an Anglican Charismatic stimulated my thoughts. Both Prof. Anderson and Dr. Cartledge were my academic and spiritual mentors during the five years in Birmingham. Their impact on my life is immeasurable.

The historical section was developed with the materials collected from the Donald Gee Centre, Mattersey and St. John's College, Nottingham. I am grateful for the assistance of the archivists there. Supplementary information was provided by Mr. Bob Balkam, who was one of the founders of the Roman Catholic National Service Committee, through email communications, and interviews with Revd. David MacInnes, Revd. Tom Walker, and Revd. Tom Smail, who were prominent charismatic leaders in the 1970s. Their personal observations, experience and discerning comments about the renewal were very helpful in constructing the historical context, which demonstrates the dedicated involvement of both the Protestant and Roman Catholic charismatics. I am most indebted to Fr. Michael and Jeanne Harper. Their welcoming hospitality, warm sharing of their charismatic experiences and generous offer of materials from the personal archive not only enriched my knowledge about the renewal, but also demonstrated their loving kindness nourished by the constant outpouring of the Spirit in their lives. In January 2010, Fr. Michael peacefully fell asleep to be with the Lord.

As he enjoys the supreme happiness in heaven, his contribution to the renewal history of Britain will continue to be a living memory on earth.

The support offered by my parents, Mr. Siu Ling Au and Mrs. Mei Fong Tsui, will never be forgotten. Their industrious hard work and self-sacrificing heart transformed my dream of studying in England into reality. Their gracious support for me studying theology despite their faith in Chinese folk religion amazed fellow colleagues and Christian friends.

Abbreviations

AG	Assemblies of God
AJPS	*Asia Journal of Pentecostal Studies*
BCC	British Council of Churches
CEN	*The Church of England Newspaper*
CMS	Church Missionary Society
CT	*Christianity Today*
ER	*The Ecumenical Review*
ET	*Ecumenical Trends*
FGBMFI	Full Gospel Businessmen's Fellowship International
FTACM	Fountain Trust Advisory Council Meeting
FTAM	Fountain Trust Advisors Meeting
FTCCM	Fountain Trust Consultative Council Meeting
Pneuma	*Pneuma: The Journal of the Society for Pentecostal Studies*
JEPTA	*The Journal of the European Pentecostal Theological Association*
JES	*Journal of Ecumenical Studies*
JPT	*Journal of Pentecostal Theology*
MR	*Modern Reformation*
OIC	*One in Christ*
RCNSC	Roman Catholic National Service Committee
SJT	*Scottish Journal of Theology*
SL	*Studia Liturgica*
TS	*Theological Studies*
WCC	World Council of Churches

Introduction

WHEN THE SPIRIT RENEWS the church, the vision for ecumenical unity follows. The Holiness Movement claimed that division was the consequence of sin and denominationalism was identified as "slavery" by one of the leaders of the Church of Christ (Holiness), C. P. Jones. Being imbued with the thoughts of the Holiness Movement, William Seymour also objected to denominationalism and endeavored to restore unity among Christians so that the gospel could be effectively expressed to non-Christians.[1] This stream of renewal, accompanied by the desire for unity, continued till the charismatic renewal in the 1950s to 1970s when the Spirit renewed the church worldwide. A sense of unity was generated through the sharing of the divine experiences in the Spirit which washed away denominational barriers at the grassroots level.

DEFINITION OF GRASSROOTS UNITY[2]

Grassroots unity is defined as unity realized at the local level. "Grassroots" implies that something develops deep down in the soil and therefore it is fundamental and basic. It contrasts with the way of pursuing unity based on theological and ecclesiological common ground among denominations, such as was developed by the Faith and Order Movement. Some theologians and ecumenists assert the importance of unity that begins and grows from the grassroots level. Hans Küng and Jürgen Moltmann claim, "This new ecumenical practice at [the] grass-roots level gives us cause for great hope." It "is not just the point of departure but the aim of *all ecumenical endeavour*. For it is only here that an ecumenical project can be transformed into ecumenical reality."[3] Hans W. Gensichen also declares, "'Ecumenicity at the grass roots' should never be neglected."[4] In

---

1. Irvin, "Drawing," 35–37.
2. Au, "Charismatic," 191–99.
3. Küng and Moltmann, "Editorial: Towards," x–xi.
4. Gensichen, *Elements of Ecumenism*, 14.

1

the booklet concerning Anglican and Methodist reunion, Hertly Price and Gordon S. Wakefield affirm that "real unity can be achieved only 'at the grass roots'—not by the enactments of remote assemblies, but by the love of neighbours."[5] Some ecumenists stress the importance of grassroots unity in the light of the inadequacy of the mainstream ecumenical movement which has relied heavily on theological dialogues at the official level. For instance, a Roman Catholic scholar, John A. Radano, asserts, "Unity cannot simply be forced upon divided Christians from above."[6] An Orthodox scholar voices the need for an alternative ecumenism which "will manifest a new 'coming together' through the encounter of men of any and every tradition and confession" instead of ecumenical agreements through dialogue.[7] Even the founder of the World Council of Churches (WCC), W. A. Visser't Hooft, also acknowledged that the weakness of the ecumenical movement was that it had been isolated from the local churches. He depicted the ecumenical scenario as "too much an army with many generals and officers, but with too few soldiers." He was very much aware of the significance of the mobilization of local churches for the ecumenical movement.[8]

Distinctive Features of Grassroots Unity

Compared to unity based on faith and order, the foundation of grassroots unity is people centered, with doctrinal agreements coming second. The contrasts between them are mainly in the area of the experiential/cerebral, and the affective/cognitive and at the local/official level. In grassroots unity, experience plays an important role, while in ecumenical dialogue doctrinal problems are the locus of discussion. The shared experience of local churches may come from worship, ministries, evangelization, or intercommunion. They become the source of the sense of togetherness and solidarity and therefore grassroots unity tends to be affective. Biblically, the sort of unity that Jesus prays for is affective. It is based on the love between the Father and the Son (John 17:24) and this love is extended to the believers, "that they may be perfected in unity, so that the world may know that You sent Me, and loved them, even

---

5. Price and Wakefield, *Unity at the Local Level*, 1.

6. Radano, "Response," 658.

7. Quoted in Harper, *Tip-toeing*, 8.

8. Visser't Hooft, "General," 26.

as You have loved Me" (John 17:23). Hence, love is the foundation of unity: within the Trinity, among believers, and between God and believers. In contrast, ecumenical dialogue is largely cognitive in orientation. This methodology is to explain doctrines of different denominations, investigate the different traditions, and negotiate an attempted doctrinal agreement in order to eliminate division. A pursuit of common experience is not perceived as being as ecumenically promising as doctrinal consensus.

Since ecumenical dialogue requires an excessive amount of theological knowledge, it only involves theological and ecclesiological elites who hold the authority of churches or the knowledge of church history and dogmas. Therefore, dialogue is an ecumenical activity conducted at the top level, or the official level, of the well-trained and well-educated in theology. The people involved in the dialogue are only a small proportion of the denominations they represent, but they define the meaning of unity, decide the methodology and determine whether it can be realized. In contrast, grassroots unity starts from the local level and involves a group of enthusiasts, or even the whole church. Every single member of the church, regardless of his or her educational background, theological knowledge, spiritual experience, gender, age, class, or race, can take part in actualizing and maintaining the unity as long as they acknowledge the necessity of a united church. Grassroots unity is not only about spreading the ecumenical vision in the congregation, but also about enabling each member to contribute to it. Unity is for, and achieved by everybody belonging to the universal church; it is not just for the ecumenical experts. As Piet Fransen reminds us, "theologians who specialize in ecumenical work and thought easily forget that real unity can only be brought about and established by the ordinary members of the Churches. They in their turn have to be prepared for it."[9]

Fransen expressed this view in the 1970s. However, the WCC just officially discussed it at its Ninth Assembly in Porto Alegre, Brazil in February 2006. One of the moderators enumerated the problems associated with institutional ecumenism in the last ten years, which have dominated the whole movement. Firstly, it has not adequately raised the awareness of ecumenism among churches but has begun "to generate indifference and even alienation." Secondly, it was not shared by the whole Christian population but was dominated by a group of ecu-

---

9. Fransen, "Intercommunion," 32.

menists. Thirdly, it was not only institutional but also became foreign to churches. In the light of these problems, the moderator believes that grassroots ecumenism is the way out from the dead end it has reached. It transforms the nature of the movement from being institutional to being "people-centered" and stresses that it should connect to life.

> Grassroots ecumenism is gaining more attraction in many regions. In fact, ecumenism is not something to be imported from the outside or developed on an institution-centred basis; rather, it must emanate from the very life of people and be owned by the people. It must touch the life of people in all its layers and dimensions. As a consequence of people-centred ecumenism, a life-centred vision of ecumenism is emerging as a feasible paradigm.[10]

Model 1: Official Ecumenical Experiments in the Local Churches

The first model is the implementation of ecumenical experiments and projects in local churches. This sort of grassroots unity involves both the laity and officials. The officials design ecumenical plans using their theological knowledge and monitor the process of implementation using their administrative training and resources. The purpose is to bring unity among denominations of a particular local area. For example, in 1967, the British Council of Churches and the Conference of British Missionary Societies organized an ecumenical study program called "The People Next Door" for churches in the whole country. It had a twofold purpose: to make known the current experiments in the ecumenical movement in local churches and "to test the relevance of the ecumenical insights in the local church situation."[11] Barry Till regarded it as "the most ambitious scheme undertaken to arouse the interest of the laity in matters ecumenical."[12] The Council also published a booklet, *Adventures in Unity: An Introduction of Ecumenical Experiment, Shared Churches and Other United Ventures in the Local Church*[13] to introduce local ecumenical projects such as sharing of church buildings,[14] "inter-

---

10. World Council of Churches, *Document No. A01.*

11. Till, *Churches Search*, 2, 463.

12. Ibid., 467.

13. Blatherwick, *Adventures in Unity.*

14. The Baptist Union, the Churches of Christ (Disciples), the Church of England, the Methodist Church, Roman Catholic Church, and the United Reformed Church registered as users of the Sharing of Church Buildings Act. Blatherwick, *Adventures in Unity*, 2.)

denominational team of ministries," and local ecumenical experiments in England in 1973–74.[15] The booklet lists forty-six areas in England where these churches were involved in these ecumenical projects.[16] Moreover, education is also a means of grassroots unity. Protestants study in Roman Catholic schools or vice versa, and thus they participate in the liturgical forms which are different from those they have in their own traditions. Some ecumenical educators raise the awareness among students by organizing visits to churches or holding ecumenical discussions.[17] Although these sorts of ecumenical activities at the grassroots level are not always recorded in church reports, they are significant for increasing the sense of unity among local churches. As Michael Horton observes, grassroots unity "is already evident practically everywhere."[18] When the ecumenical movement has been losing momentum since the 1970s and what is left currently is just a "winter of ecumenism,"[19] grassroots unity reminds us that "it is not that the ecumenical movement has disappeared. It is only that we may have been looking for it in the wrong places all this time."[20]

In fact, unity in the early church was also a kind of grassroots unity administered by officials. Since the apostles founded many local churches and they governed themselves, inevitably there were differences among them in liturgy, ecclesiological structure, and theology. However, through the communication among bishops, Christians of different areas were connected. Norbert Brox finds that by means of correspondence, bishops expressed their opinions, encouragements, exhortations, and reported updated news of their churches in order to connect with one another spiritually in the same faith.[21] The receiving churches read the letters out in front of the congregation for the sake of maintaining the fellowship. To a large extent, the grassroots unity of the early church was sustained by official communication to the people. However, without ecumenical experience and affection for their brothers and sisters, the official effort for unity would be in vain.

---

15. Blatherwick, *Adventures in Unity*, 1.

16. Ibid., 6–12.

17. Marthaler, "Grassroots," 66–67.

18. Horton, "Can."

19. Evans, *Methods in Ecumenical Theology*, 1.

20. Brown, "Ecumenism," 88.

21. Brox, *History of the Early Church*, 70.

Model 2: The Holy Spirit-Initiated Unity in the Charismatic Renewal

The second model of grassroots unity is perceived to be the directly-inspired work of the Holy Spirit at the local level in the charismatic renewal. The renewal was grassroots *per se* due to its foundation with people who experienced the Spirit personally and collectively. It was both a subjective and objective event and so it was not only a renewal for individuals but also for the whole church. Based on his renewal ministry across the country for ten years, Michael Harper affirmed this grassroots nature in the 1970s by saying, "The Holy Spirit is renewing and reviving our beloved churches at the grass roots."[22] Smail addressed this nature of the renewal at a conference of the Fountain Trust during the same period. He claimed that the charismatic renewal was not designed by officials and pushed down to the laity; rather the Holy Spirit had "started at the bottom and worked towards the top." It had been "a matter of ordinary people" at the grassroots level.[23]

The charismatic renewal was not only grassroots in nature, but it was also intrinsically an ecumenical stream. Peter Hocken identifies the renewal as "of its nature an ecumenical grace of God."[24] Kilian McDonnell asserts, "It was de facto ecumenical from the beginning and did not decide to become ecumenical at some later date."[25] Since the charismatic renewal was developed from the grassroots level, it is logical to say that the unity that it nurtured was also from the grassroots. This grassroots unity was particularly significant since it brought Protestants and Roman Catholics together. Hence Kevin Ranaghan regards this unity as "the largest grassroots ecumenical movement that Christianity has known for 450 years."[26] Hocken says, "It is the first time that Catholics and Protestants at grass roots level have truly experienced God's action together, thereby recognized that their basic unity in Christ is more important than the divisions between them."[27] The WCC also regards the charismatic renewal as "a major ecumenical development of our day" and identify their responsibility to "discern grass-roots ecumenical de-

---

22. Letter from Harper to Coggan, 17 May 1974.

23. Smail, *Doing*.

24. Hocken, "Charismatic," 320.

25. McDonnell, "Church," 3.

26. Quoted in Smail, "Editorial: More We Are Together . . . ," 2.

27. Hocken, "Charismatic," 312.

velopment of worldwide significance."[28] Since the charismatic renewal was ecumenical by nature, this grassroots unity was not a by-product, but the primary product. The renewal of worship, community and evangelization pointed to the purpose of the unity of churches.

The major force of the grassroots unity in the charismatic renewal is attributed to the Holy Spirit instead of to church officials and ecumenical theologians. Through bestowing common experiences, the Holy Spirit nurtures affection in people's hearts, which becomes the motivation for accepting one another as Christian. He intervenes directly in the long-term division and produces a sense of love among people despite the doctrinal and ecclesiastical disagreements. However, he does not instantaneously erase all the problems; rather, he brings Christians back to the fundamental common denominator of the same faith in Christ who is "the shared centre of our faith and love."[29] This was the reason for the communion of the early church, despite the plurality of practice and understanding of the faith. Charles Farah regards the ecumenical power of the Spirit as having "the force of a hurricane," which "has created an atmosphere of trust and joy among Christians not present since the days of the apostles."[30] With the ecumenical development grounded in people, and with experience from which affection is nurtured, the charismatic renewal can be regarded as a grassroots ecumenical movement leading Christians to confess the same Lord Jesus Christ and opening more opportunities for theological dialogue to deal with the doctrinal differences. Although scholars affirm the significance of grassroots unity, we also need theological agreement at the official level. Ecumenists of the grassroots and official level should not mutually discard one another but work together for future unity.

OBJECTIVE AND DIVISION OF CHAPTERS

This book studies the nature of grassroots unity within the British charismatic renewal of the 1970s and its significance for ecumenism. It argues that the unity in this movement made an important contribution to ecumenism by means of the complementarity of institution and charisms, and Christology and Pneumatology. The historical events

28. World Council of Churches, "Statement," 283.

29. Smail, "Editorial: More We Are Together . . . ," 2.

30. Farah, "Towards," 25.

of the five international conferences of the Fountain Trust are used as a basis to discuss the grassroots unity nurtured by the functioning of charisms. The first three chapters will establish the historical context of the British charismatic renewal and the grassroots unity found within it. Chapter 1 will discuss the background of the British charismatic renewal and the history of the Fountain Trust. Chapter 2 will provide historical facts about the international conferences such as speakers, participants, venues, programs, feedback from delegates, and their impact on the churches in Britain and overseas. Chapter 3 will focus on the conferences' ecumenical significance. Chapter 4 provides both historical facts and theological analysis to investigate the grassroots unity at the conferences based on two activities: worship in general and the celebration of the Eucharist. Chapter 5 will search for complementarities of institution and charisms, and Christology and Pneumatology. Chapter 6 will discuss the complementarity of ecumenical institutions and the charismatic renewal, the convergence of ecumenical streams and the continuity in modern ecumenical history. It finally suggests that the implication of the charismatic renewal for the ecumenical future lies in its legacy of hope which brings about an eschatological continuity for the ecumenical movement.

METHODOLOGY

This research applies both history and theology, with theological themes emerging from historical sources. The scene and narrative of the five international conferences in chapters one to four were established by the written and audio materials collected from the archives of the Donald Gee Centre at the Mattersey Hall, St. John's College, Nottingham, and Michael Harper's personal collection. The archival materials are supplemented by oral historical accounts acquired from interviews with charismatic leaders including Michael Harper, Tom Smail, Tom Walker, and David MacInnes. These leaders provided life stories and personal opinions concerning positive and negative ecumenical experiences, the organizational process of the conferences, and the background of the charismatic renewal in Britain. It is also used to corroborate the accuracy of the written materials, particularly concerning some controversial issues.

Since this book aims to discuss the ecumenical nature of the charismatic renewal, it is essential to understand the general history of the ecumenical movement, the World Council of Churches, Vatican II, and the establishment of their theological thinking before discerning how the charismatic renewal can fit into the ecumenical history with the concepts of complementarity, convergence, and continuity. Reports from the major ecumenical conferences, including the first and the second Faith and Order conferences in Lausanne (1927) and Edinburgh (1937), the WCC assemblies, the Pentecostal and Roman Catholic dialogues, and the documents and commentaries of Vatican II are consulted in this book.

The theological discussion is primarily focused on the complementarity of institution and charisms, and Christology and Pneumatology in the church and church unity in chapter 5. The reason for setting out arguments on these two complementarities is because ecclesiology and ecumenism have been institutionally and christologically oriented. However, charismatic renewal, with its vivid manifestation of the Holy Spirit, reminds the church of the charismatic and pneumatological elements in the constitution of the church, and hence it is regarded as a major contribution of the renewal. The complementary of institution and charisms is discussed from the perspectives of ecclesiology and Pneumatology with two dialogue partners' theories and that include Karl Rahner's open/closed system and Léon Joseph Cardinal Suenens's theories. These theologians are chosen because in their understandings of the role of the Holy Spirit in the church, they hold a good balance in their views between institution and charisms as they notice the danger of overemphasizing either of them in the church and its life. Moreover, they both raised the awareness of Pneumatology at the Vatican II, and the Cardinal himself was sympathetic to the charismatic renewal. Hence their theories are helpful to the discussion on how the charismatic renewal contributed to the complementarity of institution and charisms.

For the definitions of institution and charisms it is important to apply the theories of the traditional churches, especially the Roman Catholic Church, alongside the charismatic understandings. The reason for this is that it will help to explain the context of the charismatic renewal, which brought about a grassroots unity between Protestants and Roman Catholics. Avery Dulles's definition of institution is applied in this research as it does not just refer institution to a sociological organization, but it is also constituted by doctrinal, liturgical, and legalistic systems. Hans Küng's interpretation on charisms is adopted as he proposes four general features that explain both supernatural and natural charisms: that they are everyday phenomena, diversified, universally distributed, and still available nowadays.

The Holy Spirit as a Paraclete is used as an analogy to develop the Pneumatology of this research and it will be analyzed in the Johannine account on the Holy Spirit in the "farewell discourse." (John 14–16) This text clearly shows the multi-facetted role of the Holy Spirit in the life of the Church, that he is a revealer, teacher, and reminder of truth. Our understanding of these roles will be expanded through applying a Pauline concept of charisms in chapter 5. Moreover, the indwelling of the Holy Spirit in the church implies the complementarity of charisms and institution, that the Spirit, the giver of gifts, needs a physical institute to work within and the physical institute needs the Spirit to revitalise it.

For the complementarity of institution and charisms in ecumenism, the concept of visible unity is adopted to the discussion. The major argument in this section is that because of the tangible manifestation of charisms, the dichotomy of spiritual/institutional unity, which refers to invisibility/visibility, should be challenged. The charismatic renewal shows that charisms such as healing, prophecy, tongues, etc. are spiritual but also tangible. Hence the dichotomy should be redefined as spiritual visible unity/institutional visible unity. Conciliar fellowship is proposed as an ideal model to realise the complementarity between institution and charisms, between official and grassroots unity. It allows the co-existence of uniformity and diversity, interaction between council and local churches, and finally the cooperation between humanity and the Spirit.

In order to contextualize the complementarity of Christology and Pneumatology, I explain two traditional theological concepts: (1) St Irenaeus of Lyons's two hands of the Father, and (2) *perichoresis* in immanent and economic Trinity. Ecclesiologically, the charismatic renewal contributes to this complementarity by bringing about the simultaneous existence of *Spiriti praesens* and *Christus praesens* in the use of charisms, which reflect Jesus' work and words in the present. Ecumenically, I adopt Aloysius Pieris' model to illustrate this complementarity. There are three levels in this model: primordial experience which is pneumatological, collective memory, which is christological, and interpretation, which is ecclesial. This model itself not only represents the complementarity of Christology and Pneumatology, but also shows that both spiritual experience and ecclesial institution are necessary for ecumenism. Hence it can suitably explain how this complementarity can be realized in the charismatic renewal.

Besides the major theological discussion on the two kinds of complementarity, this book is also concerned with the theological implications of worship, the Eucharist, and the ecumenical future in the charismatic renewal. Liturgical studies are used to discuss charismatic worship and the Eucharist. Concerning charismatic worship, the first question to answer is how charismatic worship, with the features of the vivid manifestations of charisms, and spontaneity, nurtured grassroots unity, as described in the context of the Fountain Trust's conferences. Charisms characterize diversity, divine presence, and declericalization; thus enabling charismatics to serve one another, experience the presence of God together, and share priesthood at the grassroots level. They blur the boundary between clergy and laity in terms of the ministerial involvement during worship and subsequently a sense of unity grows through mutual ministry at the grassroots level. Spontaneity brings about unity because it nurtures the oneness between spirit and body within oneself, with others, and with the divine being.

Based on the experiential character of charismatic worship, the second question is how to interpret the relationship between experience and theology or beliefs in charismatic worship, which subsequently leads to grassroots unity. The ancient Latin tag, *lex orandi, lex credendi*, and its original form, *ut legem credendi lex statuat supplicandi*, are used to answer this question as it concisely highlights the intimate relationship between worship and theology. The charismatic renewal began and grew from experience through prayer and worship, rather than theology. It was charismatic experience that gave birth to theological understandings, not the other way around. It was common experience that led to common understandings and hence a sense of unity grew.

Concerning the Eucharist, the liturgical terms of epiclesis and anamnesis are adopted to analyze the theological implications of charisms and the Eucharist with a special focus on their spiritual commonalities. These two concepts are useful for this analysis as they both contain pneumatological associations. Anamnesis refers to the Holy Spirit who reminds communion participants of the crucifixion and resurrection of Jesus. Epiclesis is a prayer invoking for the presence of the Holy Spirit in the bread, wine, and participants. These two pneumatological meanings, remembrance, and the presence of the Spirit in the Eucharist, also occur in charisms. Furthermore, this book also suggests that they both share similar eschatological and ecumenical implications. Eschatologically, they both attain the absence-presence paradox as they will cease to exist when the eschaton comes. Hence their presence in the present implies their absence in the future. Ecumenically, they both have another paradox of "one-manyness" since the fragments of the bread and the diversity of charisms both symbolically represent the one body of Christ. By discussing these four commonalities, both charisms and Eucharist are means of grace and signs of unity.

Concerning the ecumenical future, eschatology is the perspective used to discuss the hope ushered in through the charismatic renewal. Jürgen Moltmann's eschatology in his *Theology of Hope* makes it a suitable text with which to interact in order to investigate this subject. His eschatology is not just about the end time of the world and the *parousia*, but also about the present day and the foreseeable future. And the hope that he is concerned with not only looks forward to the new heaven and the new earth but also occurs in the world today. This eschatological understanding is more encouraging and optimistic for the ecumenical future. It also resonates with the nature of the charismatic renewal that God's wonderful works do not just take place in the *parousia*, but also in the present, and therefore Christians can always hope for God's gracious and powerful intervention.

DEFINITION OF KEY TERMS

Charismatic Renewal

The emphasis of the charismatic renewal has varied. In the 1960s and 1970s it could be defined by the physical and spiritual, and inner and outer manifestations, namely, baptism in the Spirit and gifts from the Holy Spirit. When it continued in the 1980s, the focus was directed to power and church growth under John Wimber's evangelical campaign and his Vineyard Church worldwide. In the 1990s, the Toronto Blessing associated with accounts of animal noises, slaying in the Spirit, and other ecstatic activities, was found to be controversial among charismatics. Commenting on these phenomena, Harper said that "it is much harder to see what it is today, the signals are more confusing."[31] Hence it is important to note that the charismatic renewal that this book refers to

31. Harper, "From Michael & Jeanne Harper," 12.

is the one in the 1960s and 1970s and it is in this context that grassroots unity is discussed.

The charismatic renewal in the 1960s and 1970s was launched by two groups of charismatics, those who remained in their denominational churches and those who were called restorationists, or radical charismatics, who rejected the idea of denominational and ecclesiastical structure as they regarded them as incompatible with the new outpouring of the Spirit. They justified this thought with Jesus' metaphor that new wine should not be poured into an old wine skin. Hence, for the fullness of renewal grace, charismatics should leave the denominational churches in order to "restore" the original nature of the church as in the New Testament period, which was not constituted by institution, but was formed as a community; it was not led by clergy, but apostles. Moreover, they also emphasized the restoration of the post-conversion experience, baptism in the Spirit, and the use of charisms. Andrew Walker distinguishes two groups of restorationists, which he labels as R1 and R2. The first group tends to be exclusive and authoritarian while the other one is more inclusive and flexible in relation to other churches. Although their action of leaving their own churches and starting new ones was criticized as divisive, they defended their actions by saying what they did could fulfill the vision of unity because the denominational barriers were abolished in the community and there was oneness in Christ.[32]

This book does not deal with the Restorationist groups, but only with those who remained in their denominational churches. There are three reasons for this. First, this book aims to argue that the charismatic renewal contributed to the complementarity of institution and charisms by the emphases of the Holy Spirit and charisms. The rationale behind this argument is that institution is still essential for the establishment and functioning of the church as well as for accomplishing church unity. Institution helps to maintain order, discipline, traditions, and the doctrinal teachings of the church; hence it should be used appropriately so that it can effectively complement the charismatic and experiential elements of the life of the church. Secondly, the five international conferences show that charismatics could still keep their denominational identities and yet experience unity together, and when Protestants and Roman Catholics were joined together by the common experiences in the charismatic renewal there were significant ecumenical implications. Thirdly, most of the churches still uphold the necessity of institution in the constitution of the

32. Kay, *Apostolic Networks in Britain*, 20, 23, 39.

church and so it is necessary to deal with the question of how institution complements charisms in the charismatic renewal.

On the other hand, it took time for the term "charismatic renewal" to be finalized and widely adopted. Each stage in developing the term suggests a transformation of people's understandings of the renewal in the 1960s and 1970s. Historically, in the Western literature, the charismatic renewal has been regarded as a movement originating in the US in the 1960s. Prominent leaders in the early stages such as Dennis Bennett, an Episcopal rector of St Mark's Church, Van Nuys, California,[33] and Larry Christenson, a Lutheran minister, had made a large impact in many parts of the world, including Britain. Phenomenologically, it was similar to the Pentecostal movement, characterized by the outpouring of the Holy Spirit and the spiritual gifts. Thus when the renewal started in the US in 1959–60, its adherents adopted some Pentecostal terms such as revival, awakening, and outpouring to describe their experience, and there was no need for alternatives, as Hocken records. Then the term, "Neo-Pentecostalism" was adopted for which Hocken gives two reasons: first, the realization that these spiritual experiences were occurring in many parts of the world, and were not localized; second, a feeling of the need to bring the experiences to their churches as a consequence of such a realization.[34] Because of this awareness, Hocken thinks that the word and concept of "renewal" was developed and that it gradually replaced the previous term. Especially in the article, "The New Pentecostalism," Russel Hitt, the editor of *Eternity*, recorded the refusal by two authors to use the term, "Neo-Pentecostalism," in an article published in *Trinity* and their adoption of the term "charismatic renewal."[35] In the 1970s, the term charismatic renewal/movement was widely used for the sake of making a clear distinction between the current movement itself and the Classical Pentecostalism so that mainline churches would find it easier to accept.[36]

Apart from drawing a distinction between themselves and the Pentecostals by using the term charismatic renewal/movement rather than Neo-Pentecostalism, another question arose as to whether the movement was a renewal or revival. In 1969, Harper claimed, "We need to recognize that the charismatic renewal is not in itself revival." His *raison d'être* was that the movement of that period was for the church—to

---

33. Scotland, *Charismatics and the New Millennium*, 15.

34. Hocken, "Pentecostal," 37.

35. Hocken, "Charismatic," 48; *Streams of Renewal*, 185.

36. Hocken, "Survey," 123.

renew its ministry, structure, worship, and other aspects, while revival, as used in the Pentecostal movement, was viewed as a movement for the world.[37] Hocken suggests that revival means "coming to life" while renewal is a "revitalization" for a life that has existed.[38] In addition, in terms of continuity, revival tends to be a here-and-now concept because its focus is on the dramatic works of God falling upon human beings. It does not so much consider the past, but more the present and future in terms of eschatological visions. In contrast, renewal attempts to relate the present to the past and emphasizes God's everlasting presence and works within the church. He provides three dichotomies to conclude his understanding of the differences between revival and renewal; they are: falling upon/stirring within, discontinuity/continuity, and radical new beginning/process and development. Although conceptually it will be contradictory to put revival and renewal together to investigate either the Pentecostal or charismatic movement, his articles tend to suggest this idea because those two phenomena are historically and theologically inter-related and complementary. The picture is not so clearly seen if only one or other of the concepts is adopted.[39]

Nevertheless, the term, "charismatic renewal," was used instead of "charismatic revival" by charismatics, and by the middle of the 1970s, this term was more popular than "charismatic movement." In 1975, Smail explained, "We find ourselves speaking less and less of a movement and more and more of a charismatic renewal. The first suggests something alongside and possibly in competition with the churches, whereas the second makes it much clearer that what we seek is a renewal of the church."[40] Smail's semantic distinction between the words "movement" and "renewal" suggests that the phenomenon itself can be viewed in an aggressive way (movement) or a contributive way (renewal). The Malines document also prefers the word "renewal" to "movement" which connotes human motivation and force.[41] Concurring with Smail's distinction and the preference of the Malines document, this book will adopt "charismatic renewal" to represent the phenomenon. This is also done for the sake of consistency to avoid confusion.

37. Robinson, "Charismatic Anglican," 167–68.
38. Hocken, "Pentecostal," 35, 41.
39. Hocken, "Revival," 49–52, 54.
40. Letter from Smail to David Popely, 10 January 1975.
41. Congar, *I Believe in the Holy Spirit Volume II*, 163.

Charisms

Charisms play an essential role in the charismatic renewal as well as in personal lives. Most charismatics claim that baptism in the Spirit brings not only a transformation of their spiritual or physical lives, but also the gift of the Spirit for ministry such as healing, prophecy, teaching, etc. and for personal edification such as tongue-speaking mentioned in the First Corinthians 12. Semantically the renewal was described with the adjective *charismatic* implying the importance of prominent and even "supernatural" spiritual gifts which are frequently used. The Greek word, "charismata," in its plural form, suggests the multiplicity of spiritual gifts and is adopted as the root of the English word, "charismatic."[42] Harper said, "What is distinctive about this movement, whatever it may be called, is that many Christians are actualizing the Spirit's power in their lives, and experiencing in a new way a greater use of charismatic gifts."[43] Smail also asserted the features of spiritual gifts and God's manifestation of his power in the movement. He believed that they should be part of the constitution of the church and that Christians should reacquire them. As he explained in a letter,

> When one reads the New Testament one will find . . . a great deal about the Holy Spirit coming into people's lives as an experienced reality, on the one hand imparting the love of Christ, but on the other imparting His power and His gifts which are meant for all His disciples. The charismatic movement is simply concerned to remind the Church that such experienced love and power is God's will and provision for it, into which Christians should be entering.[44]

Charisms are certainly indispensable in the charismatic renewal. Therefore, Hocken asserts, "Without an openness to the reception of, and practice of the spiritual gifts, it would not be charismatic renewal."[45]

The Roman Catholic Church also talks about charisms but the meaning is broader than the supernatural element that charismatics refer to. As is emphasized at Vatican II, whatever builds up the church is a charism. Hence, charisms can be regarded as ministries, either for

42. Scotland, *Charismatics and the New Millennium*, 10.

43. Letter from Director of Fountain Trust to Editor of the *Church of England Newspaper*, 1 July 1973.

44. Letter from Smail to D. Cameron, 16 July 1975.

45. Quoted by Scotland in *Charismatics and the New Millennium*, 38.

the church or the world and they are essential for the growth of the church both spiritually and numerically.[46] The distribution and the effective function of charisms depend chiefly on the action of the Holy Spirit but also on the extent to which people allow the Spirit to work within the church. Therefore, institution becomes an issue. However, in New Testament times, there was not such a sharp contrast between institution and charism as at the present day. Jesus appointed the Twelve to accompany him throughout his ministry on earth and after his resurrection and Pentecost, and they became founders of churches in various places.[47] For Paul, institutionally, the church is not only built up by the apostles, but also by prophets, evangelists, pastors, and teachers who were anointed by the Spirit. The Holy Spirit also distributed gifts to the faithful, to serve within and without the church. Hence, the early church was simply constituted by a communion of the faithful with the leadership of God's chosen ones.

46. McDonnell, "Communion," 692.
47. Congar, *I Believe in the Holy Spirit Vol. II*, 39.

1

The History of the Fountain Trust

A s THE FLAME OF renewal spread in many parts of Britain during the 1950s and 1960s, some charismatics saw the need to promote the renewal through an organization. This could gather human and financial resources and build up links among charismatic Christians, churches and organizations so that the renewal could reach out geographically more widely and spiritually more deeply. To achieve this, Fountain Trust was established in 1964 in Britain and its contribution to the renewal was highly valued. From then until it closed in 1980 it built up relationships with churches and engaged in self-reflection. During this time, when new directors were appointed, there were changes of emphasis and direction both for the Trust and the renewal. The Trust's closure meant the end of a chapter of the renewal history in Britain. This chapter aims to trace these changes, but we first need to examine the background of the British charismatic renewal from which the Trust was developed.

BACKGROUND OF THE CHARISMATIC RENEWAL IN BRITAIN

The British charismatic renewal developed in the 1960s. The church had been declining drastically since the Second World War, partly because the economy had been flourishing, and a counter-culture that challenged traditional moral values had been emerging in society. It was a time when materialism and new social ideas were highly valued, but the church was failing to communicate the gospel. The church was desperate for transformation and empowerment.

The Decline of the Church

Post-war Gloom

Following two world wars in the first half of the century, the church had experienced a deep gloom and spiritual weariness among both clergy and laity. Many Christian leaders, particularly in the Church of England, had been called to serve as chaplains on the front lines, leaving loyal but elderly members to administer the church and provide spiritual guidance.[1] Those chaplains understood the cruel nature of wars, but they still had to "bless the guns" or claim that God "is on our side."[2] Anglican leaders saw how irrelevant the church was becoming and the exhaustion of its clergy. As Archbishop Garbett wrote in his diary, "May 21, 1940—Convocation appalling dreary. We discussed exchanges of benefices, cremation, lay readers, etc. while the fate of the world is being fought out."[3] When the war ended in 1945, many churchgoers were still living under its shadow. Tom Walker recalls that some of his members still felt the guilt of having killed people during the fighting. A Jewish lady could not erase the memory of Auschwitz because of a surgical scar, which had replaced a prison number tattoo.[4] Some Christians had a critical reaction against the church and Christianity. Suffering and death provoked skepticism about the reality of a loving God. Many people gave up their faith and abandoned their church-going habits. As David MacInnes recalls, "The two world wars did an enormous amount of hatchet work on the church so that a lot of nominal Christianity was cut away because it had not got any reason for remaining."[5] The wars left people with a complex mixture of pain, guilt, sadness, and unforgiveness. Questions about suffering, the existence of God and the church were not easy to answer. Spiritual healing and a renewal of power were the only hope for the revitalizing churches and individual Christians.

Formalism

While the wars brought enormous physical, psychological, and spiritual trauma to society, the church, with its formalism and dryness, could

1. Walker, *Renew Us by Your Spirit*, 15.
2. Interview with MacInnes, 28 June 2006.
3. Quoted by Walker, *Renew Us by Your Spirit*, 15–16.
4. Walker, *Renew Us by Your Spirit*, 16.
5. Interview with MacInnes, 28 June 2006.

not comfort wounded hearts. The old liturgical forms and ecclesiastical structures were not compatible with the rapidly changing society. As Harper states, "Many are dissatisfied with the church structures which may have been adequate for the pre-industrial age."[6] Worship was still traditional and dull especially in the Church of England, which was to maintain its role as the Church of the Nation.[7] Since this approach was not meeting the real spiritual needs, people were disillusioned and just left the church.[8] Bishop Huddleston recognized the problem and asserted, "The world will only hear the language of the Church and of the Christian Gospel if it can come with a freshness, a stimulus, a shining sparkle."[9] Clearly there was an urgent need for a renewal both of the structures and worship for church growth.

However, some churches believed that theological formalism could be a way to deal with the decline. Walker noticed that preachers avoided conveying a message in a simple way but used complicated theological concepts. Consequently, although Christianity became less relevant to daily life and difficult to perceive, at least, people respected the theology.[10] This kind of teaching might stimulate their cerebral thinking about belief, but it might not necessarily lead the congregation to their personal God. It was only the coming of the charismatic renewal that began to challenge the ecclesiastical and theological formalism and bring renewed life to the Church and to individuals.

Billy Graham's Preparatory Work

In the gloom caused by the wars and the formalism of the church, Billy Graham's crusade in 1954 lit the hope for the church, which paved the way for the charismatic renewal. He preached every night for three months in the Harringay Arena, and thousands of people were converted. Subsequently many young people devoted themselves to ministry. The positive results of Graham's crusade reflected the ineffectiveness of the church in evangelism after the wars because these conversions and devotions were not brought about by churches but an evangelist from the US. At the same time, churches remained unchanged and were un-

6. Harper, *New Way of Living*, 45.

7. Walker, *Renew Us by Your Spirit*, 9.

8. Interview with MacInnes, 28 June 2006.

9. Quoted by the Bishop of Coventry, "Charge," 4.

10. Walker, *Renew Us by Your Spirit*, 17.

aware of the extent of the current decline. MacInnes commented that in the 1950s, only a few prophetic voices could be heard saying, "The country is still living on spiritual capital." There had been great revival in the eighteenth and nineteenth centuries, but at the beginning of the twentieth century there was only liberal theology "which had a tendency to undercut faith" rather than renewing it. He believed that Billy Graham did preparatory work for the charismatic renewal by bringing a number of converts to the church when it had been losing its members after the wars. Based on the foundation of the faith, in the 1960s, people sought for experiential elements in their belief and the charismatic renewal fulfilled the need.[11]

Drop in membership

Although Billy Graham's work added some converts in British churches, the general decline continued. The dominating trend was a severe drop in the membership of all denominations in Britain, which went on decade after decade. From 1957, there was a similar decline in the membership of the Church of Scotland which went on until the 1990s.[12] Easter Day attendance in the Church of England had dropped to a third of what it had been in 1961. Free churches like the Baptists could not avoid the problem either. Baptist minister Douglas McBain recalled that when he began his ministry in 1957, there were 327,000 Baptists in Britain; however, by 1976, the number had dropped to 181,000.[13] The number of Methodists also decreased from 727,000 in 1930 to 416,000 in 1990.[14] The Roman Catholic Church saw an increase in membership in the post-war period, but by the 1960s it had also started losing members for the first time since the eighteenth century. It was only the Black and Pentecostal churches that were not merely immune to this trend, but were actually growing.[15] David L. Edwards concludes that there were a third of church members left between 1960 and 1985. But it was also in the 1960s that the charismatic renewal began. McBain asserted that the renewal was essential for rescuing churches from a far more serious decline.[16] Harper

11. Interview with MacInnes, 28 June 2006

12. Machin, *Churches and Social Issues*, 178.

13. Fountain Trust, *Ecumenical Issues 1*; Machin, *Churches and Social Issues*, 178.

14. Edwards, *Concise History of English Christianity*, 158.

15. Fountain Trust, *Ecumenical Issues 1*; Machin, *Churches and Social Issues*, 211.

16. Edwards, *Concise History of English Christianity*, 148; Fountain Trust, *Ecumenical Issues 1*.

declared that the way for the church to solve its "bankruptcy" was the recovery of "pentecostal power."[17] British historian G. I. T. Machin claims that the charismatics, including members of house churches, "provided the main signs of renewal of Christians."[18]

Economic Boom, Spiritual Gloom

The charismatic renewal arose when the spiritual emptiness was deepened by the economic affluence that followed two world wars. Consumerism and materialism became the dominating ideologies during the 1950s and this continued in the 1960s. These two decades were marked by a "growth in popular prosperity" where "material comfort and physical enjoyment" became a priority in people's lives. Commodities such as cars, televisions, and travel, both locally and abroad, were now affordable.[19] Society was undergoing remarkable economic growth and the Prime Minister of the time was renowned for his declaration that "We've never had it so good."[20] The affluence went on into the 1970s and the Canon of Westminster, David L. Edwards commented that "obviously Britain still belongs to the rich minority of mankind. Indeed, it is probably true to say that the British people were as a whole more prosperous in the mid-1970s than in almost any previous period, even if it was prosperity substantially financed by foreign lenders."[21] The fact that "too many had too much in terms of material goods" produced a spiritual vacuum. Tangible goods were regarded as more worthy of pursuit than the invisible God. Going shopping and travelling at weekends were more enjoyable than attending services. In that era of materialism, Walker believes that the church unavoidably saw decline.[22] The *Reports to the General Assembly of the Church of Scotland* in 1955 comments, "more than ever in such a situation is it necessary for the Church to proclaim the teaching of Christ that 'a man's life consisteth not in the abundance of things which he possesses.'"[23] Charismatic renewal developed at a time when people's minds and spirits were filled up with their

17. Harper, *New Way of Living*, 49.
18. Machin, *Churches and Social Issues*, 213.
19. Machin, *Churches and Social Issues*, 143–44.
20. Walker, *Renew Us by Your Spirit*, 17; The Bishop of Coventry, "Charge," 4.
21. Edwards, *State of the Nation*, 18.
22. Walker, *Renew Us by Your Spirit*, 17.
23. Quoted by Machin, *Churches and Social Issues*, 144.

material possessions, when God seemed to be the last concern of their lives, and when secularization grew from the seedbed of the postwar psychological devastation and material prosperity, which paradoxically mixed together. It reminded people of the forgotten God who was the giver of all things and whose Spirit could satisfy people's hearts in a way that material goods could never do. As Walker points out, "We simply note the fact that the highly spiritual and supernatural emphasis of the renewal movement has been a significant factor in drawing some of today's rationalistic pagans back to an awareness of God."[24]

The Rise of Counter-Cultures

The charismatic renewal emerged when counter-cultures were growing in 1960s British society. Young people were pursuing so-called "self-expression" and liberation from traditional values. Hippies outwardly and physically protested against the bondage of conventions with unconventional clothes, hairstyles, and behavior. Rock music and pop art were developed to counter the "high culture" such as fine art and classical music. The traditional norms of marriage and sex were challenged. From the early 1960s, the rates of cohabitation, divorce, abortion, and illegitimate birth had been increasing. The emergence of a diversity of contraceptive means encouraged sexual enjoyment without the worry of possible pregnancy. In addition, the abuse of drugs for sensual pleasure was growing. Moral norms that had been tightly sustained by the strong influence of the churches in previous centuries, was now being severely questioned. It led the Bishop of Coventry to say, "Of recent years this moral code has been weakening alarmingly. In some directions one can almost sense what amounts to challenges against conventionalized values, pleas to resist the trend arose. The charismatic renewal took place when the church was wrestling with the counter-culture and needed wisdom and strength to witness to the gospel in society.

From a different perspective, however, the development of the renewal in the 1960s was itself one of the elements of the counter-culture. The subculture offered alternatives to the conventional social norms. The traditional mind-set of the general public was shaken and new ideas, thoughts, and experiences were being welcomed.[25] Charismatic

24. Walker, *Renew Us by Your Spirit*, 17.

25. Machin, *Churches and Social Issues*, 213; Bebbington, *Evangelism in Modern Britain*, 232; Interview with MacInnes, 28 June 2006; Edwards, *A Concise History of*

renewal developed in this soil of subversion against standards and conventions that had long been regarded as ultimately correct. There were
major changes of emphasis, such as the importance of experience rather
than just cerebral understanding, of spontaneity rather than formality
in worship, and of complete surrender to the Holy Spirit rather than
human effort. The renewal altered the ecclesiastical formalism on which
the church had relied and endowed it with liveliness, freshness, strength,
and hope. After the spiritual impact of the wars, and the changes in social conventions, it presented an attractive alternative Christianity and
a form of church life that gained more and more acceptance among
mainline churches and the Roman Catholics. Its success lay in the transformation of the church by the Holy Spirit, but it was the general social
trend of welcoming new ideas that helped the renewal to flourish. Hence
the Church of England views that "the rise of the counter-culture and of
the charismatic movement were simultaneous" and that this generated
"a form of Christianized existentialism."[26]

THE DEVELOPMENT OF THE CHARISMATIC RENEWAL IN BRITAIN

When the charismatic movement began in Britain in the 1960s, it did
not initially make a big splash, nor did it have a significant impact on
many churches. In fact, it took a number of years before it was fully
recognized, and only began to be accepted as a serious force in the
1970s. Although in 1964 Harper established the Fountain Trust for
the promotion of the charismatic renewal in Britain, its growth was
"slow," and "steady but unspectacular," which suggests that it did not
catch the eye of most of the church leaders. This situation continued
until the 1970s when there was a breakthrough for the whole movement. Robinson reports that charismatic groups were then set up and
conferences took place in some mainline churches. There was the first
public Methodist Charismatic Conference attended by 135 people
with a report "Charismatic Movement in Methodism 'Goes Public'" in
1973. The "Group for evangelism and renewal" of the United Reformed
Church and the National Service Committee of the Roman Catholics

English Christianity, 147.

   26. Bebbington, *Evangelism in Modern Britain*, 233.

were formed.[27] Robinson's discovery of the growing acceptance of the charismatic renewal echoes Harper's personal experience in a Church Leaders' Conference, "Facing the Future," in Birmingham in September 1972. During the ten days of the Conference, he "was able to share with leaders in all the major denominations" and showed the film "Following the Spirit" twice in front of more than one hundred leaders. He found that they were sympathetic and supportive of the charismatic renewal.[28] There were those such as the Bishop of Warrington, John Monier Bickersteth, whom Harper described as "very friendly and very interested in what is going on."[29] He reported to a Fountain Trust Advisory Council meeting in 1972 that "There is much greater openness than ever before. All the statements and comments were complimentary, and not negative, towards the charismatic movement."[30] And so he confidently claims "surely we are living in days of great opportunity."[31]

In contrast to the Classical Pentecostal Movement, which was rooted in the working class, the charismatic renewal was predominantly a middle-class movement.[32] Jim Packer talks of the racial and stylistic differences between the two movements. If we trace the history back, one tends to be "black-style" and "'holy roller,'" while the other one is "white" and "restrained."[33] Harper admitted that in the 1970s, after ten years of the renewal, it could not permeate the working class culture.[34] A person's social background was often reflected in their qualifications. Most of the Pentecostal preachers had training in Pentecostal Bible colleges while charismatic ministers of the mainline churches had gained university degrees. The educational differences affected the relationship between the two groups.[35]

Another characteristic of the British charismatic renewal is that it was mainly led by Evangelical Anglicans. Hocken reported that at the

---

27. Robinson, "Charismatic Anglican," 185; Hocken, *Streams of Renewal*, 490.

28. Harper, *Newsletter* 43; Harper, *Newsletter* 44.

29. Letter from Harper to William Davies, 29 September 1972.

30. Minute-FTACM (2 November 1972), 1.

31. Harper, *Newsletter* 44.

32. Letter from Brian Ellis to Harper, 12 November 1973, 3; Mather, "Theology," 48; Grossmann, *Stewards of God's Grace*, 67.

33. Packer, "Piety," 20.

34. Letter from Harper to Brian Ellis, 23 November 1973.

35. Hocken, *Streams of Renewal*, 140.

Stoke Poges conference in June 1964, there were twenty participants and eight of them were Evangelical Anglicans, two Catholic Anglicans, and two were middle of the road. There were four independent Christians, one Methodist, two Baptists, and one from the Church of Scotland.[36] Moreover, the four Trustees at the early stage were all Anglicans.[37] As a Baptist charismatic herself, R. A. Pyle was frequently mistaken for an Anglican and she wondered if the Trust perceived itself as an Anglican renewal movement.[38] Nevertheless, the Trust's primary purpose was to spread the renewal among churches no matter what the denominational affiliation. It aimed at being both charismatic and ecumenical, as this was the very character of the renewal. The self-understanding of the Trust and its relations with churches are explained in the following.

A BRIEF HISTORY OF THE FOUNTAIN TRUST

Its Self Understanding in the Charismatic Renewal

Harper established the Fountain Trust because his vision was to "help to fan the flame of the charismatic renewal which was just being kindled" and to "keep it sound and balanced."[39] Its self-understanding was continually evaluated and modified so that it could keep up with the unfolding work of the Holy Spirit. Its "prime aim" was for "the renewal of the spiritual life of the Christian Church," so that its members could "enter into full possession of the important realities of the Holy Spirit."[40] The Trust recognized, within God's purposes, that its ministry could end one day, and so it did not regard itself as a permanent organization.[41] Its self-understanding can be divided into three stages.

Stage 1: Initial Period (1964–1970)

The general goal of the Trust was to spread renewal in churches, "particularly parochial-congregational renewal, within the historic Protestant

---

36. Ibid., 118

37. They were Eric Houfe, Bill Grant, Geoffrey Gould and Noel Davson. (Hocken, *Streams of Renewal*, 259, note 43.)

38. Letter from R. A. Pyle to Harper, 5 August 1975, 1.

39. Fountain Trust, "Michael," 1.

40. Letter from Ian Davidson, September 1972.

41. Minute-FTAM (6 December 1968), 2.

and Reformed churches,"[42] but its specific ideas, functions and ministry were still being clarified at this stage as can be seen in the following.

The Ecumenical Nature

When the Trust was born (29 September 1964), it was consciously endowed with an ecumenical nature. Harper announced that he felt "called to serve every section of the Church . . . to bring men of different traditions together" in the power of the Holy Spirit,[43] to fulfill this vision and to guarantee that renewal could be shared by the whole of the Body of Christ without further division.[44] Within the first ten years of the Trust, some written documents show that this idea was still sustained. For example, in the minute of an Advisory Council Meeting in 1970, we read that "the Trust was not an organization in the sense of having a membership and its work existed to transcend denominational barriers and bring together those whom God had blessed or who were seeking blessing."[45] At the international conference in Nottingham (1973), Smail claimed that if anybody asked about joining the Trust, he would say, "There is no such animal!"[46] In 1974, in a letter answering a question about the Trust, Smail pointed out that one of its features was that it did not have any membership. Instead, it was "to offer a ministry to the Churches and not to build up a support of its own." For that reason, the Trust did not have branches or a local or national group. It simply had links with churches, groups, or individuals who were sympathetic or experienced the renewal inside and outside Britain.[47]

The ecumenical character of the Trust was also apparent in the administrative structure. Besides the four Anglican Trustees under the leadership of Harper,[48] it also formed an Advisory Council in which charismatics from various ecclesiological backgrounds discussed the policies and issues relating to the charismatic renewal. The aim was to reach all

---

42. Hocken, *Streams of Renewal*, 122.

43. Quoted from Hocken, *Streams of Renewal*, 119.

44. Robinson, "Charismatic Anglican," 154.

45. Minute-FTACM (20 November 1970), 2.

46. Harper, "Editorial: Ten Years Young," 3–4.

47. Letter from Smail to John Capon, 1974; Letter from Ian Davidson, September 1972.

48. Hocken, *Streams of Renewal*, 119; Robinson, "Charismatic Anglican," 226.

the churches in Britain.[49] Due to its aim of being a service agency for renewal, Robinson comments that the Trust succeeded in overcoming "the risk of a separate denomination forming" in the process of spreading the renewal.[50]

From Being a Community to Fellowship

The Trust was envisaged as a "community" working for British churches at this early stage, but this idea proved to be inappropriate and the description was altered to "fellowship." From 1964 it struggled to find its precise role in the charismatic renewal. It was in a process of maturing and the way it could develop was not clear. As Harper said in an Advisory Council Meeting, "There had been a phase to see what would happen, particularly since 1964."[51] During this misty period, there was an apparent ray of hope in 1967 when Rev. Reg East, an "older" man ministering in a parish in Essex and closely affiliated with the Trust,[52] proposed a model of community as a "basis of the work of the Fountain Trust."[53] His idea was that the work for renewal should be done by a team, and that the team should live together, pray and support each other. The result was a plan to close the office in central London and move to North London or Hertfordshire.[54] It was agreed that the community should fulfill three goals: 1. Prayer: to make oneself available all the time to pray for any member who was in need and to be a backup for revival. 2. Rehabilitation: to help Christians who had psychological problems that were not too serious. 3. A conference center: to hold conferences with thirty delegates who were "ministers and full-time Christian workers" particularly to support the isolated. Moreover, the community was also expected to evangelize and support churches in which the Holy Spirit was doing some renewing work by sending people to "counsel and give

---

49. Hocken, "Fountain Trust," 119; Letter from Smail to John Capon, 1974.

50. Robinson, "Charismatic Anglican," 226.

51. Minute-FTACM (1 July 1967), 1.

52. Letter from Harper to His Honor Judge Ruttle, 3 November 1970. In that letter, Harper described East as "a man with a very wonderful pastoral gift. Since being baptized in the Spirit he has become more and more evangelical."

53. Minute-FTAM (6 December 1968), 1.

54. Agenda-FTACM (1 June 1967), 1. Minute-FTACM (1 July 1967), 1.

guidance." Staff of the community was supposed not only to work for renewal, but also "to minister to each other."[55]

Unfortunately, after a year and a half, this idealistic model of community was found unworkable and even harmful to the unity of the Trust. At the Advisory Meeting in December 1968, Harper reported, "The Fountain Trust had been through a difficult and confused time since the last Advisors' meeting," particularly because of a sense of disunity that had been felt in attempting to fulfill the vision of a community.[56] The problem had come to the surface at a residential conference. Harper recorded that "a deep-seated disunity" was found among Trustees and delegates and "a deterioration in the fellowship" existed despite "a time of sharing together in love." The failed process of attempting to find a house for the community had been particularly disruptive, and resulted in the resignation of a Trustee. It also limited the Trust's development, as the existing office was too small for the increasing staff and work. The sense of unity was recovered in a fellowship meeting at East's home, and afterwards the Trustees decided to alter the term from "community" to "fellowship."[57]

Strengthening Local Churches

Besides adopting the principle of being a fellowship, in 1968 the Trust was trying to identify what its ministry to churches should be, and how to respond to the needs of those experiencing the new work of the Spirit. Campbell McAlpine pointed out that the Trust could be regarded as a service agency "strengthening and helping the local churches," which should themselves be responsible for meeting the local needs, as a "Bible principle."[58] It was felt that instead of "overnight visits" the Trust would encourage churches more by staying longer in any one place to "preach and adequately teach the word."[59]

Three aims

After five years of direction seeking, the Trust eventually identified its three aims in 1969, which were stated in *Renewal* as:

55. Ibid.
56. Minute-FTAM (6 December 1968), 1.
57. Ibid.
58. Minute-FTAM (6 December 1968), 2.
59. Minute-FTAM (6 December 1968), 2, 4.

1. To encourage all Christians of all Churches to receive the power of the Holy Spirit and to glorify Christ by manifesting in their lives the fruit and the gifts of the same Spirit so that they may enrich their worship, strengthen their witness and deepen their fellowship.

2. To encourage local churches to experience renewal in the Holy Spirit and to recover the full ministry of the Holy Spirit, including that of healing.

3. To encourage Christians to expect and pray for worldwide revival.[60]

Stage 2: Maturing Period (1971–1974)

1971 was a significant year for the Trust. It was a time of rapid development of the charismatic renewal, its "coming of age" when the first international conference took place in Guildford. There was an accelerated interest in the renewal and more and more people experienced the Spirit and church leaders became more sympathetic. For the Trust, this year marked a "milestone" after "a seven-year period of steady if unspectacular growth."[61] As a result, the workload grew rapidly, and this was reflected in the huge increase in the sales and expenditures from 1970–71 to 1971–72. Some of the growth was over 100 percent.[62]

	1970–71	1971–72	Growth (percent)[63]
Book sales	£5,838	£15,864	171 percent
Magazine subscriptions	£2,503	£3,113	24 percent
Tape sales and hire	£1,530	£3,695	142 percent
Overheads (incl. salaries)	£9,889	£12,475	26 percent

60. Letter from Ian Davidson, September 1972, 1–2.

61. Harper, *Newsletter* 41.

62. Harper, *Newsletter* 43.

63. The figures of sales and expenditure were provided in *Newsletter* 43, but the percentages were my own calculation to show the growth.

Harper predicted that the work would continue to increase in the future and the office was too small for the expanding staff and work. Such growth and the associated difficulties were perceived as an encouragement rather than a burden. He and the Trust were happy to see that it was "on the move."[64]

Since the rapid development of the charismatic renewal seemed likely to continue, the Trust realized that one of its urgent tasks was to work out the theological foundations of the movement. Harper stated in 1972 that "it is very likely in the next few years the charismatic renewal will become one of the major theological concerns of the Church throughout the world." To enhance the Trust as "an effective instrument in God's sovereign purpose,"[65] he was convinced that it should be involved in theological study, so as to undergird the renewal, and to clarify the thinking of people about their unprecedented experience in the Spirit. To fulfill this aim, Harper and his wife visited Smail in Northern Ireland, hoping that he would help with the theological development. Smail was appointed as the Trust's General Secretary from September 1972 until September 1975 when he became the Director.[66] The Trust set up a library at the property in East Molesey and began holding theological workshops after the Guildford conference in 1971, which continued until 1974. This will be covered in more detail in chapter 2.[67]

Despite the encouraging growth and the increasing contribution of the Trust to the charismatic renewal in the early 1970s, Harper commented in 1972 that in the preceding eight years, "the work was a little fragmentary" and "individuals had been blessed, but we had yet to see whole churches becoming powerful agents of God's Spirit." Therefore 1974 was a year in which the Trust looked forward to seeing the church as a whole being renewed and not just individuals coming into an experience. In order to achieve this, it planned to publicize the renewal with printed materials and conferences. The leaders and the Advisory Council were prepared to be involved as much as they could to get the

64. Harper, *Newsletter* 43.

65. Harper, *Newsletter* 41.

66. Harper, *Newsletter* 43.

67. In the 1970s, there were not many libraries in the world for the charismatic renewal, apart from the one at the Oral Roberts University and Professor Hollenweger's personal collection in Birmingham. (Minute-FTACM (2 November 1972), 1. Minute-FTACM (5 April 1973), 1.

renewal to fan out "throughout Great Britain."[68] Harper in particular would reserve time for producing printed and audio materials instead of taking on other engagements.[69]

After a period of self-reassessment of the Trust[70] as a result the rapid growth of the charismatic renewal in the preceding years, and the expectation of further growth in 1974, the Trust announced its new aims, "for the renewal of the Church: in Christ, by the Spirit, to the Church, for the World."[71] The aims were stated as follows:

1. Christ centered (in Christ): it recognizes that the fundamental work of the Holy Spirit is to glorify Jesus Christ, who should be the center and pattern of all renewal.

2. Charismatic (by the Spirit): it sees the worldwide charismatic movement as one of God's way of renewal for the whole Church.

68. Minute-FTACM (2 November 1972), 2.

69. Minute-FTACM (5 April 1973), 2.

70. The reassessed items were mentioned in an Advisory Council Meeting on 8 November 1973, 1:

    1. The main points that had arisen were the national and local functions of the Trust and a right balance between the two;

    2. improvements in its ministry to minister and leaders;

    3. the need to meet a growing demand for teaching materials;

    4. ministry of reconciliation with Classical Pentecostals, evangelicals, and house churches;

    5. balance of ministry to those who were beginners in the things of the Spirit and the more mature;

    6. dangers of becoming too American, too Pentecostal, too "familiar";

    7. whether a public relations "image" was necessary or not

In *Newsletter* 48, there are also similar items mentioned about the Trust's reassessment:

    1. We want to make our own organization adequate to our ministry. We want to have the right ministry to serve and support what God is doing in His Church.

    2. We want to help those already blessed in the Spirit to know how to continue.

    3. We believe that the field of leadership training that we have now entered is going to be of increasing importance, and we are in contact with others of a like mind already working in it.

71. Fountain Trust, *For the Renewal of the Church*, 1.

It regards the recovery of the power and gifts of the Spirit as an essential part of this renewal.

3. Corporate (to the Church): it sees renewal chiefly in corporate rather than merely personal terms. Its main concern is to see churches of all denominations rather than individuals renewed by the Spirit, while recognizing that God brings renewal through individuals.

4. Compassionate (for the World): it believes that love is the heart of renewal, and that the intention of God is that church renewal should overflow to the world in terms of evangelism and social action.[72]

To realize these four aims, the Trust divided its work into four areas with four purposes. (1) Praising—The Trust intended to organize meetings for worship in London and other areas in Britain to share the renewal in the Spirit together. (2) Learning—The Trust provided courses of different lengths for church leaders covering many subjects about the renewal. In addition, conferences also provided a means for learning through "teaching, praise and fellowship." (3) Listening—producing cassette tapes containing testimonies and ministries was another way to promote the renewal. Records with songs for worship produced by Christian communities were also available. (4) Looking—the Trust also provided printed materials, primarily the bi–monthly magazine, *Renewal*, together with its companion, *Theological Renewal*, which was started by Smail in 1975 and published three times a year, carrying the "deeper implications of what is happening." In addition, books and films were also used. Despite the change of aims, the Trust maintained the policy of not recruiting members and declared during this stage that it "seeks to be nothing in itself, and believes that the results of its work will be seen under God in local parishes and congregations."[73]

Stage 3: Plateau Period to the End (1975–1980)

After the rapid development since 1971, the Trust and the charismatic renewal entered a plateau period in 1975; where there were not many excitements in terms of the numbers at conferences or miracles occurring. However, there were significant breakthroughs that had not been achieved in the previous two periods. 1975 marked the new age of the

72. Ibid., 2.
73. Ibid.

Trust. Smail became the director in that year and was concerned about the balance between renewed individuals and renewed local churches. He believed that renewal should be realized in local churches, but it was also important to "bring more people more fully into his blessings" (of the Spirit) because the second enabled the first to happen. He thought that this vision could not be worked out with some of the methods being used previously, as he claimed, "I am not convinced that altar calls at large meetings are always the right way, I am quite sure that any attempt to pressurize people into stereotyped experiences and manifestation of gifts is the wrong way."[74] Perhaps because of the change of style and emphasis, the activities of the Trust were not as well-attended as in the previous two periods. For instance, compared to the other four, the last international conference in Westminster (1979) had the fewest participants. Harper believed that the increase in renewal organizations and the rise of the House Church Movement caused the general decline in attendance. As he said, "Britain is honeycombed with renewal gatherings for praise, instruction and personal ministry."[75] Nevertheless, the Trust had created a new page of the renewal history by its ecumenical cooperation, its ministry in Wales and its social outreach.

Ecumenically, Smail continued to develop a trusting relationship with the Roman Catholics, which began in the first two periods. The final two Westminster international conferences (1977 and 1979) were organized with the RCNSC during his leadership. He also successfully invited Cardinal Suenens to attend. Moreover, the Trust was invited to organize the fourth European Charismatic Leaders' Conference in 1976 in Malines. Its theme was "Koinonia—Fellowship in the Spirit" and it was attended by more than 70 charismatic leaders at the invitation of Cardinal Suenens.[76] In addition, among the Anglican evangelicals, the ecumenical breakthrough found expression in the joint statement, *Gospel and Spirit*, in 1977 signed by sixteen Anglican ministers and Tom Smail as a non-Anglican at that time.[77] The details of the Trust's relation-

74. Smail, "Editorial: Simplicity at the Centre," 4.

75. Harper, "Prospects," 14.

76. Fountain Trust, "Leaders," 5; "Well," 4.

77. The sixteen Anglican ministers were John Baker, Colin Buchanan, John Collins, Ian Cundy, Michael Harper, Raymond Johnston, Bruce Kaye, Gordon Landreth, Robin Nixon, Jim Packer, Harold Parks, Gavin Reid, John Stott, Raymond Turvey, Tom Walker and David Watson. (Nixon, "Gospel," 18).

ship with evangelicals will be discussed in chapter 3. Looking back at this period, Smail commented that the ecumenical advance characterized the Trust's work and the charismatic renewal in that period, which was "far more important than tongues and prophecies and all the things that people went on about."[78]

During the plateau period of the Trust, there was another breakthrough, and that was in its ministry in Wales. Although charismatic prayer groups, house churches, and mainline churches had shown increasing interest in the renewal in Britain, Ken Walters described Wales as being "virtually untouched" and "slow to respond to the move of the Spirit," which contrasted with what had happened in the Welsh Revival (1904–05). *Renewal* 62 (April–May 1976) reads, "In the eleven years of its history the Fountain Trust has ministered in almost every part of Britain—except Wales." Fortunately, the opportunity came in 1976 when Smail and Colin Greene spoke to 300 to 400 people at the Salem Welsh Presbyterian Church in Aberystwyth. The message was conveyed in English and Welsh to a variety of participants such as ministers of evangelical churches and Catholic priests. Amazingly, for most of the participants, that was the first time that they had heard about the renewal and they showed high expectation and interest.[79] After this pioneering venture, the Trust enlarged its ministry in the area by organizing two official conferences in May 1975. The first one was a weekend conference on the twentieth to the twenty-second in Llandrindod Wells conducted by Jim Graham and Cecil Cousen. The second was a ministers' conference held on the following three days at the same place where Smail and Cousen spoke.[80] This ministry was still being carried on in 1980. In the summer, the Trust held a holiday conference for families at the University College of Wales in Aberystwyth.[81]

As the charismatic renewal was growing, the Trust and charismatics became more concerned about the social implications and applications of the renewal. Apart from Spirit baptism and gifts, discussion about social outreach became a main topic in the Trust's conferences. In November

---

78. Interview with Smail, 16 February 2006.

79. Walters, "Wales," 14–15; Fountain Trust, "At Last-to Wales," 6.

80. Fountain Trust, "1977," back cover; "Coming," 6.

81. The speakers were Barling, John Richards, David Pawson, Peter Marshall, Jean Darnall and Smail though he had resigned from the directorship and became the vice-principal of St. John's College. (Fountain Trust, "Fountain Trust," 10–11.)

1976, with the cooperation of Christian Industrial Enterprises, the Trust organized a conference to investigate the subject of "Christian involvement in industry and society." A diversity of experts was involved so as to discuss the issue from the perspectives of economics, theology, philosophy, and business administration.[82] At the international conference, Westminster 1977 and 1979, social concern was a major topic—ranging from local responsibility in Britain to the global vision in the third world. The Trust in this period aimed at diverting attention from the personal blessings of the Spirit to witnesses and influence in society.

After Smail's resignation from the directorship in 1979, there was neither significant change of direction nor new vision during the short period when Michael Barling held office. Eventually, the Trust's ministry was terminated at the end of 1980 when the Trustees and director felt that the task of promoting the renewal had been fulfilled.

Its Relationships with Some Christian Groups

As the Trust sought to promote the charismatic renewal effectively among the developed denominations and churches, it attempted to build up trusting relationships with them and clear up any misunderstandings. From 1964, it had tried to do this with Classical Pentecostals, mainline denominations, individual groups, evangelicals, house churches, and Roman Catholics, but the process had often been thorny.

Classical Pentecostals: Assemblies of God and Elim Pentecostal Church

As the phenomenon and nature of the charismatic renewal were similar to the Classical Pentecostals, namely the Spirit baptism and spiritual gifts, it was most important for the Trust to show that it did not attempt to compete with them, but rather, to demonstrate sincerity for cooperation. However, it had been very difficult to achieve this goal with the Assemblies of God (AG), and the response from Elim and other Pentecostal groups was not all positive. The report of an Advisory Council Meeting in 1967 notes that the misunderstandings between the AG and the Trust "had now been cleared up" and a good relationship with Elim was maintained due to the shared goal of evangelism.[83]

---

82. Fountain Trust, "Christians," 6.
83. Minute-FTACM (1 July 1967), 2.

Mistrust and tension nevertheless continued and became worse. In the editorial of *Renewal* in 1968, Harper expressed his disappointment about the conflict between the "'old' and 'new' Pentecostals" and advised both of them to learn from each other rather than making any unnecessary comparisons.[84] The 1969 High Leigh Conference, at which certain "high" church representatives experienced the Spirit, made some of the Pentecostals very uncomfortable. They were suspicious of ecumenical meetings, and particularly of one in which non-Pentecostals from various denominational backgrounds had "Pentecostal" experiences, such as a nun speaking in tongues. They wrote an article in the *Christian Guardian* to speak out against this Conference, "ecumenism and ritualism" and the term, "New Pentecostalism." This event greatly intensified the enmity of the Pentecostals who had never been "fully at one with the Fountain Trust's position."[85] Unfortunately, the mistrust was deepened at the Guildford Conference in 1971. Before the Conference started, Billy Richards, a prominent AG Pentecostal in Slough, had stated his opposition to it in an article. There were arguments about doctrine, which highlighted the Pentecostals' suspicion of the charismatic renewal during the conference. Similar to what had happened at High Leigh, the Trust's welcoming attitude and acceptance of the Roman Catholics at Guildford accelerated the Pentecostals' distrust.[86] The most open display of this was Alfred Missen's walk-out from the Conference due to his discomfort over David du Plessis's warm words about the Roman Catholics. This story will be illustrated in chapter 3. In 1972, the conflict crossed the Atlantic after Richards's booklet about his skepticism about the charismatic renewal was approved at an AG annual conference in the US. In response to this problem, the Advisory Council requested Harper to issue a statement.[87]

A meeting between the Trust and the AG held at the beginning of 1973 was a turning point in the deteriorating relationship. The Trust discovered that the AG had held some "very erroneous" ideas about it, such as that it was planning to set up a denomination itself. The AG was surprised to learn that "the director and general secretary of the Trust were only employees." The conversation successfully cleared up some of

84. Quoted in Robinson, "Charismatic Anglican," 166.

85. Robinson, "Charismatic Anglican," 165–66.

86. Email from Harper, 29 June 2005; Minute-FTACM (5 April 1973), 2.

87. Minute-FTACM (2 November 1972), 1.

their misunderstandings and "there was a much better feeling" as a result; nevertheless, the Trust maintained a distance from the AG in order to avoid rejection by other denominations.[88]

Despite the improvement in their relationship, conflict could not be avoided completely. In November of the same year, Smail reported that the AG's attitude towards the Trust had "hardened." They had written "a rather negative statement" showing that they thought of the Trust as "an authoritative body issuing statements on behalf of Neo-Pentecostalism." And they claimed that the Trust's understanding of gifts was not a definition of unity, but rather a doctrine. Smail reported that although their statement was not published before the Nottingham Conference, which the AG had attempted to do, it would be discussed in detail in their Assembly in spring 1974. Elim's attitude towards the Trust became negative as they were "more favorably disposed" to the AG's position. Nevertheless, Elim had been less hostile to the Trust and were open to the charismatic renewal. It invited David du Plessis to speak at its meeting after his pastoral credential was revalidated by the AG in the US.[89]

To deal with the increasing challenge from the Classical Pentecostal denominations, the Trust remained positive and seized any opportunity for dialogue rather than "letting the door close."[90] Although the AG opposed the Trust officially, some of the ministers did not take the same view as the majority and Douglas Quy, an executive member of AG and a minister of the Bedford Pentecostal Church, was one of these.[91] He acknowledged the miraculous manifestations in the charismatic renewal as being as valid as those in the Pentecostal movement and supported the Trust in promoting the renewal. He encouraged Harper by saying, "We are rejoicing here in evidence of miraculous power to raise sick

88. Minute-FTACM (5 April 1973), 3.

89. Minute-FTACM (8 November 1973), 3; Minute-FTACM (5 April 1973), 3.

90. Minute-FTACM (8 November 1973), 3.

91. Letter from Harper to Douglas Quy, 23 August 1972. Quy's church was founded by Cecil Polhill of Howbury Hall in 1907. He was active in church broadcasting work as well. He was the Executive Director of IBRA, a Swedish Missionary Radio project which was aimed at broadcasting the Christian Gospel in multi-language programs from Portugal, Manila, Seychelles, and S. America." He was also a consultant to the Churches Advisory Committee on Local Broadcasting and Broadcaster for AG on the BBC and ITV. (Letter from Douglas Quy to Harper, 19 December 1972; Curriculum Vitae: Douglas Quy; Fountain Trust, *Nottingham University 9–14 July 1973, Gathered for Power*, 4).

and needy from despair and helpless. Michael, we must go forward, for we have the answer to the present-day dilemma."[92] Because of that, the Trust had the confidence to request some suggestions on how to "bridge the gap between the old and new movements of the Spirit" from him.

To make progress in reconciliation, Quy accepted the Trust's invitation to speak at the Nottingham Conference (1973), with the aim of showing "the older Pentecostals" Harper's desire and effort to build up fellowship with them; and hoping for a chance to remove the hostility and to open up communication despite the underlying fears.[93] His confidence was found to be justified by the support of his church members for this speaking engagement. He was able to say, "Many elder brethren are glad to know that at this important occasion, I shall be present with you." He positively believed that "the barriers would be swept away and a door opened for a great 'gale of a wind.'"[94] Besides Quy, Wesley Gilpin, another AG minister, also accepted the invitation to be a guest in the same occasion.[95]

Other Pentecostal Groups

The Trust and the Full Gospel Businessmen's Fellowship International (FGBMFI) had built up a good relationship. In spring 1965 the fellowship sponsored Harper and his wife to go on a trip to the US to meet prominent charismatic leaders such as Dennis Bennett and some Roman Catholic charismatics in Seattle.[96] The trusting relationship still remained in 1967.[97] In contrast, the Trust had not been able to develop any relationship with the Keswick movement since 1964. Harper made it clear that the Trust as an organization for the renewal was not attempting to compete with Keswick, but since the renewal was spreading quickly, the Trust had to organize plenty of activities to meet the needs and could not avoid clashes. In 1971 alone, it held fifteen functions around Britain. Moreover, Harper felt that the Keswick leaders had been "very obdurate in their opposition to the charismatic movement" and "steadfastly through the years refused to have anything to do with" it. For him, it

92. Letter from Douglas Quy to Harper, 11 September 1972.

93. Ibid.

94. Letter from Douglas Quy to Harper, 19 December 1972.

95. Minute-FTACM (2 November 1972), 1.

96. Hocken, *Streams of Renewal*, 120.

97. Minute-FTACM (1 July 1967), 2.

was "the saddest" thing happening and despite the Trust's constant attempt to bridge the gap, the gulf was "widening every year."[98] Finally, the Trust also intended to relate to the Oneness Pentecostal groups, of which there were around thirteen in Britain in 1967. Although the Trust did not agree with their doctrine, it believed that the "false teaching and anti-church emphasis demonstrated the need for fellowship, love and sensitivity."[99]

Evangelicals

Another Christian group which the Trust found very difficult to build up a relationship with was the evangelicals. Their attitude towards the renewal and the Trust had been hardened from the beginning.[100] Although the Trust had done plenty of bridge-building, at the beginning of the 1970s they had "simply come up against a blank wall" as the evangelical leaders were not willing to "budge an inch in their policy of neglecting entirely this new work of God."[101] Consequently, "misunderstanding and hard feelings" grew. David Watson attributed this attitude to the lack of theological study of the renewal when it had started, maintaining that this had led to division among evangelicals.[102] Donald Eddison thought it was the "defensive attitude" of evangelicals that caused the difficulty, which he hoped to solve by meetings and discussion.[103] The Trust also realized that there was a "reluctance to talk about it" and gradually the division got deeper.[104] An example of this can be found in the relationship between Harper and John Stott who were respectively the representative figures of the charismatic and evangelical parties, and disagreed with each other's views about the renewal. Harper admitted that for ten years from 1965 they had seldom met each, other which obviously did not improve the situation.[105]

After all the discussion and effort, the relationship between the evangelicals and the Trust seemed to get better after 1975. Colin Buchanan

---

98. Letter from Harper to John Simons, 20 August 1971, 1–2.

99. Minute-FTACM (1 July 1967), 2.

100. Minute-FTAM (6 December 1968), 3.

101. Letter from Harper to John Simons, 20 August 1971, 1.

102. "Reality," 3, 16; "Conference," 1.

103. Minute-FTACM (5 April 1973), 1.

104. Minute-FTACM (8 November 1973), 2.

105. Harper, "Editorial: A Narrowing of the Divide," 3.

thought that this was, on the one hand, because the charismatics had become "slightly tamer than in the past." For example, they no longer insisted on the necessity of Spirit baptism for being a Spirit-filled person as much as they had at the beginning of the movement. On the other hand, the evangelicals became more accepting of the renewal, particularly the charismatic worship. They had gradually acknowledged the function of spiritual gifts and looked into the renewal theologically.[106] The reconciliation was made concrete and documented in two major events. The first one was the Swanwick conference held in November 1975 where Harper witnessed "a significant détente between the parties involved." The Anglican theologian, Jim Packer, recognized the contributions of the renewal theologically and practically, and also its weaknesses. John Stott was present, but still held generally negative views about the renewal. He agreed that he had hesitated to acknowledge the strengths of the renewal, but he wanted to encourage more communication and study of the Bible together.[107] The second event was the National Evangelical Anglican Congress (NEAC) in Nottingham in April 1977.[108] Smail was invited by the Anglican evangelicals and was regarded as an important catalyst in easing the tension, as he said that through the meeting, "evangelicals and charismatics are now really listening and speaking to one another in renewed relationship and openness."[109] The Joint Statement of the Church of England Evangelical Council and the Fountain Trust, *Gospel and Spirit*, was ready for, and endorsed by the conference. It stated,

> We have sought to understand each other's views better and to achieve closer harmony and correspondence through examining them all in the light of bible teaching. We are now issuing this account of our progress, indicating both agreements and disagreements, in the hope that it may help to promote unity where there is discord, and mutual understanding where there has been mistrust."[110]

---

106. Buchanan, *Encountering Charismatic Worship*, 21; "Is," 21.

107. Harper, "Editorial: A Narrowing of the Divide," 2–3.

108. Buchanan recorded that the theme song for the conference was "Jesus is Lord! Creation's voice proclaims it" which was chosen from a charismatic song book, *Sound of Living Water*, No. 82. It showed the evangelicals' openness towards charismatic music. (Buchanan, *Encountering Charismatic Worship*, 21, footnote 4.)

109. Smail, *Newsletter* 59.

110. Fountain Trust, "Background," 1.

This statement and Smail's attendance at the conference were significant milestones in the marathon of building up a trusting relationship with the evangelicals after going through so much uncertainty and misery.

House Churches

According to Arthur Wallis, one of the leaders of the house church movement, most of the house churches around the country neither supported the renewal nor disagreed with it, particularly the Anglican charismatic sector.[111] The Trust also recognized the weaknesses and problems of the house churches. First, it doubted the house churches' self-definition as "an anti-denominational and anti-historic church movement." They regarded themselves as the true churches as they thought that they had restored the kind of Christian fellowship in the New Testament, which the denominational and institutional churches did not have.[112] Therefore, leaders such as Bryn Jones and David Mansell believed that denominational churches could never be renewed. This was the point that the Trust was concerned about. It was worried about the house churches' conscious isolation from the historic churches, and the danger of repeating the same mistakes that the historic churches had made throughout many centuries. In actual fact this did happen, as the Trust observed. Secondly, the Trust doubted the possibility of "100 percent commitment and dedication to Christ" that the house churches taught. The Trust acknowledged that there were plenty of people only giving a "nominal commitment" in the historic churches, but the commitment that the house churches required would pressurize individuals and consequently reduce the number of people in the church. Third, although the house churches grew very fast and were constituted by relatively more young people than the historic churches, the Trust discovered that those young people were cut off from the reality of life and the society. For instance, some of them felt unprepared to deal with the university environment where temptations and pressures were perceived to be everywhere. The Trust thought that this could be due to the protective environment of their communities in the house churches and the lack of theological teaching about the interrelation between the church and

111. Letter from Arthur Wallis to Harper, n. d.
112. Minute-FTCCM (8 June 1977), 3.

society. Consequently, "a kind of spiritual introversion" was developed among individuals.[113]

The Trust neither attacked nor corrected these theological and ecclesiological weaknesses of the house churches, but it initiated meetings and discussions to build up relationships with a hope that the house church leaders would modify their theological teachings and the way they saw traditional churches. For example, Bryn Jones was invited to speak at a meeting of the Trust in October 1977[114] and in the following year, Smail visited Jones's church in Bradford, which belonged to the "Bradford Circle."[115] He was given the "warmest reception and freedom of ministry." Nevertheless, he insisted on the necessity of "speaking the truth in love."[116] Through these encounters, Smail believed that the Trust's connection with the house churches would be built up and any future discussion could be based on "a context of first-hand knowledge of one another and our work."[117]

Roman Catholics

It had been hard for the Trust to reconcile and build up relationships with the Christian groups mentioned above; but in sharp contrast, the relationship with Roman Catholics was always easy and they had been the Trust's allies since the 1960s. Their cooperation could be divided into two periods, those of Harper (1964 to 1975) and Smail (1975 to 1979).

Harper's positive attitude towards the Roman Catholic charismatics paved the way for the Trust's future relationship and cooperation with the Roman Catholics. In 1965, as has been mentioned above, Harper and his wife visited and spoke to the Roman Catholic charismatics in Seattle. This gave them a new insight into God's renewing work

113. Ibid.; Minute-FTCCM (10 May 1978), 3; Letter from Smail to John Bedford, 5 June 1978.

114. Smail, *Newsletter* 61.

115. This church was a combination of three churches: Open Brethren church, Clayton Road Fellowship and Wally North's New Covenant Fellowship and it was formed in October 1975. Members of the church had rented a theatre for worship and other activities, but in 1976, since "the present premises were acquired in the form of the former Anglican diocesan headquarters," the members scattered in Britain and were guided by the leaders in Bradford. So the name "Bradford Circle" was given. (Mather, "Theology," 14.)

116. Letter from Smail to John Bedford, 5 June 1978.

117. Smail, *Newsletter* 61.

among the Roman Catholics. In September 1969, an American Catholic couple, Bob and Laurin Balkam, who had been baptized in the Spirit in 1968, came to England with their six children (they had two more later). After their arrival, Balkam contacted Harper as the Trust was the only "Pentecostal source" that he had known before his departure. In December Harper invited him to a Trust's meeting at a Baptist Church in Elephant and Castle, London, where he met his first Roman Catholic charismatic friend, Esmond Gwatkin, who had been baptized in the Spirit at an AG meeting in Portsmouth. In 1970, Balkam was invited to participate in the committee of the Guildford conference and he was the only Roman Catholic among the five members. Harper continued to invite the Balkams to "share as fully in Fountain Trust activities" as they liked and to become part of the Trust with other Roman Catholics. But Balkam had already envisaged developing a charismatic organization to promote a renewal with "visible" and "distinctly Roman Catholic expression" so that it could be acknowledged by the Roman Catholic officials. Balkam and other Roman Catholic charismatics organized activities mainly for Roman Catholics such as a "Day of Renewal" on 19 September 1971. The International Ecumenical Charismatic Conference in 1972, and another conference at the University of Surrey in 1973, both had Roman Catholic and Episcopalian speakers from the US. In November 1973, Balkam proposed to some Roman Catholics that they should have a Catholic charismatic organization, and in the same month, the National Service Committee in England and Wales was founded and chaired by Fr. Mike Targett.[118] This organization enhanced connections between prayer groups and local bishops, arranged charismatic conferences, and offered charismatic teaching.[119] It also maintained a cooperative relationship with the Trust and they invited each other to participate in their ministries. Balkam was personally grateful for Harper's "generous assistance and encouragement" during the 1970s. After four decades he still regarded him as his good friend.[120]

The Trust's activities had not lacked Roman Catholic participation. At the international conferences at Guildford, Nottingham and Westminster 1975, the number of Catholic delegates was higher each

118. Email from Bob Balkam, 16 November 2005; Email from Bob Balkam, 18 November 2005.

119. Mather, "Theology," 22.

120. Email from Bob Balkam, 18 November 2005.

time. At a summer school at Sussex University, there were Roman Catholic participants and their main concern was unity. Although Catholic and non-Catholics were discussing the divisive doctrines, they could express their opinion "freely and frankly" and so Smail said, "We shall not easily forget the new sense of closeness that we found with our Roman Catholic brethren there."[121]

In addition, Harper also had personal outreach to the Roman Catholic charismatic renewal. He attended three sessions of the Roman Catholic-Charismatic dialogue in Zürich (19–24 June 1972), Rome (18–23 June 1973), and Venice (21–26 May 1975), the World Leaders' Conference in 1973 and the charismatic conference of the Roman Catholics on 16–18 May 1975 in Rome,[122] where 127 Roman Catholic leaders attended and he was one of the five Protestants. Based on his observation at this conference, he concluded that the renewal was spreading much faster among the Roman Catholics than in other historic churches and there were some "impressively good" leaders in the Roman Catholic charismatic circle. For example, there was a Mexican, Salvador Carillo, who presented his paper on Spirit baptism, which was highly appreciated. However, Harper felt that there were still ecumenical obstacles because some Roman Catholics did not recognize any ecumenical relation with non-Catholic churches. One of these was Edward O'Connor, who resigned from the Roman Catholic Renewal Committee. In addition, doctrinal and hermeneutical problems still hindered ecumenical progress.[123]

When Smail became the Trust's director, he successfully maintained the ecumenical relationship with the Catholic charismatics that Harper had built up. After the first year of his leadership in 1976, he concluded that the Trust had "made new and very precious connections with English charismatic Roman Catholics."[124] In the summer of 1977, the RCNSC was invited to assist with the organization of the international conference in Westminster and in the autumn, the Trust held a night school in Westminster Cathedral with Cornerstone, a Roman Catholic educational organization. The attendance was about 160 people from many denominations, which was much higher than the seventy

---

121. Smail, *Newsletter* 50.

122. Harper, *Newsletter* 43; Smail, *Newsletter* 46; *Newsletter* 52.

123. Minute-FTACM (8 November 1973), 1.

124. Smail, *Newsletter* 57.

that they had expected. At the end of that year, Smail announced that the editorial board of the *Renewal* magazine had involved a Roman Catholic representative so that the Roman Catholics would have a platform to "more fully speak" to their co-workers of the renewal in the country.[125] The cooperation was continued until Smail's resignation in 1979 when they held the final international conference together in Westminster. For those three years of cooperation, Smail commented, "The sort of Catholic, non-Catholic thing was taken for granted that there were quite close relationships."[126]

Besides strengthening the Trust's relationship with Roman Catholic charismatic organizations, Smail also developed friendship with Roman Catholic leaders including Cardinal Suenens, Veronica O'Brien, and Bob Balkam, who regarded him as a "wonderful friend."[127] He recalled one occasion when the Cardinal and he spent the whole evening discussing Marian and other controversial doctrines. Despite disagreements they remained one in fellowship and the Cardinal still accepted Smail's invitation to attend the two Westminster international conferences in 1977 and 1979. After Westminster 1975, Smail also developed a good friendship with a Jesuit, Paul Lebeau, who was closely associated with the Cardinal and spoke at that conference. On the Pentecost of 1977, they and other Roman Catholics went for a pilgrimage to Jerusalem to celebrate the fiftieth anniversary of the priesthood of the Cardinal where they enjoyed "ecumenical love." Smail himself became more devoted to ecumenical work after the journey.[128]

Its Directors

The Trust underwent two transitions of director, which changed the direction and emphasis of the renewal ministry. After eleven years of his ministry in the Trust, in 1975, Harper decided to leave and to minister as a curate at Holy Trinity Church, Hounslow. He gave two reasons for leaving. First, he believed that transferring the leadership would enable the renewal to reach a new stage. Secondly, being a minister in a local

125. Smail, *Newsletter* 61.

126. Interview with Smail, 16 November 2006.

127. Letter from Tom Forrest to Smail, 13 February 1979, 2; Email from Bob Balkam, 20 November 2005.

128. Interview with Smail, 16 November 2006; Letter from Smail to Cardinal Suenens, 13 June 1977.

church would allow him more time to visit churches in and outside Britain and to write. He would help with the teaching ministry in Hounslow and the church would also support his travelling and writing ministry relating to the charismatic renewal, which would be more practical than theoretical. He would still maintain connections with the Trust as a consultant editor and contributor to *Renewal*, chairman of the Advisory Council and speaker at meetings and conferences. Jeanne Harper would give assistance in the musical area. [129] Harper's contribution to the renewal was highly acknowledged by the Trust and those who benefited from his ministries in Britain and overseas. Smail regarded him as having "been able to present the promise and reality of renewal in the Spirit with such courage and balance to the churches" and he appreciated his acceptance of, and obedience to, God's vision "at risk and cost" in establishing the Trust to promote the renewal in Britain. John Perry praised Harper for being "very wise and often fearless to the work of the Fountain Trust." Considering the public desire to express gratitude, the Trust set up a "Harper Presentation Fund" from May to the end of August 1975 for gifts.[130]

When Harper ceased to be the director, Smail was regarded as the most suitable person to succeed the position for four reasons. First, with his personal experience in the Spirit and his profound theological training, it was believed that he could build up theological understandings of the renewal. Experientially, he was baptized in the Spirit under Dennis Bennett's ministry in 1965 when he had been a minister of Thornile Church at Wishaw near Glasgow.[131] Theologically, he was of outstanding ability.[132] Secondly, his Scottish background and connection with Northern Ireland helped in bridging relationships between the Trust and churches of these two areas, which enabled the Trust's ministry to spread out more widely in Britain. He was ordained in the Church of Scotland in 1953 and served in Scottish parishes for fifteen

129. Robinson, "Charismatic Anglican," 205; Fountain Trust, "From Michael & Jeanne Harper," 4; "Michael," 1; An attached letter from Harper, *Newsletter* 53; Letter from Harper to Neville B. Cryer, 12 June 1975.

130. Letter from John F. Perry to Harper, 20 June 1975; Smail, *Newsletter* 53.

131. Fountain Trust, "Press Release of Fountain Trust," 24 April 1972.

132. He obtained an MA degree in Philosophy with first class honors at Glasgow University. Then he got a BD in systematic theology with distinction at New College, Edinburgh, where he was awarded a scholarship to study at the University of Basle, Switzerland, under Karl Barth for one year. (Fountain Trust, "Press Release of Fountain Trust"; Letter from Smail to Douglas A. Smith, 2 May 1974.)

years. In 1968, he was called to minister in a Presbyterian church outside Belfast in Northern Ireland where his ministry was regarded as being of "good and regular standing" in a certificate given by the Presbytery of North Belfast.[133] Thirdly, his abundant experience of ministering in churches for nearly twenty years would help the Trust with local ministry. Finally, his membership of the Presbyterian Church and later on of the United Reformed Church in Walton-on-Thames in 1974 would assist the Trust's work ecumenically.[134] With his academic qualifications, churchly connection, pastoral expertise, and spiritual experience, Smail was acknowledged to be the most suitable person to succeed to the directorship. As Harper said, "There is no-one we would rather be at the helm than Smail, and commend him to your prayers and future support."[135] Smail's work would focus on the life of renewal in the local churches and training leaders and people who had significant positions in the church.[136] As he said, "We can help to ensure that what the Spirit is doing is not confined to small groups on the fringes of church life, but also has free course at the centre."[137]

At Christmas in 1978, it was announced that Smail had resigned from the Trust and would accept a lectureship in St John's College, Nottingham starting in September 1979, and that the associate director, Michael Barling, would succeed him.[138] Smail's change of ministry was instigated by the Principal of the College at that time, Colin Buchanan, who encouraged him to consider lecturing in Christian doctrine. After discussing this with the Executive of the Trust, he accepted the offer within a month.[139] He said that this decision was "one of the easiest and most inevitable" ones he had ever made. He described his ministry in the Trust during the seven years[140] as "wandering" in which he experi-

133. Letter from Smail to Douglas A. Smith, 2 May 1974; Awarded Certificate to Smail from the Presbytery of North Belfast, Presbyterian Church in Ireland, Belfast, 27 June 1972.

134. Fountain Trust, "Press Release of Fountain Trust"; Letter from Smail to Douglas A. Smith, 2 May 1974.

135. An attached letter from Harper, in Smail, *Newsletter* 53.

136. Fountain Trust, "Michael," 1.

137. Fountain Trust, "Renewal," 1.

138. Fountain Trust, "Move," 5; Smail, *Newsletter* 64;Letter from Smail to Cardinal Suenens, 23 April 1979, 1.

139. Smail, *Newsletter* 64.

140. He was the General Secretary in 1972–75 and Director in 1975–79.

enced "a lot of suffering, considerable disappointment as well as a little disillusionment to mix with the continuing wonder and hope at the reality of what God keeps on doing."[141] He admitted that he had had some "illusions" about the renewal, but throughout those years, they had been swept away, and he felt that it was time for him to go back to reality.[142] He regarded the new task of training people as "a great joy and privilege," particularly at St John's, where the training contains three elements: "evangelical conviction, academic theology and charismatic experience." This was done in an "ecumenical context" though it was mainly for training ministers for the Church of England. Moreover, this job gave him a better opportunity to engage with other ministries at the weekend and during the term break in summer, and particularly to maintain the ecumenical and European connections that had come his way in the previous years. Regarding the Trust's situation, he thought that it was difficult for it to fulfill all the needs of local churches with "constant itinerancy," and it was time to have new directions and insights from a new leader. Smail's contribution to the renewal was significant in establishing theological reflection on both the renewal and its ecumenical work. The Trust acknowledged his work by saying that he had "given strong and valuable leadership not only to the Fountain Trust but also the renewal in general." The Trust expressed its thanks to him and his wife in a presentation during the Westminster Conference on 3 August 1979. After leaving the Trust, Smail continued to edit the *Theological Renewal* (1975–83).[143] At the end of 1979, the Trust heard that Smail's teaching was appreciated by the students in the College, and he had chosen to be ordained a priest in the Church of England in the College Chapel on 5 December 1979.[144]

Michael Barling was appointed to succeed to the directorship of the Trust in September 1979. Although he was not so well known at that time, the Trust believed that he could meet the needs of the charismatic renewal at that stage since he was a person with "ministry of teaching and renewal, recent parish experience and administrative gifts." He had been an Anglican vicar and was baptized in the Spirit in 1969 during

141. Smail, *Newsletter* 64.

142. Minute-FTCCM (6 June 1979), 1.

143. Fountain Trust, "Move," 5; Smail, *Newsletter* 64.

144. Barling, *News and Prayer Letter*, 66; Letter from Smail to MacInnes, 9 August 1979.

Harper's ministry at St. Paul's, Portman Square where he was a curate.[145] At the international conferences of Westminster 1975, 1977, and 1979, he was a member of the conference committees and had proved to be well qualified to solve complicated administrative problems. His directorship finished when the Trust was disbanded at the end of 1980.

Its End

After sixteen years, although the Trust had been a significant medium for motivating the charismatic renewal in Britain, the Executive Committee and Trustees decided to close it with general consent. It was announced on 1 September 1980 that the Trust would be wound up on 31 December in that year. All the activities would be stopped on that day except the night school. *Renewal* and *Theological Renewal* would be continued and would be edited by their founders, Harper and Smail respectively, but they would no longer be published under the Trust.[146] *Theological Renewal* would be published by Grove Books and *Renewal* was saved by Edward England, who was a close friend of Harper and had a publication career. He bought *Renewal* for £5 with the debts and Harper edited it for three years. *Theological Renewal* was continued until November 1983 because of the lack of theologians writing about the charismatic renewal and the difficulty of keeping correspondence under the circumstance of publishing it three times a year. In contrast, *Renewal* went "from success to success" so that it reached 16,000 circulations at its highest point and lasted until 2000.[147]

Michael Barling claimed that the closure of the Trust was not because of any pressure such as finance, but because of revelation received over several months while praying. The Trustees sensed that God did not want his work to be confined by any human organization. They took this to mean that it was time to bring the Trust to an end, and that if it continued, it would become a stumbling block in "God's eyes.'" The director, Michael Barling believed that disbanding the Trust would enable new life to begin, new work to blossom. He declared, ". . . it is our conviction that the winding up of the Trust will be a positive contribution towards

145. Smail, *Newsletter* 64; Fountain Trust, "Odd," 4.

146. Barling, "Editorial: Unless," 2–3; "Editorial: Farewell," 2; Fountain Trust, "News," 4.

147. Interview with Harper, 10 November 2005; Interview with Smail, 16 February 2006; Fountain Trust, "News", 4; Harper, "30 Years," 11.

the renewal of the Church." Although the Trustees, and he himself, did not know how closing the Trust would help with God's new works, they insisted that it was a mission from God and they should implement it with "a joyful obedience."[148] In reviewing the Trust's work in the previous sixteen years, Barling suggested that there were two dimensions that the Trust had contributed to the charismatic renewal. Firstly, he believed that it had been given a special privilege by God to motivate the renewal in historic churches through the Holy Spirit. Churches had been renewed and had rediscovered the significance of the Holy Spirit both experientially and theologically. Secondly, Barling suggested that ecumenically, it also made a considerable contribution as it was aware of the divisive potential of the charismatic renewal and had resisted the strong pressure to establish a denomination. It had done this by organizing a team of leaders with a variety of ecclesiological backgrounds and had refused to adopt any system of membership. In addition, it had also seized every opportunity to achieve reconciliation both with the Evangelicals and Pentecostals by tackling the misunderstandings that had arisen. Their efforts at avoiding further division among churches had been recognized and appreciated.[149]

The closure of the Trust was a sad day for some because of the spiritual blessings it had brought in the past. But others admired the decision because they agreed with the Trustees that its tasks had finished. They also felt that it should not be kept for personal sentimental reasons as a repetition of the past could become a hindrance to the launching of new initiatives.[150] That the Trustees could consider the whole matter of closing the Trust, and believe that this would be for the good of renewal in the future, can be explained by their understanding of its role when it was established. One of the members of the Advisory Council, Campbell McAlpine, had foreseen its closure long before as God's purpose. The minute of the Trust's meeting in 1968 reports that he "felt that there might come a time when the Trust's work would be at an end in God's will, and that the lessons He gives were to help us learn that the scope of any work of His was in His hands."[151] The Trustees had kept reviewing their work every eighteen months and one of the questions they con-

---

148. Barling, "Editorial: Unless," 2–3; Fountain Trust, "News," 4.

149. Barling "Editorial: Farewell," 2–3.

150. Ibid., 2–4.

151. Minute-FTAM (6 December 1968), 2.

tinually asked was whether the Trust should be continued. They "were terrified" of being like some Christian organizations, which were useless but did not die. After sixteen years, the Trustees and Barling felt that the Trust had fulfilled its task and felt justified in deciding that it should be wound up.[152]

Although the Trustees claimed that the termination was God's will, and that this was confirmed by the "harmony and complete unanimity by the Trustees and the Executive,"[153] two inner pressures on the Trust are worth considering as factors in its closure. The first one was the financial difficulty about which Barling had warned. In the Trust's *News and Prayer Letter* (December 1979), he described the difficult financial situation in detail and said, "I have to report that last year the accounts show a loss of nearly £8,000." He reported that in the previous years expenses had grown, with a 64 percent increase for administration, and a 35 percent increase for travel. Meanwhile income had not kept pace with the outgoings. In May 1980, four months before the announcement of the Trust's closure, Barling warned, "The figures for the following six months, i.e., up to March 80, are even worse!" Regarding this critical financial pressure, he said that the Trust had to be careful with their use of resources and the house at Beauchamp Road had to be sold. The financial crisis even led them to consider canceling some activities and was seen to put the whole future of the Trust at risk, although at that stage there seemed to be no thought of closing the Trust altogether. At that point, Barling was sure that "FT should continue in the ministry God has given us" and he urged those who were concerned to think about devoting more resources, both financially and spiritually, for the Trust.[154]

Secondly, before the closing of the Trust, the leadership team and staff had lost several experienced and gifted persons. In 1979, Bob Gordon ceased to have any connection with the Trust and started work for the Evangelical Alliance in Harrow. Executives and Trustees like Douglas McBain, Brian Soan, and Julian Ward also left in the same year.[155] John Richards resigned the associate directorship of the Trust in May 1980 and began to enhance the communication among people or

152. Interview with Smail, 16 February 2006.

153. Barling, "Editorial: Unless," 3.

154. Barling, *News and Prayer Letter* 66, 67.

155. Barling, *News and Prayer Letter* 66.

organizations that were involved in healing ministry, which had been confirmed by the prayers of the Executives of the Trust. He would retain connection with the Trust. The secretary, Sylvia Lawton, who had served in the Trust for many years left and worked with CMS. Ian Jolly, the editorial assistant of *Renewal* magazine, also decided to leave for a job in a firm of surveyors.[156] Although some of the vacancies could be filled,[157] losing such a large number of significant people together with their spiritual insights, theological knowledge, expertise, and personal experience in less than eighteen months was a huge discouragement. It inevitably affected the commitment, zeal, and assurance of the continuation of the ministry.

Despite being the founder of the Trust, Harper had not been consulted about the closure. He believed that it was a wrong decision, had nothing to do with God's will and was simply a human lack of vision and confidence. At the end of the 1970s, the Trustees and some charismatics had felt that the renewal had "peaked" and had reached an "apogee" as Colin Buchanan put it.[158] However, Harper's panorama of the renewal was different. He thought that it was neither "peaked" nor ended in the 1970s, but on the contrary, had undergone "acceleration." He foresaw that during the 1980s there would be "greater manifestations of the power and presence of Jesus Christ among his people." He expressed this view in an article for *Renewal* in 1980 and still held it in 2005 during my interview with him.[159] He felt that those leaders of the Trust had failed to get a renewed vision for the needs of the 1980s, but still held on to the original one from the 1960s when the Trust was first established. In contrast, Smail agreed with closing the Trust as he explained that if the task was to introduce the charismatic renewal within the mainline churches, its aim had been achieved, and its job done by the end of 1970s.[160] Although Harper and Smail had different views on the closure of the Trust, they both believed that the appointment of Barling had caused it. Both thought that he was not the right person for the job. As

---

156. Fountain Trust, "New," 5; Barling, *News and Prayer Letter* 67.

157. For example, George Hoerder took over the central administration of the Trust, and Mrs. Ruby Waterman did the typing as a part-time job. (Barling, *News and Prayer Letter* 67.)

158. Interview with Harper, 10 November 2005.

159. Harper, "Prospects," 14; Interview with Harper, 10 November 2005.

160. Interview with Smail, 16 February 2006.

far as Smail was concerned, he did not have the national connections that Harper and he had brought. As far as Harper was concerned, he did not have the "strength" and "calling" for the position. He was not the "visionary" that the Trust needed after Smail who "had become fed up with it."[161]

The Ecumenical Loss of Its Closure

Both Harper and Smail acknowledged that the Trust was an important instrument for linking denominations and so its closure meant an end to the ecumenical developments that had been so successfully and widely cultivated. They both regarded the Trust as an "umbrella" that had grouped and gathered denominations including Roman Catholics together when the renewal was prospering. Especially by the end of the 1970s, the renewal was growing within Anglican, Baptist, Presbyterian and Methodist churches, as well as the house churches. Moreover, people had started doing their own thing for renewal within their own denominational groups so there was a kind of "split" taking place. Since the Trust had always resisted the idea of being a denomination and in-sisted on being neutral as a vehicle to facilitate the charismatic renewal, it could gather representatives of different churches to work together. The Advisory Council became an arena for charismatic leaders of dif-ferent denominations to discuss issues. Its conferences were a means of gathering laity from a variety of backgrounds to learn and experience the renewal together. Since there was no other organization with quite the same character as the Trust, this kind of ecumenical consultation and cooperation for the renewal ended when it was disbanded. Individual churches including the historic, Pentecostal and house churches would just concentrate on their own ministries without cooperating with one another. Consequently, they all lost a lot and gained very little. Smail saw that the ecumenical dimension had "got lost . . . never quite came back again" after the Trust's closure. Harper's criticism was that the Trust closed at a "very strategic moment at the end of the 70s to the 80s," and that this was a "wrong" and "unnecessary" decision, "a sad story."[162] He

---

161. Interview with Harper, 10 November 2005.

162. Interview with Harper, 10 November 2005; Interview with Smail, 16 February 2006.

and Andrew Walker believed that it had "left the Renewal without a clear focus" when it approached the 1980s.[163]

CONCLUSION

The charismatic renewal in Britain took place within a society undergoing religious, economic, cultural, and moral transitions in the post-war period to which the established churches were not able to respond. It was widely spread out and systematically promoted in the country through the Fountain Trust, which was founded and developed by the devotees of the renewal. Although the renewal and the Trust did not gain support and acknowledgement from all British churches and they underwent attack and antagonism, plenty of churches were renewed and individuals' lives were transformed in sixteen years (1964–80). The Trust also successfully encouraged churches to reach out into the realm of ecumenism and search for further possibilities of interdenominational cooperation. The Trust was the symbol of the charismatic renewal and they existed, grew, and ventured new ministry together; hence, the closure of the Trust implies the end of renewal. Undeniably, there were waves of renewal in the 1980s and 1990s, but the ray spread out by the Fountain Trust was distinct and it only belonged to the 1960s and 1970s.

163. Walker, *Restoring the Kingdom*, 51.

2

The Five International Conferences

DURING THE 1970S THE Fountain Trust held five international conferences biennially starting in 1971. They took place at the University of Surrey, Guildford (12–17 July 1971), the University of Nottingham (9–14 July 1973), and at Westminster (28 July–2 August 1975, 1–5 August 1977 and 30 July–3 August 1979) for five to six days during the summer. Since the Fountain Trust had been established in 1964, it had held many local conferences in various major cities and towns in England and Scotland. However these five conferences were different in character as they were aimed at being both international and ecumenical. There follows a description of these conferences in terms of the aims, participants, venues, programs, feedback, and results.

AIMS

The Trust organized these conferences because it hoped that churches would not just be renewed superficially but right down to their foundations,[1] through "charismatic worship, ecumenical encounters, international fellowship, and in-depth teaching."[2] Furthermore, the conferences were also intended to be ecumenical which was "indeed the very purpose."[3] Harper confidently claimed that the conferences would "demonstrate a unity made possible by the experience of the Holy Spirit" despite the disagreements regarding certain areas of doctrine. This ecumenical intention was announced to the public before the Guildford Conference began,

1. Rough notes-Guildford (14 October 1970); Letter from Harper to Michael Pusey, 29 October 1970, 2.

2. Fountain Trust, "Leaflet and Booking Form of the Conference," n.d.

3. Harper, "Editorial: Christian," 5; Letter from Harper to Michael Pusey, 29 October 1970, 2.

> The purpose of the conference is to draw together Christians from every church tradition from Roman Catholic to Pentecostal, and from many countries of the world, to learn more about the power of the Holy Spirit and the way in which our churches can regain it in its fullness.[4]

The aims of these conferences varied according to the visions of the director. During Harper's directorship, which ended in September 1975, the three international conferences in Guildford, Nottingham, and Westminster had two common characteristics: 1. Fellowship and community in the Spirit; and 2. The manifestation of the power and glory of the Spirit. These two features were clearly reflected in the titles. Guildford (1971) was given the title "The Fellowship of the Holy Spirit," because the Trust wanted to be coherent to the prayer week for Christian unity of Godalming Council of Churches in the autumn of 1971 which was themed with the same title.[5] The theme of Nottingham (1973) was "Gathered for Power," which was the title of Graham Pulkingham's book. Pulkingham was the Rector of the Church of the Redeemer in Houston, Texas. This conference had a "strong Texan flavour" because the Church of the Redeemer's music team—Fisherfolk, and Pulkingham were so much involved in it. Also, a film, *Following the Spirit*, was shown at the conference and Harper's book, *A New Way of Living*, which described the renewal of that church, was available for sale during the conference. Harper believed that with the involvement of that church, delegates would experience the "new and exciting areas" of the charismatic renewal "in increasingly creative ways." [6] In addition, the Trust claimed that "it is through the gathered community that God's power is most freely and fruitfully manifested."[7] Harper was personally convinced that "the whole question of the church as a community of people expressing the Body of Christ" was a matter of concern for everybody.[8] Westminster (1975) was entitled "Glory in the Church" suggesting that "the glory of

---

4. Fountain Trust, "Press Release: International Conference," n. d.

5. Letter from Bob Balkam to Harper, 18 May 1970; Letter from Harper to Leslie Davison, 9 July, 1970; Minute-Guildford (12 June 1970).

6. Harper, "Letter," 1.

7. Letter from the Director of the Fountain Trust to Cliff Longley, *The Times*, London, 2 July 1973; Fountain Trust, "Leaflet and Booking Form of the Conference," n.d.

8. Letter from Harper to Larry Christenson, 26 July 1972.

God should be manifested through His people in the world."[9] This theme was also used for the whole series of celebration activities for the Trust's tenth anniversary from 1974 to 1975. The first celebrating activity was "Festival of Praise" in St Paul's Cathedral in London on 12 October 1974 followed by a series of "Glory in the Church" weekends which lasted until Westminster 1975. The weekends were held in various major cities and towns in Britain including Newcastle-on-Tyne (1–4 November 1974), Bristol and Bath (29 November–2 December 1974), Birmingham (7–10 February 1975), Manchester (18–20 March 1975), Liverpool and Manchester (18–21 April 1975), and Plymouth (2–5 May 1975). Smail recorded that "the fellowship with Roman Catholic brethren was most refreshing." Participants in these weekends were involved in public services on both Friday and Saturday nights. They had lectures and seminars on Saturdays. The last event of the celebration was Westminster 1975 which was specially arranged as the culmination of all the celebration activities.[10]

After Smail succeeded to the directorship in 1975, the focus of the other two international conferences was altered. He put the emphasis on renewal in the local churches and their responsibility for evangelism and social concern.[11] For example, in his sermon at an evening service in Westminster 1975, entitled "The Recipe of Reality," he emphasized that renewal should be brought about by the work in local churches, and should not only be "singing, hugging and hand raising." He reminded the delegates of the Christ on Calvary and the cross, and taught that charismatics should integrate the gospel and the Spirit, and let renewal be seen by the world. As he said, "The charismatic renewal must never become a movement by itself or for itself. It belongs to the life of the church, to the local church far more than to a large conference." He took the title "Growing in the Church—An International Conference on Renewal in the Local Church" for the fourth conference in 1977, believing that "If the glory is there the growth must follow."[12] For him, "growth" meant "growing into the world—how the church can become more fruitfully

9. Harbour, "Glory," 4.

10. Fountain Trust, "Press Release", January 1975; "Itinerary: Harper and Smail," *Newsletter* 50; "Itinerary: Smail," *Newsletter* 51; "Itinerary: Harper and Smail," *Newsletter* 51.

11. Fountain Trust, "Renewal," 1; "Reality," 16.

12. Smail, *Newsletter* 57.

and decisively involved in areas of social need and concern."[13] He particularly directed the conference to concentrate on the renewal in local churches, on the basis that the "Charismatic renewal stands or falls by what happens in local parishes and congregations. What matters is their ability to be deeply rooted in God's Grace and Christ's gospel, so that they may grow into healing fellowship, evangelical outreach and social impact."[14] Therefore, the phrase "Renewal in the Local Church" was added after "An International Conference" in the subtitle. It targeted the local church leaders as the main source of delegates in order "to help them to give renewal and its ministries corporate shape" in their own churches.[15] Through prayer and praise, delegates learnt by experience how the local church could be renewed "in their worship, fellowship, evangelism and social concern."[16] The last international conference, "Joy in the City: An International Conference on Renewal and its Outreach in Society" also had a similar emphasis. The phrase "Joy in the City" was taken from the book of Acts 8:8, "So there was much rejoicing in that city" after Philip had preached the gospel which was accompanied by signs of healing and exorcism in Samaria (v.5–8). Smail wanted to encourage charismatics to focus "on the need for a renewed and revitalised social impact within the life and ministry of the church"[17] because "[t]hese are not alternatives, but that the one is very much the empowerment for the second, and any renewal which forgets this will inevitably become eccentric and inward looking."[18] In addition, Smail insisted that charismatics should not only be concerned about what they personally could gain from the renewal as it could lead to "self-indulgence." As he explained in a letter to Michael Green, saying, "The central theme as 'Joy in the City' where we are trying to turn people's attention from personal problems and the obsession with healing, which could so easily swamp the renewal movement, into a new obedience to the call of the Spirit towards evangelism and prophetic

13. Minute-FTCCM (8 June 1977), 1.

14. Fountain Trust, *Growing in the Church*, 2.

15. Letter from Smail to Mrs. Agnes Sanford, 23 February 1976; Letter from Smail to Tom Walker, 23 February 1976; Letter from Smail to Rev. Howard Belben, 5 March 1976; Letter from Smail to Harper, 5 March 1976.

16. Fountain Trust, "Press Release: Growing in the church, April 1977."

17. Minute-FTCCM (8 December 1977), 1.

18. Letter from Smail to the Bishop of London, 18 July 1979.

action in the world."[19] "Turn the renewal inside out"[20] was the slogan of this conference. He planned to invite those who had experience of local ministry and a vision for renewal in the local church to be speakers. He found the American style of "star presentations and miracle services"[21] incompatible, and said frankly, "I want to avoid both the MacNutt sort of American image, and the theological scholar who is very profound but does not communicate on the popular level."[22]

PARTICIPANTS

These five international conferences attracted from several hundred to more than a thousand people from Britain and other countries. For Guildford, there were 650 delegates[23] while at the second one in Nottingham the number was double that, 1500, which includes 1252 residents and 250 to 350 day visitors.[24] At Westminster 1975, the number climbed to 1800.[25] The Trust's international conferences became more and more popular within those five years. From the time that the conferences were open for registration, the bookings, both from inside and outside Britain, grew steadily and the quota for each conference was filled up very quickly. For example, in December 1970, six months before the Guildford conference took place, Harper had already an-

19. Smail, *Discipline*; Letter from Smail to Michael Green, 23 April 1979.

20. Letter from Smail to Michael Scanlan, 10 November 1977; Letter from Smail to Michael Green, 10 November 1977; Letter from Smail to Catherine Marshall LeSourd, 10 November 1977; Letter from Smail to Catherine Marshall LeSourd, 3 March 1978; Letter from Smail to William T. B. McAllister, 31 March 1978; Letter from Smail to D. K. Gillett, 4 August 1978; Letter from Smail to the Archbishop Helder Pessoa Camara, 28 August 1978; Letter from Smail to Larry Christenson, 15 September 1978; Letter from Smail to William J. Brown, 6 February 1979; Letter from Smail to the Bishop of London, 6 February 1979; Letter from Smail to Tom Forrest, 6 February, 1979; Letter from Smail to Suenens, 23 April 1979, 2; Fountain Trust, "Joy in the City", 1; Smail, *Newsletter* 64.

21. Letter from Smail to Jim Glennon, 4 August 1978.

22. Letter from Smail to Fr. Paul Lebeau, 23 February 1976.

23. This figure includes 460 residents and the rest was day visitors. Fountain Trust, "Guest List: Guildford"; Davison, "Memorandum," 1.

24. Fountain Trust, "Guest List: Nottingham ," 1–27; Letter from Harper to David MacInnes, 11 December 1972; Letter from Secretary to Harper Mr. Dixon, 28 June 1973.

25. Letter from Truda Smail, 6 June 1975.

nounced, "The bookings for this conference are going very rapidly."[26] In April 1973, he said, "We have had an unprecedented demand for places and we are already nearly full", by which he meant that over 1,000 people had registered. So he then had to close English bookings because the accommodation in the University of Nottingham was "practically full."[27] Nevertheless, applications did not stop coming and by the end of May, there were still a "tremendous number of people" on the waiting list. The quota for the first Westminster conference was enlarged to 2,400 due to the "heavy demand for places" at Nottingham and bookings were "coming in very nicely."[28] Although in 1977 and 1979 Smail did not try to get another numerical breakthrough, and was concerned more about the quality of delegates, the number was still over 1,000. It was reported that delegates' maturity was "equally high" compared with the quality of the speakers' teaching.[29] There were 1,715 delegates in 1977 who participated fully, and 200 came to the evening services only.[30] In 1979, an attendance of 1,214 was recorded.[31] These were mainly British, and the rest were from many parts of the world, although the majority of non-British were from Western Europe and Scandinavia. Within these countries, Sweden was the major supporter.[32] There were also quite a number of Americans and Canadians as well as Australians and New Zealanders. At Westminster in 1975, the Temple Trust in Australia brought 50 peo-

---

26. Letter from Harper to Thurnace York, 22 December 1970.

27. Letter from Harper to Rune Brännström, 10 April 1973; Letter from Harper to Lewis Simonfalvi, 10 April 1973; Letter from Harper to Hans Jacob Frøen, 10 April 1973.

28. Letter from Harper to David Bartlett, 24 May 1973; Fountain Trust, "Booking Form: Westminster 1975"; Letter from Harper to the Bishop of London, 2 June 1975; Letter from Truda Smail, 6 June 1975.

29. Minute-FTCCM (8 December 1977), 1.

30. Fountain Trust, "Guest List: Westminster 1977"; Minute-Westminster 1977 (6 July1977); Letter from Smail to speaker, 1977.

31. Fountain Trust, "Guest List: Westminster 1979."

32. For instance, a Swede, Rune Brännström, of the Kriten Ungdom, Jesus Centre asked for 100 places at the Nottingham Conference for a group of young people three months before it began. However, Harper could only offer him 50 and asked him to return the application forms by the end of April to secure the places. These young people had to come by buses instead of by flight because the Trust could not offer a special price for parties, but it showed their determination to come to the conference for renewal. (Letter from Harper to Rune Brännstöm, 10 April 1973; Fountain Trust, "Press Release from the Fountain Trust," 2 July 1973, 1.)

ple to the conference.[33] This organization had kept up communications and maintained a close relationship with the Trust, and it advertised the Conference in its publications and activities. Those who came from Asia and Africa were mainly Singaporeans, Indians, residents in Hong Kong (mainly non-Chinese), and South Africans. At Nottingham, there were some people from the Middle East including Israel and Iran, and from South America, Brazil, Argentina, and Bermuda.[34] Details are shown in the appendix.

These international conferences were "a truly kaleidoscopic gathering—with many bright colors."[35] They took place during Harper's leadership and the wide international participation was due to four factors. Firstly, following Guildford, organizations similar to the Fountain Trust had been established in other countries and their close relationship maintained with frequent communication. This gradually built up an unofficial but effective charismatic network. That was one of the ways the conferences were advertised internationally and attracted groups of foreign participants. The Temple Trust in Australia was one of the examples. Secondly, Harper's personal contact with charismatics in many countries also helped to increase the variety of countries and number of participants at the conferences. For example, Harper's visit to India, Australia, and Singapore between the end of January and the end of March in 1975 gave him the opportunity to get acquainted with the local charismatic leaders and to open up further cooperation. During those two months, he was invited by four bishops of the Church of South India to speak to ministers and theological students in Vijayawada, Hyderabad, Madras, Bangalore, and Madurai. Then he was invited to speak at the National Charismatic Conference at the University of Melbourne on 20–25 January 1975 and stayed for one month to visit Canberra, Tasmania, Adelaide, and Perth. On the way back to Britain, he stayed in Singapore for a week.[36] He made a second visit to India in November of the same year and was warmly welcomed by Bishop Sundar Clarke. When he attempted to invite leaders from the non-Western world to Westminster 1975, with the support of a bursary fund, he contacted the Church of

33. Letter from Ralph Bancroft to Truda Smail, 18 March 1975.

34. Fountain Trust, "Guest List: Nottingham."

35. Letter from Director of Fountain Trust to Editor of the *Church of England Newspaper*, 1 July 1973.

36. Fountain Trust, "Travelling Man," 6.

South India and the Bishop of Singapore, Chiu Ban It, and asked them to nominate one or two potential leaders.[37] Chiu himself, apart from speaking at the conference, also brought a party of twenty from Singapore and Malaysia to Westminster 1975.[38] Thirdly, the provision of simultaneous interpretation in 1975 removed the linguistic obstacle for people who had a limited command of English.[39] Translation into French, German, Danish, and Swedish was provided for lectures and seminars.[40] The Trust also put those delegates who needed interpretation of a particular language together for the evening services.[41] Although the facilities were expensive, at £700, it was felt to be worthwhile for such a well-represented international conference.[42] However, at Westminster 1977 and 1979, this facility was not provided as it was thought to be impracticable.[43]

Apart from tackling the language difficulty, the Trust was willing to assist some Christian leaders financially. In 1973, Harper had been prepared to assist a Hungarian Pentecostal, Lewis Simonfalvi, by paying for his conference fee and transportation costs from Budapest to London, and then the return fare from London to Nottingham. Simonfalvi explained that because of the weak Hungarian currency and the barriers to travelling under the communist régime, he needed Harper's assistance both with money and also with an invitation letter to present to the immigration office for a visa. Unfortunately, Simonfalvi could not come for reasons which he did not explain, and he was "depressed" about it.[44] The whole incident reflected Harper's determination and effort to invite as many people in the world as he could, and not to exclude those behind the

37. Letter from Sundar Clark to Harper, 15 May 1975, 2; Letter from Harper to Sundar Clarke, 21 April 1975; Letter from Harper to Chiu Ban It, 21 April 1975.

38. Letter from Chiu Ban It to Harper, 30 December 1974.

39. Letter from Harper to Hans-Jacob Frøen, 22 November.

40. Harper expected that there would be approximately 100 'from each of German, French and Swedish- speaking countries. (Letter from Harper to D. White, 18 November 1974.) Fountain Trust, "Glory in the Church," 3; Minute-Westminster 1975 (1 October 1974), 2; Letter from Harper to overseas, 15 October 1974; Letter from Harper to J. Malm, 11 November 1974.

41. Fountain Trust, "Glory in the Church," 3; Letter from Harper to Ruth Champness, 12 September 1974.

42. Minute-Westminster 1975 (31 January 1975), 3.

43. Fountain Trust, "Growing in the Church," 3; Fountain Trust, "Joy in the City," 2.

44. Letter from Lewis Simonfalvi to Harper, 14 February 1973; Letter from Lewis Simonfalvi to Harper, 19 April 1973; Letter from Harper to Lewis Simonfalvi to Harper, 1 May 1973; Letter from Lewis Simonfalvi to Harper, 5 June 1973.

iron curtain despite the predictable political obstacles to their coming. For Westminster 1975 the Trust set up a bursary fund to overcome the financial difficulties for church leaders from non-Western and Eastern European countries.[45] It was constituted by donations and covered the expenses of transport, accommodation, and other necessities.[46] Because of the limited amount of money available, however, it was only open to young leaders who could be equipped at the conference for their future ministries.[47] The Trust not only offered money and flight tickets, but also arranged visits to some charismatic churches and other European countries when requested after the conference.[48] There were seven charismatic leaders from Asia and Africa who benefited from this fund: Dr. Louis Tay, a Singaporean Chinese and an Anglican minister chosen by Chiu Ban It,[49] Zao Poonon, a Baptist minister in Bangalore,[50] G. D. Poornachandrarao, a vicar of St. Andrew's Anglican Church,[51] and P. A. Sathiasatchy, a layman of Bishop Sundar Clarke's church in the diocese

---

45. Fountain Trust, "Bursary Fund," 5; Smail, *Newsletter* 52; Minute-Westminster 1975 (1 October 1974), 5; Letter from Harper to Chiu Ban It, 21 April 1975; Letter from Harper to Louis Tay, 16 May 1975.

46. By the end of January, it had already accumulated £1728, of which there was one donation of £1000. Another source of the Fund was from a couple, Brenda and John Fulcher, in Kenya who donated £100. (Minute-Westminster 1975 (31 January 1975), 1; Letter from Harper to Brenda and John Fulcher, 3 June 1975.)

47. Letter from Harper to Felix Dias-Abeyesinghe, 5 May 1975; Letter from Harper to Sundar Clarke, 8 May 1975.

48. Letter from Harper to Louis Tay, 3 June 1975.

49. Letter from Chiu Ban It to Harper, 5 May 1975, 1–2; Letter from Harper to David Pawson, 15 May 1975.

50. Poonen's experience of Spirit baptism and tongues spread very quickly in India. He shared his experience with John Stott in a letter and they ministered together during Stott's visit in India. His charismatic ministry led many people of his church received the baptism of the Spirit and tongues. However, there was also opposition against his ministry. The church authorities forbade the teaching of Spirit baptism and they did not want Harper and Harald Bredesen who had led twelve people to experience Spirit baptism in Poonen's congregation to speak any more. As a result, Poonen was prepared to resign. (Letter from Zac Poonen to Harper, 28 April 1975, 2; Letter from Harper to David Pawson, 15 May 1975; Letter from Zac Poonen to Harper, 3 June 1975.)

51. He was regarded by the Bishop of the Church of South India as a "very fine dedicated young clergyman". At Westminster 1975, he witnessed the works of the Spirit in people's lives from many countries as he said, "The Spirit is indeed moving all over the world." (Letter from Harper to Ananda Rao Smauel, 19 May 1975; Fountain Trust, "What the Week Has Meant to Me?," 2.)

of Madras,[52] Robert de Maar, a black Anglican minister of the Church of Reconciliation in Manenberg, South Africa, who was nominated by the Archbishop of Cape Town,[53] Julius Adoyo,[54] and Elijah Malenje[55] who were both leaders of the Trinity Fellowship in Kenya.

VENUES

The first two conferences were residential and delegates stayed at the student hostels of the Universities of Surrey and of Nottingham during the week. The last three conferences were all in Westminster, "the heart of the church and state" where many religious and political buildings are situated such as the Houses of Parliament, Westminster Abbey, Westminster Cathedral, and the Jerusalem Chamber (where the King

52. Clarke described him as a "keen," "very dedicated and committed" member. He had a positive attitude towards the charismatic renewal and the Spirit's power. Clarke expected him to bring the renewal back to the church. (Letter from Sundar Clark to Harper, 15 May 1975.)

53. Robert de Maar was very thankful for the Trust's offer as he said, "Word fail to express a deepfelt Gratitude." When preparing the trip to England, he came across a "not unusual" problem of a passport. Black South Africans were always given a passport one day before they departed. He had had this trouble in the previous year when he wanted to go to the All Africa Conference of Churches in Lusaka, Zambia. Nevertheless, through the persuasion of the Archbishop of Cape Town and the Provincial Executive Officer in Johannesburg to the Minister of Interior, the problem was solved successfully and de Maar was given a passport in the early July. (Letter from the Archbishop of Cape Town to Harper, 7 July 1975; Letter from the Archbishop's secretary to Harper, 8 July 1975; Letter from Robert de Maar to Harper, 12 July 1975; Letter from the Archbishop of Cape Town to Harper, 15 July 1975; Letter from Robert de Maar to Harper, n.d.)

54. Harper had the idea of inviting Julius Adoyo because when he was traveling in a tube in London, he was told by a passenger that he should invite Adoyo if the Trust was to invite somebody from Africa. When Harper requested Godfrey Dawkins, the General Secretary of the Trinity Fellowship, to nominate two Africans, Dawkins suggested Adoyo. Therefore, Harper thought that it was God's will for Adoyo to come and so he sent the invitation to him. However, Adoyo faced a difficulty from his Bishop as he had already had leave once in that year. The Bishop only offered his permission if Adoyo could fulfill two conditions that "he forfeit his allowance for that time" and he would not go to any conference for at least one year. In order to attend the Conference, "this vast and very important gathering in the life of the Church for this days," he accepted those conditions. (Letter from Godfrey Gawkins to Harper, 10 September 1974; Letter from Godfrey Dawkins to Harper, 13 May 1975; Letter from Harper to Julius Adoyo, 3 June 1975; Letter from Julius Adoyo to Harper, 3July 1975; Letter from Godfrey and Elisabeth Gawkins to Harper, 4 July 1975.)

55. Godfrey Dawkins described him as "one of the most consistent Christian characters" whom he knew. (Letter from Godfrey Gawkins to Harper, 13 May 1975.)

James Authorized Version was finalized). That symbolically demonstrated an intimate relation between the renewal and society, and implied that the fruits of the renewal should benefit society, which was actually emphasized in the last two Westminster conferences.[56] All the activities of those Westminster conferences were scattered around in different buildings of the area: Central Hall, Caxton Hall (Great Hall and York Hall), St. Margaret's Church, St. John's Church, and Westminster School Hall.[57] These Westminster conferences were "more fluid"[58] than the Guildford and Nottingham conferences, as they took place in a variety of buildings rather than on one university campus.

This arrangement had its drawbacks, however. Some delegates felt that there was a lack of solid fellowship because participants rushed from one place to another by public transport. Also, since London itself was a tourist centre with many attractions, it created distractions for delegates at the charismatic conferences where they were supposed to concentrate on spiritual matters.[59] Moreover, this venue was administratively-challenging compared to a university campus, where a set of lecture rooms, a great hall, and residential hostels were ready for the various activities of the conferences. Also, the number of participants at Westminster 1975 was nearly double that of Nottingham 1973 and so it was more difficult to make arrangements for all the delegates.[60] Fortunately, Michael Barling, the vicar of St. Andrew's, Sidcup, helped resolve the complexity of the problems it raised. Smail regarded him as the "answer" to all the administrative problems as he was "trained and expert on how to put so many people in so many halls for so many lectures" and, when completed, the plan for doing so was "as clear as day." His proposed timetable for the morning lectures of Westminster 1975 "was received with admiration" at the conference committee meeting. Barling started planning Westminster 1975 from September 1974 to make sure that everything

56. Fountain Trust, "Booking Form," n. d.; "Growing in the Church", 2; Joy in the City,1; Letter from Smail to David Watson, 10 November 1977; Harbour, "Glory," 4.

57. The Central Hall consisted of the Great Hall, Lecture Hall, Assembly Hall, Fellowship Room and library. In 1975, the rental cost of the building for the Conference was £2464. ("Memorandum," 1.) Fountain Trust, "Press Release," January 1975; Fountain Trust, "Conference Brochure," 6.

58. Minute-Westminster 1975 (1 October 1974), 1.

59. Letter from Mr. and Mrs. M. Carney to Smail, 21 September 1977.

60. Smail, *Newsletter* 54.

ran "like clockwork." Despite all the admiration, he regarded himself as the "conference odd-job man."[61]

As these conferences were not residential, the Trust offered several suggestions for accommodation, such as camping, caravanning, university hostels, or hotels. Delegates could also consider staying in homes under the scheme called "Operation Cornelius" which recruited Christians in London who were willing to provide bed and breakfast.[62] The Trust first adopted this method in 1975. Harper described it as "a new kind of conference, international in its scope but within the budget of most ordinary people."[63] It also helped to "increase fellowship and decrease cost."[64] The final two Westminster conferences became completely non-residential. The Trust simply prepared a list of Londoners who were willing to provide bed and breakfast and then left the delegates to make their own arrangements. In 1977, it became a policy for future conferences not to provide accommodation for delegates, because the cost of doing so was "prohibitive."[65]

PROGRAMS

Although the aims of the conferences varied according to the two different directors, the programs for all the five conferences were similar. From 1975, the Trust invited some bishops to welcome the conference on the first evenings. For example, the Bishop of London, Gerald Ellison, representing the diocese, spoke at Westminster 1977 and 1979 and the Bishop of Southwark, Arthur Mervyn Stockwood, also did so at the 1977 event.[66] In the following four or five days, the conference program was

---

61. Smail, *Newsletter* 52; Fountain Trust, "Odd," 4; Minute-Westminster 1975 (31 January 1975), 1.

62. Fountain Trust, "Booking Form," n. d.; Smail, *Newsletter* 51; Letter from Truda Smail to G. Davies, 15 November 1974.

63. Minute-Westminster 1975 (1 October 1974), 1.

64. Smail, *Newsletter* 52.

65. Minute-FTACM (9 December 1976), 1.

66. Fountain Trust, "Press Release (January 1975)"; Letter from Harper, to A. D. Roake, 9 January 1975; Letter from Harper, dictated and signed in his absence, to the Bishop of London, 2 June 1975; Letter from Harper to the Bishop of London, 15 August 1975; Letter from the Bishop of London to Smail, 9 February 1979; Letter from Smail to Suenens, 23 April 1979, 1; Letter from Smail to the Bishop of London, 18 July 1979; Smail, "Editorial: The More We are Together," 2.

so packed that delegates "had no need to feel at a loose end."[67] Each day started with a morning service that was separated into different liturgical forms to cater for delegates of different traditions, though in the main there was a Protestant service and a Roman Catholic Mass. The Trust specially invited Cardinal Suenens to conduct the Mass at Westminster 1977 and 1979.[68] After the service, the delegates would go to lectures, by various speakers, each of whom was responsible for a specific topic. The lectures usually lasted for one hour, and were mainly for teaching rather than discussion, as there could be as many as 200 to 250 people in any one lecture.[69] But at Westminster 1979, lectures were longer, lasting for one and half hours so that people could raise questions in the last thirty minutes.[70] In the afternoons there were seminars to discuss some precise issues concerning renewal. They were aimed at being "very practical and specific, dealing with particular issues and not broad-based topics."[71] They usually began with a short introduction by a speaker and then discussion followed.[72] Alternatively, delegates could participate in a workshop to learn practical skills relating to their church ministry such as worship leadership, dancing, drama, banner-design, and art. The most prominent contributor was the Fisherfolk worship team who had a variety of skills and strengths and was invited to the conferences of 1973 and 1975.[73]

67. Fountain Trust, *Renewal*, No. 46 (August–September 1973), 21.

68. Fountain Trust, "Programme: Nottingham," 1; "Detailed Programme," 1; "Gathered for Power," 8; "Conference Brochure," 3; "Daily Mass," 2; "Booking Form," n. d.; "Westminster 1977," 2; "Fountain Trust International Conference," n. d.; "Joy in the City," 4; Minute-Westminster 1977 (20 April 1977), 1; Letter from Smail to Suenens, 23 April 1979, 1; Letter from Suenens to Smail, 9 May 1979, 2.

69. Fountain Trust, "Speakers' Information: Nottingham," 1; Letter from the Secretary to Harper to Frank Lake, 29 June 1973.

70. Letter from Michael Barling to speakers, April 1979; Letter from the Fountain Trust to speaker, June 1979.

71. Minute-Westminster 1977 (14 January 1977), 1; Minute-Westminster 1977 (25 February 1977), 1.

72. Fountain Trust, "Speakers' Information: Nottingham," 1; Letter from the Secretary to Harper to Frank Lake, 29 June 1973; Letter from Smail to the speakers, n. d.; Minute-Westminster 1977 (25 February 1977), 1.

73. Fountain Trust, "Detailed Programme: Nottingham," 1–2; "Programme: Nottingham," 1; "Joy in the City," 5; "Glory in the Church," 6; Harbour, "Glory," 6; Minute-Westminster 1975 (31 January 1975), 2; Letter from Lisa Reynolds to Smail, 13 August 1977.

In the evenings, most of the registered delegates and some interested outsiders participated in public services in a cathedral or public hall, except at Nottingham, where these were held at the university's Sport Centre. [74] At Guildford these services were held in the Cathedral of the Holy Spirit. It was relatively new as it had only been built ten years before the Guildford Conference started. According to David Pawson, since the architect of the Cathedral thought that after twenty years there would not be any preaching, he "designed it for music and visual effect." Emile Dallière admired the Cathedral, saying, "And there, above the altar, at the very apex of the choir vaulting, was the rose window with its motif of the dove descending."[75] Delegates had amazing experiences of God in this Cathedral specially dedicated to the Holy Spirit. For instance, Dennis Ball, a charismatic leader in England, heard "the most beautiful sound of music and singing" after the worship, when the choir or musical instruments had stopped performing. More surprisingly, a man next to him said, "'So you hear it too!'"[76] A couple claimed, "We were so thrilled to . . . feel and know the power of God with us—specially in the Cathedral."[77] David Watson was full of praise, "The Cathedral services were fantastic—it is still hard to believe what happened there."[78] Harper personally was so touched by the worship that he said, "for most of those present the cathedral services will surely live longest in the memory."[79]

Harper used his American connections to arrange the services. He invited Merv and Merla Watson from Toronto to lead worship at Guildford[80] and the Fisherfolk from Houston at Nottingham and Westminster 1975.[81] By contrast, Smail seemed not to appreciate the imported worship style from America and so appointed his daughter, Mary Smail, to organize a Fountain Trust music team to lead the worship. Most of the delegates enjoyed their worship and found it "wonderful."[82]

74. Letter from Harper to John Horner, 18 October 1971.

75. Letter from David Pawson to Harper, 30 April 1970; Dallière, "Guildford International Conference," 7–8.

76. Fountain Trust, "Guildford," 32.

77. Letter from Mr. and Mrs. Jack Evans, 19 July 1971.

78. Letter from David Watson to Harper, 20 July 1971, 1.

79. Harper, "Coming-of-Age," 3–4.

80. Fountain Trust, "Press Release: International Conference 2."

81. Harper, "Letter," 1; Holl, "Glory in the Church," 5.

82. Letter from John Fowell to Smail, 8 August 1977; Letter from Smail to D. M.

Mr. and Mrs. Whitaker thought that Mary Smail's singing "was a real contribution to the worship."[83] J. Pereboom appreciated the singing of the whole team, saying that it was "good, spontaneous and stimulating," and so people were "with it."[84] Peggy William admired the way the musicians knew "the right moment to stop or continue."[85] The music team made another contribution at Westminster 1979 with the musicians of St. John's College, Nottingham where Smail was going to teach.[86] A communion which was conducted in the "Series III" Anglican form was specially arranged in the final evening service to symbolize the ecumenical significance of the renewal.[87] This practice was continued when Smail was the director despite his Presbyterian background and found it "good that the celebrant should be Anglican and have Episcopal status." The celebrant was the Bishop of Southwell (John Denis Wakeling) at Nottingham, the Archbishop of Cape Town (Bill Burnett) at Westminster 1975, the Bishop of Pontefract (Richard Hare) at Westminster 1977, and Michael Whinney at Westminster 1979.[88] These final Eucharists triggered complex feelings within the congregation since Roman Catholics were not allowed to receive communion even though they had enjoyed fellowship with the Protestants throughout the conferences. Details of this ecumenical problem will be discussed in chapters 3 and 4.

FEEDBACK FROM DELEGATES

These five international conferences received a very positive appraisal from delegates, as shown by their letters to the Trust. Of the five conferences Guildford was the most impressive. Simon Tugwell said that it "was most exciting, and a blessing" to him although he could only participate

Adams, 19 August 1977.

83. Letter from D. Whitaker to Smail, 21 August 1977, 2.

84. Letter from J. Pereboom to the Fountain Trust, 9 August 1977, 1–2.

85. Letter from Peggy William to the Fountain Trust, 8 August 1977.

86. Fountain Trust, "Joy in the City," 2; Smail, *Newsletter* 64.

87. Letter from Harper to David Barlett, 24 May 1973; Letter from Smail to Lesslie Newbigin, 23 April 1979.

88. Letter from Smail to David Pytches, 12 March 1979; Letter from Harper to the Bishop of Southwell, 26 July 1972; Letter from the Bishop of Southwell to Harper, 1 January 1973; Letter from Harper to the Dean of Westminster, 3 June 1975; Letter from Harper to the Bishop of Southwell, 28 June 1973; Fountain Trust, "Conference Brochure," 2; "Michael," 1; "Speaker," 2; "Joy in the City," 4; Holl, "Glory in the Church," 10; Minute-Westminster 1977 (20 April 1977), 1.

in part of it.[89] Kevin Ranaghan described Guildford as "fantastic" and a "tremendous gift from God." He continued to praise God for what had happened at Guildford whenever he thought about it.[90] Ivar Lungren, a Swedish charismatic, claimed that "the conference was wonderful and of great importance for the future."[91] F. P. Möller, a South African Pentecostal minister, thanked Harper for the "marvelous," "enjoyable and blessed time" at Guildford and asserted that "What happened at Guildford is nothing less than a miracle, a doing of God!"[92] After more than thirty years (1971–2005) when Harper recalled what had happened at Guildford, he just said, "Guilford Conference in 1971was awesome and remarkable."[93]

In the same way, Westminster 1975 was beneficial and full of blessings for most of the delegates.[94] It was regarded as "wonderful," "super," "splendid," "profitable," "an unforgettable experience," and "a tremendous encouragement."[95] Some of them appreciated the way the conference covered "the breadth and depth of the many areas of life."[96] They not only gained understanding about renewal, but also saw how it could be worked out in practice.[97] They felt motivated to pray for renewal in their local churches.[98]

Delegates at Westminster 1977 described the conference as "wonderful," "thrilling," "helpful," "challenging," "memorable," "fruitful," and

89. Letter from Simon Tugwell to Harper, September 1971.

90. Ranaghan, *Maturity of the Body of Christ*.

91. Letter from Ivar Lungren to Harper, 28 July 1971.

92. Letter from F. P. Möller to Harper, 29 July 1971.

93. Harper's personal note for the author, 22 July 2005; Interview with Michael and Jeanne Harper, 8 August 2005.

94. Smail, *Newsletter* 54.

95. Letter from S. V. Winbalt Lewis to Harper, 2 August 1975; Letter from Miss J. G. Simpson to Harper, 3 August 1975; Letter from Bill and Gladys Kuty, 4 August 1975;Letter from Lornaand Ken,14 September 1975, 2; Letter from Beryl M. Parker to the Fountain Trust, 5 August 1975, p.1. Letter from Beryl M. Parker to the Fountain Trust, 5 August 1975, 5–6; Letter from Edwin to Michael and Jeanne Harper, 8 August 1975; Letter from Pamela Lucas to the Fountain Trust, 29 August 1975; Letter from Ken to Harper, 4 August 1975.

96. Letter from Trevor J. Marzetti to Harper, 8 August 1975.

97. Letter from Mary Alison to Smail, 21 August 1975.

98. Letter from S. V. Winbalt Lewis to Harper, 2 August 1975.

"useful."[99] It was a week full of blessings "in no small measure."[100] Tom Walker observed that plenty of the delegates "were touched deeply."[101] No wonder a delegate said, "If that is what a Fountain Trust conference is like, what I want to know is when is the next?"[102] Moreover, having attended Westminster 1975, one delegate noticed the great improvement in the organization of Westminster 1977, of which he said that there was "left little if anything to be desired in this respect."[103] Other delegates also admired the smooth running of the conference and they were grateful for the hard work of the whole team behind the scenes.[104] These positive appraisals given by local and international delegates suggest that these five conferences successfully and impressively promoted the renewal and had a significant impact on churches in Britain and other countries.

IMPACT

Church Leaders in the United Kingdom

The five international conferences brought about a change in the attitude of church leaders toward the charismatic renewal. The influence of Guildford was particularly significant. As Cecil Cousen, one of the Trustees, said, "Since Guildford, no Christian can ignore the charismatic renewal" although they might disagree with it. He added, ". . . the charismatic renewal has infiltrated further into all denominations.

99. Letter from Collin McCampbell to Smail, 5 August 1977; Letter from Philip Sourbut to Smail, 6 August 1977; Letter from Pauline Ruffett to Smail, 9 August 1977. Letter from Collin McCampbell to Smail, 5 August 1977; Letter from A. K. Pring to Smail, 18 August 1977; Letter from Mr. D. Whitaker to Rev. and Mrs. Smail, 21 August 1977; Letter from J. Martin-Doyle to Smail, 9 September 1977; Letter from Mr. and Mrs. Mike Carney to Smail, 21 September 1977.

100. Letter from Collin McCampbell to Smail, 5 August 1977; Letter from Gordon V. Clark to Smail,12 August 1977; Letter from John Forwell to Smail, 8 August 1977; Letter from D. M. Adam to Smail, 6 August 1977; Letter from J. Pereboom to the Fountain Trust, 9 August 1977, 2; Letter from Renale Vetter to the Fountain Trust, 11 August 1977.

101. Letter from Tom Walker to Smail, 6 October 1977.

102. Letter from D. Whitaker to Rev. and Mrs. Smail, 21 August 1977.

103. Letter from J. Pereboom to Smail, 9 August 1977.

104. Letter from J. Martin-Doyle to Smail, 9 September 1977; Letter from Peggy William to Fountain Trust, 8 August 1977; Letter from Pamela Mellyard to Smail, 8 August 1977.

Catholics are involved, the Church of Scotland has given us its blessings, and Methodists are showing greater interest."[105] Indeed, Cousen did not exaggerate what had happened since Guildford. Many leaders of different denominations and Christian organizations had become more open towards the renewal.

Anglicans

Since most of the Trust's leaders were Anglicans and maintained connections with their own churches, the international conferences produced the greatest impact on the Anglican Church and a number of bishops or ministers began to express their interest in the renewal after Guildford. For example, in October 1971 the Bishop of Guildford, George Reindorp, arranged a conference with the Trust with the theme of "Pentecostalism" in the Cathedral of Guildford for the Anglican clergy of the diocese.[106] According to David Pawson, the Bishop spoke about Spirit Baptism at the Mothers' Union in the diocese, and he thought the Bishop had been positive in his assessment.[107] It was very obvious that there was a change in his attitude from before the conference in July 1971. Eric Jennings, a minister of the Bourne Vicarage in Surrey, said that the bishop had been "very prejudiced" against the renewal though he was "willing to learn";[108] Jennings had hoped that his misunderstandings would be altered by the book, *Gifts and Graces*, which he had sent. In fact his desire to see the bishop's attitude towards the renewal transformed was realized exactly one year later when he "responded wonderfully to the fellowship of the Conference and gave . . . a great welcome."[109] For the Trust, this change was very encouraging because he could influence the local clergymen. In addition, there had been forty-five local people participating in the conference,[110] and it was reported that "some of the Guildford churches derived considerable benefit from" it with "very good repercussions" and a "strong impact was made on the diocese of Guildford."[111] David

105. Coomes, "1500," 1.

106. Letter from Harper to Emile Dallière, 19 October 1971; Minute-FTACM (12 November 1971), 1; Letter from Harper to Dennis Bennett, 5 October 1971.

107. Letter from David Pawson to Harper, 4 October 1971.

108. Letter from Eric Jennings to Harper, 11 July 1970.

109. Letter from Eric Jennings to Harper, 21 July 1970; Bittlinger, *Gifts and Graces*.

110. Ibid.

111. Letter from Harper to John Horner, 18 October 1971; Letter from Harper to

MacInnes, who was involved in the renewal, was pleased about it and acclaimed, "It is a most astonishing miracle."[112]

For Colin Urquhart, who had been "an unknown Anglican vicar of an unknown parish" at St. Hugh's in Luton, Guildford was his first experience of the charismatic renewal and he was still "bathing in the glory" after the conference.[113] In fact, he had wanted to leave soon after the first meeting, but because he did not want to waste the money that he had paid for the whole conference, he stayed albeit reluctantly. During this time he experienced the power of the Spirit and the love of the fellowship. It confirmed for him that the baptism in the Spirit that most of the people in his church had experienced was God's will, and he was shown in a prophecy what his future ministry was to be.[114] A year later, his parish church began a new form of church life as a community where Christians learnt to connect and live with one another.[115] He witnessed how his church members experienced the Spirit so that "when God was renewing the lives of our people individually within our church, everything was absolutely playing saintly. It was the Vicar's dream. You know people just falling into blessing, people being healed all over the place. It was lovely!"[116]

Apart from these two Anglican ministers, Harper recorded that after 1971 there were seven bishops who were involved in the renewal. In 1972 the Archbishop of Canterbury, Arthur Michael Ramsey, mentioned the renewal appreciatively in sermons and lectures.[117] For Westminster 1975, the Bishop of Pontefract, Richard Hare, exclaimed in a letter, "How enormously I enjoyed what I saw of the Westminster conference" and he was particularly impressed by Francis MacNutt's teaching.[118] He became deeply involved in the charismatic renewal and at Westminster 1977 he was invited to celebrate the final communion. Bill Neaty, a rector from North Yorkshire, commented on Westminster

David Watson, 29 July 1971; Minute-FTACM (12 November 1971), 1.

112. Letter from David MacInnes to Harper, 29 October 1971.

113. Fountain Trust, "Guildford," 31; Urquhart, "Rejoiced," 32; Letter from Colin Urquhart to Harper, 8 October 1971.

114. Urquhart, "Rejoiced," 32.

115. Urquhart, *Renewal in the Local Church Fellowship* (1975).

116. Ibid.

117. Harper, "Editorial: From Guildford to Nottingham," 2.

118. Letter from the Bishop of Pontefract to Smail, 10 September, 1975.

1975, "It was the most wonderful conference I have attended in nearly thirty two years ministry in the Church of England."[119] A. K. Pring, a rector from Buckinghamshire, experienced "a memorable and fruitful time" and foresaw the "far-reaching benefits" for his future ministry at Westminster 1977.[120]

Roman Catholics

On the Roman Catholic side, there was also active involvement in the charismatic renewal after Guildford. Bob Balkam organised the first "Day of Renewal" at Heythrop College on 19 September 1971 and Bishop Victor Guazzelli was invited to come.[121] On the second "Day of Renewal" in December of the same year, Harper was invited to speak and this enabled the Trust to be more involved in the Roman Catholic Renewal, which was progressing at that time.[122] The birth of the National Service Committee in November 1973, after the Guildford conference, was a milestone. Balkam attributed this development to Guildford 1971, saying, "The family tree of Catholic charismatic renewal in England and Wales certainly has roots in the Surrey hills."[123] After this, the RCNSC and the Trust frequently cooperated in the renewal, particularly at the Westminster conferences in 1977 and 1979. Although the Trust was closed down in 1980, the Committee still serves the Roman Catholic charismatic renewal today.

Leaders of Mainline Churches

Many leaders of some mainline churches were influenced and edified at the international conferences. Lord George MacLeod of the Church of Scotland was sympathetic to the renewal and he spoke at Nottingham. John Horner, a Methodist minister who had attended the international conferences since Guildford, said he was most edified at Westminster 1975 "from the fellowship, from the speakers and from the Fisherfolk."[124] A Baptist minister from Worcester, John Bedford, ex-

119. Letter from Bill and Gladys Neaty to Smail, 4 September 1975, 1–2.

120. Letter from A. K. Pring to Smail, 18 August 1977.

121. Email from Bob Balkam, 16 November 2005.

122. Letter from Ray Bringham to Harper, n.d.; Letter from Harper to Ray Bringham, 22 November 1971.

123. Balkam, "Roots ," 33.

124. Letter from John Horner to Smail, 5 August 1975.

claimed, "We're praising the Lord for all the Good things that happened at the Westminster Conf. [1975]"[125] Another Baptist, Gordon Clark, felt being "better equipped" to work for the church after Westminster 1977.[126] With their experiences at the conferences and their support of the renewal, the flame of renewal spread within their local churches and the renewal prospered.

British Council of Churches

One of the leading Christian organizations at that time, the British Council of Churches (BCC),[127] also showed its support for the renewal after Guildford. In September 1971, Bishop Sansbury of the Executive Committee invited Leslie Davison to talk about his report on the conference to the Executive members, as he had been sent to represent the Council unofficially. He expressed his wish to Davison saying, "The churches will be big enough to contain the Movement and not to expel it."[128] In 1974, the General Secretary of the Council expressed his praise and acknowledgement of the value of the movement in *Renewal*, on the occasion of the Trust's tenth anniversary.[129] The Trust hoped that the Council's understanding of renewal would increase, particularly with the help of Dr. Walter Hollenweger, who had settled in Britain after his appointment at the University of Birmingham in 1971.[130]

International Church Leaders

One of the characteristics of these five conferences was that they were international and their influence reached overseas. Of all of them, Guildford had the greatest charismatic impact. It is not an exaggeration to say that Guildford was like another Azusa Street Revival, in that the wave of renewal was rapidly moving out from its place of origin, and spreading dynamically to many other parts of the world. The renewal not only reached other places but, more important, was to grow there. The following is an examination of the impact of Guildford on the de-

125. Letter from John Bedford to Harper, 8 August 1975.

126. Letter from Gordon V. Clark to Smail, 12 August 1977.

127. It is now called Churches Together in Britain and Ireland.

128. Letter from Davison to Harper, 3 September 1971.

129. Robinson, "Charismatic Anglican," 186; Harper, "Editorial: From Guildford to Nottingham," 3.

130. Minute-FTACM (12 November 1971), 1.

velopment of renewal in Sweden, Norway, Australia, New Zealand, and South Africa, in so far as the record of their renewal was sufficiently detailed and available in the archive.

Sweden

After experiencing the renewal at Guildford, Ivar Lundgren, a journalist for a Swedish Pentecostal daily newspaper, *Dagen*, brought the message back to his country and initiated the renewal by holding conferences.[131] He described the conference as "wonderful and of great importance for the future." He published six major articles about it including reports of interviews that he had conducted during the conference.[132] Since he was "so enthusiastic about what he saw" at Guildford, he organized conferences with similar settings in order to bring renewal to many local churches in the country.[133] The conferences were also represented ecumenically by the speakers, and organised by committee members from various traditions. He corresponded with Harper saying that there would be at least one Lutheran bishop on the committee for the conference in Stockholm in the following autumn. For that "ground breaking conference," he invited Harper and some Roman Catholic priests to speak so as to promote the charismatic renewal in Sweden.[134] The ecumenical character of the charismatic renewal also penetrated into the major Swedish Pentecostal church. Lewi Pethrus, the prominent Pentecostal leader in Sweden, invited Harper and a Roman Catholic priest, George de Prisio, to speak in his "Filadelfia" Pentecostal Church in Stockholm in 1971.[135] It was the first time that a Roman Catholic had been invited to speak

131. Harper's personal note for the author, 22 July 2005, 2. In Swedish, *Dagen* means "the day." According to Ahonen and Johannesson, this newspaper circulates 23,000 copies every day and it was an important ecumenical medium because it connects Pentecostals and evangelical churches and maintains unity among Pentecostals. (Ahonen and Johannesson, "Sweden," 256.)

132. Letter from Livar Lundgren to Harper, 28 July 1971; Minute-FTACM (12 November 1971), 1.

133. Fountain Trust, "Guildford," 31.

134. Harper's personal note for the author, 22 July 2005, 2.

135. Interview with Michael and Jeanne Harper, 8 August 2005; Interview with Harper, 11 November 2005. In Sweden, Pentecostal churches were called "Filadelfia" or "Pingstkyrkan." Pethrus' church was the largest Pentecostal Church in Sweden and it had the biggest "religious auditorium in Europe" which can accommodate 4000 people. (Ahonen and Johannesson, "Sweden," 255–56; "Influence ," 6.)

from the platform of his church.[136] Apart from conferences, Lundgren also used written materials to publicise the renewal in Sweden. He considered publishing 12,000 copies of Harper's book, *None Can Guess*, for a book club in Sweden by a major Christian literature publisher belonging to *Dagen*.[137]

Norway

A similar story also happened in Norway. The flame of renewal was brought back to the country from Guildford by a Lutheran minister, Hans-Jacob Frøen. He and other Lutherans organised a group similar to the Fountain Trust which they called "Agape for the world" and published a magazine, *Deeper Life*, first published before Christmas 1974.[138] At the beginning of June, Harper and his wife were invited to speak in the country.[139]

Australia

The renewal not only spread upward to Northern Europe from Britain, but also downward to the southern hemisphere. Being amazed and inspired by Guildford, Alan Langstaff, a Methodist from Sydney, established the Temple Trust with similar functions to the Fountain Trust, to promote the renewal in Australia. He intended to enable the renewal to be "peacefully integrated in the Church."[140] Langstaff resigned from his Methodist church at the end of 1973[141] and by that time, he had made a lot of links with leaders of the renewal in all the major and capital cities including Perth, Adelaide, Melbourne, Canberra, and Brisbane.[142] Because of their support, the Temple Trust could widen its ministry and Langstaff could invite more speakers from abroad. For example, Rodman

136. Harper's personal note for the author, 22 July 2005, 2.

137. Letter from Ivar Lundgren to Harper, 5 November 1971; Harper, *None Can Guess*.

138. Letter from Harper to Larry Christenson, 19 October 1971; Letter from Hans-Jacob Frøen to Harper, 6 November 1974; Interview with Michael and Jeanne Harper, 8 August 2005.

139. Minute-FTACM (12 November 1971), 1; Letter from Harper to Ivar Lundgren, 12 November 1971.

140. Letter from Harper, 6 March 1973; Letter from Harper to J. Abraham, 4 April 1973; Minute-FTACM (5 April 1973), 4.

141. Letter from Harper to Rev. and Mrs. Ray Muller, 4 April 1973, 1.

142. Letter from Alan Langstaff to Harper, 25 April 1973, 1.

Williams and Graham Pulkingham came to speak in September and November 1973 respectively.[143] Harper not only accepted an invitation to speak at conferences, but also was willing to cooperate with Langstaff closely as he thought that Langstaff had "a very responsible approach" which gave him the "utmost confidence" in him.[144] He was "perfectly happy" to sell the Fountain Trust's publications including *Renewal* and tapes through the Temple Trust.[145] Moreover, the Temple Trust also held conferences to promote the renewal. It organised the first National Charismatic Conference with a Baptist minister called Howard Carter at the University of New South Wales, Sydney. The conference gathered 900 people from Australia and Papua New Guinea, and 1,500 Anglicans, Roman Catholics, Pentecostals, and free churches participated at the final youth rally. It was the first time that Australian charismatics had gathered together. Langstaff and Carter's efforts in organizing this ecumenical and charismatic event were highly acknowledged.[146] In January of both 1974 and 1975, the Temple Trust also organised two other national conferences in Canberra and Melbourne respectively.[147]

New Zealand

In New Zealand the flame of renewal was rekindled by an ex-Anglican vicar, Ray Muller. He worked at the Fountain Trust for one year in 1971 when the Guildford Conference was being prepared and held. After going back to New Zealand, he established "Christian Advance Ministries" which was also similar to the Fountain Trust. In January 1973, a conference was held at Massey University, Palmerston North, where he had been "a very successful chaplain." Kevin Ranaghan, Bob Frost and, Harper were invited to speak.[148] It gathered one thousand delegates, with Anglicans and Catholics in the majority and attracted plenty of

143. Letter from Alan Langstaff to Harper, 29 June 1973.

144. Fountain Trust, "Guildford," 31; Letter from Harper to Frank Watts, 22 May 1973; Letter from Harper to J. Abraham, 4 April 1973.

145. Letter from Alan Langstaff to Harper, 25 April, 1973, 1; Letter from Harper to Alan Langstaff, 22 May 1973, 1.

146. Fountain Trust, "It's Time in Australia," 21–22.

147. Letter from Alan Langstaff to Harper, 25 April 1973, 1; Letter from Alan Langstaff to Harper, 29 June 1973; Smail, "Itinerary: Harper."

148. Letter from Harper, 6 March 1973; Fountain Trust, "History Repeated in New Zealand," 19.

ordained and lay leaders to attend.[149] Positive evaluations were given by both Protestants and Catholics. They appreciated the serious theological examination of the renewal and a sense of unity during the Eucharist in the mornings and the evening meeting.[150] Similar to Guildford, the conference had "widespread and continuing repercussions" among churches including the Roman Catholic Church and was identified as a "significant turning point" for the renewal in the country. This had a remarkable influence on the country which had "largely failed to make a noticeable impact on the larger churches," although it had been strong for several years in non-mainline churches. Campbell McAlpine and Arthur Wallis were regarded as the pioneers of the charismatic renewal in New Zealand. In 1959, McAlpine preached in Baptist and Brethren churches in the country. Wallis was active in Brethren and evangelical sectors. He organized a conference at the Massey University in 1964, which gathered charismatics and Pentecostals together. The charismatic renewal in the country was mainly launched by individuals rather than an organization. Muller's attempt to establish "Christian Advance Ministries" helped to gather resources and finance to spread the renewal more widely in the country.[151]

Together with the Temple Trust and Christian Advance Ministries, the Fountain Trust had developed a partnership with another three charismatic agents in other countries: Charismatic Renewal Services (US), Fishermen Incorporated, and Ecumenical Academy (Schloss Craheim, West Germany). Harper foresaw the great potential of these six to cooperate more frequently and interactively in the future.[152]

South Africa

In South Africa, "very great blessing, new insights, wider vision" were brought from Guildford by its representatives of whom Derek Crumpton was a prominent one.[153] He spent one year preparing for the renewal and established the "Christian Interdenominational Fellowship" in East

149. Fountain Trust, "History Repeated in New Zealand," 19.

150. Fountain Trust, "Press Comment on Massey University Conference," 20–21.
Those evaluations were given by an Evangelical Protestant magazine, *Challenge Weekly*, and a Roman Catholic paper, *The Tablet* and were cited in *Renewal*.

151. Knowles, "New Zealand," 189–90.

152. Letter from Harper to Rev. and Mrs. Ray Muller, 4 April 1973, 2.

153. Letter from Jim and Val Kincaid to Michael and Jeanne Harper, 30 July 1971.

London.[154] This organisation and its Caring Centre penetrated into the Baptist, Methodist, Afrikaans-speaking Reformed churches, and the Roman Catholic circles. Many of them turned from being against the renewal to being baptised by the Spirit. The Fellowship organized conferences that attracted an attendance of around one hundred people of various backgrounds. In 1972, almost seventy people participated in the meetings and many of them were baptized by the Spirit and experienced "an increasingly powerful moving of God." The Fellowship grew "at an astounding rate."[155] Apart from the organization, Crumpton's personal ministry was also significant, particularly in teaching. He was invited to speak at a Baptist Family Convention in Pretoria where he seized the leisure time to share the charismatic message with some delegates, and many of them were baptized by the Spirit. He also led some Roman Catholics to "a real experience of salvation by faith in Christ and then into the charismatic experience." He explained the biblical basis of the Spirit baptism with priests and nuns and some of them attended the meetings of his organisation.[156] Officially, he was invited to speak in a seminar led by Bill Burnett who was the Bishop of Grahamstown, and by David du Plessis in a Pentecostal Mission's event and was asked to teach in Baptist churches.[157] Crumpton's contribution to the renewal in South Africa was noteworthy. Ten years after the Guildford conference, when Harper recorded the history of the event in *Renewal*, he said, "Derek Crumpton, who was to go back to South Africa to pioneer renewal and to prepare the way for the breakthrough a year or so later which was to sweep many church leaders into the experience of renewal."[158]

It is possible that there were still many stories of renewal resulting from Guildford in many other countries that Harper and the Trust did not even know about. But from the stories recorded above, it is obvious that the flame of renewal did not just spread around Britain, but moved across national borders so that overseas churches were renewed as well. It is also clear that the methods of spreading the flame in Britain were worth learning, since charismatic leaders of other countries also

154. Fountain Trust, "Guildford," 30; Letter from Derek Crumpton to Harper, 2 November 1972, 1.

155. Letter from Derek Crumpton to Harper, 2 November 1972, 2.

156. Ibid.

157. Letter from Derek Crumpton to Harper, 29 March 1973, 1.

158. Fountain Trust, "Guildford," 30–31.

promoted the renewal through establishing similar organizations, conferences, and publications. These organizations gradually developed a network with the Fountain Trust so that they could exchange resources and news of the local renewal development and mutually support one another financially and spiritually.

Theological Awareness

In all the five international conferences, theology had never been devalued. The schedule of each conference, which was constituted by intensive lectures and seminars on a variety of subjects, suggested that the Trust affirmed the importance of theological knowledge and reciprocal discussions, which implicitly countered the "anti-intellectual elements in renewal movement."[159] This setting of the conferences conveys a message to the delegates that they should avoid being content with and indulging in the experiential realm of the renewal, but rather find a balance between experience and truth. Through learning and discussions, it was assumed that delegates could attain theological knowledge relating to the renewal and their personal experiences so that they could be protected from potential dangers.

The emphasis on theology had occurred since Guildford. Emile Dallière appraised the quality of the theological teaching as being of "an exceptional biblical purity, absolutely sound and authentic." Speakers were patient to explain and their "lectures were presented with great clarity, dynamic in approach and powerful in conviction." Some people were baptised by the Spirit during the lectures. Those attending were eager and humble to learn rather than being intent on provoking disputes.[160] J. Rodman Williams, as one of the speakers, was "grateful" and "delighted" to see the growing theological interest among delegates who carefully looked into certain theological issues during the lectures and conversations. For him, this trend of serious theological investigation regarding the renewal was crucial because it prepared for "the vast importance in the future of continuing study and reflection."[161] Harper said, "The movement expressed at Guildford the desire to study and become deeply acquainted with the biblical foundations of the Christian faith" and thus

---

159. Harper, "Coming-of-Age," 2–3.
160. Dallière, *Guildford International Conference*, 4–5.
161. Williams, "Genuine," 9.

he pointed out a "didactic character" of the conference.[162] This could be regarded as a harbinger paving a theological road for the future development of the British renewal. The renewal was therefore strengthened by continuous theological investigation and a serious attitude towards the truth. The set-up of the theological workshop during the conference provided a good example. For three days, "highly qualified theologians" including Simon Barrington-Ward, Howard Belben, William R. Davies, James D. G. Dunn, John Orme Mills, David Pawson, John Richards, Simon Tugwell, and J. Rodman Williams, investigated the definition of Spirit baptism, the relationship between theology and experience, charismatic renewal, and church structures. It proved to be successful that the members of the group wanted to continue it every year. Harper was looking forward to more "serious studies" and the fruit borne.[163] The second meeting took place in January 1972 followed by a residential meeting at Selly Oak Colleges, Birmingham on 12–15 December. It was attended by Simon Tugwell, Simon Barrington-Ward, James Dunn, and Walter Hollenweger (who replaced Leslie Davison) as the chairperson. The third one was held at St John's College, Nottingham on 1–4 January 1974.[164] Each time during those few years Harper invited more people to join the group on condition that they had "a dedicated interest and concern in the charismatic renewal without . . . pre-judging any particular theological position."[165] When the workshop was run until 1975, Smail felt that the meetings had "rather collapsed" and "got lost on the indefiniteness of its agenda." Nevertheless, he did not devalue the setting of theological investigation and he consulted James Dunn for remedies to make the discussion more focused. The growth of the workshop showed that the theological importance of the renewal was reaffirmed.[166]

---

162. Harper, "Coming-of-Age," 2–3.

163. Fountain Trust, "Guildford, England, 1971"; "Theological Workshop: Address List"; "An Invitation of the Theological Workshop from Harper, n. d."; "An Invitation of the Theological Workshop from Harper, June 1973"; Harper, "Coming-of-Age," 3; Williams, "Genuine," 9; Davison, "Memorandum," 2; Letter from Harper to D. MacInnes, 10 November 1971; Letter from Harper to Simon Tugwell and John Mills, 7 July 1972; Letter from Harper to James Dunn, 19 July 197; Minute FTACM (12 November 1971), 2.

164. Minute-FTACM (12 November 1971), 2; "An Invitation of the Theological Workshop from Harper," n. d.; "An Invitation of the Theological Workshop from Harper," June 1973.

165. "An Invitation of the Theological Workshop from Harper," n. d.

166. Letter from Smail to James Dunn, 8 August 1975.

The trend of theological study was continued at Nottingham where a theological workshop was led by Smail and J. Rodman Williams. Although it could only be a small setting since it was difficult to gather the entire crowd of delegates, Smail strongly advised people to come, saying that it could be worth abandoning their original plans for that morning so as to participate in a profound theological study.[167] As a result of these theological discussions, Emmanuel Sullivan appreciated the leaders of the conference recognizing the importance of theology, but they did not overemphasize theology at the expense of experience. For him, theology was a means of rescuing "Pentecostal spirituality from becoming a mindless Christianity inhabited by the devils of fanaticism, elitism, erroneous exegesis, and false prophecy."[168] In addition, the number of cassettes of the lectures and seminars that were sold suggested the rapid growth of theological interest among delegates. On the fourth day of the conference, 800 cassettes were sold; and within two days, the number amounted to 3,800. The cassette copiers had to keep going all the time to meet the demand.[169]

When Smail was the director of the Trust, the emphasis on teaching at conferences became even stronger. For Westminster 1979, Smail stated clearly in his letters to speakers that "serious teaching" was the "main emphasis" of the conference.[170] In the first place a new session for Bible Study was added into the program, and it took place before the lectures, seminars, workshop, and services began. It indicated that the Trust affirmed the uniquely unshakable position of the Bible and that all the teaching should be based on that rather than solely on personal experience. In addition, lectures were lengthened from the usual one hour to one and a half hours, to allow more time to learn, to think, and to discuss. All these teaching sessions were arranged in order to achieve the purpose of motivating people to take action in evangelism and social concern, and to transform the world with the renewal. This was stated in a Consultative Council Meeting, that ". . . a renewed church should

167. Letter from the Secretary to Harper to J. Rodman William, 16 May 1973; Letter from Smail, July 1973.

168. Sullivan, "Seeing," 25.

169. Fountain Trust, "Gathered for Power," 10; *Renewal*, No. 46 (August–September 1973), 22.

170. Letter from Smail to Canon Michael Green, 10 November 1977; Letter from Smail to Catherine Marshall LeSourd, 3 March 1978; Letter from Smail to William J. Brown, 6 February 1979.

be able to conform the world to the structures of the gospel. This is an emphasis upon the Word becoming [incarnate] in the people['s] lives and is not a reversion to fundamentalism or conservative evangelism."[171] To ensure that the teachings on evangelism and social concern were effectively and contextually expressed, the Trust invited speakers who not only had profound theological knowledge but also abundant experience in the area of concern—people such as Lesslie Newbigin and Tom Forrest who had been missionaries in South India and South America for years and were also missiologists.

The conferences reflect the way in which the Fountain Trust saw the role and significance of theology within the renewal. It rejected the idea of being satisfied with a cozy atmosphere in a warm fellowship in the Spirit, and insisted on the profound and careful study of truths. The emphasis on theological exploration grew stronger during Smail's directorship. Perhaps the comment of a so-called "liberal" theologian, Leslie Davison, about the theological work for the renewal, is a suitable conclusion for this section. He said, "If this movement is to enrich the life of the Church it must open itself to fullest critical examination and make sure that the Truth within it shines out clearly without distortion. Much sifting has yet to be done."[172]

Social Concern

Social concern had been regarded as an essential area of the renewal at the international conferences. At Nottingham, three speakers talked about this topic which was believed to be increasingly important.[173] One was Larry Christenson who talked about "A Charismatic Approach to Social Action" dealing with the relationship between charismatic experiences and social action, and how to respond to social needs with spiritual power.[174] The other one was Lord George MacLeod, who was a pacifist and had gradually seen the significance of the charismatic renewal. He believed that "a recovery of spiritual vision" through the renewal would provide a solution for the problems created by the industrialized, commercialized, and environmentally polluted society, which politicians

171. Minute-FTCCM (8 December 1977), 2.

172. Davison, *Pathway to Power*, 11.

173. Letter from Harper to Larry Christenson, 24 May 1973.

174. Letter from Larry Christenson to Harper, 18 May 1973; Fountain Trust, "Gathered for Power," 2; "Programme: Nottingham," 2.

were incapable of handling. He thought that "the general witness of the Church is simply not faithful enough to bridge the gap," and so he hoped that the conference would arouse social concern and renew the delegates as "in Christ" with a growing affection for society.[175] He encouraged delegates to be "active in politics and social action"[176] and more important, to change society by peaceful means instead of violence. He said, "If the world was not to see 'a violent revolution of necessity', it must see a 'non-violent revolution, a revolution of love, by consent.'"[177] This made a great impact on the delegates. One such, David Coomes, said, "I left Nottingham believing that I had seen there the seeds of that non violent revolution."[178] Sullivan also commented that he could feel "the growing sense of social responsibility and even political maturity" at the conference, but it still needed to be nurtured and those who were renewed Christians should manifest the holiness that they experienced, in society as well as in the Church.[179]

Another major figure involved in social concern at both Nottingham and Westminster 1975 was Bill Burnett. He had been the Bishop of Grahamstown in South Africa and was inducted as the Archbishop of Cape Town and Primate of the Church of the Province of South Africa in 1974. Harper described him as "one of the most influential of charismatic leaders" in the 1970s. He was baptized in the Spirit when he was praying in his private chapel. He said, "When the Holy Spirit came upon me in his power . . . my knees weakened and I sank down on the floor in adoration . . . I also found myself praising God in a new language."[180] He then spread the message of Spirit baptism in his diocese and his experience "made headlines in most major newspapers." An increasing number of people became interested and involved in the renewal under his influence.[181] He also persuaded some Anglican ministers such as Peter Campbell, the rector of Queenstown, to "come out into the open

---

175. Fountain Trust, "Four Conference speakers," 5.

176. Coomes, "1500," 1.

177. Coomes, "Nottingham," 19.

178. Robinson, "Charismatic Anglican," 188.

179. Sullivan, "Seeing," 25.

180. Fountain Trust, "Gathered for Power," 5; Fax transmission, "Obituary," 29 August, 1994, 2–3.

181. Letter from Derek Crumpton to Harper, 29 March 1973, 1; Fountain Trust, "Press Release," 1.

air" when the charismatic renewal was not well accepted.[182] Harper described Burnett as having been "already thoroughly committed to the movement."[183] Moreover, Burnett had been a prominent opponent of apartheid and now he saw that this was not only a matter of social and political injustice, but also of spiritual warfare.[184] The renewal made him realize that God was concerned about the oppressed and He also loved the oppressors. This gave the impression to many that he had adopted a compromising position on the political issue.[185] In a Press Conference, the Archbishop expressed his opinion about racial issues by saying, "The Holy Spirit is renewing people in South Africa but there will have to be vast structural changes in the country if Christian justice between black and white is to come about."[186] His personal experience and his talk at Nottingham and Westminster 1975 on social action aroused delegates' awareness of the issues in the wider society.[187]

At Westminster 1975, delegates were also able to hear teaching and stories about social issues from Cecil Kerr, an Anglican clergyman from Northern Ireland. He was baptized in the Spirit when he was chaplain at Queen's University in Belfast in 1971. He then began a charismatic prayer group composed of students from various denominational backgrounds. He was the founder and warden of the "Christian Renewal Centre" in Rostrevor, Northern Ireland, which was aimed at bringing about reconciliation between Protestants and Catholics in Ireland.[188] At the conference, he talked about social action in a seminar under the title "The World: Reconciliation." He said that "Ireland's darkest hour was yet to come" and there would be "many more killings, shooting and bombings," and therefore, "don't expect too much too quickly, after centuries of bitterness."[189] Nevertheless, he believed that the Holy Spirit was "moving in re-creation, bringing life, joy and peace to a world sadly lacking these qualities." To

182. Letter from Derek Crumpton to Harper, 2 November 1972, 1.

183. Letter from Harper to Bernard Palmer, 11 May 1973.

184. Letter from the Bishop of Grahamstown to Harper, 30 May 1973.

185. "Reality," 3.

186. Fountain Trust, "Conference Aims," 1.

187. Holl, "Glory in the Church," 4; Letter from Harper to the Archbishop of Cape Town, 13 September 1974; Fountain Trust, "Glory in the Church," 4, 6; "Westminster: Speakers' Subjects"; "Charismatic Event (July 1975)"; Letter from the Archbishop of Cape Town to Smail, 30 January 1975.

188. Fountain Trust, "Prayer," 4.

189. Ibid.

face the conflicts in Ireland, people might rely on political solutions but they still needed the inner healing of the Spirit. He believed that if there were more people praying, peace would come one day.[190] His talk made a great impression on the hearers. As one of the delegates, Barbara Holl, remarked, "What depth of understanding there was there, what enlightenment of his heart and mind by the Holy Spirit."[191]

The teaching on social responsibility at Nottingham brought the renewal to a more mature level. It extended its concern from the internal realm of personal spiritual renewal to the one of social justice and welfare. This concern continued at Westminster 1975. Since there was a rising interest during the conference, the Trust specially arranged "an informal and non-residential weekend consultation" entitled "Spirit and Society" in central London on 13–14 December of that year.[192] When the renewal went on to the late 1970s, the Trust believed that social action should be facilitated by the ministry of prophecy and prayer, as was stated in a Council meeting minute,

> The prophetic ministry and the life of prayer need to combine to make the renewal a much more challenging and powerful force in the land. If one of the ends we are moving towards is a revitalized and reawakened Christian witness in our land then we need to become a prayerfully prophetic people who speak a living true word to the real needs of our society rather than produce endless facile stop-gap measures.[193]

The emphasis on social concern continued until Westminster 1979. Smail invited the Colonel of the Salvation Army Men's Social Services in London, William McAllister,[194] to speak about "the local church and social concern." He also arranged for another William from the US to deal with this issue. William Brown, the executive director of the Trinity Christian Community in New Orleans, Louisiana, had seen the practical effect of renewal "in the inner city situation and in a difficult racial background" with his church.[195] Smail was sure that Brown's experience

190. Fountain Trust, "Glory in the Church," 4, 6; "Charismatic Event (July 1975)"; "Prayer Can Avert Ireland Disaster," 4; Letter from Cecil Kerr to Harper, 6 July 1975, 2; "Reality," 3; Coomes, "Optimism," 1.

191. Holl, "Glory in the Church," 4.

192. Fountain Trust, "Spirit," 9.

193. Minute-FTCCM (8 December 1977), 2.

194. Letter from Smail to William McAllister, 31 March 1978.

195. Letter from William Brown to Smail, 6 March 1979; Letter from Smail to

and ideas about how the renewal could make an impact on society were "exactly" what the conference needed and that he could inspire those in the congregation who might have a similar situation and concern.[196] Finally, there was a lecture concerning the importance of prayer and prophecy in response to any need in society and the world and how delegates could be equipped by those two ministries.

A REFLECTION OF THE FIVE INTERNATIONAL CONFERENCES

The five international conferences reflected the development of the British charismatic renewal. Their emphases demonstrated the focus of the renewal at each stage, the spiritual circumstances of charismatic churches and how the Trust reacted to them.

Guildford 1971: Coming of Age

Guildford brightened the future of the British charismatic renewal, which had previously looked dull and unclear. James Dunn described it as "the coming-of-age,"[197] others called it "a spiritual breakthrough,"[198] "a milestone," and "a signpost" of the movement.[199] It had "some widespread repercussions" which sustained and greatly accelerated the progress of the renewal.[200] Harper said, "The flames are fanned" and "we have seen things escalate very quickly in England with our international conference at Guildford," which meant that the Trust was "very much involved in the charismatic movement."[201] Thus, one of the Trustees, Cecil Cousen, confidently claimed, "Most of all, the charismatic movement was now firmly 'on the map.'"[202] Arthur Wallis felt it was a privilege to contribute

---

William Brown, 6 February 1979; Fountain Trust, "Speakers at Westminster 1979."

196. Letter from Smail to William Brown, 6 February 1979.

197. Fountain Trust, "Guildford," 30.

198. Fountain Trust, "Leaflet and application form of the Nottingham Conference."

199. Harper, *Newsletter* 41.

200. Letter from Harper to Brother Andrew, 4 October 1971; Letter from Harper to Ray Bringham, 22 November 1971.

201. Letter from Harper to Simon Tugwell, 29 September 1971; Letter from Harper to Dennis Bennett, 5 October 1971; Letter from Harper to Bishop Bazley, 29 November 1972.

202. Cousen, "Ten," 34.

because it was an event "making history at Guildford."[203] The reason for these rapid developments was that for the first time, people realised the importance of the charismatic renewal in the church.[204] The gifts and power from the Holy Spirit especially were recognised as the answer to what the church had been searching for in a time of powerlessness and declining attendance. Smail sharply pointed out this problem at a Fountain Trust conference,

> Ask the young people, why they don't go to church and you will get one answer: nothing ever happens and it's also boring! . . . Far more devastating to the reality of Christ work among us, that nothing happens, that there isn't effective relationship, so that the thing that the Head desires and all that get actually done and could be seen to be done.[205]

The church realized that it needed a renewal from the Spirit; the dry bones needed a fresh breath from the Creator so that they could work effectively and fruitfully for the Head of the body. And there in Guildford, ministers and laymen from churches of Britain and overseas witnessed the works of the Spirit which could revitalize the Church. Leslie Davison, in the Report on the Conference for the BCC, said, ". . . it is very evident that here is a new and powerful movement at work throughout the Christian world which is again demonstrating that the vitality of the New Testament Church can be recaptured."[206]

Guildford seemed to soften, moisten and fertilise the sterile soil in Britain in which the Fountain Trust had sowed the seeds of renewal since 1964. People had seen the work of the Holy Spirit with His "truly remarkable" freedom in the conference.[207] Harper believed that the significance of the Spirit in churches' and people's lives would be growing. Meanwhile, the workload of the Trust had increased because as Harper noted, "Certainly many doors have opened since the conference, and opportunities are abounding to witness concerning the power of the Holy Spirit in the Church today."[208] After Guildford, the renewal was able to grow and become mature. This was to be seen at Nottingham two years later.

203. Letter from Arthur Wallis to Harper, 21 July 1971, 1.

204. Robinson, "Charismatic Anglican," 188.

205. Smail, *Humanity.*

206. Davison, "Memorandum," 3.

207. Letter from Harper to the Lord Rank, 28 July 1971.

208. Letter from Harper to James Dunn, 29 July 1971.

Nottingham 1973: A Milestone of Maturity

If Guildford was regarded as the coming of age of the charismatic renewal in Britain, then Nottingham was a crucial step in the maturing of the renewal. Both Michael and Jeanne Harper commented that Nottingham did not share the same climax as Guildford which denoted "something historic that was happening."[209] However, if the renewal was to grow and not be self-satisfied about what had been achieved at Guildford, then it must reach a higher level of maturity, rather than simply repeating the "coming-of-age." There was some disagreement about this matter of maturity. The Editor of the *Church of England Newspaper* and Emmanuel Sullivan, the official observer of the BCC at the conference, held opposite views. The Editor was uncertain whether Nottingham had brought the renewal to maturity, although Sullivan testified that it had been evident at the conference. The Editor's point was that if the renewal was making a mature impact on churches, the "rediscovery" of the Spirit's power should result in outreach. Sullivan thought that the experience of the Spirit at Nottingham was "richer and deeper" than at Guildford. He also felt that it had become lest individualistic and more of a collective and interactive event, and one which was "integrated within their lives, now a fixed pattern of life in Christ." The Editor had suggested, furthermore, that a mature renewal should result in continuing "the rediscovery of the Church as the charismatically ordered body of Christ." Sullivan affirmed that this rediscovery had occurred at the conference and was being given attention. Finally, the Editor questioned whether the renewal was mature enough to contribute to "the wider life of the Church" and Sullivan responded positively by saying, "I left Nottingham with fresh hope for the whole church. I left with the conviction that God is doing something wonderfully new among His people. And I said, 'Praise God!'"[210] Nottingham did bring the renewal to another milestone of maturity. A greater ecumenical capacity, a sharper awareness of the need for social concern and a deeper theological investigation at the conference, showed that charismatics and the Trust were not individualistic, nor self-satisfied with the spiritual experience, but were opening themselves to face the challenges of wider ecumenical developments and social and theological adventures.

209. Interview with Michael and Jeanne Harper, 8 August 2005.
210. Sullivan, "Seeing," 21, 25; "Editorial: Whiter," 7.

Westminster 1975: Renewal on a Plateau

This conference reflected the fact that the renewal had reached a peak between 1973 and 1975 where everything was stable, there was little change, and it was time to evaluate what had developed so far. The Spirit's power was no longer such a surprise. More and more members of the laity and clergy in local churches around the country were reported to have been baptized and renewed by the Spirit, or had testified to that. Most of the issues about the renewal such as the theological study of the charismatic experiences, gifts, social concern, and the relationship of charismatics with their own churches had been rethought and discussed many times. There had been changes to liturgy and worship, which people had enjoyed. Physical and psychological healings had borne their fruits. The title, "Glory in the Church," suggested that after ten years, the Trust and the renewal saw themselves as having reached a mountain top where they would see the glory, so what else could happen? Was there a new topic to think about? Was there a new message to preach? Were there new songs to sing? Were there new divine healers? In fact, all these things had happened in what was quite a small circle of people, not the whole Christian community in the country. As Harper warned, "We must not fall into the trap of getting too euphoric about what has happened; the renewal is still very small in England." The size of the renewal was still small in 1976 as it was discussed at the Advisory Council Meeting. When Smail was about to succeed to the directorship, he felt that the renewal "should begin to think about itself" in terms of its theology of the gospel, not just be satisfied with enthusiasm.[211] One example, according to Colin Buchanan at a conference in Reading in 1976, was that the Trust taught about "how to control and discipline" spiritual gifts rather than seeking for and ministering them. Prophecies had to be discerned carefully rather than be accepted without question.[212] In an editorial of the same year, Smail even said, "Two-thirds of the exercise of spiritual gifts is phony."[213] Smail's succession was a turning point in the way the Trust focused on the renewal. He led the Trust and charismatics generally to evaluate critically what had happened in their lives and churches, and to look at how they should prepare and adjust for the future.

211. Fountain Trust, "Michael Hands over the Rein," 1; Minute-FTACM (9 December 1976), 3.

212. Buchanan, *Encountering Charismatic Worship*, 21, footnote 2.

213. Smail, "Editorial: Treasure," 2.

Westminster 1977: Retrospection and Ready for the Future

Although this conference was spiritually edifying to delegates and enriched their understanding of renewal, it could not conceal the intrinsic problems of the renewal. Before it took place, delegates were asked to choose which lectures they wished to attend, and nearly 50 percent of them had chosen "Growing into Wholeness" which dealt with healing. Noting this, Smail said to the speakers in a letter, "I leave you to ponder the implications." He believed that those who opted for other sections were "really interested in them!"[214] His comment indicated that those who applied for that session did so out of curiosity more than real concern about the issue. And after ten years of the renewal, people were still at the a stage of being more interested in miracles than investigating questions relating to the body of Christ—its fellowship, evangelism, understanding of truth, and relationship with God.

Moreover, after the conference, when the Trust did an evaluation, Smail and other members had a revelation in their prayer time, which was that in the previous two years, the renewal had been coming across the "wilderness" as the exodus of the Israelites. Disappointment grew when the expectations of miracles were unfulfilled. It was recorded that most of the places that had experienced the renewal were "under very testing attack." All the effort was going to preserving what the church had already received from God or fighting to recover what had been lost, rather than moving forward to another stage.[215] Furthermore, in 1976 Smail noticed that there had been charismatics and churches that were not genuinely renewed, but pretended to be. He was also concerned about the growing danger of charismatic gnosticism. He concluded that 1976 "had been a very testing time for all leaders in renewal."[216] In addition to his view, David Phypers also felt that charismatics had been enjoying themselves in "a cosy diet of warm, loving fellowship with their own 'in' group" rather than reaching out of their comfort zone to save the lost with the Spirit's renewal power.[217] As a director observing all this, Smail interpreted the problems as positive signs indicating the pruning process that the renewal was going through. He believed that because the

214. Letter from Smail to the speakers, n.d.
215. Smail, "Editorial: Lights," 2–3; Minute-FTCCM (8 December 1977), 2.
216. Minute-FTACM (9 December 1976), 1; Minute-FTCCM (8 June 1977), 3.
217. Phypers, "Charismatic," 30.

renewal had been fruitful, it needed to be pruned so that it would bear more fruit.[218] The Trust also thought that the renewal was "on the brink of a new stage of development" which required solid faith, profound understanding of the Word, strong prayer, and prophetic ministry, and a re-evaluation of institutional structures that might block the working of the Spirit.[219] Motivated by this hope, the Trust courageously continued to lead churches through this painful process in order to reach a more fruitful stage.

Westminster 1979: A March towards a New Stage

This conference, "Joy in the City," reflected the Trust's intention of leading the renewal into a new stage. It wanted to adjust the focus of delegates to see that the way to build their faith was not through "easy triumphalistic panaceas,"[220] but through obedience, in order to give up self-indulgence, take up self-discipline, stop using the power of renewal to fulfill personal interests, and start following God's commandments.[221] One of the things that charismatics ought to be doing was reaching out to the world through social action and evangelism. That was the emphasis of the conference and the Trust hoped that people would "go out, get on with the job, put into practice back home" what they had learnt at the conference.[222] Smail believed that this emphasis resulted in a decrease in the number of participants because it was not pandering to any egotistic concerns such as healing, but about evangelism, focusing on the world and others. He spoke out about this saying, "If the conference is about instant healing now you could have booked the Albert Hall every night and it would have been packed. But if you had the conference on "Joy in the City" and getting out into the world, all the people that are just interested in themselves with their problems and their nice experience, they are not there."[223] Nevertheless, Smail was not discouraged by the decrease in numbers, but actually was fascinated by the growth of maturity among delegates.[224] One of the marks of that maturity could be

---

218. Smail, "Editorial: Growth," 3.
219. Minute-FTCCM (8 December 1977), 2.
220. Ibid.
221. Smail, *Discipline.*
222. Fowke, "Go," 6.
223. Smail, *Discipline.*
224. Ibid.

seen in Ruth Fowke's description, "No emotionalism, solid teaching and appropriate emotion."[225] With the focus on evangelism and social action out of an attitude of obedience, the Trust believed that charismatics could become less self-centered. And that was the point of departure for proceeding to a new stage of the renewal.

CONCLUSION AND EVALUATION

The Fountain Trust's five international conferences had both strengths and weaknesses. First, as far as strengths were concerned, there was a holistic approach in the conferences because the program included not only spontaneous worship in which people experienced the Holy Spirit, but also practical activities in workshops, and learning through serious theological teaching and discussion. The conferences were aimed not only at renewing local churches and leaders in Britain, but also spreading the flames overseas. They not only focused on the inner growth of individuals and churches, but regarded this as preparation for a social impact. Secondly, the conferences reflected the self-awareness and self-critical attitude of the Trust. They reminded delegates of the potential danger of emotionalism and fanaticism which could overshadow the divine purpose of the renewal. Theological teaching was important to safeguard renewal from the indulgence of triumphalism as it equipped delegates to discern anything that was going in the wrong direction. Thirdly, although they reflected the weaknesses and problems of the charismatic renewal during the 1970s, they were simultaneously arenas for correction and equipping people for further stages of the renewal through theological teaching. They helped the renewal to grow continuously with a solid foundation. Fourthly, they carried a strong ecumenical dimension, which abolished denominational barriers through common experiences in the Spirit. This point will be covered in more detail in the next chapter.

However, there were weaknesses in the conferences. They were dominated by Anglicans and Roman Catholics and the free churches were in the minority. This was primarily because most of the staff of the Trust were Anglicans and they had close relationships with the RCNSC. Consequently free churches were not so well informed about the conferences and the renewal itself, which caused the renewal as a whole lim-

225. Fowke, "Go," 6.

ited to Anglican churches and the Roman Catholic Church. Moreover, the early conferences tended to adopt an American worship style. At Guildford, Harper invited a Canadian couple, Merv and Merla Watson, to lead the worship and at Nottingham and Westminster 1975, the Fisherfolk. It was only when Smail became the director of the Trust and British Christians led their own worship. Overly relying on American worship style could have weakened the solidarity of the conferences because not all British Christians were entirely comfortable with the American style and that might have affected the attendance. Also, it might have caused British charismatics to be less creative in composing new songs and developing their own worship style and may have led to a lack of authenticity in British charismatic worship. Furthermore, the influence of the conferences on the charismatic renewal overseas had been decreasing. It was only the Guildford conference that influenced some Australians, New Zealanders, South Africans, and Swedes to take the fire to their own countries. The Trust then assisted them by sending printed and audio materials, and advising them on establishing a charismatic organization and preparing conferences. Although there were also international delegates at the other four conferences, they did not have the same effect of encouraging them to spread the renewal fire through organizations, conferences, and theological education in their own countries.

3

The Grassroots Unity
of the Five International Conferences

THE FIVE INTERNATIONAL CONFERENCES clearly demonstrate the essence, characteristics, strengths, and weaknesses of grassroots unity developed in the charismatic renewal. Huge numbers attended, and there was a great diversity of ecclesiological backgrounds both among the speakers and participants. The cooperation between Protestants and Roman Catholics was unprecedented, at least in British church history. The activities, which included worship and the Eucharist, nurtured both an intense sense of unity as well as revealing the deep pain derived from the remaining unresolved ecumenical issues. This pioneering ecumenical approach was inevitably rejected by some people who had held a negative view of other traditions; but at the same time there was such a melting pot of ecclesiastical diversity that many of the objectors were eventually ecumenically converted. This chapter is aimed at exploring these ecumenical aspects of the five international conferences.

ECUMENICAL SPEAKERS

At Guildford, the Trust had challenged the conventional practice in Roman Catholic and Protestant churches of only having speakers of their own denominations. Instead, the criterion of inviting a person to speak at the conference was their experience and theological reflections upon the renewal regardless of their denomination. Renewal, in this case, was the means of bringing people with different backgrounds together, to serve God and those attending with their expertise. In that way, all the speakers can to some extent be regarded as ecumenists because they were willing to share a common platform with others from different ecclesiastical backgrounds. For these five international conferences, the Trust invited sixty-three prominent theologians and leaders of the charismatic renewal in Britain and from overseas, and from the Roman Catholic Church and mainline Protestant denominations, to speak. Some of them came more than once. Anglicans were in the majority, with twenty altogether, and the second highest number was of Roman Catholics, with twelve. The rest of them were Protestants including Baptists (4), Presbyterians (5), Methodists (4), Lutherans (2), Pentecostal (1), and Salvation Army (1). There were some independent speakers and one Orthodox preacher. Each conference had a "galaxy" and "an impressive range of speakers and teachers" numbering about fifteen.[1] Details of the speakers and their subjects are given in the following section.

Two Key Ecumenists

Among the speakers, there were two prominent ecumenists highlighting the ecumenical nature of the international conferences—David du Plessis and Cardinal Léon Joseph Suenens. Du Plessis had felt called to spread the renewal message among mainline Protestant churches and the Roman Catholic Church. In the 1970s, he was the co-chairman of the Roman Catholic-Charismatic dialogue.[2] The Trust invited him to speak at Guildford and Nottingham under the titles "An Ecumenical and Economical Pentecost" for a seminar and "Gathered to Unite the People of God" for an evening meeting, where he talked about the Spirit and gifts in an ecumenical context.[3] He was also responsible for a lecture about "the Pentecostal movement and its contribution to the whole church."[4] Du Plessis himself symbolised the ecumenical character of the renewal and hence his attendance and talks at the international conferences effectively raised the ecumenical awareness among those attending, which the Trust had hoped for.

From the Roman Catholic side, Cardinal Léon Joseph Suenens, the Archbishop of Malines-Brussels in Belgium, was a prominent charismatic ecumenical leader. During the 1970s, he increasingly acknowledged the importance of the "grassroots charismatic renewal" for two aspects of the church—the institution itself and its spiritual life. He saw

1. Smail, *Newsletter* 64.

2. Fountain Trust, "Gathered for Power," 4.

3. Fountain Trust, "Fellowship of the Holy Spirit," 7; Davison, "Memorandum," 1.

4. Letter from Secretary to Harper to David du Plessis, 16 May 1973; Fountain Trust, "Programme: Nottingham,"; "Detailed Programme," 2.

some "extraordinary ecumenical implications" of the renewal—not just in the theological symposium, but, more important, in Christian daily life. From the testimonies he heard about the ecumenical result of the renewal, and he affirmed that it would be "a great impetus for Christian unity." He also prayed for his own Spirit baptism, with the help of friends who had had this experience in Belgium.[5] When Smail invited him to speak at Westminster 1977, he "gladly" accepted, seeing it as supporting and witnessing to the growing unity between the Protestants and Roman Catholics in British charismatic renewal. The joint organisation of the RCNSC and the Trust particularly demonstrated the ecumenical growth between Roman Catholics and Protestants.[6] At Westminster 1977, he was responsible for a lecture on the Spirit and social action and took part in a seminar about ecumenical issues. On the following evening he gave a sermon on the topic of "the Charismatic Renewal as the work of the Holy Spirit."[7] One delegate said that he sensed the Cardinal's dedication to unity in his speech.[8] At Westminster 1979, he spoke to the whole conference in a Bible study and worship session in the morning. His talked about the biblical insights into the Spirit's work in renewing society.[9] The Cardinal clearly demonstrated his commitment to ecumenism and the charismatic renewal by speaking at the international conferences with multi-denominational attendance and sharing the platform with non-Catholic clergy twice. His attendance represented the Vatican's openness to charismatic renewal not just for Roman Catholics, but also for Protestants, and their readiness for any ecumenical advance following Vatican II. His sermons to both groups of Christians showed his acknowledgement that the non-Catholics were also members of the body of Christ and that they all experienced the same Spirit. His teaching on social concern suggested that both Catholic and non-Catholic charismatics could not avoid the fact that the fruit of renewal must include social witness and ecumenical cooperation.

5. "Looking," 7, 10–11; Suenens, "My Encounters," 28.

6. Letter from Smail to Suenens, 14 January 1976; Letter from Suenens to Smail, 25 February 1976; Letter from Smail to Suenens, 7 October 1976.

7. Letter from Smail to Suenens, 25 April 1977; Letter from Suenens to Smail, 4 May 1977; Letter from Smail to Suenens 13 June 1977; Fountain Trust, "Westminster, Growing in the Church," 3; "Suggested Programme for Suenens."

8. Letter from J. Pereboom to the Fountain Trust, 9 August 1977, 2.

9. Letter from Smail to Suenens, 17 May 1979.

Anglican and Episcopal Speakers

There were twenty speakers from the Anglican tradition in Britain and overseas. David Watson, a curate at St. Cuthbert's Church, who later became the vicar of St Michael-le-Belfrey in York,[10] ministered in an evangelistic evening meeting for young people and more than forty were converted at Guildford.[11] At Westminster 1975, he challenged delegates to spread the renewal in their local churches, so that non-Christians could experience God through charismatic fellowships and lively worship. He also stressed the healing of divisions between evangelicals and charismatics, which had been caused by inadequate theological interpretation in the early stage of renewal.[12] He preached about Jesus' prayer for unity from the Gospel of John 17 at the first evening service for the opening ceremony, which demonstrated the ecumenical significance of renewal about which delegates needed to ponder throughout the week.[13] David MacInnes's evangelistic concern was also expressed in his talks at Nottingham and Westminster 1979. He was the son of an Anglican Archbishop of Jerusalem, a Precentor of Birmingham Cathedral and Religious Advisor to Associated Television (ATV).[14] Gavin Reid, who spoke at Westminster 1975, was a Secretary for Evangelism in the Church Pastoral Aid Society and the author of *The Gagging of God*,[15] *The Elaborate Funeral*,[16] and *A New Happiness*.[17] He described himself as being indifferent to the charismatic renewal in the 1960s and uneasy about Christians pushing others to be baptised in the Spirit. But following the Nottingham Conference, his attitude changed as he found that the focus of the renewal was not so much on individual satisfaction but

10. Fountain Trust , "Booking Form," n.d.; "Glory in the Church"; "Charismatic Event (July 1975.)"

11. Letter from Harper to David Watson, 6 April 1971; Fountain Trust, "Fellowship of the Holy Spirit", 7; Davison, "Memorandum," 1.

12. "Reality", 3, 16; "Conference Aims," 1.

13. Fountain Trust, "Westminster: Speakers' Subjects"; "Speakers from all over the World", 2; Letter from Harper to Gavin Reid, 16 April 1975.

14. This television company operating in the Midlands. Curriculum Vitae: David MacInnes; Fountain Trust, "Gathered for Power," 3; "Programme: Nottingham," 2; "Detailed Programme," 1–2; Letter from David MacInnes to Harper, 19 April 1973.

15. Reid, *Gagging of God*.

16. Reid, *Elaborate Funeral*.

17. Fountain Trust, "Glory in the Church," 3, 5; "Speakers," 3; Letter from Gavin Reid to Harper, 1 July 1975; Reid, *New Happiness*.

on the growth of the church. He had then come to experience renewal in his own life while praying and worshipping, but this had not made him forget the task of preaching the gospel, and the calling for justice in the world.[18] After pondering and experiencing the renewal, he neither fully rejected nor fully supported it. He remained neutral, though sympathetic toward it with certain reservations.[19]

Besides evangelism, there were three Anglicans who were gifted in healing and deliverance ministering at the conferences. John Richards had been a Curate in different churches and during his service as a secretary to the Bishop of Exeter's Commission on Exorcism, he wrote a popular book, *But Deliver Us from Evil*, which is regarded "as the standard work on the ministry of deliverance." He was appointed associate director of the Trust in 1977.[20] He spoke at Westminster 1975, 1977, and 1979 and discussed deliverance and exorcism from social, psychiatric, and theological angles.[21] He suggested that casting out demons was not the major problem of exorcism, but what really mattered was "after-care." Hence the church should be a healing community where people could experience the abundant life as Jesus promised.[22] Another exorcist was David Smith, who was a layman of David Watson's church and had had "a balanced and successful itinerant ministry" for ten years. He chaired the seminar about exorcism at Westminster 1975.[23] Jim Glennon, an Australian Anglican canon, spoke at Westminster 1979 on the same topic. In the invitation letter, Smail expressed his appreciation of Glennon's approach to healing because it was not the same as the American style of "star presentations and miracle services" but his main concern was about ministry in local churches. His "firm roots in the Anglican tradition" even appealed to Smail.[24] Glennon totally agreed with Smail's appraisal and said, "I am more concerned to say how this ministry can be

---

18. Fountain Trust, "Happier," 6.

19. Letter from Harper to Herbert F. Stevenson, 22 August 1975.

20. Fountain Trust, "New," 6; "The Day at Westminster," 2; Richards, *But Deliver Us from Evil*.

21. Fountain Trust, "Speakers," 2; "Glory in the Church," 5–6.

22. Fountain Trust, "Outline," n. d.; "Westminster, Growing in the Church," 3–4; "Joy in the City," 5.

23. Fountain Trust, "Glory in the Church," 5–6.

24. Letter from Smail to Jim Glennon, 4 August 1978.

exercised by the local church than to have people falling over, etc., etc., at the time."[25]

Furthermore, some Anglican speakers were specialists in worship and church community. Graham Pulkingham, an Episcopal clergyman from the US, was invited to speak at Nottingham on this topic and conducted the final Eucharist at the conference. He was raised a Roman Catholic but transferred to the Episcopal Church and became the Rector of the Church of the Redeemer in Texas.[26] When Pulkingham had to decline the invitation to speak at Westminster 1975 due to an urgent need for medical treatment in the US,[27] the Trust invited Harold Parks to take the responsibility of speaking about worship at a seminar. He was the vicar of Christ Church in North Finchley and one of the Trustees.[28] Colin Urquhart was the vicar of St Hugh's Church, Lewsey, near Luton. He participated in the Guildford Conference and soon after that his church in Luton experienced renewal, which was recorded in his book *When the Spirit Comes*.[29] Meanwhile, he had developed a traveling ministry in Britain and overseas.[30] He spoke about worship at Westminster 1975, 1977, and 1979[31] where he suggested that leading worship could be creative rather than solely "singing endless choruses." The task of worship leaders was to lead the congregation to worship "with reality" and with an open heart to the Spirit and others.[32] Tom Walker was "an obvious candidate" to teach about worship and spoke on the subject at Westminster 1977 with Urquhart.[33] He regarded this speaking engagement as "an enormous privilege" and "a totally refreshing experience."[34] He was the vicar at St. John's in Harborne, Birmingham,

25. Letter from Jim Glennon to Smail, 17 August 1978.

26. Fountain Trust, "Gathered for Power," 4; "Programme: Nottingham," 2; "Detailed Programme," 1–2.

27. Holl, "Glory in the Church," 4.

28. Fountain Trust, "Last-minute," 4.

29. Urquhart, *When the Spirit Comes*.

30. Fountain Trust, "Growing in the Church," 4; "The Day at Westminster," 2; Smail, *Newsletter* 56.

31. Fountain Trust, "Booking Form," n.d.; "Glory in the Church," 4–5; "Westminster: Speakers' Subjects"; "Joy in the City," 5.

32. Minute-Westminster 1977 (25 February 1977), 1.

33. Fountain Trust, "Westminster, Growing in the Church," 2–3; Letter from Smail to Tom Walker, 23 February 1976.

34. Letter from Tom Walker to Smail, 6 October 1977.

which went through both blessings and difficulties for years as a result of the renewal.[35]

There were some Anglicans speaking about mission and society. Bill Burnett was invited to speak at Nottingham and Westminster 1975. Cecil Kerr illustrated the conflict and suggested possible solutions for reconciliation between Protestants and Roman Catholics in Northern Ireland. Lesslie Newbigin of the Selly Oak Colleges in Birmingham lectured on mission with particular reference to his work in South India at Westminster 1979. Although he did not identify himself as "charismatic," he had frequent contact with Pentecostals and charismatics and was concerned about their relation with church life.[36] Another lecturer, David Gillet, the director of extension studies at St. John's College, also talked about mission at the same conference.[37]

Both the Roman Catholic Bishop of Menevia, Langton Fox, and the Anglican Suffragan Bishop of Pontefract, Richard Hare, were concerned about the ecumenical potential of the renewal and they lead a seminar at Westminster 1977. Hare also conducted the final communion in the last evening of the conference.[38] At Westminster 1979, Michael Green, the rector of St. Aldate's in Oxford, was invited to lead the daily Bible study in the mornings.[39] He illustrated the issues of social concern, evangelism, community, and unity in renewal by focusing on three cities in the biblical period, Jerusalem, Ephesus, and Philippi from Acts, Ephesians, and Revelation.[40] Paul Felton, a Scottish Anglican priest in Cumbrae, talked about the relation between renewal and economic, social, and family

35. Fountain Trust, "The Day at Westminster," 2; "Growing in the Church," 4.

36. Letter from Smail to Lesslie Newbigin, 13 March 1978; Letter from Lesslie Newbigin to Smail, 25 March 1978; Fountain Trust, "Speakers at Westminster," 1979."

37. Fountain Trust, "Joy in the City," 5; "Joy in the City: Outreach," 2; "Speakers at Westminster 1979"; Letter from Smail to David Gillett, 4 August 1978.

38. Letter from Richard Hare to Smail, 19 May 1977; Fountain Trust, "Westminster, Growing in the Church," 3.

39. Letter from Smail to Michael Green, 2 May 1979; Letter from the secretary to Smail to Michael Green, 8 June 1979; Fountain Trust, "Joy in the City," 4; "Speakers at Westminster 1979."

40. Letter from Michael Green to Smail, 16 May 1979; Letter from Michael Green to Smail, 29 May 1979.

life[41] and spoke at Westminster 1977 on the Christian family.[42] Michael Harper was invited to speak at the same conference as a minister of Holy Trinity Church in Hounslow. He talked about "Love as the Root and Ground of Growth (Ephesians 3)" and led a seminar on "A New Look at ministry."[43] He also gave a "rich treatment of 1 Cor. 12, 13, 14" in the last lecture.[44] Finally, the Trust invited a Chinese Bishop of Singapore, Chiu Ban It, to lecture on the prophetic role of the church and lead a seminar on evangelism with David Watson and Gavin Reid at Westminster 1975.[45] Chiu served on the Anglican Consultative Council, was chairperson of the Christian Conference of Asia, and a member of Central Committee of the WCC and the Commission of World Mission and Evangelism. He made a comment about himself, "I have been about."[46] Despite all these official engagements, what had made the biggest impact on his life was his spirit baptism at a WCC conference on evangelism in Bangkok in 1973. Since then he changed his understanding of scriptures, preaching, worship, and ministry drastically. He was also empowered to begin a healing ministry, which he had been called to do when he was ordained as Bishop. From that time, healing became "a natural part" of his minis- try and he sometimes prayed for the sick with the vicar during services.[47] Many people became Christians and the "luke-warm" Christians were renewed. Reflecting on the WCC and the Christian Conference of Asia, he realised that these organisations were doing God's work on the basis of human knowledge rather than God's power.[48]

Methodist Speakers

The Trust invited four Methodist ministers to speak at the international conferences. For Guildford, despite the controversies, the conference

---

41. Minute-Westminster 1977 (25 February 1977), 1; Fountain Trust, "The Day at Westminster," 2; Letter from Smail to Paul Felton, 23 December 1976.

42. Fountain Trust, "Growing in the Church," 3–4.

43. Fountain Trust, "Westminster, Growing in the Church," 3.

44. Letter from Michael Bennett to Smail, 11 August 1977.

45. Fountain Trust, "Glory in the Church," 4, 6; Letter from Harper to Chiu Ban It, 5 May 1975; Letter from Chiu Ban It to Harper, 13 June 1975.

46. Fountain Trust, "Singapore," 2–3; "Bishop," 4.

47. Letter from Peter Young to Harper and David Watson, 28 March 1973; Fountain Trust, "Charismatic Event (July 1975);" "Singapore," 3.

48. Fountain Trust, "Bishop," 4.

Committee insisted on inviting Leslie Davison who was regarded by some as too liberal to speak. This conflict will be described in the last section of this chapter. Davison gave four lectures about the Spirit and gifts from the current Protestant perspective.[49] For Nottingham, the Trust invited William Davies to speak. He was a senior lecturer in Religious Studies specializing in church history and Old Testament at Padgate College of Education, and he experienced the Baptism in the Spirit when he was the President of the College Chapel in 1970. He was a joint editor of the *Dunamis* magazine.[50] He was given the special topic of "Holiness and Revival" dealing with the connection of the contemporary charismatic renewal with the eighteenth-century revival and John Wesley's teaching on holiness.[51] At Westminster 1975, John Horner, who was the superintendent of the Methodist Mission at Albert Hall in Nottingham and had attended the Guildford and Nottingham conferences, was invited to speak about Christ and the Spirit.[52] At Westminster 1977, Smail invited Howard Belben, the Principal of Cliff College in Derbyshire, to speak in

49. Davison, "Memorandum," 1; Letter from Harper to Leslie Davison, 26 April 1971; Letter from Harper to Leslie Davison, 9 July 1970; Letter from Leslie Davison to Harper, 13 July 1970. The contents of the four lectures were written in his book, *Pathway to Power.* The first one focused on "the history of the Doctrine of the Spirit up to the formulation of the great Creeds." He explored the historical facts and linked the history to the contemporary charismatic renewal, particularly the experiential issues. In the second lecture, he focused on the history of gifts with an attempt to discover "the development and use of the charismata at different times" in the scriptures. For lecture three, he talked about Wesley's theology on holiness in the eighteenth century as he believed that it was one of the origins of the Pentecostal Movement and was also related to the charismatic renewal. In the final lecture, he discussed how the holiness and revival movements influenced each other in the nineteenth century and how the charismatic renewal developed from this integration. (Davison, *Pathway to Power*, 10–11.)

50. In the letter of 3 November 1972, Davies mentioned that Charles Clarke's newsletter would be combined with *Dunamis.* Clarke was going to be joint editor with Ross Peart and hence Davies would co-edit *Dunamis* with Clarke. (Letter from William R. Davies to Harper, 3 November 1972.)

51. Fountain Trust, "Gathered for Power," 2; "Programme: Nottingham," 2; Letter from William Davies To Harper, 3 October 1972; Letter from Harper to William Davies, 16 May 1973.

52. Letter from John Horner to Harper, 25 October 1971; Fountain Trust, "Glory in the Church," 4, 6; "Westminster 1975,"; Letter from John Horner to Harper, 25 June 1975; Letter from John Horner to Smail, 5 August, 1975; Holl, "Glory in the Church," 4.

order to keep "the Methodist flag flying."[53] He talked about discerning God's will and chaired a seminar together with Jan van der Veken.[54]

Presbyterian Speakers

From the Presbyterian circle, there were four speakers involved at the international conferences. J. Rodman Williams, a Professor at the Presbyterian Theological Seminary in Texas, was invited to speak on the doctrine of the Holy Spirit at Guildford.[55] Two years later he came to Nottingham, and was by then the President of Melodyland School (Bible and Theology) in Anaheim, California, which was established in 1973.[56] He had also taken part in the founding of an Ecumenical Research Centre and the Roman Catholic-Pentecostal/Charismatic dialogue.[57] At Nottingham, he lectured on "the charismatic movement in the Protestant churches and its contribution to the whole church" and led a seminar about renewal entitled "The New Reformation." He also gave a short talk at an evening service under the theme of "Gathered to Unite the People of God" and was involved in a theological workshop during the conference.[58] As mentioned previously, George MacLeod of the Church of Scotland (Presbyterian) also spoke at Nottingham about social issues. For Westminster 1975, the Trust invited Jim Brown, a minister from Parksburg Presbyterian Church in Pennsylvania, to speak on Spirit baptism, charismatic life, and gifts at a seminar. He was known as one of the first Presbyterian ministers to be baptised in the Spirit in the US.[59] At Westminster 1977, Andrew Morton, a Scottish Presbyterian who

53. Fountain Trust, "The Day at Westminster," 2; "Growing in the Church," 3; Letter from Tom Walker to Smail, 26 February 1976; Letter from Smail to Howard Belben, 5 March 1976.

54. Letter from Howard Belben to Smail, 25 April 1977; Letter from Smail to Howard Belben, 9 May 1977; Fountain Trust, "Growing in the Church," 3–4.

55. Davison, "Memorandum," 1; Fountain Trust, "Fellowship of the Holy Spirit," 7.

56. In his letter to Harper, Williams mentioned, "We have just launched a School of Theology with 125 in the first class!" (Letter from J. Rodman Williams to Harper, 17 January 1973.)

57. Curriculum Vitae: J. Rodman Williams; Fountain Trust, "Gathered for Power," 5.

58. Letter from Secretary to Harper to J. Rodman Williams, 16 May 1973; Fountain Trust, "Programme: Nottingham," 2.

59. Fountain Trust, "Glory in the Church," 4, 6; "Westminster 1975"; Letter from Jim Brown to Smail, 10 June 1974.

worked in the BCC as a social responsibility secretary,[60] talked about how Christians might relate to the world and the country.[61] For Westminster 1979, the Trust invited an Irish Presbyterian, David McKee, to speak on evangelism. He served at the Christian Renewal Centre, which Cecil Kerr had established for reconciliation between Protestants and Roman Catholics in Ireland.[62] Smail believed that McKee could give very good lectures on evangelism with his Irish background and that the audience would hear "some good Reformed voice."[63]

Baptist Speakers

Four speakers from the Baptist circle were involved at the international conferences. At Nottingham, the Trust invited David Pawson, a minister from Millead Centre in Guildford, to lecture on "Liberty in the Spirit" based on Galatians.[64] He thought that the lecture would be "a bit of biblical ballast" for the audience.[65] This idea came into his mind first of all at Guildford, and he thought that the epistle was "a very needed corrective within the charismatic movement" as it contained the teachings on the gifts and the fruit of the Spirit in relation to salvation, faith, and works.[66] He was also assigned a sermon at an evening service under the theme of "Gathered to hear the Word of God."[67] At Westminster 1975 Jim Graham,

60. Fountain Trust, "The Day at Westminster," 2; "Growing in the Church," 4.

61. Fountain Trust, "Westminster, Growing in the Church," 3–4.

62. Letter from David McKee to Michael Barling, 2 April 1979; Fountain Trust, "Speakers at Westminster 1979."

63. Letter from Smail to David McKee, 10 March 1978; Fountain Trust, "Joy in the City," 5.

64. He "definitely" accepted the invitation of speaking at Nottingham two years before the conference actually took place by saying, "I will look forward very much to being at Nottingham." After one year he seemed to forget about the promise that he had made with Harper, as he said, "I must confess that I had not fully realised that I had definitely promised to be with you, but would appreciate it if you could let me have more details about this and what kind of thing you would like me to do," and so Harper reminded him of his promise. (Letter from David Pawson to Harper, 4 October 1971; Letter from David Pawson to Harper, 5 September 1972; Letter from Harper to David Pawson, 18 October 1972.)

65. Letter from David Pawson to Harper, 30 January 1973; Fountain Trust, "Programme: Nottingham," 2.

66. Letter from David Pawson to Harper, 29 July 1971; Letter from David Pawson to Harper, 30 January 1973.

67. Letter from Secretary to Harper to David Pawson, 16 May 1973.

a minister from Gold Hill Baptist Church near Gerrards Cross, was invited to talk about the fruit of the Spirit and worship.[68] At Westminster 1977, two Baptist ministers were involved. One was Douglas McBain, one of the Trustees and a minister from Lewin Road Baptist Church in Streatham, London, which had experienced "a considerable measure of corporate renewal." He lectured on "God's word and fresh vision for Renewal" and participated in a seminar on the ecumenical issues. Ken Pagard was a minister from Chula Vista Baptist Church in California, which experienced a great renewal and launched a "community-household living within the context of parish life." At the conference, his lecture and seminar focused on his experience and knowledge of this sort of church life.[69] His approach was both experiential and biblical and so Michael Bennett commented that his view on experience was "scripturally verified" and all his lectures were "fully prepared and well documented." Both McBain and Pagard won praise from the delegates in the last lecture concerning the church's future.[70]

Lutheran Speakers

Lutheran speakers only appeared at Nottingham. Arnold Bittlinger was the Director of the Ecumenical Academy in Schloss Craheim and a member of the Vatican-Charismatic dialogue in 1971. He spoke about theological issues concerning the renewal in a lecture and took the subject of "God's stewards" in a seminar dealing with the relationship between Christian ministry and renewal.[71] Another Lutheran was Larry Christenson, the pastor from Trinity Lutheran Church in San Pedro in California, and he had a vital part in kindling the flame of renewal in Britain. His lecture was "A Charismatic Approach to Social Action"[72] which Harper thought would be helpful to the situation in Britain as social action was believed to be increasingly important.[73]

68. Fountain Trust, "Glory in the Church," 4, 6; "Westminster: 1975."

69. Fountain Trust, "Westminster, Growing in the Church," 3; "Growing in the Church," 4; "The Day at Westminster," 2; Minute-FTCCM (8 June 1977), 1.

70. Letter from Michael Bennett to Smail, 11 August 1977.

71. Curriculum Vitae: Arnold Bittlinger; Fountain Trust, "Gathered for Power," 2; "Programme: Nottingham," 3.

72. Letter from Larry Christenson to Harper, 18 May 1973; Fountain Trust, "Gathered for Power," 2; "Programme: Nottingham," 2.

73. Letter from Harper to Larry Christenson, 24 May 1973.

Other Denominational Speakers

Douglas Quy was the only Pentecostal who was one of the main speakers at the international conferences. Harper cautiously proposed the invitation to Quy of being a guest. Instead of writing to the Assemblies of God Headquarters, he wrote to Quy directly to avoid troubles. Quy was "happy to accept" the invitation without getting the consent of the AG because it was a "Fellowship of Churches, with no central government or legislative body." He also suggested that Harper could invite him to speak at the Conference as it would help to improve the relationship between the AG and the Trust. His four lectures were about the gifts of the Holy Spirit and healing in relation to his special concern about the current healing campaigns such as "Christian Missions of Divine Healings." He thought that "[r]emarkable healings" possibly contained the elements of extremism and fanaticism. [74] He gave a speech on "Gathered to receive the Spirit of God" with Smail at the first evening meeting, which was about the contribution of the Pentecostal movement to the worldwide churches. Smail talked about the "new" Spirit movement, while Quy talked about the contribution of the "old" drawing out "the relationship between the old and the new."[75] Finally, Colonel William McAllister from the Salvation Army spoke at Westminster 1979 about renewal and social issues.

Independent Speakers

Apart from speakers coming from various ecclesiastical backgrounds, there were some who came without representing any denomination. At Guildford, Ralph Wilkerson, a pastor from the Christian Centre in Melodyland in California, gave lectures on "The baptism of the Spirit and its result" and the unceasingness of miracles.[76] His colleague, Robert Frost, who was a biologist, spoke about "the charismatic community." Arthur Wallis, who was regarded as "a respected leader in the house churches, and valued teacher and expositor among all the churches,"[77]

---

74. Letter from Harper to Douglas Quy, 23 August 1972; Letter from Douglas Quy to Harper, 11 September 1972; Letter from Douglas Quy to Harper, 19 December 1972.

75. Letter from Secretary to Harper to Douglas Quy, 16 May 1973.

76. Davison, "Memorandum," 1; Fountain Trust, "Fellowship of the Holy Spirit," 7; Letter from Christine Rennie to Ralph Wilkerson, 26 May 1971.

77. Fountain Trust, "Growing in the Church," 4; "The Day at Westminster," 2.

spoke about worship in the Spirit and revival at Guildford,[78] and prayer warfare at Westminster 1977.[79] Cecil Cousen was recognised as "a respected and regular speaker at Fountain Trust conferences."[80] He had been the editor of *A Voice of Faith* for twenty years but the magazine was discarded in 1977 and developed his own ministry afterwards. [81] He spoke about and practiced healing at Nottingham, lectured on the gifts of the Spirit at Westminster 1975, and explained wholeness in marriage at Westminster 1977. Another frequent speaker was Frank Lake. He was the founder and Director of the Clinical Theology Association and had trained Christians for counselling with understanding, skill and "compassion of Christ." Many people had sought for psychological healing from the association, and its staff and office had grown rapidly. Many people were released from their implicit problems at one of its conferences named as "The Charismatic Prayer Group and the Healing of Forgotten Pain."[82] For him, healing was a crucial but "complex" issue in renewal. His lectures were both theological and psychological. At Nottingham, he taught about how to counsel individuals and the contribution of the charismatic renewal in dealing with sickness and suffering. He believed that the gift of healing was what the world needed, including physical healing, and the transformation of personal characters, which enabled maturity and holiness to grow. At Westminster 1975 and 1977 he continued his teaching on healing and relationships. But for Westminster 1979, he was not in the speaker team[83] and the Trust invited another psychiatrist, Ruth Fowke, to deal with the topic of healing from an academic perspective.[84]

There were some independent speakers who were concerned about or actually involved in social or missionary work. For Nottingham, the

78. Letter from Arthur Wallis to Christine Rennie, 8 June 1971; Fountain Trust, "Fellowship of the Holy Spirit", 7; Davison, "Memorandum," 1.

79. Letter from Arthur Wallis to Smail, 2 June 1977; Fountain Trust, "Growing in the Church," 2–3.

80. Fountain Trust, "Westminster, Growing in the Church,"3; "The Day at Westminster," 2.

81. Smail, *Newsletter* 59.

82. Fountain Trust, "Programme" Nottingham," 1–3; "The Day at Westminster," 2; "Glory in the Church," 4–6; "Westminster, Growing in the Church," 3–4; Letter from Frank Lake to Sylvia Lawton, 17 May 1973.

83. Letter from Smail to David MacInnes, 31 March 1978.

84. Fountain Trust, "Joy in the City," 2; "Joy in the City, London," 5.

Trust successfully invited Loren Cunningham, the founder of Youth with a Mission (YWAM), to speak about "Faith and Vision" in youth ministry for four lectures and "Gathered to reach the world for God."[85] At Westminster 1975, Roy Calvocoressi, who worked for Christian social action in Cyprus and British industry,[86] together with Campbell McAlpine, spoke about social action and God's work in the world respectively.[87] Since McAlpine had spoken at the first Fountain Trust conference where twenty-eight people attended in 1964, Harper invited him specially to Westminster 1975 to celebrate the tenth anniversary of the Trust.[88] At Westminster 1977, Simon Barrington-Ward was invited to teach about mission.[89] He was the general secretary of the Church Missionary Society in Birmingham and was described as "an expert on missionary strategy and evangelism."[90] For Westminster 1979, Smail invited William Brown, the executive director of the Trinity Christian Community in New Orleans, Louisiana, to talk about the effect of renewal "in the inner city situation and in a difficult racial background" in his church.[91] Smail was sure that Brown's experience and ideas about how the renewal could have an impact on society was "exactly" what the conference needed and he could inspire those attending who might be in a similar situation.[92] At the same conference, Don Double, as an evangelist of the Good News

85. It is an interdenominational evangelical ministry recruiting volunteers to serve every corner of the world. It establishes Schools of Evangelism for training workers and leaders and the first one is in Lausanne, Switzerland where the international coordinating centre is located. Until 1973, YWAM had reached 130 countries with tens of thousands of volunteers, fifteen schools world-wide and a ship for training, medication and transporting volunteers to the South Pacific and Asian area. From 1969, Cunningham had been the International Director of the organization. Up to 2002, YWAM had sent 50,000 short-term and 11,500 full-time workers, set up more than 240 Discipleship Training School and the University of the Nations awarding degrees, obtained four mercy ships and served more than 220 countries in the world. (Robinson, "Youth," 1223–24; Fountain Trust, "Gathered for Power," 2; Curriculum Vitae: Loren Cunningham.) Fountain Trust, "Programme: Nottingham," 2; "Detailed Programme," 2.

86. Fountain Trust, "Glory in the Church," 4, 6; "Speakers," 2.

87. Fountain Trust, "Glory in the Church," 3–6; "Speakers," 2.

88. Letter from Harper to Campbell McAlpine, 4 April 1975; Fountain Trust, "Glory in the Church," 5; "Speakers," 2.

89. Fountain Trust, "Westminster, Growing in the Church," 3–4.

90. Fountain Trust, "Growing in the Church," 3; "The Day at Westminster," 2.

91. Letter from William Brown to Smail, 6 March 1979; Letter from Smail to William Brown, 6 February 1979; Fountain Trust, "Speakers at Westminster 1979."

92. Letter from Smail to William Brown, 6 February 1979.

Crusade, which was a member of the Evangelical Alliance, was invited to speak about the Spirit's involvement in evangelism.[93] Smail thought that he could contribute a lot in the lectures as he had "practical experience in charismatic evangelism."[94] At one of the evening services of the conference, he preached about repentance as he believed that it was the secret of joy, which charismatics had neglected.[95]

An Orthodox Speaker

At the international conferences there was only one Orthodox speaker, Fr. Athanasios Emmert. He had been the pastor of the Holy Spirit Orthodox Church, which he had established himself, and belonged to a missionary parish in the Antiochian Archdioceses of New York and All North America. In 1972, he was invited by David du Plessis to represent the Orthodox Church at the Vatican-Charismatic dialogue in Zürich. In 1973, he gave up the pastorship in the US and was invited by Arnold Bittlinger to serve at the Ecumenical Academy in Schloss Craheim, because J. Rodman Williams and Ralph Wilkerson who could possibly help in ecumenical works were busy working for the theology school in Melodyland.[96] Harper was eager and determined to invite him to speak at Nottingham, as he explained in the invitation letter, "It would be terrible not to have representation from the Orthodox Church and there is no person I would rather have than you." Being encouraged by du Plessis, Emmert accepted the invitation. He talked about the charismatic renewal in the Orthodox Church, its contribution to other churches, and worship in the Spirit according to the Orthodox tradition.[97]

93. Letter from Don Double to Smail, 1 April 1978; Letter from Don Double to Michael Barling, 9 May 1979; Fountain Trust, "Joy in the City," 2; "Speakers at Westminster 1979."

94. Letter from Smail to Don Double, 10 March 1978.

95. Letter from Don Double to Michael Barling, 9 May 1979.

96. Curriculum Vitae: Athanasios Franklin Stuart Emmert, 1–2; Fountain Trust, "Gathered for Power," 2–3; Letter from Athanasios Emmert to Harper, 1 November 1972.

97. Fountain Trust, "Programme: Nottingham," 2; Letter from the Secretary to Harper to Athanasios Emmert, n.d.; Letter from Harper to Athanasios Emmert, 18 October 1972; Letter from Athanasios Emmert to Harper, 1 November 1972; Letter from Harper to Athanasios Emmert, 22 November 1972.

Roman Catholic Speakers

At the five international conferences, Roman Catholic speakers were the second largest team after the Anglicans, with twelve involved. Most of them were famous Catholic theologians or charismatic leaders. Despite the strong opposition from some Protestant leaders, which will be mentioned in the last section of this chapter, Harper insisted on inviting an American Catholic charismatic, Kevin Ranaghan, to speak at Guildford as he was certain that Ranaghan's approach "would be just the right one for England at the moment."[98] From his personal experience, he spoke about how his church in the US was growing into maturity through the renewal and becoming a "thoroughly Charismatic and thoroughly Catholic" community. He also elaborated on the history of the Catholic charismatic renewal in the US, with testimonies of transformation that had taken place, both personally and collectively, and gave a talk on "the re-discovery of spiritual gift."[99]

After Guildford the Trust continued to invite Roman Catholics to speak at other international conferences and when it came to Nottingham Harper said, "We want a strong team of Catholics present." He invited Albert de Monléon who was a Dominican priest teaching theology and the charismatic renewal at the Centre d'Études Istine for ecumenical studies in Paris and a leader of the French Charismatic Renewal which was "growing rapidly" and "beautifully."[100] De Monléon also attended the Guildford conference.[101] Simon Tugwell strongly encouraged Harper to invite de Monléon as he was "a very sound and alive Christian" and "it would be absolutely splendid" if he could accept the invitation.[102] It took Harper three attempts to successfully invite him. In the first invitation, Harper said, "It would give us very great delight if you could manage it and I know that many others will appreciate your ministry there." But De Monléon hesitated to accept since he was not confident in speaking at a big conference and was uncertain about the arrangement at Providence

98. Letter from Harper to Bob Balkam, 21 July 1970.

99. Letter from Kevin Ranaghan to Harper, 24 April 1971; Davison, "Memorandum," 1; Letter from Christine Rennie to Kevin Ranaghan, 26 May 1971.

100. Fountain Trust, "Gathered for Power," 3; Letter form Harper to Albert de Monléon, 27 July 1972; Letter from Albert de Monléon to Harper, 20 September 1972; Letter from Albert de Monléon to Harper, 28 December 1972, 1–2.

101. Fountain Trust, "Catholic Attending: Guildford."

102. Letter from Simon Tugwell to Harper, 1 May 1972.

College. In the second invitation, Harper asserted, "I do hope that you can come" because it was very important. In the third time, he said, "We would certainly miss you if you were not able to be there."[103] Both he and the Trust were "overjoyed" when he eventually accepted. He talked about "the charismatic movement in the Roman Catholic Church and its contribution to other churches" in one lecture and then a four-session seminar on "Jesus and the Spirit" dealing with the theology of the Son and the Spirit in the Trinity.[104]

At Westminster 1975 there were two Roman Catholic speakers. Francis MacNutt, a Dominican from St Louis, US, was a leading figure in healing ministry in Catholic circles. He had begun his ministry of physical and spiritual healing in 1967 in the US, and it had taken him to South America and other African countries; over 75 percent of his time was spent travelling round the world.[105] He taught about and practiced healing in lectures, seminars, and an evening service. Richard Harbour recorded that MacNutt "wore his white Dominican robes that night 'to give a little Resurrection life to you Protestants in black.'" One of the features of his teachings and conviction about healing was that "Jesus can do it." [106] He claimed that healing ministry should be both physical and spiritual because physical problems could so easily hinder the flow of love for others; inner healing was the way to solve the intrinsic problems of people in the world who were "unhappy and fearful."[107] Moreover, he insisted that healing should not be "put on the fringe of the church's life" since it was a means that Jesus applied to preach his words. Another Catholic speaker was Paul Lebeau. He was a Belgian Jesuit priest teaching at the Institute d'Études Theologiques and "closely associated with

103. Letter from Harper to Albert de Monléon, 17 May 1972; Letter from Harper to Albert de Monléon, 6 July 1972; Letter from Albert de Monléon to Harper, 15 July 1972; Letter from Harper to Albert de Monléon, 27 July 1972; Letter from Harper to Albert de Monléon, 28 September 1972.

104. Letter from Albert de Monléon to Harper, 28 December 1972, 1; Fountain Trust, "Programme: Nottingham." 2.

105. Fountain Trust, "Girl," 1.

106. Harbour, "Glory," 4, 6; Fountain Trust, "Speakers," 2; "Glory in the Church," 4–6; "Conference Brochure: Westminster," 2; "Booking Form," n.d.; "Charismatic Event (July 1975)"; Letter from Francis MacNutt to Harper, 8 July 1974; "Reality at Westminster," 3.

107. Coomes, "Optimism," 1; "Reality", 3; Harbour, "Glory," 6.

Suenens."[108] Smail described him as "a theologian of considerable weight as well as being a most attractive Christian brother."[109] He was assigned to talk about social action, which he was keen on as "man's dignity and divine vocation" had not found its right place in the world.[110]

At Westminster 1977, besides Suenens, the Trust invited four other Catholic representatives, and that created the largest Catholic speaker team among all the five international conferences. Jan van der Veken was a theologian teaching at the Roman Catholic University of Louvain in Belgium and worked with Suenens in the composition of the Malines document to provide guidelines for renewal.[111] Smail requested him to lecture on "The work of God and the work of man in Renewal" to illustrate some of the points in the document, and raise a "basic theological necessity" that renewal involved the power of God and human effort. In other words, it should avoid both "supernaturalism" and "naturalism" which resulted from putting the emphasis solely on God's power or on human effort. More important, the lecture was to bring out how renewal theology was related to charisms in practice. Apart from the lecture, he was also responsible for a seminar concerning gifts, discernment, and guidance.[112] Ian Petit was a Benedictine priest and famous in the Irish Renewal.[113] He had been involved in the previous international conference as chaplain or conductor of Mass, and at Westminster 1975 he spoke as a chairperson of the RCNSC on "The Charismatic Dimension and Catholic Tradition" and also gave a seminar on the "Release of the Spirit."[114] Through Bob Balkam, Dr. Jack Dominian, a Roman Catholic doctor and psychologist, was invited to speak.[115] He was interested in understanding charismatic experiences from a psychological perspec-

108. Letter from Smail to Paul Lebeau, 31 January 1975; Fountain Trust, "Glory in the Church," 5; "Charismatic Event (July 1975)"; "Speakers," 3.

109. Letter from Smail to Cecil Kerr, 10 February 1975.

110. Fountain Trust, "Glory in the Church," 3, 6; Letter from Paul Lebeau to Smail, 25 January 1975.

111. Fountain Trust, "The Day at Westminster," 2.

112. Letter from Smail to Jan van der Veken, 23 December 1976; Fountain Trust, "Westminster '77," 2; "Growing in the Church," 3–4.

113. Fountain Trust, "The Day at Westminster," 2; "Growing in the Church," 4.

114. Fountain Trust, "Growing in the Church," 2–3.

115. Minute-Westminster 1977 (25 February 1977), 1; Memo from Bob Balkam, 13 December 1976.

tive and believed that a bridge could be built between these two areas.[116] He developed this thinking in an article published in the *Expository Times* and at the conference he illustrated it under the topic, "The Psychological Health of Charismatics."[117] Smail believed that this lecture would help charismatic leaders and prayer groups to be aware of the "false supernaturalism" and "false naturalism." After the conference, his talk was admired as having been "constructive and positive."[118] Apart from the clinical side, the Trust was concerned about the spiritual aspect of healing and so it invited a Roman Catholic nun to teach and practice it. Briege McKenna, a young Franciscan nun, was becoming famous for her healing ministry in the US and Ireland, especially in regard to incurable diseases such as cancer. In fact, she was not the first choice for the Trust but was brought in to replace Agnes Sanford who had declined the invitation, because of her age (eighty) although she had originally accepted it.[119] McKenna gave a lecture and a seminar on the healing ministry and conducted a healing service at an evening meeting.[120] She was regarded as "the central figure of the conference" and "a real gift of God."[121] Barrington-Ward described her leading of healing ministry as being marked by "her inspired ordinariness and naturalness" and "simple assurance . . . that God is enough." People received ministry and were able to "minister to each other." He personally felt that "the reality of the faith, peace and joy" from worship was very obvious in that healing service.[122] Michael Bennett felt "a sense of authority, which was helpful" in her spiritual counselling.[123] An Anglican rector was blessed

116. Letter from Jack Dominian to Smail, 15 August 1977.

117. Letter from Smail to Jack Dominian, 23 December 1976; Letter from Jack Dominian to Smail, 24 January 1977; Minute-Westminster 1977 (21 October 1976), 1; Fountain Trust, "The Day at Westminster," 2; "Growing in the Church," 3.

118. Letter from Smail to Jack Dominian, 23 December 1976; Letter from Jack Dominian to Smail, 15 August 1977; Letter from Agnes Sanford to Smail, 2 May 1977; Letter from Smail to Briege McKenna, 27 May 1977;

119. Letter from Smail to Agnes Sanford, 10 June 1977; Letter from Smail to Michael Scanlan, 10 November 1977; Fountain Trust, "The Day at Westminster," 2; Minute-FTCCM (8 June 1977), 1.

120. Letter from Smail to Briege McKenna, 27 May 1977; Fountain Trust, "Westminster, Growing in the Church," 2–4.

121. Letter from Smail to Michael Scanlan, 10 November 1977.

122. Barrington-Ward, "Faith," 2, 8.

123. Letter from Michael Bennett to Smail, 11 August 1977.

in her "lovely ministry."[124] A German delegate enjoyed the gentleness of her ministry in the service.[125] The wife of a Salvation Army captain felt a process of healing of her cervical spondylosis following the service.[126] And a delegate also wrote to the Trust that she experienced a great inner healing.[127] The contribution of the Catholic speakers was highly appreciated. A delegate regarded their talks as "useful and interesting."[128] An Anglican minister felt that they had given "deeper and better thought" than the Protestants.[129]

At Westminster 1979 Suenens spoke again and there were three other Roman Catholic speakers. Through the connection with Bob Balkam, the Trust was able to invite another prominent Roman Catholic speaker, Tom Forrest.[130] He was the director of the International Communication Office in Brussels for the Catholic charismatic renewal[131] and Smail described him as "much involved in the Catholic renewal." Since the Trust wanted the conference to hear about the renewal in the Third World and Forrest was well-experienced in the South America mission field, it eagerly invited him to speak at the conference.[132] He gave a lecture on "church and city including reference to the Third World" and also in the first evening service. The other two Catholic speakers were Paul Lebeau and Ian Petit who had been invited to the previous international conferences. Their lectures were about the local church, social concern, and prayer.[133]

These five international conferences can be regarded as ecumenically successful because they gathered a group of speakers that comprised Protestants and Roman Catholics. Via the common ground of the renewal, they could work together for the conferences regardless of their

124. Letter from A. K. Pring to Smail, 18 August 1977.

125. Letter from Hans-Dieter Gramm to the Fountain Trust, 12 September 1977.

126. Letter from Kath Holmes to Smail, 17 August 1977.

127. Letter from Pamela Mellyard to Smail, 8 August 1977, 4.

128. Letter from J. Pereboom to the Fountain Trust, 9 August 1977, 2.

129. Letter from Roger Hardcastle to Smail, 21 August 1977, 3.

130. Letter from Smail to Tom Forrest, 6 February 1979.

131. Letter from Tom Forrest to Smail, 13 February 1979, 1; Fountain Trust, "Speakers at Westminster 1979."

132. Letter from Smail to Tom Forrest, 6 February 1979; Letter from Smail to the Bishop of London, 18 July 1979.

133. Fountain Trust, "Joy in the City," 4–5.

doctrinal differences and they could speak to an audience that was made up of a diversity of traditions. Perhaps what Jeanne Harper recalled at Guildford could be said to typify the mutual acceptance and ecumenical communion at the conferences, when she commented, "I remember there was an electric stream when the first Catholic speaker got up and said, 'Dear brothers and sisters.' Something's really nice."[134]

ECUMENICAL PARTICIPANTS

Guildford was the first test of ecumenical fellowship and it proved to be successful. There were fourteen denominations including four major Christian traditions: Roman Catholics, Orthodox, Protestants, and Pentecostals at Guildford.[135] Most of them were charismatics, but some had not had that kind of experience before; so the conferences, bringing together charismatic leaders and laymen as well as theologians, were good opportunities for enquiring and learning about the renewal.[136] This ecumenical character continued in the following four international conferences; however, for the Trust, the ecumenical nature was defined primarily by Roman Catholic attendance. Harper endeavored to help the Roman Catholics who had financial difficulty in coming to Guildford. For example, once he received a letter from Simon Tugwell about his financial difficulty Harper was "very anxious" about the Roman Catholic attendance as he thought that they "should have every opportunity of coming and there should be as good a representation as possible." Therefore, he determined to tackle the financial obstacle by offering Tugwell a free place on behalf of the Trust and also one or two more for the Roman Catholics who had similar problems. Furthermore, he consulted his two Catholic partners, Bob Balkam and E. Gwatkin, about the possibility of getting sponsorship from Roman Catholics who acknowledged the Catholic Charismatic Renewal and were willing to subsidise their fellow Catholic members to join the conference, especially "members of the religious orders" for whom the admission fee was "prohibitive."[137] He made this request in early January 1971, six

134. Interview with Michael and Jeanne Harper, 8 August 200.

135. Fountain Trust, "Press Release: International Conference," 2.

136. Davison, "Memorandum," 2.

137. Letter from Simon Tugwell to Harper, 2 January 1971; Letter from Harper to Simon Tugwell, 5 January 1971; Letter from Secretary to Harper to E. Gwatkin, 6 January 1971.

months before the conference, to ensure that those Roman Catholics who had financial problems would be sponsored before the booking was full.[138] Moreover, besides a list of the total attendance, there was also a special list recording the Roman Catholic participants at Guildford and it recorded that twenty-eight of them were from Britain, and the rest came from France (3), Spain (1), Holland (1), Denmark (4), and the US (3).[139] For the Trust, Guildford was a significant and successful step for the future of ecumenical gatherings because of the Roman Catholic attendance. In the following international conferences, Smail also identified their ecumenicity with Roman Catholic participation. Concerning Westminster 1977, he said, ". . . at which at least a third of the participants were Roman Catholics, and which must have been one of the largest and most significant ecumenical events to date in Britain."[140] Similarly for Westminster 1979, before the Conference actually took place, the Trust believed that it would be significantly ecumenical because there would be a large crowd of Roman Catholics. Smail had confidently anticipated that one fourth to one third of the attendance would be Roman Catholics and the rest Protestants from major denominations. Hence, Smail described the conference as "widely ecumenical," "ecumenical oriented," "fully ecumenical," "one of the largest lay ecumenical gatherings so far in this country," "a very large ecumenical representation," and "very large ecumenical gathering."[141]

These five international conferences also had a strong ecumenical character because they involved theologians and leaders from different churches, some of them from overseas. At Guildford, Roman Catholic leaders like Albert de Monléon from France and Kilian McDonnell, Director of the Ecumenical Institute in Minnesota, attended the conference. Both of them had participated in the Roman Catholic-Charismatic

138. Letter from Harper to Bob Balkam, 5 January 1971; Letter from Secretary to Harper to E. Gwatkin, 6 January 1971.

139. Fountain Trust, "Catholics Attending: Guildford."

140. Smail, "Editorial: The More We Are Together . . . ," 2.

141. Letter from Smail to Catherine Marshall LeSourd, 3 March 1978; Letter from Smail to William Brown, 6 February, 1979; Letter from Smail to the Bishop of London, 6 February 1979; Letter from Smail to David Watson, 10 November 1977; ; Letter from Smail to Don Double,10 March 1978; Letter from Smail to David McKee, 10 March 1978; Letter from Smail to David MacInnes, 31 March 1978; Letter from Smail to Larry Christenson, 15 September 1978.

dialogue in Rome in June 1971.[142] Some of the church leaders and theologians were Pentecostals, such as Alfred Missen, General Secretary of the Assemblies of God (though he eventually walked out after the opening ceremony), Wesley Gilpin of the Elim Bible College, and F. P. Möller, Director of the Apostolic Faith Mission of South Africa. A variety of Protestant traditions was represented, including some of the Anglican ministers and lay leaders who experienced the baptism in the Spirit at Guildford.[143] There was John Neale, the Canon Missioner of the Diocese; Simon Barrington-Ward, Principal of Crowther Hall; Wallace Haines of the International Christian Leadership; Howard Belben, Principal of a Methodist College, Cliff College; and James Dunn, from the Department of Theology at the University of Nottingham, who saw the significance of Pentecostalism for churches.[144] Arnold Bittlinger, the Director of the Ecumenical Academy of West Germany, also attended at Guildford.[145]

At Nottingham, Harper endeavored to invite leaders of different churches to be represented in the conference. In the Protestant realm, he approached the three major churches in Britain: the Church of England, the Church of Scotland, and the churches in Wales. From the Anglican side, he invited the Bishop of Southwell to welcome the conference in the opening ceremony and to concelebrate with other church leaders at the Eucharist with Anglican liturgy on the final night. The Bishop accepted the invitation for both tasks.[146] Besides that, Harper also appointed Ray Muller from New Zealand, who was also involved at Guildford, to be an Anglican Chaplain at the conference.[147] Moreover, Harper wished to have representatives from the Church of Scotland, and Smail, who had a connection with the Church, was the most suitable person to give the invitation.[148] He also thought that it was important for the churches

---

142. Letter from Harper to the Archbishop of Canterbury, 6 July 1971.

143. Letter from Harper to Bob Balkam, 11 May 1970.

144. Letter from James D.G. Dunn to Harper, 12 December 1970.

145. Fountain Trust, "Press Release: International Conference 2."

146. Minute-FTACM (5 April 1973), 2; Letter from Harper to the Bishop of Southwell, 26 July 1972; Letter from the Bishop of Southwell to Harper, 1 January 1973; Letter from Harper to the Bishop of Southwell, 9 January 1973; Letter from the Bishop of Southwell to Harper, 16 January 1973.

147. Fountain Trust, "Gather for Power," 8.

148. He approached H. Walker of the Home Board, Bill Shannon of St. Ninian's and Rev. James G. Matheson of the Stewardship and Budget Department. They all had interest in the charismatic renewal. He did not expect them to represent the Church

in Wales to be represented at the conference. He invited Rev. Graham Horwood of Rhondda, Glamorgan, whose church had a prayer meeting where ten people had received the Spirit baptism within a period of several months in 1973. In the parishes of Ystad and Hopkinstown, Pontipridd, there were also similar groups seeking the filling of the Spirit. Therefore, Harper requested Horwood to invite those he knew to the conference saying that he would reserve places for them despite the limited number of vacancies.[149]

On the other hand, Harper also actively invited the Roman Catholic leaders who were sympathetic or actually involved in the renewal. He assigned Ian Petit as the Roman Catholic Chaplain for the conference to be responsible for the Mass every morning at seven. Other Catholic leaders like Benedict Heron, Fr. Bernard Brady, the Catholic Chaplain of the University of Nottingham and other priests also helped with it.[150] In addition, Harper asked for a representative of the BCC which eventually sent Emmanuel Sullivan, a Roman Catholic Franciscan and the Secretary of the Committee for Unity in Prayer, to attend the conference. Harper regarded him as the most outstanding Roman Catholic observer of the renewal besides Kilian McDonnell. He wrote a booklet for the BCC, *Can the Pentecostal Movement Renew the Churches?*,[151] to discuss the relation between the Pentecostal and ecumenical movements. It had received a "heartening" response from charismatics. Harper commented that it was "one of the fairest and most constructive pieces of writing on this subject yet to appear" and he thought that Sullivan gave "a slightly qualified 'yes'" to the question of the title. Harper also raised an interesting point that "the BCC should have to turn to a Catholic to write on such a subject, and an American at that." It reveals a fact that

---

of Scotland officially at the conference but to bring a personal report on renewal to the Church. However, none of them were able to come. Then he contacted Dr. Rudolph Ehrlich, the Convener of the Panel of Doctrine which was studying Pentecostalism at that time. Ehrlich sent the Trust's invitation to his panel members and the response was positive. (Letter from Smail to H. Walker, 17 January 1973; Letter from Smail to James G. Matheson, 3 April 1973; Letter from Smail to James G. Matheson, 25 April 1973; Letter from James G. Matheson to Smail, 19 June 1973; Letter from Smail to James. G. Matheson, 23 June 1973.)

149. Letter from Graham Horwood to Harper, 14 May 1973; Letter from Harper to Graham Horwood, 22 May 1973.

150. Letter from Harper to Ian Petit, 28 June 1973.

151. Sullivan, *Can the Pentecostal Movement Renew the Churches?*.

since the 1970s, there was a lack of British writing about the charismatic renewal apart from Simon Tugwell's *Did You Receive the Holy Spirit?*[152] Sullivan was "grateful" for the invitation to participate in the conference and agreed to contribute an article to *Renewal* about his impression of it.[153] Last but not least, some Catholic Charismatic theologians were also invited, such as Tugwell and McDonnell, although neither of them could come.[154] Interestingly, Harper wished that the Prince of Wales could witness this international and ecumenical event and sent him invitation. However, because of his commitment as a Naval Officer at that time, the Prince declined.[155] Having a variety of church leaders at the international conference had become the norm and so there was no lack of church leaders to attend the remaining three. For example, at Westminster 1977, Veronica O'Brien from Malines agreed to come with her secretary. Her presence strengthened the ecumenical character of the conference at which a crowd of Roman Catholics were present.[156]

At Guildford, Harper warmly welcomed Tugwell, who was one of the Roman Catholic participants, by saying, "We would be delighted for you to be part of our fellowship there and link closely with us."[157] A delegate who came to Guildford with his "real hatred of Romans" was transformed dramatically at the moment where he talked to a man whom he had thought was a Roman Catholic but was in fact an Anglican priest (Eric Sellgren).[158] It was understandable that the differences of theological and doctrinal conviction still existed among them as it was unrealistic to think that historical divisions could be erased in a few days, but delegates at Nottingham were able to be open minded towards different ideas. Coomes described the delegates at Nottingham in the following way:

152. Harper, "Editorial: From Guildford to Nottingham," 2–3.

153. Letter from the Secretary to John B. Leake to Harper, 30 January 1973; Letter from Sullivan to Harper, 14 April 1973; Letter from Harper to Bernard Palmer, 11 May 1973.

154. Letter from Simon Tugwell to Harper, 1 May 1972; Letter from Harper to Kilian McDonnell, 24, April 1973.

155. Letter from Harper to the Prince of Wales, 19 January 1972; Letter from David Checketts to Harper, 27 January 1972.

156. Letter from Wilfrid Brieven to Sylvia Lawton, 13 April 1979; Letter from Suenens to Smail, 9, May 1979, 2.

157. Letter from Harper to Simon Tugwell, 5 January 1971.

158. Sellgren, "God," 33.

> [They] were not uptight about every doctrine, tradition and experience, not rooted to every jot and tittle of the law, not so poised on a knife-edge of authority that every criticism seemed destined to destroy faith, future and personal peace. Here were Christians who, when criticised, as they often are (justly or unjustly), don't go on the defensive, don't recoil in horror, don't whip back with angry words, but who are able to laugh at their excesses, analyse the critics, and, if it is just, act upon it.[159]

Douglas Quy commented that the grassroots unity manifested at Nottingham 1973 "would have been unthinkable ten years ago" and he praised God for that.[160] For Sullivan, Nottingham gave him a fresh hope for the ecumenical future. He observed that "there was ecumenical witness throughout the conference but [proselytism] never raised its ugly head." He affirmed what Suenens said, "not for Vatican III, but Jerusalem II."[161] Loren Cunningham witnessed that ecumenical community at Nottingham and prayed that the Trust would continuously be an "anointed instrument to bring unity within the Body."[162] Delegates of Westminster 1975 also tasted the sweetness of unity. For example, Mrs. Pamela Lucas said that she enjoyed the fellowship with many Roman Catholics who had experienced "deeper blessings" in the conference.[163] Barbara Holl regarded herself as a "reserved" lady, but during the conference, she felt "a warmth of fellowship from total strangers—who just happened to be our brothers and sisters in the Lord!" Moreover, she noticed that in the Eucharist, she was offered the wine by "a non-Conformist, coloured pastor" who was holding the Cup for her; hence, she said, "This was the true meaning of Ecumenism."[164] The conference also showed Richard Harbour the nature of oneness in Christ. His attitude towards the Roman Catholics was changed and he recalled that he had lunch with two sisters and they all felt sad about the doctrines separating Protestants and Catholics. Such separation was obviously manifested in the final communion. After all these, he said, "Reconciliation is not

159. Coomes, "Nottingham," 19.

160. Coomes, "1500," 1.

161. Sullivan, "Seeing," 20–21.

162. Letter from Loren Cunningham to Harper, 3 August 1973.

163. Letter from Pamela Lucas, 29 August 1975.

164. Holl, "Glory in the Church," 9–10.

papering over the cracks."[165] Considering the historical conflict and centuries of isolation, this openness and mutual acceptance between Protestants and the Roman Catholics at the international conferences was something that had been rarely found in church history. These attitudes had been expressed naturally without any artificial packaging in the Spirit.

ECUMENICAL ACTIVITIES

Worship

The sense of unity was strongly felt in the daily worship. At Guildford, delegates from all ecclesiastical backgrounds gathered together for a "Morning Praise";[166] and the Roman Catholics held their Mass each afternoon and welcomed everybody to join. They "enjoyed a very warm fellowship" as Balkam recalled[167] As the Trust considered the need for different liturgical forms of worship to cater for delegates with a diversity of backgrounds, they officially prepared both Protestant services with Anglican or Reformed traditions and Catholic Mass for the morning service at Nottingham 1973, Westminster 1975, and 1977.[168] Westminster 1979 was rather special because there was no separate simultaneous worship section for Protestants and Roman Catholics, but only a daily Mass at 8:30 a.m. followed by a worship and bible study session for the whole conference. This was led by Suenens on the first morning and by Michael Green on the remaining three.[169] These arrangements gave delegates opportunities for new worship experience and reminded them of the need for respecting differences for the sake of unity in Christ. Sullivan expressed this view about Nottingham 1973, which also applies to the other international conferences. As he put it, "The emphasis at Nottingham was on a unity already *possessed* which we have to learn to

---

165. Harbour, "Glory," 7–8.

166. Dallière, "Guildford International Conference," 3.

167. Email from Bob Balkam, 16 November 2005.

168. The Reformed liturgical form was held only at Nottingham. (Fountain Trust, "Programme: Nottingham," 1; "Detailed Programme,"1; "Gathered for Power," 8.)

169. Fountain Trust, "Joy in the City," 4.

express visibly in more and more ways without any disloyalty to our conscientious convictions and the disciplines of our various churches."[170]

If the morning worship was a lesson in learning to respect one another's differences, then the evening services were arenas for ecumenical realization. All the delegates and those of the public who came in experienced and witnessed the work of the Holy Spirit as they sang and praised together. Subconsciously and gradually, a sense of unity grew among the congregations. Emile Dallière, the brother of the famous leader of the French Charismatic Renewal, Louis Dallière,[171] paralleled this sense of unity at Guildford which he experienced on 14 July 1971, France's national day, with "The Fall of the Bastille," which marked the beginning of French Revolution.[172] When the French people were celebrating the liberty they had obtained from the collapse of the monarchy in 1789, those Christians at Guildford were rejoicing in the freedom of unity resulting from the demolition of boundaries by the Spirit. He recalled that in that night, "everyone present was aware that something special was happening" and "the diversity of religions, churches, races or pigments of skin" dissolved when the gift of tongues was performed by most of the congregation. The heavenly language spoken in the Spirit washed away the boundaries between Christians and so he said that "the tower of Babel had been well and truly demolished." Furthermore, the preachers of that evening were Kevin Ranaghan and two Roman Catholic priests who were naturally accepted by the congregation which was made up of many Protestants. Hence he said, "And there is no doubt at all that the unity experienced with such reality on the evening of 14 July in the Cathedral stands as a great step forward."[173] Harper also recalled that everybody "had a tremendous sense of being present at history in the making."[174]

At the international conferences for the charismatic renewal, worship was a major arena for unity to grow through common experience in the Spirit, which brought out the presence and power of God. Charisms such as speaking and singing in tongues, prophecy, healing, and intercession functioned for mutual edification and encouragement through the power of the Spirit and the sense of unity was nurtured in the congrega-

170. Sullivan, "Seeing," 21.
171. E-mail from Harper, 5 October 2005.
172. Dallière, "Guildford International Conference," 8.
173. Ibid., 10; Fountain Trust, "Guildford," 32.
174. Letter from Harper to Nina Putman, 6 October 1971.

tion. Delegates' testimonies and comments on their experience of unity and the ecumenical implications will be illustrated in the next chapter.

The Eucharist

Besides worship, the Eucharist was the ecumenical activity, which materialized the metaphor of the one body of Christ. To realize a Eucharistic unity with people from various denominations, the Trust implemented "concelebration" in Anglican liturgy.[175] It was first used at Nottingham and was proved to be practically feasible and symbolically meaningful; hence the Trust continued to adopt this ecumenical practice at the three Westminster conferences. At Nottingham, the concelebration was conducted by the Bishop of Southwell and Harper was responsible for the priestly sections, which included declaring the Absolution, giving the final blessing and presiding over the "actual sentences of Consecration" while he and other non-Anglican leaders proclaimed the words of consecration at the same time.[176] Although the Bishop agreed to this arrangement, he clearly stated that he would only do it in that exceptional case by saying, "I am ready to accede to your request about others than Anglicans joining in the words of consecration on condition that it is noted that this forms no precedent either within or outside this diocese." He also agreed to use the Anglican rite even though it was held in an "extra-diocesan building" (by which he meant the Sport Centre of the University of Nottingham) which was not "consecrated" and therefore it was "technically illegal" at that time.[177] Eventually, the service, as the "climax" of the whole conference, was regarded as "incredible" and "fantastic." Delegates obviously felt the filling of the Holy Spirit and were joyfully dancing, singing, and hugging one another without "pressure, coyness and embarrassment."[178]

175. It was based on a tradition in the early church where the bishop conducted the Eucharist with his presbyters and they said the same words and performed the same actions together. Nowadays it is practiced at ecumenical meetings where ministers from various backgrounds consecrate the bread and wine and distribute to the congregation according to the same rite. (Till, *Churches Search for Unity*, 499.)

176. Letter from Harper to the Bishop of Southwell, 26 July 1972; Letter from the Bishop of Southwell to Harper, 1 January 1973; Letter from Harper to the Bishop of Southwell, 28 June 1973.

177. Letter from the Bishop of Southwell to Harper, 3 July 1973.

178. Fountain Trust, *Renewal*, 25.

Among the five international conferences, the final communion at Westminster 1975 most obviously revealed the division between Protestants and Roman Catholics. Considering loyalty to the canon law, Roman Catholic speakers including Francis MacNutt, Paul Lebeau, and other Catholic clergy who had been involved at the Conference decided not to partake in the concelebration. Their withdrawal discouraged some of the delegates as Protestants and Roman Catholics could not sacramentally experience unity "although they had shared the week's worship . . . to the full" and "had dropped all the denominational and party labels for four days." Harper recalled that "there were some very moving scenes of deep contrition of the continued divisions in the body of Christ" which "touched the conference deeply." For instances, to empathize with the grief of their "dear Catholic friends," some delegates from the Baptist, Methodist, and other mainline Protestant churches did not partake in the Eucharist.[179] Barbara Holl said, "I shall remember the tears streaming down the faces of two Roman Catholic nuns who were seated next to me" and hence for her, it was "one of the saddest parts of the entire Conference."[180] John Richards, one of the speakers, described the Eucharist as "a shattering spiritual experience" and expressed his sadness by saying, "the sudden awareness of the only partial participation of the R.C.'s 'tore' me, there is no other word for it!"[181] He remembered that he "wept in a way unrelated to normal weeping."[182] In the face of this reality of division, MacNutt said positively, "We may not yet be able to share the same Eucharist, but we can wash each other's feet."[183] Harper warned that we should not deceive ourselves and pretend that the unity was there. Division *was the real thing.* We should face the unfavourable reality and "press on in faith towards the full unity of the Body of Christ."[184]

Although full communion could not be practiced at Westminster 1975, people at the conference still endeavored to express the unity

---

179. Holl, "Glory in the Church," 10; Letter from Harper to the Bishop of London, 15 August 1975; Letter from Mallie Calver to Harper, 8 August 1975, 3; Harper, "Editorial: No Cosy Marinas," 3.

180. Holl, "Glory in the Church," 10.

181. Letter from John Richards to Harper, 4 August 1975, 1.

182. Richards, "Tears," 33.

183. Harbour, "Glory," 8.

184. Harper, "Editorial: No Cosy Marinas," 3.

that they had longed for. For example, the Bishop of London allowed non-Anglican ministers to concelebrate "the Choral Eucharist" with the Archbishop of Cape Town by proclaiming the words of consecration and "holding out their hands over the elements."[185] Moreover, the chalices used on that night were borrowed from different sources, one of those being a Roman Catholic priest. This particular chalice had been secretly used by the Roman Catholics in the seventeenth century. But in that communion service, it was used openly with other chalices representing "a symbolic gesture of the desire of so many for reconciliation."[186] Furthermore, Smail revealed that the Roman Catholic delegates eagerly invited everybody to join their morning Mass every day in the Westminster basement without hesitation. They would be "upset" if the non-Catholics did not go. And their priests distributed communion to the whole congregation every morning despite breaching the canon law.[187]

Both the Roman Catholic authority and the Trust had learnt the lesson from the communion at Westminster 1975 and they had looked for ways in which the delegates could still follow canon law and could accept the reality of division easily. At Westminster 1977, the Roman Catholic authority allowed everybody to participate in the morning Mass, but not to receive communion. This order brought more pain to the grassroots, as Smail recalled, "The Charismatic Catholics were very upset about that and very apologetic that they haven't been able to do for us what they had done two years before."[188] Moreover, the Trust also handled the final communion carefully. They determined not to let the Roman Catholics feel that they were being isolated, while helping them to be psychologically prepared to accept the reality of not being able to participate. The eucharistic issue not only concerned the organizers on how to arrange it properly, but also the delegates on why this was the way that it had to be. At Westminster 1977, there were two seminars dedicated to discuss ecumenical issues, which had been made obvious since the charismatic renewal. The Bishop of Pontefract, Richard Hare, who was going to preside at the Eucharist in that last evening, explained his standpoint on this controversial issue by saying,

185. Letter from the Bishop of London to Harper, 4 July 1975.
186. Letter from Harper to the Bishop of London, 15 August 1975.
187. Interview with Smail, 16 February 2006.
188. Ibid.

> Can I say a word about the Eucharist on Friday night? Obviously at any Eucharist . . . this is an occasion of repentance. I myself am not willing now, since the passing of canon B15 & A, six years ago, to celebrate the Eucharist without giving the invitation to everyone that communicate who is baptized and in good common understanding with our tradition.

Then he said that he was going to give the following invitation at the Eucharist.

> If you are baptized within a Trinitarian tradition, and if you are a communicant within your own congregation, then it is the Lord's Table and not ours and the Lord says come to my peace and be ready. Come and get it as the Americans say. But there are those for reasons of conscience or obedience, do not feel able to accept this invitation, and if you are among those, then please pray for the unity at which the invitation ends.[189]

In that evening, he did give this invitation by announcing that the Eucharist was an "open table" and that everybody was welcome to participate. Many Roman Catholics felt obliged not to receive communion, but some did join.[190] Those who could communicate experienced blessings by being able to share the bread and wine.[191] But some had not been able to forget the divided table from which the pain derived.[192] The Eucharist was regarded as a "climax" and "heart" of the conference[193] and Smail praised that the way the Bishop had handled it, saying it was "magnificent";[194] however, Westminster 1977 still could not avoid the sadness derived from the unrealised sacramental expression of unity, which occurred at Westminster 1975.[195] At Westminster 1979, the sensitivity about Roman Catholic participation still existed, but similar announcement was made that Roman Catholics could decide whether

189. Fountain Trust, *Ecumenical Issues II.*

190. Letter from Smail to the Bishop of Croydon, 23 February 1979; Letter from Smail to Bishop David Pytches, 12 March 1979; Interview with Smail, 16 February 2006.

191. Letter from Peggy William to Fountain Trust, 8 August 1977; Fountain Trust, *Renewal*, 71 (October–November 1977), 9.

192. Letter from Ray J. Simpson to Smail, 8 August 1977.

193. Fountain Trust, *Renewal*, 71 (October–November 1977), 9; Letter from Hans-Dieter Gramm to the Fountain Trust, 12 September 1977.

194. Letter from Smail to Richard Hare, 12 August 1977.

195. Smail, "Editorial: The More We Are Together . . . ," 4.

they participated or not according to their conscience.[196] The matter of communion was problematic and reflected a contradiction between the unity brought about by the charismatic renewal at a grassroots level and the more rigid doctrinal stance of the authorities in the traditional churches. There will be a more comprehensive analysis of this point in chapter 4.

ECUMENICAL COOPERATION

The conference committee for Guildford consisted of members from three different traditions: Anglican, Methodist, and Roman Catholic. They were Michael Harper, Eric Jennings, who was an Anglican minister of the Bourne Vicarage of Farnham in Surrey, Leslie Davison who was a Methodist and the General Secretary of the Home Mission Department of the Methodist Church at that time, and Bob Balkam, a lay Roman Catholic. Before this committee was formed, there had been an ecumenical problem. At a meeting for the Guildford Conference on 12 June 1970 attended by Ken and Eleanor Morgan, Bob Balkam, and Harper, it was decided to invite Geoffrey Carver and Noel Doubleday to be members of the committee. Doubleday and his wife were present at a meeting for the Conference on 3 July 1970, but then he wrote a letter to Harper saying that he would not join the committee because he was "rather hesitant" about unity with the Roman Catholics. Although he thought that the Spirit could unite Christians crossing over any barrier, the Roman Catholic doctrines could still be an obstacle to unity because the speech of the Pope in that period gave him an impression that if the "separated brethren" did not accept the doctrines of the Roman Catholic Church, there would be no opportunity for unity. [197] However, what happened at Guildford proved that unity with Roman Catholics was not completely impossible. The grassroots unity that Protestant and Catholic charismatics experienced through the power of the Holy Spirit was not accomplished by the official church, but it was certainly an ecumenical breakthrough.

196. Letter from Smail to David Pytches, 12 March 1979; Letter from Smail to Lesslie Newbigin, 23 April 1979; Letter from Smail to the Bishop of Croydon, 23 February 1979.

197. Notes-Guildford (3 July 1970); Letter from Noel Doubleday to Harper, 14 July 1970; Letter from Eric Jennings to Harper, 21 July 1970; Letter from Leslie Davison to Michael Harper, 4 October 1971; Fountain Trust, "Fellowship of the Holy Spirit," 7.

The result and feedback from the conference presented in chapter 2 proved the success of this pioneering ecumenical cooperation. When Smail became the director the ecumenical cooperation with the Roman Catholics became more official through the RCNSC.[198] For example, since the Trust invited them to join in with the organizing committee for Westminster 1977, Balkam and Ian Petit forsook the plan of holding their own conference in the summer of 1977.[199] This venture was regarded as a "major ecumenical breakthrough,"[200] "the most ecumenical" conference in Britain[201] and was "very much a joint enterprise fully shared by the Protestant and Catholic sections of the renewal in Britain."[202] After two years, the RCNSC was invited to cooperate with the Trust again for Westminster 1979 and the Roman Catholics were given a higher profile in the preparation for this conference. For example, on the leaflet and booking form of the conference, the words "arranged by Fountain Trust in association with the Roman Catholic National Service Committee" were clearly printed, but this was not the case for Westminster 1977.[203] In nine out of nineteen letters collected by the author so far, to speakers or to guests and lay people from Smail and Barling, the involvement of the RCNSC was clearly mentioned,[204] while in the correspondence for

198. Letter from Smail to Walter Hollenweger, 5 November 1976; Letter from Smail to J. Dominian, 23 December 1976; Letter from Smail to Jan van der Vekan, 23 December 1976; Fountain Trust, "Growing in the Church," 1; Minute-FTCCM (8 June 1977), 1.

199. Letter from Smail to Ralph Martin, 7 October 1976; Letter from Smail to Suenens, 7 October 1976; Minute-FTACM (9 December 1976), 1.

200. Minute-FTCCM (8 December 1977), 1.

201. Fountain Trust, "Press Release: Growing in the church, April 1977."

202. Letter from Smail to Ralph Martin, 7 October 1976.

203. Fountain Trust, "Joy in the City," front page; "Growing in the Church," front page.

204. Letter from Smail to Catherine Marshall LeSourd, 10 November 1977; Letter from Smail to Michael Scanlan, 10 November 1977; Letter from Smail to Michael Green, 10 November 1977; Letter from Smail to David Watson, 10 November 1977; Letter from Smail to the Archbishop Helder Pessoa Camara, Brazil, 28 August 1978; Letter from Smail to Tom Forrest, 6 February, 1979; Letter from Smail to Larry Christenson, 15 September 1978; Letter from Michael Barling to Dennis J. Bennett, 18 October 1978; Letter from Michael Barling to Norma Hearth, 5 January 1979; Letter from Michael Barling to Kent E., 22 January 1979; Letter from the Fountain Trust to Maurice, Barnett, Simon Barrington-Ward (Church Missionary Society), Bishop of Kenington, David Bubbers, Wesley Gilpin (Elim Bible College), Kenneth Greet, Clifford Hill (Evangelical Alliance), Don Irving (Church Society), Gordon Landreth (Evangelical Alliance),

Westminster 1977, it was not stated in most of the letters.[205] Moreover, Smail emphasized the strong ecumenical character of Westminster 1979 by describing it as "a very large ecumenical gathering," "a completely ecumenical gathering," and "fully ecumenical."[206] These expressions showed that their ecumenical cooperation had become more mature and official by the time of Westminster 1979.

Besides the major planning for the conferences, the Trust also invited some Roman Catholics to be involved in some minor but important elements. For instance, the banners of all the international conferences were designed by some Catholic nuns. For Guildford, the Trust requested Sister Gertrude, a Benedict nun of the Priory Close in Southgate, to borrow some "beautiful banners which did make so much difference to" the conference.[207] For the rest of the four international conferences, the Trust invited Sister Regina, who was a Benedictine nun from Cockfosters and "a trained artist," to design and produce banners which had different slogans. For Nottingham 1973 the slogans were "Gathered for Power," "The Water of Life," "Psalm 103 (104)," "God's People on the Way," and "Sing the Lord a New Song." For Westminster 1975 the themes of the banners were "The Baptism of Jesus, Matthew 3:16–17," "The Spirit Moving over the Chaos, Genesis 1:2," meaning God creates the world in order from chaos, "The Tower of Babel, Genesis 11: 1–9," and "The Day of Pentecost, Acts 2." The "confusion of tongues" after building the Tower represented the disunity of the Church and on the day of Pentecost the apostles speaking in tongues in the Spirit represented the unity. "The Live Coal Taken from the Altar, Isaiah 6:6–7," meaning the "the purifying, sanctifying, healing touch of God." [208] Moreover, the Trust assigned both Protestant

R. O. Latham, James B. Lawson (St. Andrew's Garrison Church of Scotland), A. L. Macarthur, Fraser McLuskey (St. Columba's Church of Scotland), Harry O. Morton (British Council of Churches), Derek Pattinson (CoE General Synod), David S. Russell (General Secretary of Baptist Union), Harry Sutton (Evangelical Alliance), and David Taylor (Nationwide Initiative in Evangelism), n. d.

205. In fact, I was not able to get hold of all the copies of all the invitation letters from the Trust to church leaders, only four of them. In those four letters from Smail to Agnes Sanford, Tom Walker, Arthur Wallis, and Jack Dominian, the involvement of the RCNSC was mentioned just in Dominian's letter.

206. Letter from Smail to Larry Christenson, 15 September 1978; Letter from Smail to Catherine Marshall LeSourd 10 November 1977; Letter from Smail to Tom Forrest, 6 February 1979.

207. Letter from Harper to Sister Gertrude, 20 July 1971.

208. Coomes, "1500," 1; Fountain Trust, "Gathered for Power," 11; "Westminster,

and Catholic ministers to be chaplains, so that Christians from different ecclesiastical backgrounds would be offered relevant spiritual advice. For example, Ray Muller and Cecil Marshall were chaplains for Protestants at Nottingham 1973 and Westminster 1975 respectively and Ian Petit was the Catholic chaplain at both conferences.[209]

ECUMENICAL CONFLICTS AND CONVERSIONS

Before all this ecumenical experience, affection, and cooperation happened, some people had uncompromisingly borne the ecumenical vision and toiled for it despite severe criticism and constant discouragement. Before the Guildford conference actually started, some ministers in the Surrey area including Michael Pusey, Harold Owen, and Fred Pride were disturbed by the fact that a liberal, Leslie Davison, was going to address to the conference.[210] They felt uncomfortable with the modernistic views in his book, *Sender and Sent: A Study of Mission*,[211] and his speech at a Trust's Public Relations meeting held on 14 October 1970 to inform the local ministers of Surrey about the Guildford conference.[212] Pusey could not accept him saying that "the Ecumenical, Liturgical & Protest Movements with the Charismatic movement are all 'of the Holy Spirit'" because it might have an adverse effect on new believers.[213] Owen, who regarded himself as a former Baptist liberal who understood liberal ways of thinking, criticised Davison for rejecting the "substitutionary doctrine of atonement" in his recent publication. He worried that if the opponents of the Pentecostal and charismatic movement knew that the conference had speakers dishonouring the atonement, they would make "mincemeat of us once again." He therefore blamed Harper for creating a difficult situation for people in the renewal circle.[214] Pride

Growing in the Church," 6; Letter from Sister Regina to Smail, 4 February 1975; Minute-Westminster 1975 (31 January 1975), 3; Minute-Westminster 1977 (25February1977), 2.

209. Fountain Trust, "Welcome to Westminster," 2.

210. Michael Pusey was a pastor of the Farnborough Baptist Church, Harold Owen, a minister of the Woking Baptist Church and Fred Pride the leader of Abinger Fellowship which held regular conferences in Abinger Hammer. (Harper's personal note for the author, 22 July 2005, 1.)

211. Letter from Arthur Wallis to Harper, 13 November 1970; Letter from Michael Pusey to Harper, 22 December 1970; Davison, *Sender and Sent*.

212. Notes-Guildford (3 July 1970), 1.

213. Letter from Michael Pusey to Harper, 16 October 1970, 1.

214. Letter from Harold G. Owen to Harper, 29 December 1970, 1–2.

also frankly said to Harper that he was "doing a grave disservice not only to the charismatic movement in this country but to the cause of Christ," because he had heard that the advisors for the Bible week of the Abinger Fellowship, which would be held a few weeks before the conference in Abinger Hammer, "were profoundly disturbed" by the fact that a man "whose credentials have not yet been proved as to their basic and fundamental doctrines" was invited to speak publicly.[215] They were also suspicious about Roman Catholic involvement in the conference. Owen disagreed with inviting Kevin Ranaghan, the author of *Catholic Pentecostals*, to speak at the conference, because he found his book confusing and he believed that Ranaghan would not "honour the Blood of Christ . . . nor the Word of Truth."[216] He also could not accept that the Trust shared ministry with a Roman Catholic, Bob Balkam, in the conference committee.[217]

As the Director of the Trust, Harper was the major target of these criticisms and was responsible for defending the Trust's decisions. Recalling this incident after twenty-five years he said, "I did not have an easy time."[218] He pleaded with those who complained about Davison to be fair in their judgment. Regarding Pusey's criticism, he suggested that while generally the ecumenical and liturgical movement were accepted as "of the Holy Spirit," he honestly said that he was not sure what Davison meant by the "Protest Movement." Nevertheless, he firmly stated that Davison should not be judged negatively simply because that part of his statement was unclear.[219] In reply to Owen's letter, he made a careful assessment of pages 117, 128, and 205 of Davison's book, and corrected Owen's misunderstanding of Davison's statement about the substitutionary doctrine of the atonement. In these pages, he could not see that Davison was rejecting the doctrine but, rather, was commenting on other people's points of view regarding the doctrine. He argued that even if Davison did reject the doctrine, he could still be invited to speak

---

215. Letter from Fred Pride to Harper, 4 January 1971, 1–2.

216. Letter from Harold G. Owen to Harper, 29 December 1970, 2; Ranaghan, *Catholic Pentecostals*.

217. Letter from Harold G. Owen to Harper, 28 August 1970, 1; Letter from Harold G. Owen to Harper, 29 December 1970, 2.

218. Harper's personal note for the author, 22 July 2005, 1.

219. Letter from Harper to Michael Pusey, 29 October 1970, 1–2.

at the conference to talk about something other than the atonement.[220] Responding to Pride's letter, Harper affirmed his invitation to Davison as he recognised the Holy Spirit's work not only among the evangelicals but also among liberals, and he believed that they were also being used by the Spirit to make contributions. He reminded Pride that they should avoid the Pentecostals' mistake of consciously or unconsciously regarding themselves as having "the monopoly of the Holy Spirit."[221]

Besides directly answering those complainers' questions, Harper also explained his choice of those two controversial speakers at the Advisory Council Meeting. Regarding Ranaghan, he said that he had witnessed the Holy Spirit's work among the Roman Catholics in the US and so it was important for British charismatics and foreign participants to hear about it. As for Davison, Harper knew him personally and was pleased about his experience in the Spirit.[222] The Council agreed to the invitation to Davison and Ranaghan as speakers for the conference and Harper wrote a private and confidential memorandum to Pusey, Owen, and Pride to explain their decision.[223] Pusey's attitude towards Davison was changed completely and he came to regard him as a leader of the renewal;[224] but some of them still insisted on their objections after reading the memorandum.

Criticisms did not stop coming during the conference. David Pawson praised Davison's first two lectures as "brilliant," "stimulating," and the historical research was "superb," but he felt uncomfortable in the last one primarily because some of Davison's theological statements were made without sufficient support from his own personal experience. Some people had also been surprised that Davison's experience in the Spirit was not as deep as they had thought; and some were perplexed by his stress on liberal leanings being maintained by the renewal. Hence, Pawson asserted that Davison should seek for a deeper experience in the Spirit so that his theology would be transformed. He criticized Davison as "the odd man out on the team" "trying to identify with the movement without getting too involved." However, he did not have difficulty with the Roman Catholics. In fact, he also rejoiced about their experience in

220. Letter from Harper to Harold G. Owen, 2 January 1971, 1–2.

221. Letter from Harper to Fred Pride, 10 January 1971, 2.

222. Minute-FTACM (20 November 1970.)

223. Harper, "Memorandum."

224. Letter from Michael Pusey to Harper, 22 December 1970, 1.

the Spirit and their transformed understandings of scriptures, commenting "The exciting thing about the RC's at the conference was that they could hardly have been more fundamentalist in their addresses!"[225]

Guildford was a conference paradoxically mixing ecumenical conflicts with conversions. One of the stories was about Alfred Missen, who was upset by David du Plessis's "adoration of the Roman Catholic Church." He thought that du Plessis, as a Pentecostal, should realize that his pioneers had undergone a great deal of suffering for years to safeguard the purity of doctrine, but he seemed to take little account of the hardship that Pentecostals had experienced at their hands and about this he was "very unhappy."[226] Since he wanted to avoid any impression that his attendance at the conference might be seen as a "compromise" with the Roman Catholics both by himself and the AG, he decided to walk out the following morning. After he left, he reminded Harper that by coming to the conference he was not giving his assent to what had been said by du Plessis, and he went on, "It would be unfortunate if my attendance were taken to signify approval of some of the things said last night."[227] In addition, he said that he did not want to be present among those who dressed up with "flowing white robes with a long flowing white beard to match" whom he perceived to be Orthodox or those who had "denominational ties." But he underwent a dramatic and thorough ecumenical conversion within ten years. His view of the Roman Catholics and traditional churches was completely changed and saw that God's work among the non-Pentecostals at Guildford fostered a sense of unity. He regretted walking out saying, "What a tragedy if after it all we walk away from one another and move back again into our denominational enclaves." He also stated that "It is my prayer that the spirit of Guildford will live on. It is my faith that, despite all our fumblings, the prayer of Jesus in John 17.20–23 will be fulfilled."[228]

Another ecumenical conversion happened to David Watson. As a faithful evangelical, he had been deeply influenced by the stress on "the inwardness of true religion," so he found that it was difficult to speak on

225. Letter from David Pawson to Harper, 23 July 1971, 1; Letter from David Pawson to Harper, 29 July 1971, 1.

226. Letter from Alfred Missen to Harper, 13 July 1971, 1; Harper personal note for the author, 22 July 2005, 1; Email from Harper, 29 June 2005; Missen, "I walked out," 34.

227. Letter from Alfred Missen to Harper, 13 July 1971, 2.

228. Missen, "I walked out," 34.

the same platform with Roman Catholics who emphasized "systematic sacramentalism" at Guildford.[229] He was worried that his major calling as an evangelist—preaching the gospel—would be damaged by sharing the platform with a Roman Catholic priest and his evangelical credentials would be suspected by fellow evangelists in Britain.[230] However, his worry proved to be unwarranted. He spoke with Ranaghan and preached to a congregation which consisted of Roman Catholics. During the discussion with the Catholic charismatic leaders, he was surprised to discover how similar their understanding of the gospel was, and how firm their belief in the Bible, as he said,

> There was an astonishing agreement as to the truth of the Gospel. But of course, the Holy Spirit is the Spirit of Truth, and I found to my joy that these Catholic Pentecostals were Christ-centred and Cross-centred, with a great dependence on the authority of the Bible. We had, somewhat to my surprise, the closest fellowship in the Lord, based firmly on his Word as well as on a common experience of his love.[231]

He also enjoyed worship with Roman Catholics based on fraternal love and felt that the denominational walls collapsed. John Gunstone identified Watson's ecumenical role during and after the conference as being to bridge the relationship between evangelicals and Roman Catholics where there had been a big gulf despite the Roman Catholics' ecumenical openness since Vatican II.[232]Although Watson experienced this fellowship with the Catholic charismatics at the conference, he could not accept the fact that they were still affiliated with "a basically corrupt church." But after hearing God directly challenging his attitude, he confessed his critical feelings towards them and his lack of love. In the following years, he got involved in ministries in Northern Ireland for the reconciliation of Protestants and Roman Catholics with Monsignor Michael Buckley and Mairead Corrigan.[233]

These controversies had been severe trials particularly for Harper, as it is shown in his prayer request to Pride in a letter saying, "I have personally had to endure criticism and persecution from many people—

229. Sansom and Saunders, *David Watson*, 182.

230. Ibid., 183; Gunstone, "A Strong," 16.

231. Quoted in Sansom and Saunders, *David Watson*, 183.

232. Sansom and Saunders, *David Watson*, 182–83; Gunstone, "A Strong," 16.

233. Sansom and Saunders, *David Watson*, 184.

and I know it is impossible to please everyone. But I long to please HIM, not myself."[234] Owing to Harper's insistence on the decision that he and the Advisory Council believed to be right, a new realm of unity was created—not only between Protestants and Roman Catholics, but also between evangelicals and liberals, when people opened their hearts to the Spirit. Davison and Ranaghan's contributions at the conference were approved by the official conference observer of the BCC, Emmanuel Sullivan, as he wrote in a memo for the Council, saying, "Rev. Dr. Davison and Kevin Ranaghan deserve special commendation for their integrated and academic approach. Both seem highly competent to speak on this charismatic phenomenon; both are aware of difficulties associated with the phenomenon."[235]

CONCLUSION AND EVALUATION

The five international conferences demonstrated that the grassroots unity derived from the charismatic renewal was different from the mainstream ecumenical movement motivated at the official level. This could happen primarily because of Harper's vision for an ecumenical charismatic conference at Guildford and his courage in inviting Roman Catholics and a liberal who had been stigmatised by conservative evangelicals. After this pioneering attempt at Guildford, the other four international conferences continued this ecumenical character and people felt that it was natural and appropriate. There were no more complaints about speakers from diverse denominations sharing the same platform. Mutual recognition through common experiences in the Spirit continued. Sacramental expression of oneness through concelebration still took place though some of the Roman Catholics did not participate in it. For Westminster 1977 and 1979, the Trust even officially cooperated with the RCNSC which reflected a solid trust between Protestants and Roman Catholics and a more advanced ecumenicity. Undeniably this grassroots unity, nurtured by common experience, could not tackle all the historical ecumenical problems such as the Eucharist, but it created an arena for Christians from different denominations to gain a deeper understanding and to resolve misunderstandings and biases. Hence ecumenical conversions unceasingly happened and further cooperation and communication were

234. Letter from Harper to Fred Pride, 5 November 1970, 1.
235. Sullivan, "Memo."

made possible. These five international conferences opened a new page in ecumenical history, which was characterized by the grassroots unity of the charismatic renewal in the 1970s. It is easy to get a sense of unity in a few days of intense experience and learning of the Spirit at conferences, but to prolong and create a wider ecumenical impact among local churches is another story. After the closure of the Fountain Trust there was no "umbrella" organization gathering charismatic representatives from various denominations and grassroots unity was left without further development and nourishment; and it gradually died away.

Although there was a galaxy of speakers from many denominations and countries, the subjects of these five conferences were mostly about the basic elements of the truth regarding the charismatic renewal, such as Spirit baptism, healing, exorcism, charisms, community, evangelism, social concern, and worship. They had not yet touched on how to relate the renewal to the tradition of the church. Such things as liturgy and sacrament, and a balanced christological and pneumatological view of the renewal still needed to be explored. Admittedly the Trust was conscious of the danger of triumphalism, but in the conferences it had not got into serious teaching on relating the renewal to Christian sufferings, discipleship, and bearing the cross to follow Christ. Delegates would only be receiving the beginning of truth without being led into maturity and a life of devotion.

4

An Analysis of the Grassroots Unity at the Five International Conferences

Worship and the Eucharist were two grassroots activities that demonstrated unity and disunity at the five international conferences. They reveal the contributions and challenges that the charismatic renewal has brought to ecumenism. This chapter analyzes how worship and the Eucharist derive grassroots unity contextually and theologically.

A GRASSROOTS ACTIVITY (1): WORSHIP

Worship played a significant role in the charismatic renewal. Colin Buchanan maintains that worship is "the key to the Charismatic Movement" which sustained the life of the renewal.[1] I. R. Stackhouse also acknowledges the importance of worship in the renewal and states ironically, "Without worship it is hard to envisage what charismatics would have left to contribute to the wider body of Christ."[2] Obviously worship is not the whole of the charismatic renewal, but it is the dominant part of it. Worship is not the only reason for the rapid spread of the renewal from church to church, parish to parish, and country to country; but it is the first reason given, though other reasons follow. Charismatic renewal embraced a form of worship that played a major part in radically changing or gradually shaping the identity as "charismatic."

If worship is indispensable for the charismatic renewal, then the grassroots unity which developed from it is intimately connected to that worship. There is no lack of testimony to this connection from the five international conferences. At Guildford, David du Plessis observed

1. Buchanan, *Encountering Charismatic Worship*, 9.
2. Stackhouse, "Revivalism," 35.

that this unity among delegates was found all the time at every event, from prayer meetings in the morning to the sessions in the evening.[3] At Westminster 1975, a Roman Catholic, Barbara Byrne, said that she experienced "a great joy" in worshipping with Christians from other traditions. Christopher M. Kobba from the Cameroons had a strong sense of "the spirit of love and joy" and affirmed that there was a depth of corporate worship among Protestants and Roman Catholics. Mrs. Marjorie O'Neil also experienced the corporate worship with almost two thousand Christians which brought a great joy to her.[4] Referring to the morning Mass in which they participated at the same conference, Mr. and Mrs. James believed that God was able to transform human hearts and to unite His people through the Holy Spirit during worship.[5] At Westminster 1977, Pamela Mellyard felt that she was being lifted up by the singing of the whole congregation in Christ and was reminded that she should look upon Jesus for everything at all time and in all situations.[6] Colonel William McAllister's wife described how the sense of unity grew during the worship, which was a "challenge and blessing and [the] tremendous joy."[7]

Charismatic renewal in the 1970s gave birth to a grassroots unity based on the centrality of worship which was essential for the life of every Christian. Generally worship involved the whole Christian community, the laity as well as the clergy. But charismatic worship was distinctive because of the noticeable acts of the Holy Spirit. The word "noticeable" suggests tangibility, sensibility, and visibility; and the word "acts" implies initiative. Charismatics believed that the Holy Spirit took the initiative to fill the people of God and endowed them with spiritual gifts according to his will. He brought the divine proximity to worshipers, so that they could dwell in God and explore his glory and mercy. They were therefore prompted to praise him with words and physical movement, with rationality and affection, and with the spirit and mind (1 Cor 14:15). God generously gave these experiences to Protestants, Roman Catholics, and Christians of any denomination, as long as they confessed the Lord Jesus as the Savior. They found themselves having

3. Du Plessis, "Unity," 4.

4. Fountain Trust, "What," 2–3.

5. Letter from James to Harper, 1975, 3.

6. Letter from Pamela to Smail, 8 August 1977, 3–4.

7. Letter from Captain (Kath Holmes) to Smail, 17 August 1977.

similar experiences in the Spirit and realized that, in fact, they were all members of the body of Christ despite doctrinal differences. The Holy Spirit took the initiative to demolish the wall which had separated His people and to bring Christians together in fellowship. Grassroots unity was therefore experienced by laity through the common experiences of the Spirit and the growing affection for one another in charismatic worship. The body of Christ was renewed not only through the new power granted from on high, but through a new love for one another, which overrode the prejudices against other Christians inherited from their historical denominations. As a result a new Christian community was born. The five international conferences show how this grassroots unity was nurtured in charismatic worship, particularly through the use of spiritual gifts and free expression in worship.

Contextual Analysis of Charisms

Speaking and Singing in Tongues: Sounds of Unity

In the worship of the five international conferences, speaking and singing in tongues produced a sense of unity among delegates because it brought about the vivid presence of God. There are testimonies of delegates at Guildford describing the unprecedented unity nurtured by that spiritual speech which was given to Christians of all traditions. For example, Michael Harry recorded that his wife Svetlana, whose native language was similar to Russian, heard a Spanish Catholic priest using a Slavic language to worship. By that he was amazed by the power of the Spirit which brought transformation to his life and began to recognize the ecumenical work of the Spirit through the renewal.[8] Dallière also witnessed the unity when everyone was speaking in tongues in worship regardless of their ecclesiastical backgrounds. He contrasted this glossolalic worship of one accord with the "incomprehension and confusion" caused by God's withdrawal of the common language which consequently derived division around the Tower of Babel. He also drew a parallel between the destruction of the Bastille prison during the French Revolution in 1789, from which people were liberated from monarchial oppression and enjoyed equal citizenship, and the fall of walls between Christians

---

8. Fountain Trust, "And Now," 33.

effected by speaking in tongues, through which Christians were freed to love each other and became one in Christ.[9]

Unity was strongly experienced when delegates were enjoying the beauty of singing in tongues. At Guildford, Alan Shadwick depicted the moment when singing in tongues broke out in the service saying, "Soon, at a point when all the people were standing, a murmur of song began—a kinds of crooning in strange words which rose and after a few minutes gently fell away."[10] Eric Sellgren was also deeply moved by that magnificent moment.[11] Dallière describes the dramatic scenario where delegates praised in tongues under the guidance of the Holy Spirit and were united in Christ.

> I do recall that it began rather timidly, then gathered [strength] and finally swelled to become one great spiritual song uniting the whole gathering of eleven to twelve hundred people, filling the nave of the Cathedral with wave after wave of praise, generally very soft and sweet in quality and with a poignant harmony. As the song died away a deep feeling of holiness.[12]

The "celestial beauty" of speaking and singing in tongues also embraced the congregation in Westminster 1977, as Andrew Morton, a representative of the BCC, reported.[13] Apart from the general evening worship, worshippers felt united in the Spirit when they were singing in tongues at daily Masses. As Anglicans, Mr. and Mrs. James had only had a few experiences of attending Masses that were conducted in Latin with incense and bells. However, the Mass at Guildford, which was led by a lady who sang modern Christian songs and hymns accompanied by her guitar, gave them a new experience of Catholic liturgy and a vivid sense of unity. But what strongly united the mixed congregation of sixty Roman Catholics and non-Catholics was the moment of singing in tongues. The couple described how it was as if people's hearts were being "lifted up to heaven in gratitude to God that the long last barriers were coming down and we were becoming free to love each other in the same Lord."[14]

9. Dallière, "Guildford International Conference," 8.

10. Shadwick, "Spiritual," 16.

11. Fountain Trust, "And Now," 33.

12. Dallière, "Guildford International Conference," 6–7.

13. Morton, "Depths," 10.

14. Letter from James to Harper, 15 August 1971, 3.

Those testimonies show that the criterion of unity is God's presence, into which people can spontaneously enter through speaking and singing in tongues. The charismatic working group of the Church of England suggests that tongues brought a reassurance of God's presence and "a sense of security" to His people.[15] Heribert Mühlen reckons tongues not only as a "physical experience" of Spirit baptism which Classical Pentecostals emphasize, but also an "objective sign" of the inner presence of the Holy Spirit.[16] When the Spirit fills and works inside the person, he prompts the utterances through his/her physical parts; hence, tongues are always primarily an inner work of the Spirit and secondarily a physical divine manifestation. Paul exhorts the Colossians to worship God "with . . . spiritual songs, singing with thankfulness in *your hearts* to God" (Col 3:16). He also says, "If I pray in a tongue, my spirit prays" (1 Cor 14:14). Harvey Cox not only identifies tongues as a "primal speech"[17] suggesting the purpose to be that of manifesting the presence of God, but also as acting as "a language of the heart"[18] by which he means that the words come from the innermost realm of the person where the Spirit works. Smail also recognizes the dual nature of tongues, particularly singing in tongues which involves a "renewed mind" as well as a "renewed heart." The divine speech accompanied by a spiritual melody expresses not only the "superficial feelings," but also "the deep primal emotions at the hidden center of our being in our self-offering to the living God."[19] As speaking and singing in tongues manifest the holistic—physical and spiritual, outer and inner—work of the Spirit, His presence becomes so intimate, "as close as one's own larynx and vocal chords."[20]

Donald Gelpi claims that the presence of God can cultivate "charismatic openness to the Spirit,"[21] and, I would suggest, furthermore, an openness to people, which opens up a chance for grassroots unity. At the five international conferences, grassroots unity occurred when worshipers realized that they were sharing the goodness of God. As the glossolalic speech and songs were generously given by the Spirit to ev-

---

15. Church of England, *Charismatic Movement*, 32.

16. Mühlen, "Charismatic," 344.

17. Cox, *Fire from Heaven*, 81–97.

18. Ibid., 82.

19. Smail, "In Spirit," 96.

20. Cox, *Fire from Heaven*, 95.

21. Gelpi, "Theological," 191.

erybody regardless their traditions, their hearts were linked together by the angelic language and melody; all ecclesiastical differences become so unimportant and the sense of togetherness and mutual acceptance grew. Both the working group of the Church of England and Harper perceive that singing in tongues is "a marvellous way of expressing unity" or "unity-in-diversity."[22] Such unity, rooted at the grassroots level among charismatics, having the support of the clergy, and catalyzed by speaking and singing in tongues, was undeniably a contribution of the charismatic renewal to the ecumenical movement.

Healing: Witnessing the Power of God and Human Weaknesses Together

The healing ministries at the international conferences not only brought vital deliverance for those suffering illnesses, but also a great sense of wonder for those who were eyewitnesses. They collectively saw the releasing power of God reaching out to His people of whatever denominations and that led to a gradual acknowledgement of one another as members of the Body of Christ. At Guildford, delegates witnessed a girl's leg which had been shorter then growing an inch in length, a man was able to speak after the healing of his larynx, and a woman found the arthritis which she had had for a long time had disappeared.[23] In one service, Harper led the congregation to pray for healing for a boy aged four years who suffered severely from leukemia.[24] Tom Walker, who attended Nottingham 1973, witnessed several cases of healing and found people were drawn together because of this.[25] At Westminster 1977, the whole congregation was able to minister to one another when Sister Briege led delegates to the healing ministry with her "simple assurance" that "God is enough."[26] Andrew Morton noticed the psychological healing in that service which touched on the long lasting wounds deep down in people's hearts. Personal conflicts with God were revealed and resolved. There were circumstances where tears poured out.[27]

---

22. Church of England, *Charismatic Movement*, 36; Harper, *These Wonderful Gifts*, 98.

23. Granowski, "Hope."

24. Shadwick, "Spiritual," 16.

25. Telephone Interview with Tom Walker, 21 December 2006.

26. Barrington-Ward, "Faith," 3.

27. Morton, "Depths," 5.

A sense of growing unity was brought by healing, not only because of common experience of wonder at what God was doing, but also because of common witness of human weaknesses and helplessness. Moltmann suggests that worship reveals the contrast between God's divine power and human weaknesses. When the glory of the resurrection and God's sovereignty which brings "freedom of the messianic era" are magnified in worship, the pain, suffering, failure, and problems of people's everyday lives are revealed. As he says, "The service of worship reveals the heights of life, but also the poverty of the depths of our own lives. These dissonances are part of its harmony." He continues, "Where the nearness of God is experienced in the Spirit, there is also awareness of life's godlessness."[28] Gordon Lathrop also states that worship reveals "the full truth about ourselves," which he lists as sorrow, hunger, loneliness, sin, and death, but the God of mercy can bring the opposite into our lives.[29] Both Moltmann and Lathrop remind us of the fact of God's almightiness reflecting human weaknesses in worship; however, I would emphasize that this contrast becomes extreme when the gift of healing is relieving the sufferers of devastating physical or psychological problems; when it simultaneously shows the infinite power of God and the limitation of human knowledge. Healing declares that God is a source of hope to whom the distressed can turn for a significant qualitative transformation in their lives. It brings alive the meaning of God's consoling words that "my grace is sufficient for you, for power is perfected in weakness" (2 Cor 12:9).

In a worship assembly, seeking God's healing is not only a matter of concern to those who are sick, it is a burden which is shared by the whole congregation, as was seen in Sister Briege McKenna's ministry when people showed great care in ministering to one another. Therefore, when healing is performed by God's mercy and grace, the joy and wonder are shared by the entire assembly too. As Paul says, "If one member suffers, all the members suffer with it; if one member is honored, all the members rejoice with it" (1 Cor 12:26) because "the members may have the same care for one another." (1 Cor 12:25) The sacrifice of thanksgiving to God in worship is not only presented by the healed, but by the whole congregation. Grassroots unity is nurtured through this process of collectively recognizing human weaknesses, of having empathy for

28. Moltmann, *Church in the Power*, 261–62, 273.
29. Lathrop, "Knowing," 44.

the suffering brothers and sisters, of earnestly seeking for God's mercy by acknowledging His awesome power, and finally, of offering praise and gratitude together. Mühlen rightly sees that healing "is promised *to the Church as a whole*."[30] This promise of God's remedial hand is extended from the imperfections of human bodies to the wounded and divided Body of Christ.

Prophecy: A Collective Edification from the Same God

Richard Harbour recorded that during the services at Westminster 1975, God spoke to the congregation with tongues followed by interpretation and prophecy such as one entitled "All my cross to go deeper into your lives."[31] This poetic prophecy affirms the unshakeable position of the church which is the gateway of God's glory, regardless of the accumulated faults of the church, and its decline in size and spiritual strength. It was printed in *Renewal* after the conference.

> You stand before great gates my children.
> Do not regard how old they are,
> or how overgrown.
> They have been put there for you and for all my people.
> They are not closed for ever, as some believe, never to be used again.
> They will open to you are the slightest touch.
> Your path lies up to them.
> Stretch out in faith and push with the strength which comes from my
> right hand.
> When they open, you will see my glory.
> Your path to the gates may be hard,
> sharp with stones and flints;
> But you will leap over it with hart's feet.
> The great gates are my church,
> the entrance to my kingdom.
> Do not look for any other gates than those which are before you.
> You stand before my church.
> Push, and you will enter in and share my glory.[32]

Prophecy is the divine-human communication which creates and consolidates the unity of God's people. At the worship of the five conferences, Protestants and Roman Catholics were addressed by the same

---

30. Mühlen, *Charismatic Theology*, 163.

31. Harbour, "Glory," 6.

32. Fountain Trust, "Prophecy," 7.

God about His concern through the same Spirit. They received the same encouragement, exhortation, and consolation through the divine message. Paul identifies the function of prophecy as being for edification—building up the church (1 Cor 14:2, 4) until "we attain to the unity of the faith" (Eph 4:13). That is the mark of true prophecies.

Intercession: An Empowered Action of Love in a Koinonia

At Guildford, Margaret Granowski testified to "a deeper signs of love" when people noticed needs of any sort and offered to pray for one another. Personal ministries, healing, and help were given to those who were in need.[33] At Nottingham, Tom Walker witnessed that during the prayer section of worship, some people went forward to receive prayer from the clergy while others stayed in their seats and prayed for those who had gone forward. This shows the concern and love for one another that was apparent in the whole community.[34] At Westminster 1975, a delegate who had been bound by the power of evil, "finally left really happy" because of a talk by Bill Burnett, and also "very particularly through the loving prayerful ministry of two friends."[35] For her, the intercessory ministry was clearly a touching and personal way to receive the word and work of God. This "prayerful ministry" initiated by the Spirit provided an opportunity for her and the intercessors to talk about something personal which might not have been easy to articulate in front of other people.

Intercession is an act of love, reaching out to those who are in need in the Body of Christ, and thus nurtures unity at the grassroots level. Prayer is a gift from God and an authority granted by God to those who belong to him, whether they have been baptized in the Spirit or not. It is a means for communication with the heavenly Father and a sign of a personal relationship with him. Smail explains its meaning by saying, "The Lord makes us a gift of prayer which gives expression to the fact that we are adopted into sharing his own relationship to God, as sons and daughters to a Father."[36] People who are given a special gift and calling of intercession are sensitive to the needs of others and feel compelled by the Spirit to pray according to His guidance. It is true that not everybody has this gift, but there is no doubt that every Christian can

33. Granowski, "Hope."
34. Telephone Interview with Tom Walker, 21 December 2006.
35. Letter from Beryl M. Parker to the Fountain Trust, 5 August 1975, 1–2.
36. Smail, *Giving Gifts*, 205.

pray for others and God will listen. This concern and affection for others is nourished particularly in charismatic worship "yielding a sensitivity to human need," as Albrecht puts it, even towards strangers, when the Holy Spirit is moving among the whole assembly. This sensitivity is triggered by a personal encounter with God in worship and the relationship which develops from it.[37] The sense of concern for one another seemed to be stronger than denominational labels; hence unity grew out of this mutual concern with love in the Spirit motivating His people to minister to one another with prayer.

Moreover, the congregation becomes "the house of prayer" (Lk 19:46) dwelt in by the Holy Spirit when Christians intercede for one another. Each individual is a temple for the Spirit (1 Cor 6:19) and individuals gather together in Christ to build up his Body (1 Cor 12:27), which is also a "holy temple in the Lord" (Eph 2:21), as Yves Congar puts it.[38] The living Spirit fills the hearts of those who pray with the love of Christ so that they can have the same love for others. With the foundation of love, the Spirit inspires those who pray with concern for the needs of others, and their intercession is honestly and earnestly presented to God. However, the Holy Spirit does not work in this way in only one person, but draws in everybody from the worshipping congregation, and thus there was the situation of people backing up with prayers those who had gone to the front at Nottingham. As Smail noted, the Holy Spirit "does not only inspire prayer in the heart: he gives a heritage of prayer and praise to the whole Christian community."[39] Intercession enables another sort of experience in the Spirit for both the intercessor and the one who receives prayer. The intercessor becomes the medium of God's love, which is transferred to the person prayed for. The gratitude that bursts out inside the one who receives is not only for God, but also for the intercessor. With the inspiring love of the Holy Spirit and his gift of intercession during charismatic worship, the house of worship becomes the house of prayer inside which grassroots unity grows.

---

37. Albrecht, *Rites in the Spirit*, 227.

38. Congar, *I Believe in the Holy Spirit Vol. II*, 113.

39. Smail, *Giving Gifts*, 212.

Theological Analysis of Charisms

One Spirit, But Many Gifts: Unity and Diversity in the Charismatic Context

At the international conferences a variety of gifts were granted by the Spirit for serving one another, including healing, prophecy, intercession, and speaking and singing in tongues. There are more gifts enumerated by Paul in 1 Cor 12 and Eph 4, but he emphasizes that they are all from "the one and the same Spirit" (1 Cor 12:11), and in Moltmann's words, "the uniformity of the Spirit's energies."[40] He claims that for Paul, gifts suggest "the energies of the new life."[41] Thus gifts convey the divine equipment with power, enabling each member of the Body to serve God, the Church and the world. To defines gifts, Smail says, ". . . for the truth of the matter is that God by his Spirit wants to do things through us. That's the definition of a charismatic gift. God, the Holy Spirit, doing something that can be seen . . . that I couldn't do by myself, doing something through me, that proclaims that Jesus is risen, that's the definition of a charismatic gift."[42] The diversity of gifts is designed for the diversity of ministry (1 Cor 12:5); the reason for giving all these gifts to different people rather than allowing them to be owned by a few individuals is to enable a collective involvement in God's ministry, so that nobody can be proud of themselves. In most of the spheres of human society, diversity tends to easily create chaos and conflict rather than uniformity. The problems that arose in the Corinthian church were not caused only by the misuse of one gift, but many gifts which complicated the chaotic situation. Thus unity in diversity implies the potential crisis of division in diversity at the grassroots level, but the Holy Spirit is the Spirit of harmony, peace, and unity. He generously chooses to distribute a variety of gifts to different members of the church rather than a single one, according to His will "for the common good" (1 Cor 12: 7, 11). Uniformity brings monotony, dullness, and allows little freedom and creativity. It is lifeless. Diversity accompanies dynamic, flexibility, and multiplication of grace. It henceforth brings life. Although Jesus Christ is the Head of the Body, he does not rule the Church as a dictator, but rather, he ascended on high to "captive the host of captives" and descended to give gifts to

40. Moltmann, *Experiences in Theology,* 329.

41. Moltmann, *Church in the Power,* 295.

42. Smail, *Doing.*

his people (Eph 4: 8–9). So that in one Spirit, from an ecclesiological point of view, the church is developed through ministries with various gifts which are coordinated to serve the world and expand the Kingdom of God. From an ecumenical point of view, through a corporate ministry with a diversity of gifts in one Spirit, unity is cultivated within the Christian community at the grassroots, and it is strengthened by their common experiences in the Spirit and affection for one another.

Unity in diversity in the charismatic context does not have the same meaning as it does in the mainstream ecumenical movement. Diversity refers to the variety of gifts and the source is the Holy Spirit. But diversity in ecumenism refers to a variety of ecclesiastical and institutional practices and the theology behind them. In the process of developing these practices, it is primarily human beings who take the initiative to create and consolidate them. Diversity in the charismatic renewal grows among a diversity of people who are filled by the Spirit at the grassroots level; while diversity in the mainstream ecumenical movement is discussed in dialogues at the official level. These are two different ecumenical methodologies, but they are complementary. This point will be expanded in the next chapter.

Charisms, the Presence of God, and Grassroots Unity

The previous section discusses the fact that tongues manifest the vivid presence of God. In fact, all charisms, by their nature, have this character and so bring about the fellowship at the grassroots. The essential meaning of koinonia is that God is present, as expressed in the promise of Jesus that, "for where two or three have gathered together in my name, I am there in their midst" (Matt 18:20). Koinonia is not the same as a secular social gathering, but is distinguished by being a gathering in Jesus' name and with his own presence. Therefore, God is the reason for koinonia. Moreover, he is also a mediator of koinonia by drawing converts together in his name to worship. Although those involved are just strangers at the beginning, they are able to pray and share together because they believe in the same Lord. However, Jesus has ascended to heaven. How can we know that he is present in the fellowship? The answer is partly because Christians believe in Jesus' promise in the scripture, but also because God sends his Holy Spirit among Christians and visibly manifests himself with spiritual gifts. Paul says, "But to each one is given the manifestation of the Spirit for the common good" (1 Cor

12:7). Mühlen notes that when Paul defines tongues and prophecy as signs in 1 Cor 14:22, he uses the word "semeion" meaning "a sign of presence, the appearance, the manifestation of the Spirit of Christ himself (1 Cor 12:7)." He stresses that the presence of the Spirit is not only reflected in tongues and prophecy but actually in all the spiritual gifts.[43] He also notes that when healing is performed, Jesus' concern for the sick is manifested and the whole congregation experienced peace, joy, and "liberating freedom." He thus recognizes that healing is not only a process of personal physical restoration, but "the expression of the social experience of God."[44]

In the worship of the five international conferences, delegates testified to the presence of the Spirit through spiritual gifts. Charisms used in worship have the effect of bringing human beings close to God, and thus personal sins and collective division are clearly revealed, and the desire for repentance and for unity becomes strong. Charisms show the love of God bringing peace and restoration, in contrast to human selfishness, which leads to division. In this sense, the ministry of charisms becomes a process of self-rediscovery, exposing the lack of love and kindness within one's heart, and showing that it is time to seek reconciliation with God and others. Because of that, the concept and practice of koinonia is expanded from simply being a coming together of those Christians who share the same doctrines and traditions, to a fellowship with those who have opposite theological emphases, and towards whom they would previously have had negative attitudes. The same God that they know about from their own traditions is present with the others, and the same Spirit is working among them through his gifts. Jesus promises being with his own people and unity grows out of this koinonia in Jesus' name among the grassroots.

Charisms, "De-clericalization," and Grassroots Unity

Peter identifies the Christian community as "a chosen race, *a royal priesthood*, a holy nation, a people for God's own possession." (1 Pet 2:9) 1 Pet 2:5 says that they are also living stones for building up "a spiritual house for *a holy priesthood*, to offer up spiritual sacrifice acceptable to God through Jesus Christ." In the Old Testament, priests were chosen by God to serve him and the whole company of Israelites. Among the twelve

43. Mühlen, "Charismatic," 336, 340.
44. Mühlen, *Charismatic Theology*, 163.

tribes, the Levites were particularly chosen, as Num 3:6 says, "Bring the tribe of Levi near and set them before Aaron the priest that they may serve him." The Levites were responsible for the duties in the tent on behalf of all Israel, holding services in the tabernacle and taking care of the furnishings of the tent for meetings (Num 3:7–8). They also had to set up and set out the tabernacle during the exodus (Num 1:50). Lay people would be killed if they came too close to the tent (Num 1:51). Moreover, the whole tribe of Levi not only had the privilege of working for God, but they were also called the possession of God. Num 3:11 says, "I have taken the Levites from among the sons of Israel instead of every firstborn, the first issue of the womb among the sons of Israel. So the Levites shall be mine." And God commanded Moses, saying, "You shall take the Levites for Me" (Num 3:41). The scriptures quoted in First Peter imply that a person who is spiritually born again to be a Christian is like a descendant of Levi who was born to be priest. In other words, this is an innate priesthood. But the New Testament priests do not need to look after the tabernacle and furnishings and offer sacrifices to God by slaughtering animals. They are equipped with charisms to build up the "spiritual house," the Body of Christ and to serve God and one another. Their sacrifices of worship are given to God "in spirit and truth" (John 4:24). To be God's people is not confined to a particular race, but is available for everybody who has faith in Jesus.

However, in practice, the priesthood of every Christian has been taken over by "priests" within the ecclesiastical structure. The hierarchical structure creates two classes, that of clergy and laity. The purpose of the clergy is to ensure the functioning of the church in terms of its administration, finance, and the numerical and spiritual growth of members. In this sense, lay people, in Congar's term, are "clients" of the ordained.[45] As far as worship is concerned, some of the lay people are "assigned" minor tasks to do such as preparing hymn books, arranging flowers, and nursing children during services,[46] but ministers are still the ones running the program. Worship becomes a "spectator sport," as John Killinger points out.[47] The root of the problem still relates to the fact that the priesthood is seen as belonging solely to the ordained, while Peter's concept of universal priesthood is nowadays not realized. The

---

45. Congar, *I Believe in the Holy Spirit Vol. II*, 208.

46. Church of England, *Charismatic Movement*, 41.

47. Killinger, *Leave It to the Spirit*, 42.

charismatic renewal restored the priesthood of laity through charisms, which highlighted the significance of grassroots unity. Each member of the Body of Christ is a priest endowed with different gifts for different ministries, because "charisma are used as *ministries*."[48] Each of them is able to contribute to the Body in the practical and spiritual realms and maintain the healthy functioning of the Body rather than it being the domain of the clergy only. Congar regards the church as being "de-clericalized" by the restoration of charisms. The Church of England also recognized the significance of "every member ministry" brought by the charismatic renewal.[49] Even the charismatic renewal itself has never been just the vision of the clergy. As Smail pointed out, "Renewal has been a matter of ordinary people."[50] Their priesthood is restored when the charisms are used and unity is nurtured by ministry that comes from the grassroots. This de-clericalization derived from the charismatic renewal enables unity to be achieved by every member of the Church through their experience of the Spirit and their growing love and concern for one another.

Contextual Analysis of Spontaneity

Free Expression to God

The second reason for the grassroots unity nurtured in worship at the five international conferences was the spontaneity that occurred. Because they relied on the Spirit in worship and the simplicity of the worship program, delegates were able to express their worship freely with their bodies. At Guildford, the Cathedral was filled with delegates every night for worship. There was a free atmosphere where delegates could wholeheartedly express their love and devotion to God.[51] They raised their arms without hesitation to magnify the God of strength, wonder, love, and mercy. In one service, Shadwick saw that the Cathedral became "a forest of arms upraised in praise and openness to the Spirit" when they sang "All hail the power of Jesus' name." In addition, free expression in worship was also featured by the frequent use of dance. They were able to praise God with the movement of the entire body. Shadwick recorded

48. Congar, *I Believe in the Holy Spirit Vol. II*, 208.
49. Ibid.; Church of England, *Charismatic Movement*, 41.
50. Smail, *Doing*.
51. Harper, "Coming of Age," 4.

that at an afternoon worship at Guildford, people of all ages started dancing as they sang, "The Holy Ghost will set your feet a dancing." They "were tapping feet and raising arms as if to receive something from the blue sky."[52] The worship at Nottingham was regarded as "incredible" and "fantastic" because delegates were filled by the Holy Spirit and the "aisles were filled with dancing, hugging, singing Christians, but naturally and with no pressure, coyness or embarrassment."[53] At Westminster 1975, Margi, one of the members of the Fisherfolk worship team, danced every morning during the conference.[54] At Westminster 1977, Roger Hardcastle saw how people enjoyed dancing at the end of the service and commented that dancing was "good & helpful" for worship.[55] Whether they were delegates or worship leaders, whether they were young or old, with the guidance of the Spirit, the stream of worship ran spontaneously from their hearts to their bodies to praise God. Their worship was full of joy and passion for God whose presence filled their hearts as well as the whole community.

Free Expression to Others

The overflowing stream of worship expressed by the body enabled people to worship with one accord and freely express their love to others of the Body of Christ. The spontaneous worship brought a new openness to people, as Dallière witnessed at Guildford "no one had to feel as a purveyor of strange or dangerous novelties."[56] Margaret Granowski was amazed that at Guildford, Christians who had been segregated from one another by theological controversies for centuries could freely worship together.[57] At Westminster 1977, Andrew Morton saw that worshippers ceased to be mindful of the social conventions about demonstrative behaviors, and expressed themselves freely toward God and other people—they lifted their arms to God and used them to hug one another.[58] At Westminster 1975, Barbara Holl, who regarded herself as a reserved person found her way of worship transformed and a new openness to

---

52. Shadwick, "Spiritual," 14, 16.
53. Sullivan, "Seeing," 25.
54. Holl, "Glory in the Church," 6.
55. Letter from Roger Hardcastle to the Fountain Trust, 21 August 1977.
56. Dallière, "Guildford International Conference," 5.
57. Granowski, "Hope."
58. Morton, "Depths," 5.

people. She had felt it more and more natural to extend her arms and open her palms to sing and pray. She was also surprised that she was leaping and jumping around St John's Church after an afternoon worship. She reached a new level of worshipping God to which she could not have broken through by herself. Moreover, she was able to open herself more to people. She held hands with other delegates and she was able to accept "a charismatic bear-hug" from a Canadian whom she described as "the enormous bearded Viking of a man," and she felt comfortable with it. Furthermore, she was able to seek reconciliation with others. In the middle of the final service, she approached a person and said, "Forgive me." They kissed each other and she returned to her seat. She concluded that the whole transformation was one of God's "present-day miracles" which showed her the ecumenical character of the charismatic renewal. As she said, "What a warmth of fellowship from total strangers—who just happened to be our brothers and sisters in the Lord!"[59]

Theological Analysis of Spontaneity

The freedom of charismatic worship restores three sorts of unity: the unity of body and soul as a human being, the unity with the triune God, and the unity between members of the Body of Christ. The first two kinds of unity are the conditions for the third kind.

Unity of Oneself as a Human Being in Charismatic Worship

Free expression in charismatic worship allows the Spirit to restore a person, a creature, to a being in the complete likeness of the creator, which should be "very good" (Gen 1:39). Killinger criticizes churches for having dichotomized body and mind so that they have given a high value to mind and shown distrust of the body, even demonizing it.[60] In conventional circles, bodies are supposed to be under strict control during worship and, therefore, dancing, lifting up arms, and opening palms are forbidden. Worship has often been an activity of mind only, following a standard liturgical form which is all rationally familiar and predictable.[61] Killinger argues that "intellectualism simply cannot sustain the truth about God. If God cannot be felt in the body, in the entire psy-

---

59. Holl, "Glory in the Church," 5–6, 9–10.

60. Killinger, *Leave It to the Spirit*, 35.

61. O'Neil, "Catholic," 26.

chosomatic unity of the person, then he cannot really be said to have an efficacious existence in the life of the person."[62] This restriction of physical expression during worship was enforced by the way churches were arranged, especially after the Reformation. Long wooden pews indicated to worshippers that they were to stay where they were throughout the service. Killinger ironically describes this as "a symbol of the gaol-like imprisonment of worshippers."[63] Pulpits or altar tend to be built far away from the congregation suggesting the supreme position of the priests rather than a communal worship of God.[64] The traditional arrangement in church implied a separation of both the mind and body, and also of the clergy and laity.

In contrast to the traditional style of worship, charismatic renewal is a release of physical expression which leads to a harmony of body and soul. The body is released from its intellectual cage and freely expresses emotion towards God, according to the soul. Once body and soul are united, people can worship God with all their hearts, all their souls, and all their strength. Arms are lifted up to express feelings of awe towards God; palms are opened to welcome God himself and his works; dancing represents the beauty of God's gentleness or the excitement of His wonder and love. With the guidance of the Spirit, soul, and body are coordinated simply for the sake of praising the almighty God. Christopher Cocksworth rightly notes that "there is no purely spiritual activity. Every action, emotion and affection is a complex interplay between our bodies, minds and spirits." For him, the physical expressions of worship make us both "receivers of the Spirit's work upon us and as transmitters of the worship the Spirit inspires in us."[65] Worship in the Spirit proves the inadequacy of the dichotomization of body and soul because when the Spirit fills the worshipers with awe, excitement, and gratitude towards almighty God, a lip-service of thankfulness is certainly not enough. Charismatic renewal restores the holistic original being of human and enhances their vertical communication with God.

62. Killinger, *Leave It to the Spirit*, 38.

63. Ibid.

64. O'Neil, "Catholic," 33; Harper, "Principles," 37.

65. Cocksworth, *Holy, Holy, Holy*, 189.

Vertical Communication: Unity with God

Physical movements echoing heartfelt gratitude or excitement towards God bring worshipers to a new level of worship. They do not need to disguise their innermost strong feelings towards God by worshiping with words that are in keeping with social conventions, but can whole-heartedly express their true selves in front of God. As James I. Packer comments, "At all events, charismatic worship aims above all to achieve *genuine* openness to God at the deepest level of our personal being," (italics mine)[66] and the unity between God and a person becomes possible. The vertical communication with God is therefore made effective as the inner works of God begin. Healing happens outwardly on the body, as well as inwardly, deep inside a broken heart. Visions are revealed. Tongues, interpretations of tongues, prophecies, and words of wisdom and knowledge are proclaimed. Where there is a great deal of freedom in worship God is able to work as much as he wills. If the Spirit can work whatever he thinks is enhancing and edifying to the congregation when people are willing to open to him, then certainly the healing of division in the Body of Christ can also be done, both in individuals' hearts and in the whole assembly. Hence, the unity with God brings unity with others into reality at the grassroots.

Horizontal Communication: Unity with Members of the Body of Christ

The unity of body and soul, and unity with God of the individual, leads to unity with members of the Body of Christ. The supreme closeness to God brought about by the free expression in worship enables worshipers to experience the divine love of God. This love motivates them to love their neighbors freely in the Spirit. As John says, "We love, because He first loved us" (1 John 4:19). However, in the Spirit, sometimes words are not enough for horizontal communication among worshipers. They need to be accompanied by physical gestures such as embracing, kissing, and holding hands, which can be regarded as concrete signs of love. Physical expressions of love for one another can bring assurance of God's love and a strong sense of security within the Body of Christ. It is a place where support, comfort, and forgiveness in God can be found. The whole community manifests God's presence and love, for as John says,

---

66. Packer, *Keep in Step*, 180.

"No one has seen God at any time; if we love one another, God abides in us, and His love is perfected in us" (1 John 4:12). Grassroots unity is built upon the stream of love with simple bodily expressions, which flows from the spontaneous worship to God in the Spirit, as the love for each other is growing.

A New Form of Liturgy

Free expression in charismatic worship creates a unity of liturgical forms for Christians from different traditions which enables the grassroots unity to grow. Gunstone claims that, "The difference between formal and spontaneous worship is not as great as we might imagine" and they even amalgamate "into a lovely unity."[67] Such liturgical unity brings about the grassroots unity between Christians of various denominations because they have found common ground in worship—following the Holy Spirit. This was obvious at the five international conferences. Although delegates were from various ecclesiastical backgrounds and the Trust only adopted the Anglican liturgical form for most of the services, they could still worship the Lord with one accord because what was guiding them to worship was not the liturgical form, but the Holy Spirit. This form, which had been so heavily relied on for worship and building up Christian identity, returned back to its original purpose which was to be a form made for people and not people for the form. Worship no longer consisted merely of lip-service, but of an action involving the body and the spirit, and words and gestures. As Aidan Kavanagh states, "a liturgy exists first of all not to be read or studied but to be done."[68]

Moreover, when the worship is free in the Spirit, the form no longer restricts the Spirit but becomes a means for him to work within his people. It then becomes a common liturgical form and an ecclesial property which charismatics share and utilize together. As Gunstone says,

> . . . charismatics have very ecumenical tastes in liturgy. When they share in the worship of other denominations, they are less concerned to mark down the differences between that worship and their own; they are more appreciative of the way the Holy Spirit has led that particular tradition to respond to God's Word in its liturgy.[69]

67. Gunstone, *Greater Things*, 85; *People for His Praise*, 93.

68. Kavanagh, *On Liturgical Theology*, 96.

69. Gunstone, *People for His Praise*, 91–92.

Therefore, grassroots unity is able to grow freely without the barriers of liturgical form in the charismatic worship. Free bodily expressions and complete surrender to the Holy Spirit are the agreed instruments and attitude to the worship of holy God.

Lex Orandi, Lex Credendi in Charismatic Worship

Lex Orandi, lex credendi is a Latin tag, simplified from a Catholic monk, Prosper of Aquitaine (390–463)'s statement, *ut legem credendi lex statuat supplicandi*, which means "let the law of prayer establish the law of belief."[70] This suggests that liturgy was a means of grace and a demonstration of Christian faith in front of non-Christians or heretics, particularly in the traditional Good Friday intercession.[71] Prosper's argument suggests that the function of liturgy is to bring God's redeeming grace to the lost and to proclaim Christian belief to counter Pelagians' teaching especially. Moreover, Geoffrey Wainwright claims that for Prosper, this statement does not just refer to the textual liturgy where written prayers are read out, but liturgy as "a total ritual event."[72] Orthodox liturgist Alexander Schmemann also understands *lex orandi* as a liturgical event where a divine-human encounter takes place rather than being simply a liturgical order.[73] Hence, *theologia prima* (primary theology) can develop. Kavanagh defines it as the theology born from liturgy through constant adjustment during the event. He claims that there is "collision, chaos, and a certain violence" in each liturgy and participants keep adjusting it so that there will be improvement in the liturgy that follows. The adjustment is made both consciously and unconsciously and enables liturgy to evolve and grow gradually. Theology is therefore developed through the adjustment.[74] Kevin Irwin also raises the concepts of adjustment and evolution in liturgy to refer to the fluidity of liturgy. As

70. Wainwright, *Doxology*, 224; Irwin, *Context and Text*, 3.

71. On Good Friday, the church prayed, "Grace may be given to unbelievers; that idolaters may be freed from the errors of their impiety; that the Jews may have the veil removed from their hearts and that the light of truth may shine on them; that heretics may recover through acceptance of the catholic faith; that schismatics may receive afresh the spirit of charity; that the lapsed may be granted the remedy of penitence; and finally that the catechumens may be brought to the sacrament of regeneration and have the court of the heavenly mercy opened to them." (Wainwright, *Doxology*, 225–26.)

72. Wainwright, *Doxology*, 227.

73. Chan, *Liturgical Theology*, 49.

74. Kavanagh, *On Liturgical Theology*, 74.

he says, ". . . liturgy is an evolving reality whose main contours have been shaped by liturgical tradition, but whose component elements have been and continue to be adapted and adjusted."[75] The fluidity and adjustment are conditioned by the understanding of liturgy as an event rather than solely a textual practice. Because of this fluidity, first-hand experience of God in liturgy is allowed to take place and thus the theology growing out of the liturgy is primary and living, influential and transformative to life. Hence *theologia prima* can simply mean the knowledge of God acquired from the divine-human encounter in liturgy.

Liturgists such as Geoffrey Wainwright argue that Prosper's statement in the tag form can be understood in reverse, and that it is also correct to say that the law of belief establishes the law of prayer, particularly for Protestants who tend to emphasize doctrines over liturgy and set the liturgical rules according to doctrines.[76] But Kavanagh insists on the irreversibility of the statement and he therefore rejects the tag form. Since linguistically "the law of belief" is predicated with the verb *statuat* which suggests the subordination to and consequence of "the law of prayer," it is not logical to say that the consequence can become the source. He accepts the explanation that the law of belief can influence the law of prayer, but disagrees that the law of belief "*constitutes* or *founds*" the law of prayer; so it is only correct to interpret Prosper's statement as the law of prayer establishing the law of belief.[77]

To apply Prosper's statement to explain charismatic worship, I suggest that Kavanagh's interpretation of the statement is more suitable. As Prosper states that liturgy as an event rather than a textual practice proclaims Christian faith to the lost in the world and therefore establishes the law of belief, the eventfulness of charismatic worship can also produce new understandings of Christian belief and *theologia prima*. Charisms such as speaking and singing in tongues, healing, prophecy, intercession, etc. that happened at the international conferences in the British charismatic renewal were actually a direct encounter with the transcendent and given by the transcendent. The free bodily expressions during worship were the result of, and response to, this divine-given encounter, where the physical expressions of praise were no longer bound

75. Irwin, *Context and Text*, 32.

76. Wainwright, *Doxology*, 218, 251.

77. Kavanagh, *On Liturgical Theology*, 91–92.

by the conventional rules in liturgy. Worshipers gained a vivid primary experience of God and therefore a living theology was developed.

In addition, the international conferences demonstrate that this primary experience and theology occurred not just in a particular group of Christians at the service, but among Christians from diverse traditions including Protestants and Roman Catholics, and therefore a sense of unity grew. They experienced the same *lex orandi* together in charismatic worship as they surrendered to the Spirit, following which charisms might be given and the body freed to worship. This corporately discovered *lex orandi* overrode the variations of liturgical dogmas and practices across traditions and constituted a set of common *lex credendi*. Ecclesiologically, they realized the church as the Body of Christ constituted by members not just of their own church, but of many other churches. The church could not function properly and effectively just by the ministerial office, but required also the charisms granted by the Holy Spirit. The vivid presence of Christ reminded the worshipers that he was the head of the church, not the bishop or Pope. Pneumatologically, they also discovered that the Spirit worked according to his will and distributed charisms to every one in the church so that they could serve God and one another. He also filled the lives of individuals for ministering renewal and deliverance. He interceded for each one "with groanings too deep for words" (Rom 8:26) and helped them to understand more about the triune God. Ecumenically, they realized that the Holy Spirit was capable of removing prejudices and hatred and endowing fraternal love. They discovered that denominational labels representing their identities no longer disguised their intrinsic common identity as the children of God. These three aspects of knowledge were acquired through their experiences in worship. Undoubtedly adjustment took place among those worshipers from various traditions as they consciously or unconsciously laid down certain denominational norms and practices, so that they could worship with one accord and gained a new understanding of those things.

Moreover, charismatic worship demonstrates what Kavanagh argues, which is that the law of belief can only influence the law of prayer but not constitute or found it. This is simply because there was not an established charismatic theology to give birth to charismatic worship, but rather vice versa. The grassroots unity that was nurtured from the worship was not a result of charismatic theology. The unprecedented experiences in the Spirit during charismatic worship were the source of a new understanding of God and the body of Christ and subsequently of new interpretations of scriptures and new language to explain the phenomena, such as "filled by the Spirit," "touched by the Spirit," and "resting in the Spirit." These new linguistic expressions were used by charismatics for communication and they indirectly consolidated the unity that was already built up. This echoes John H. Leith's emphasis on *lex orandi* that "it comprises essential data for theological reflection; that it provides (together with Scripture) the language and idioms for theological articulation; and that the community of prayer, defined as "worshipping" and "believing," is a source, principle context, and primary audience for Christian theology."[78] The new knowledge of God articulated in the new language derived from charismatic worship has gradually conventionalized and become the law of belief. That *influences* the way worship continues and then adjustment may take place so that the *theologia prima* may be further developed. Worshipers' knowledge of God and experience keep being renewed by the Spirit and by the unity that is growing at the grassroots. Liturgy in charismatic renewal becomes "the work of the people," in Kenneth W. Stevenson's phrase,[79] in that they experience God, articulate the experience with new languages and increasingly become one in Christ through the common experience and language in worship.

Conclusion

The five international conferences show that the grassroots unity was nurtured in charismatic worship enhanced by the functioning of charisms and by free expression to God and others. Charismatic worship marked by spontaneity and vivid manifestations of charisms enriches the meaning of *lex orandi, lex credendi*. Under the guidance of the Holy Spirit, Christians from various traditions were able to worship with one accord because of the shared experience and mutual edification of charisms. These commonalities brought about a new understanding of God, the church and unity.

---

78. Kay, "*Lex orandi*," 15.
79. Stevenson, "Lex Orandi," 241.

A GRASSROOTS ACTIVITY (2): THE EUCHARIST

Although worship at the international conferences created both a sense and a reality of Christian unity, paradoxically, they also revealed a painful fact that this unity was not perfect and division still existed around the Lord's Table. As was described in chapter 3, the division brought a tremendous sadness to delegates, especially at Westminster 1975. Roman Catholic Church speakers such as Francis MacNutt were not concelebrating the Eucharist with those of other denominations on the stage. Roman Catholic delegates wept at not being able to share the communion with their Protestant brethren and sisters. The following section will draw out the meaning behind the failure of sharing the final communion at the international conferences. The analysis will be twofold: firstly, the contextual analysis, focusing on the unfulfilled sacramental expression of unity at the international conferences, and, secondly, a theological analysis, discussing the ecumenical implications that the charismatic renewal and the Eucharist both share.

Contextual Analysis

An Exposure of an Incomplete Unity

It is undeniable that delegates of the international conference experienced a tremendous sense of unity, which the mainstream ecumenists had never imagined to be possible. However, under the critical test of the final communion, the unity was proved to be incomplete; it was *per se* emotional and experiential, which was not the whole answer to the deep-rooted divisions derived from doctrinal disagreements throughout centuries. The unity shown in the charismatic renewal was a temporary event, and not yet a permanent reality. It did not close the chapter of Christian division in history. Suenens saw how the doctrinal problems had been disguised by the sense of unity in the charismatic renewal and warned that, "We must not give way to an euphoric ecumenism which, in the joy of rediscovering Christian brotherhood, would overlook the doctrinal difficulties yet to be resolved."[80] The Eucharist is one of the toughest ecumenical issues, since denominations insist on their own theological, liturgical, and ecclesiastical "truths" about the sacrament. To

---

80. Suenens, *Ecumenism and Charismatic Renewal*, 45.

achieve full communion came to be far more difficult than charismatics ever imagined, as Smail declared at a conference of the Fountain Trust,

> What we thought would be easy has proved to be difficult. What we thought would be fast has turned out to be far more slow. What we thought would happen at the way of some kind of charismatic…that is going to change the whole situation overnight, we've seen to be required much more prayer, much more sacrifice, much more sensitivity, much more patience, much more hard work than we imagined or perhaps even that we've been prepared to give.[81]

Apart from the actual difficulty of achieving unity that the final communion reveals, it also shows that in ecumenism, experience, and doctrine, and grassroots level and the official level, are always in confrontation. No matter how real the unity has been that was nurtured by experience at the grassroots level, people at the official level still struggle to achieve doctrinal consensus and believe that it is the gateway to ultimate unity. The authorities of some churches still insist on the truth of certain doctrines and on the importance of others, agreeing with that truthfulness before unity can be achieved. Hence, the unity manifested in the charismatic renewal which was based on experience of the Holy Spirit at the grassroots level is noteworthy, but is not regarded as a basis for ecumenical dialogue. Unity will remain incomplete if the confrontation between experience and doctrine and between the grassroots and the official level in the ecumenical movement still exists, and if ecumenists find that they cannot deal with the indispensability of both.

The Roman Catholic Dogma

The Roman Catholic Church's persistent refusal to revise the Eucharistic doctrine over centuries directly caused the difficulty of achieving any kind of sacramental unity at the international conferences. At the Faith and Order conference in Lund (1952), the Roman Catholic Church rejected the Protestants' proposal of intercommunion as "the medicine of our division" and a stepping stone to full communion.[82] They insisted that the Eucharist could only be celebrated together when unity was achieved. As a Roman Catholic representative of the conference, Yves Congar, clearly affirmed, "There cannot properly be 'inter-communion.'

81. Smail, *Humanity*.
82. Torrance, "Eschatology," 304.

There is or there is not Communion."[83] He based his statement on the ecclesiastical idea of the Church as both an institution and a communion. As an institution, the Church is established by three elements: faith, sacraments, and "apostolic powers instituting a ministry of teaching, worship and government of communities." Hence, the Eucharist has its place in the very constitution of the Church as an institution. As a communion, the Church is perceived as a single body composed of members who share the same faith, practice the same sacraments, and accept the apostolic authority of ordained priests to minister to the congregation. Therefore, dividing that one body means destroying the church as a communion with the result that there is no point in celebrating the Eucharist together.[84] Since the idea of intercommunion compromises the eucharistic principle of acknowledging the Church as an institution and a communion, the Roman Catholic authority prohibits its members from taking part in any form of communion with their "separated brethren" until the day of perfect unity comes and there will be full communion.

In addition, Vatican II officially expressed its rejection of sharing any liturgical ritual with the "separated brethren" for the sake of unity. The Council allows and encourages Roman Catholics to participate in ecumenical gatherings and prayer meetings for unity with non-Catholics as "they are a genuine expression of the ties which still bind Catholics to their separated brethren." However, the ties are not allowed to reach as far as the realm of the Eucharist to express the sense of unity. The statement says, "Yet worship in common (*communication in sacris*) is not to be considered as a means to be used indiscriminately for the restoration of unity among Christians" but "it should signify the unity of the Church; it should provide a sharing in the means of grace." Therefore, Christians should wait until the time when "little by little, as the obstacles to perfect ecclesiastical communion are over," they can celebrate the Eucharist together as a sign of the perfect communion.[85]

Suenens, although acknowledging the remarkable ecumenical impact of the renewal which he elaborated in the two Malines documents, publicly affirmed the position of his church regarding communion in one of the seminars at Westminster 1977. His reason for objecting to

83. Congar, "Amica Contestatio," 144.

84 Ibid., 142–44.

85. Vatican Council II, "Unitatis Redintegratio," 352, 384.

the intercommunion was in line with Congar who also insisted on the intimate connection of the church and the Eucharist, as he explained:

> Because Eucharist is the reality of the body of Christ and the church is also the body of Christ. It's one and the same reality in this sense that it is the church making eucharist and it is eucharist making the church. So you cannot divorce because of the depth of the mystery. It's one and the same mystery in two different aspects. I cannot say take the Eucharist and refuse your church because they are one.[86]

In another seminar about ecumenical issues at the same conference, Roman Catholic Bishop Langton Fox also took the same position as Suenens, as he asserted, "To receive the communion together is for us the expression of communion fully achieved." He advised conference delegates to be patient: "We should wait until we have this communion together in faith before we should receive the Holy Communion together."[87] Although the Cardinal and the Bishop were supportive of the charismatic renewal,[88] as leaders of the Church, they had to stand firm on their Church's position and remind the Catholic charismatics of the doctrines, despite the developed sense of unity and the possible grief at their sacramental withdrawal. The sense of unity that flourished at the grassroots level in the charismatic renewal was found unfulfilled in the sacrament of the Eucharist and this demonstrated the sharp discrepancy between the grassroots and official level of ecumenical progress. The unity achieved at the grassroots was still restricted by the disunity of the official level. Canon laws still had to be followed, and Protestants and Roman Catholics still had to celebrate the sacrament separately regardless of their desire for a common celebration. The Catholic Truth Society of London understandingly describes the reality that "to abstain from Communion at their Eucharist may be painful, but the pain is part of the tragedy of our divisions."[89] In the 1980s, the Roman Catholic author-

86. Fountain Trust, *Ecumenical Issues II.*

87. Fountain Trust, *Ecumenical Issues I.*

88. Langton Fox was named by the bishops at the first Newman Conference as the "Ecclesiastical Assistant to Catholic Charismatic Renewal." Cardinal Hume affirmed his position by saying, "'We don't name Ecclesiastical Assistant to anything we don't approve of.'" Fox was active in the RCNSC and frequently attended meetings. The Committee gained a lot of assurance of its work by Fox's sharing, discussion and prayer. (Email from Bob Balkam, 16 November 2005; 18 November 2005.)

89. *Intercommunion*, 15.

ity still held the same position regarding intercommunion. John Paul II stated that it could "send conflicting signals or to mislead people . . . It would not mitigate the pain of separation if we avoided the cause of this pain, which is the separation itself." For him, it would be more appropriate for the church to seek for a common faith first and therefore "common celebration" through dialogue.[90]

The Identity Crisis of Roman Catholic Charismatics

The final communion services at the international conferences created an identity crisis for Catholic charismatics. The noun "Catholic charismatic" is compounded of two words which convey contradictory ecumenical implications. The adjective "Catholic" represents a church which regards itself as the only true church in the world having inherited the apostolic faith. For this church, unity occurs only when other non-Catholic churches return to it and acknowledge its ecclesiastical, liturgical, and sacramental doctrines. The ecumenical responsibility is laid on the non-Catholic churches to be the ones to approach the Catholic Church for the sake of unity. In other words, this is a one-dimensional approach for unity. The second component of the noun "charismatic" suggests that the outpouring of the Holy Spirit is not merely given to "the only true church," but also to all churches confessing Jesus Christ. Christians mutually recognized one another as members of the Body of Christ because of the common experience in the Spirit and so the approach of unity becomes multi-dimensional.

Surprisingly these two contradictory elements were brought together in the charismatic renewal and they existed simultaneously in the same person. Roman Catholics became charismatic through the experience in the Spirit and obtained a new identity. However this also began a conflict within them because they were presented with a choice between loyalty to the Roman Catholic Church and the realization of unity for which they longed. As Veli-Matti Kärkkäinen accurately notes, "The Catholic Charismatic Movement is shaped as much (or more) by its commitment to the Catholic Church as it is by its commitment to a type of spiritual experience."[91] The sadness that arose at the final communion services at the international conferences was one of the results of this double commitment. Catholic charismatics had to choose between breaching

90. Quoted in Larere, *Lord's Supper*, 77.
91. Kärkkäinen, *Pneumatology*, 94.

the rule of their church, which might well create a sense of guilt, and refusing to take the bread and wine which discouraged non-Catholics and brought great pain to the whole congregation. Although this identity crisis was initially personal to the Roman Catholics, it produced a negative effect on non-Catholic charismatics who were frustrated by the dilemma. Consequently the grassroots unity which had developed from the common experience and the mutual edification of charisms was disrupted by this identity crisis of the Catholic charismatics.

Some of the Protestant charismatics felt uncomfortable with the Catholics abstaining from the Eucharist in order to be loyal to their church rather than being obedient to Jesus' command. For example, Susan Pernet, a delegate at Westminster 1975, questioned,

> Where is the born-again Catholic who will take heed of his Lord's command and receive the elements in company with other members of the body of Christ, and who will obey God rather than the rules of his church? Is the Catholic still looking at his church's teaching on the Lord's Supper rather than the teaching of Scripture? Dear Catholic brethren, we are burdened by the shackles you bear and long to see you take your stand for Jesus in the light of his word. The blessings will surely follow.[92]

Another delegate at the same conference, R. A. Pyle, wrote to Harper to express her "shock" at still being labeled as "separated brethren" who were supposed to return to the Roman Catholic Church despite the "rich time of fellowship." Like Pernet, she believed that the eucharistic teachings in the New Testament should be the only foundation for the sacrament rather than complicating it by adding denominational and historic doctrines and regulations.[93]

Not only Protestant lay people believed that the celebration of the Eucharist should be based on "the simplest reason" of being united in Christ, but ministers did as well. In the seminar when Suenens explained the eucharistic position of the Roman Catholic Church, Bishop Richard Hare condemned this saying that it was "a lack of faith" not to share communion together at the Eucharist until official consent had been given. He said that as long as there is "sufficient unity in faith and to express that unity in the Spirit which has already given" Christians of different traditions should celebrate the Eucharist together. He urged a

92. Pernet, "Catholics," 9.
93. Letter from R. A. Pyle to Harper, 5 August 1975, 1–2.

cessation of all the "divisions in the name of Christ" which led further on to a divided world.[94] Douglas McBain, as a Baptist minister, also expressed a similar view, saying that because the Lord's Supper belonged to the Lord, it should be open for all Christians to participate in and to have fellowship with him.[95]

The grassroots unity which was nurtured mainly by positive emotions of love and mutual acceptance was challenged by the negative emotions of skepticism and judgements based on people's own understandings of the Eucharist. This shows that the nature of this grassroots unity was fragile, and that it was easily challenged not only by the doctrines from the official circles outside the conferences, but also from the inner disharmony within the congregation. Nevertheless, it does not mean that the grassroots unity was in vain because the mutual acceptance that it develops is still the basis for dialogue and for further understanding of each other. This kind of fellowship will be prolonged and become mature if churches can deal with controversial and divisive issues with perseverance and patience.

A Neglect of the Eucharist

The five international conferences had an overemphasis on charisms and at the same time neglected the significance of the Eucharist. That led to an incomplete understanding of unity in two ways. First, pneumatologically, charisms were seen to be the signs of the presence of the Holy Spirit while sacraments were frequently not perceived to have this significance. However, if the Holy Spirit is the energy of the charismatic renewal of the church, then the Eucharist should have been recognized as part of his renewal agenda. That it was not seen to be so could be due to the fact that the charismatic renewal took place mainly in Protestant churches which do not put the same value on the sacramental role of the Holy Spirit, as Lukas Vischer observes to be the case during the Reformation, "The doctrine of the Holy Spirit was treated in a new but not more comprehensive way."[96] Owing to the partial perception of the presence of the Spirit in the charismatic renewal, the way to understand the ecumenical work of the Holy Spirit is limited to the experiential spectrum while the sacramental realm remained underdeveloped.

94. Fountain Trust, *Ecumenical Issues II.*

95. Fountain Trust, *Ecumenical Issues I.*

96. Vischer, "Epiclesis," 33.

Secondly, ecclesiologically, the focus on charisms also caused a loss of a holistic view of the church. The renewal seemed to create a picture of the church built on "first apostles, second prophets, third teachers, then miracles, then gifts of healings, helps, administrations and various kinds of tongues" (1 Cor 12:28) with the power of the Holy Spirit, but it forgot the eucharistic foundation which the Roman Catholic and Orthodox Church have emphasized. One Russian Orthodox priest asserts, "The Church exists in and for the Eucharist."[97] Du Plessis asserts that the Pentecostal and charismatic movement transforms the church in a miraculous way, but he wonders why these two movements have not "demonstrated a rich and full manifestation of chapters 12, 13, and 14 of the first Epistle to the Corinthians." He discovers the reason to be the unsolved problem of the Eucharist mentioned in chapter 11.[98] The Lord's Table is still divided; that means the church, the Body of Christ is still divided and that is the problem that prevents the gifts from functioning to their fullness (chapters 12 and 14), the love coming to perfection (chapter 13) and the renewal to reaching its completeness. C. P. M. Jones also raises a similar point about the interrelatedness of chapters 11 to 14. Paul's teaching on order in chapter 14 for the exercises of charisms is similar to his instructions for conducting the Eucharist in chapter 11. His preference for prophecy over tongues so that the congregation can say Amen with gratitude to the grace of God (1 Cor 14:16) can also be applied to the Eucharist which is *per se* a shared act of thanksgiving. He therefore believes that the Eucharist and the charismatic congregation were not separated in the early church.[99] Congar acknowledges that the renewal created a "reintegration in unity," but notices that it could not tackle some ecumenical problems such as the Eucharist. He warns that without considering the sacramental, christological and visible elements but only the pneumatological ones, we will only pursue unity under the principle of "immediacy," and aim to "achieve unity in grace" without "the instituted means of grace."[100] It is undeniable that the charismatic renewal has ecumenical potential which is based on the grassroots experience, but to enable this potential to be used to its fullness, a holistic ecclesiological and ecumenical view is necessary. And that means both

---

97. Kallistos, "Communion," 188.

98. Du Plessis, *Renewal of Christianity*, 5.

99. Jones, "Eucharist," 193.

100. Congar, *I Believe in the Holy Spirit Vol. II*, 206.

pneumatological and christological, spiritual and visible, and charismatic and institutional of the church and church unity should be considered. This point will be fully discussed in chapter 5.

The Eucharistic Impossibility Became a Possibility

Although the grassroots unity in the charismatic renewal was found to be incomplete and vulnerable when it came to the challenge of the final communion, and charismatics did not pay much attention to the intimate relation between the Eucharist and unity, there is still significance for ecumenism. In practice, intercommunion did happen, although on a small scale, during the international conferences. At Guildford and Westminster 1975, there were occasions where Roman Catholic priests secretly invited Protestants to join the Eucharist. Mr. and Mrs. James recorded that in the first Mass at Guildford, only Roman Catholics were given the bread and wine, but that was changed in other Masses. They said, "At the second, the officiating priest was broken down himself to such an extent that he said he could not refrain from offering all his brothers and sisters the Body & Blood of Christ, and on this 3rd day they were freely given & all shared together by receiving."[101] A similar incident was repeated at Westminster 1975 when Protestants were warmly invited by the Roman Catholics to join their Mass every morning and to celebrate the Eucharist which was consecrated by a Roman Catholic priest. Unfortunately this secretive practice was discovered and the authority forbade the joint celebration with Protestants in the Mass at Westminster 1977. The Catholic charismatics apologized deeply for the prohibition. Nevertheless, the charismatic renewal did create a bonding between Roman Catholics and Protestants, which sprang out of affection for one another, and made them want to seize every opportunity to celebrate the Eucharist together as a sign of unity, even at the expense of violating the canon law. Although intercommunion is almost an impossibility, ironically it was the Catholic priests who broke the rules in the charismatic renewal.

Theological Analysis

The Eucharist is a sacrament and a means of grace which is instituted by Christ, so that the church remembers him and continues to be sheltered

---

101. Letter from James to Harper, 15 August 1971, 3.

by his salvation; charisms are gracious gifts which are granted by the Holy Spirit to build up the church. From an ecumenical point of view, they are both means and symbol of unity, and particularly in the charismatic renewal where grassroots unity was brought about by the manifestation of charisms. This section is to discuss four characters shared by the Eucharist and charisms. They are both anamnetic, epicletic, eschatological, and ecumenical.

The Anamnetic Character

Although anamnesis is the purpose of the Eucharistic celebration, the manifestation of charisms also carries the same meaning. Anamnesis means remembrance and this is the word Jesus used when he says, "Do this in remembrance of me" (Luke 22:19).[102] He asks the believers to remember his sacrifice for humankind through breaking the same bread and drinking the same cup. The request for remembrance of God's salvation in the Eucharist is parallel to the purpose of celebrating the Passover for remembering God's deliverance of the Israelites from Egypt. The salvific acts in the Old and New Testaments are intrinsically a covenant that God has made with humankind and he will never alter or withdraw it. Thus, through anamnesis, the redeemed are once again reminded of this covenant and their faith in God is reaffirmed. Particularly in the Eucharist, taking the bread and drinking the wine, according to John, represent a relationship with "the Son of Man" who is the bread from heaven given to humankind (John 6:27, 53) who abide in Christ and Christ abides in them. They are also promised eternal life (John 6:54, 56). Hence, the anamnetic purpose of the Eucharist is to reaffirm the divine relationship with the Savior and to reassure Christians about the promise that he has made.

Anamnesis aims at bringing the past events into the present, but it is not nostalgic. Nostalgia drives people to remember the past selectively, particularly the pleasant and enjoyable episodes of the whole incident, and that blinds them from seeing the complete and authentic picture, and prevents them from making fair and balanced evaluations. However, the Holy Spirit, who is the Paraclete and is named as "the remembrance,"[103] does not recall our memory of the past according to our own interest, but to his own will in order to build us up. Therefore with the work of

---

102. Beckwith, "Jewish," 77.
103. Stookey, *Eucharist*, 100.

the Holy Spirit, the anamnestic function of the Eucharist draws the participants not only back to the dreadful suffering that Jesus bore, but also to the glory of the resurrection that followed, and the joy of thousands of souls being redeemed through this once and for all sacrifice for humankind. Through this holistic remembrance of the past and symbolic act of taking the bread and drinking the wine, participants once again confirm their faith in the Savior, remain in hope of eternal life, and offer a sacrifice of thanksgiving to God.

Charisms which are endowed by the Holy Spirit also have the anamnetic purpose of the Eucharist in focusing on Jesus' redemption. Tongues are spiritual utterances praising the works of God and the interpretation of tongues helps to make sense of the praise for human understanding; while healing is believed to be the physical aspect of salvation; and exorcism manifests the authority of Jesus. These gifts of the Holy Spirit represent Jesus' triumph over evil through the power of the cross and through the resurrection. When "He ascended on high, He led captive a host of captives, and he gave gifts to men . . . for equipping of the saints for the work of service, to the building up of the body of Christ" (Eph 4:8, 11). Each charism has its own function of edifying individuals as well as the church, but, meanwhile, each of them reminds both the performers and receivers of the perfect gift of Jesus' salvation. Scott McCormick suggests that anamnesis directs Christians to view salvation not only as a past event, but also as a process continuing in the present, when he speaks of "his re-creating, life-giving gift being repeatedly offered and repeatedly received."[104] His understanding of the anamnesis of the Eucharist rightly fits the intrinsic meaning of charisms, which are continually performed and continually received to manifest the glory of salvation.

The collective anamnesis of Jesus through charisms and the Eucharist is a collective experience which triggers a collective memory of and affection for the crucified Lord. The charisms and Eucharist also confirm the collective identity as Christians and their shared faith. They remind Christians that all the wonderful manifestations of charisms would not have happened if the salvation had not been accomplished by Jesus Christ. The celebration of the Eucharist is instituted by Christ for all the redeemed, and charisms is bestowed by the Spirit on all of them. The Eucharist symbolizes unity with all Christians breaking the same bread and drinking the same wine, while charisms create unity when

104. Quoted in Biddy, "Re-envisioning," 235.

they are used for building up the body. Hence, the unity growing out of these two activities is the fruit shared by people, and by their very nature both activities are essential to grassroots unity.

The Epicletic Character

Epiclesis is a prayer of invocation to the Holy Spirit to descend upon and to be present in the bread and wine during the Eucharist, as well as uniting the communicants.[105] This prayer in the Eucharist has been particularly important in eastern liturgy. As Vischer notes, it is "the climax of the whole liturgical action."[106] For example, St. John Chrysostom's prayer reads, "'Send down thy Holy Spirit upon us and upon the gifts placed before thee.'" St Basil's prayer invokes not just the presence of the Holy Spirit, but also unity, as it has the words, "'And to unite us all as many as are partakers in the one bread and cup, one with another, in the communion of the one Holy Spirit.'"[107] Similarly, in Roman Catholic liturgy, the Holy Spirit is first invoked for the transformation of the bread and wine into Jesus' presence before the consecration. Then afterwards the communicants invoke the "unity in depth" which can only be given by the Holy Spirit. And this unity referred to is the visible unity. [108]

The Holy Spirit is believed to be the one who enables the Eucharist to be effective[109] and epiclesis is the means to achieve this purpose. This is because the Holy Spirit links the past with the present, and makes real the Jesus who was crucified and now is alive. He is "the One who makes the historical words of Jesus present and alive."[110] Moltmann comments that the Eucharist is "the mark of the history of the Spirit."[111] The Holy Spirit also enables us to understand the eschatological implication of the

---

105. Davies, *Spirit, the Church and the Sacrament*, 137; Smail, *Giving Gift*, 194; Henderson and Primavesi, "Witness," 430; World Council of Churches, *Baptism, Eucharist and Ministry.*

106. Vischer, "Epiclesis," 30.

107. Zizioulas, "Eucharist," 224, note 70.

108. Fountain Trust, *Ecumenical Issues II.* This idea of the epiclesis was explained by Cardinal Suenens during the seminar. However, according to Yves Congar, traditionally, epiclesis was not part of the Roman Catholic liturgy since Gregory the Great. It was added into the eucharistic liturgy with the consent of the bishops during the Vatican II. (Congar, *I Believe in the Holy Spirit Volume III*, 251, 256.)

109. Congar, *I Believe in the Holy Spirit Vol. III*, 250; Pinnock, *Flame of Love*, 123.

110. World Council of Churches, *Baptism, Eucharist and Ministry*, E14.

111. Moltmann, *Church in the Power*, 257.

Eucharist which is that the living Jesus will come back to this world and believers will share the banquet with him. The epiclesis connects us with Jesus through reminding us of the past, celebrating the Eucharist in the present and foreseeing the *parousia*. It creates a koinonia between each communicant and Christ in the Eucharist. As Albert C. Outler claims, "It has been the epikletic action of the Holy Spirit that made of each such occasion a true sign of our koinonia in Christ."[112]

Moltmann's eucharistic concept of the Trinity is coherent to the meaning of epiclesis, which suggests that the Holy Spirit is doing ground work among human beings in order to create an upward connection with the Father. His concept of the Trinity contrasts the monarchial one which focuses on the descent of love, and the good attributes of the Father that come to human beings through the Son and the Holy Spirit (Father→Son→Holy Spirit). He proposes an ascent of our response to the works and love of God which is inspired by the Holy Spirit. He stirs up human hearts to give thanks, praise, and adoration to the Son and the Father (Holy Spirit→Son→Father),[113] and particularly in the Eucharist, through the anamnesis of Christ's sacrifice. This upward connection initiated by the Holy Spirit and expressed in the epiclesis indirectly opens up an ecumenical possibility at the grassroots level.

The request for the presence of the Holy Spirit in the Eucharist requires the self-surrender of human beings, which is the beginning of unity. Epiclesis represents an attitude of a complete surrender of self-will without any attempt at manipulating the Lord. It reminds the church that Christ still is and should be the head of the body, and here in Jesus' supper, he is the host. If epiclesis is truly an honest and earnest prayer of the communicants and celebrants of the Eucharist, the Spirit of unity will be able to mend the broken Table by open communion for every member of the Body of Christ and gradually unity will come. Wainwright foresees that "common participation in the one Eucharist will allow the Lord creatively to bring us closer to the perfect peace and unity that will mark the final kingdom."[114] Vischer suggests that the epiclesis should be used in every church's Eucharist because it is a seeking for the Holy Spirit. He believes "that everything which can be said about the work of the Spirit in the church also applies to the union of the separated churches." It can

112. Outler, "Pneumatology," 372.

113. Moltmann, *Spirit of Life*, 298–300.

114. Wainwright, *Eucharist and Eschatology*, 143.

be "a sign of the freedom given by the Spirit." Although the epiclesis has been emphasized in Orthodox eucharistic liturgy, he believes that this plea for the presence of the Holy Spirit should be adopted by all churches and this common epicletic emphasis can be a reference point for unity because of the shared focus on the Holy Spirit that it gives. One of the reasons for this is that churches will then not only look at their own historical continuity but at the continuity of the whole Church of Christ which has been guided by the Holy Spirit.[115] Hence the epiclesis reduces the individualistic attitude of churches and raises the awareness of the oneness of the church.

The plea for the presence of the Holy Spirit, the attitude of self-surrender and the possible fruit of unity derived from the epiclesis of the Eucharist can all be found in the use of charisms. To be able to use the charisms effectively, charismatics request the Spirit to fill them and work through them unceasingly, and that requires a complete obedience and surrender. This is a life-long invocation just as the Eucharist is a life-long anamnesis of Christ with the epicletic prayer being used in the process. Charisma and the Eucharist both remind the church of the Holy Spirit who is the gift from God, as Visher and Smail assert, and "has the divine willingness to give" life, power, and unity to the church.[116] Hence, charisms are epicletic and the epiclesis is charismatic. As John Gunstone claims, "The *epiclesis* expresses what we (charismatics) believe should be expressed, when the Eucharist becomes so much a 'renewal service' of the most significant kind."[117] They are mutually coherent and more importantly, they both point to a common goal of unity among Christians.

The Eschatological Character

Charisms and the Eucharist are both eschatological as they are being used and celebrated until the end time comes. They both point to the eschaton. The remembrance activity with the plea for the presence of the Holy Spirit in the Eucharist will cease when Jesus comes back. As Paul says, "For as often as you eat this bread and drink this cup, you proclaim the Lord's death until He comes" (1 Cor 11: 26). Therefore, when believers are celebrating the Eucharist in the present, with the memory of Jesus'

115. Vischer, "Epiclesis," 34, 37–39.

116. Ibid., 34–35; Smail, *Giving Gift*, 14–17, 22.

117. Gunstone, "Spirit," 13.

sacrifice in the past, they are looking forward to the future when Jesus comes back and they drink the new wine with him in the kingdom of the Father (Matt 26:29). It is a shared anticipation and a hope for the future of all believers. Moltmann even states, "The supper of the hoping church is a 'foretaste' of the messianic banquet of *all mankind*" (my italic).[118] John Zizioulas sees that the epicletic invocation of the Holy Spirit's presence and work at the Eucharist demonstrates the historical Jesus in the present and points to the hope of his actual presence at the end time. He identifies the Eucharist as "the eschatologisation of the historical word, the voice of the historical Christ, the voice of the Holy Scripture which comes to us, no longer simply as 'doctrine' through history, but as life and *being* through the *eschaton*."[119] From the eschatological perspective, the Lord's Table is a place where Christian unity should be realized. It is a means of grace effecting the sweetness of unity among the participants. It is because of this shared hope that Christians maintain their faith and still break bread and drink wine. It is because of this shared hope that the church which is the body of Christ still exists, and it is because of this shared hope that it is meaningful for Christians to prepare themselves as a church for the coming King. Therefore, the eschatological hope symbolized by the Eucharist should always be ecumenical and always be represented by the whole body of Christians.

Similarly the spiritual gifts which are characteristic of the charismatic renewal also carry an eschatological meaning which has further ecumenical implications. According to Paul, all the spiritual gifts will cease to function at the end time of the world. As he says, "If there are gifts of prophecy, they will be done away; if there are tongues, they will cease; if there is knowledge, it will be done away" and "when the perfect comes, the partial will be done away" (1 Cor 13:8, 10). The presence of charisms in the present implies their absence in the future, but before the end time comes, they serve as manifestation of the glory and might of God, and as the means of mutual edification among Christians which in turn strengthens the unity. Hence, the charisms which are emphasized in the charismatic renewal, like the Eucharist, also suggest a collective anticipation of the arrival of the "perfect" where charisms will cease but the unity developed on earth will last forever for "love never fails." (1 Cor 13:8)

118. Moltmann, *Church in the Power*, 253.
119. Zizioulas, *Being As Communion*, 22.

The Ecumenical Character

Both the Eucharist and the charisms have ecumenical significance. According to Paul, they both carry the "one-many" relationship. For the Eucharist, he says, "Since there is one bread, we who are many are one body; for we all partake of the one bread" (1 Cor. 10:17). The *Didache* provides an analogy of this "one-many" relationship of the Eucharist as follows, "As this fragment lay scattered upon the mountains and became a single [fragment] when it had been gathered. May your church be gathered into your kingdom from the ends of the earth."[120]

About charisms Paul says, "For just as we have many members in one body and all the members do not have the same function, so we, who are many, are one body in Christ, and individually members one of another" (Rom 12:4–5). For functions he refers to charisms outlined in verses 6–8 and there is a similar argument in 1 Cor 12. Paul does not see the contradiction of "one" and "many" as they refer to different entities and the oneness of an entity relies on the "manyness" of another entity to be constituted. In addition, the "manyness" of that entity can be diverse in many aspects but there should be one ultimate commonality. Hence one and many are not mutually exclusive but ought to be mutually dependant. The presence of this "one-many" relationship in both the Eucharist and the charisms is significant for Christian unity. Since the body of Christ cannot be constituted just by one person, but many people; not just one culture, but many; not just one race, but many; not just one social background, but many; not just one gender, but both male and female; and finally not just one charism, but many charisms. Although there is "manyness" existing in each member of the body of Christ, there is only one faith shared by all of them. Because of the "manyness," there is diversity rather than uniformity, and by virtue of the oneness of faith, there is unity. Due to the one faith, they break the one bread and drink the one cup signifying the one Savior whose flesh was pierced and whose blood was shed for all. Due to the one confession of Christ, they are endowed by the Holy Spirit with many charisms to constitute the one body of Christ. This "one-many" relation of the Eucharist and charisms is obvious at the grassroots level. This is because the one bread and cup are not just taken by the celebrant on behalf of the whole congregation, but each member of the church is entitled to

---

120. "Doctrine of the Twelve Apostles," 10.

partake of them. It is also because charisms are granted to each member and they are empowered to be involved in ministries of the church and build up the one body of Christ. Hence, through participating in the Eucharist and a ministry when charisms are exercised, each member is creating and demonstrating unity.

Conclusion

The broken table throughout the centuries exposes the visible division among churches and it also occurred during the charismatic renewal. As Gunstone notes, the charismatic renewal "has not swept away doctrinal differences between Christians on the eucharist."[121] Because of charisms and common experiences in the Spirit, grassroots unity took place among Christians of diverse traditions during the charismatic renewal; but because of the Eucharist, the grassroots unity was found to be incomplete and vulnerable. In fact, both the Eucharist and charisms are anamnetic, epicletic, eschatological, and ecumenical. Hence these two outward signs of unity and means of grace are indispensable for the church and are crucial for its unity, particularly at the grassroots level. Ecumenists and charismatics should not neglect either of them but pay equal attention to both for the prospective unity of the church.

FINAL CONCLUSION

This chapter has discussed the grassroots unity nurtured in the charismatic worship at the five international conferences through the functioning of charisms, including speaking and singing in tongues, healing, prophecy, and intercession. It also explained that grassroots unity was developed from the spontaneity during worship which produced an intimacy with God and between people. Moreover, I have attempted to apply the ancient tag *lex orandi, lex credendi* to explain charismatic worship. Its spontaneity and openness to God enable *theologia prima* to occur and the tag can only be interpreted as saying that the law of prayer establishes the law of belief, not the other way around, in charismatic worship.

Worship in the five international conferences demonstrated unity at the grassroots level, but the Eucharist exposed its weaknesses and vulnerability when it faced the dogmatic insistence of the Roman Catholic

---

121. Gunstone, "Spirit," 13.

Church that it could only be celebrated together when the unity of the church was achieved. The divided table during the conferences also developed an identity crisis among Catholic charismatics. The incidents showed that doctrinal agreement at the official level was necessary to complement the grassroots unity. Nevertheless, concelebration which took place in public services and intercommunion which was practiced in secret in morning Masses indicate the fact that grassroots unity, to some extent, enabled the eucharistic impossibility to become a possibility within certain doctrinal boundaries.

Theologically, I develop a charismatic understanding of the Eucharist with the concepts of anamnesis and epiclesis, and discuss the shared eschatological and ecumenical implications of the Eucharist and charisms. Although the five international conferences show that charisms during worship brought about unity at the grassroots level and the Eucharist divided the congregation, they are *per se* the signs of unity and means of grace; hence, they are not mutually exclusive but can complement each other. The Eucharist institutionally constitutes the church; charisms actively sustain the life of it. The Eucharist implies the christological element and charisms the pneumatological in ecclesiology. The next chapter will depart from the historical context of the five international conferences and theologically investigate the complementarity of institution and charisms, and Christology and Pneumatology in the church and the church united in the charismatic context.

5

In Search of Complementarity
in the Charismatic Context

CHARISMATIC WORSHIP WAS SPONTANEOUS in its use of charisms while the Eucharist was essentially part of the formal church institution.[1] Charisms represent the work of the Spirit and hence are the pneumatological element of the church while the Eucharist focuses on Christ's redemption and is to do with the church's basic christological stance. However, the church has been criticized for focusing on the institutional aspect of its life and neglecting the charismatic; ecclesiology has concentrated on Christology without so much recognizing the importance of Pneumatology. It is true that the charismatic renewal reminded the church of the pneumatological element and it nurtured a grassroots unity, but this unity did not last. This indicates that to build up the church and bring about unity, there is a need for both charisms and institution, and for both Pneumatology and Christology. To attempt to do so with just one or the other is not sufficient. They are complementary. Hence, this chapter is an attempt to search for the complementarity between charisms and institution, and Pneumatology and Christology for the church (Ecclesiology) and the church united (Ecumenism) from a charismatic perspective.

INSTITUTION AND CHARISMS

Ecclesiology

The word "institution" carries two meanings. First, it refers to formal organizations, which are the churches, and ecumenical organizations. Second, in the church, according to Avery Dulles's definition, it can refer

1. Zizioulas, *Being As Communion*, 22.

to four structural elements: (1) doctrines in the forms of creeds, catechism, etc.; (2) worship, containing sacraments, liturgy, and ritual; (3) government, such as offices and hierarchy; (4) laws.[2] Charism as it was defined in the introduction of the thesis means the so-called "supernatural" gifts manifested in the charismatic renewal as well as those beneficial to the spiritual and numerical growth of the church. Ecclesiologically, institution and charisms should be complementary, for as Congar asserts, "they lead to the same end, which is the building up of the work of Christ."[3] Protestant and Roman Catholic theologians warn that the either-or mentality regarding the existence of institution and charisms in the church will put the church in danger.[4] Charisms imply freedom, spontaneity, liveliness, creativity, and renewal while institution implies order, discipline, jurisdiction, and effectiveness. The church needs both elements and should keep them in balance; otherwise, it will either become chaotic, corrupted, and alienated from the truth by the overemphasis on charisms or inflexible, restrictive, and eventually ossified by the overemphasis on the institution.

Karl Rahner provides a model of the open and closed system of the church, which is useful for analyzing the complementarity of charism and institution. A closed system he defines as, "A complex of realities of various kinds which, despite their variations, are related to one another and contribute towards a common task, [which] is defined and directed from a point within the system itself." In this closed system the church is constructed as an "absolute monarchy or totalitarian system" where all ministries are administered by the officials or, in the case of the Roman Catholics, by the Pope who has absolute authority. In other words, the church relies enormously on human effort and the involvement of transcendent force such as the Holy Spirit, is very limited. In contrast, an open system is featured by, in Rahner's phrase, "the dominion of God," and its functioning is "rather charismatic than institutional in character." Based on this system, he concludes that the charismatic aspect of the

---

2. Dulles, "Earthen Vessels," 159.

3. Congar, *I Believe in the Holy Spirit Vol. II*, 11.

4. Protestant theologians make this point such as Pinnock, *Flame of Love*, 140; Evans, *Church and Churches*, 138. Roman Catholic theologians mention about this point such as Suenens, *Ecumenism and Charismatic Renewal*, 32; O'Keeffe, "Investigation into the Charismatic Movement," 209; Whitehead, "What is the Nature of the Catholic Charismatic Renewal?"

church is "inherent in the very nature of the Church as such."[5] In addition, he recognizes that the charismatic movement plays a significant role in keeping the church in an open system, for as he says,

> . . . while the institutional factor in the Church is a legitimate entity, it nevertheless remains encompassed by the charismatic movement of the Spirit in the Church, the Spirit who again and again ushers the Church as an open system into a future which he himself, and no-one else, has arranged, and in a manner which can never adequately be planned for beforehand, by any man or any institution.[6]

This Spirit-operating open system is not an abstract entity, but it contains a physical structure to enable the ecclesia to grow. Rahner's open system suggests a complementarity between the institution and charisms with an active involvement of the Holy Spirit. The charismatic renewal characterized by the spontaneity of the Holy Spirit brings into view the intrinsic value of charisms, which have been subordinated within the institution, to create an open system.

As far as Cardinal Suenens is concerned, the complementarity of institution and charisms lies in the fact that they are both the gifts from the Holy Spirit. He perceives institution as a physical base for charisms to work in, and gives the analogy of the institution as a tree with roots, trunk, bark, and branches, and the charisms as sap. The sap can support the whole tree with its nutrition and enables flowers and fruits to grow because it is protected by the tree and absorbed within it rather than exuding away. Hence, without institution, there is nothing to protect the charisms and provide a framework within which they can work. He also suggests that institution ensures the continuity of the church in the past, present, and future. For the past, the institution serves the purpose of keeping the church rooted in the tradition, so that it has a solid foundation to receive any renewal in the present. For the present, the institution is important for discerning any danger and avoiding any error. For the future, the institution provides strength for the church to grow and bear fruits.[7] Charisms rely on institution, as that is the place in which they function and that is where they nurture the church. Institution also helps to avoid "over-emotionalism, illuminism, exaggerated supernaturalism"

5. Rahner, *Theological Investigations Vol. 12*, 88–89, 97.

6. Ibid., 97.

7. Suenens, "Holy Spirit," 257–58.

when charisms are used in the church. On the other hand, charisms are like "leaven" boosting the community with "vitality, freedom, thanksgiving and praise, witness and renunciation" and avoiding rigidity and formalism.[8] To get the best out of the complementarity of institution and charisms, those in authority in the institution should bridge the charismatic and institutional divide. That is what Suenens saw himself called to, when he was ordained as a bishop.[9] He urges that "we must at all costs avoid giving the impression that the hierarchical structure of the Church is an administrative apparatus with no intimate connection with the charismatic gifts of the Holy Spirit which are diffused throughout the Church."[10] Theoretically, Rahner and Suenens claim that institution and charism should be complementary, and at the ecumenical dialogue during 1985–89 between Roman Catholics and Pentecostals—the institutionally-oriented and the charismatically-oriented church respectively—there was an attempt to search for this complemenatrity. Pentecostals admitted to their over-emphasis on the Spirit at the personal level, while forgetting the church level.[11] They also recognized their lack of ecclesiological knowledge, both in the congregation and leadership, about the importance of the institution for the functioning of the church and it is recorded that "Pentecostals acknowledge both the reluctance that many of their members have in submitting to ecclesial authority and the difficulty which their charismatic leaders have in working through existing ecclesial institutional channels which could protect them from acting irresponsibly or in an authoritarian manner."[12] Nevertheless, the end of the report notes that they do not see that institution and church order intrinsically hinder the work of the Spirit, but they regard them "as the

8. Suenens, *Ecumenism and Charismatic Renewal*, 32.

9. Suenens, "Holy Spirit," 254–55.

10. Quoted in O' Connor, *Pentecostal Movement in the Catholic Church*, 186.

11. Gros, Meyer and Rusch, *Growth in Agreement II*, 746. This dialogue was represented by the Pontifical Council for Promoting Christian Unity of the Roman Catholic Church and some Pentecostal leaders who were officially appointed by their churches. This was the first time Pentecostal churches were sending representatives to the dialogue including the Apostolic Church of Mexico (1986), the Apostolic Faith Mission of South Africa (1985–89), the Church of God (Cleveland) (1985–88), the Church of God of Prophecy, USA (1986–88), the Independent Assemblies of God International, USA (1987), the International Church of the Foursquare Gospel, USA (1985–89), and the International Communion of Charismatic Church, USA (1986). (Gros, Meyer and Rusch, *Growth in Agreement II*, 735).

12. Gros, Meyer and Rusch, *Growth in Agreement II*, 746.

will of the Lord for his church" according to the New Testament. They also affirm them as an ecclesial necessity through which the Holy Spirit works for the benefit of the church, and "they recognise that the Spirit operates not only through charismatic individuals but also through the permanent ministries of the church." This recognition is coherent with the Roman Catholic's concept of institution. They insist that some elements within the ecclesiastical structure are granted by God and are indispensable, and "that they belong to the very essence of church order." They see the Spirit working with rather than without the structure, which is the same as that in Suenens's model. Both of them agree with the necessity of institution as part of the construction of the church, but they also see that the institution needs to be constantly renewed by the Spirit; it needs a fresh breath for its life.[13] Pentecostals who are relatively charismatically oriented discover the orderliness brought about by institution, while Roman Catholics who are relatively institutionally oriented recognize the liveliness brought by charisms in the Spirit.

The complementarity between institution and charisms seems to be theoretically-proved, but in reality the church has been so dominated by the institution that it has forgotten charisms as the other basic component. Mühlen explains that this is partly due to the political influence of Constantine when Christianity penetrated into every public and private sector. The result was the pursuit of charisms to empower the church for mission diminished, even at the cost of persecution and martyrdom, and they came to be regarded as part of the "mysticism of the monasteries." Some charisms such as teaching, healing, prophecy, and caring for the needy have been preserved but most of those that functioned in the early church were lost. Order and discipline were overemphasized as the gifts of the Spirit, particularly in the Western churches, while other gifts were neglected.[14]

Congar elucidates three major elements of the institution from a christological perspective in Roman Catholicism. First, Jesus gathers the people who have faith in him. Second, he leads his people into a communion through sacraments such as baptism and the Eucharist. Third, through his calling to the disciples, his election of Peter as the rock of the church and his endowment of the Twelve with the apostolic ministry, he forms a structure with "hierarchical powers" for this com-

13. Ibid., 747–50.
14. Mühlen, *Charismatic Theology*, 147, 121.

munity.[15] The church is a '*societas perfecta*' which is comprised of offices governed by bishop, priests and ministers and a Pope as the ultimate authority of the entire hierarchy.[16] As far as Congar is concerned, hierarchy is an essential element of the Roman Catholic Church and its structure, but its hierarchology results in the neglect of lay involvement, and that raises questions about the very nature and being of the church. But he also notices that although Protestant churches stress community rather than hierarchy, they "are in practice almost as clericalized as the Catholic Church."[17] Another Catholic theologian, Avery Dulles, makes the criticism that institutionalism, which overemphasizes the institutional substances in an ecclesiastical system, has adversely affected the church for centuries. For him, it is a "deformation" and it subordinates the importance of graces and charisms of the Spirit in the church.[18]

Nowadays, the term "charism" has been rediscovered, but its definition has been widened to include the institution itself as a charism. Prophecy, tongues, healing, etc. are categorized as non-institutional charisms while leadership and hierarchy are categorized as official charisms.[19] As Vatican II explains about the church, the Holy Spirit "furnishes and directs her with various gifts, both hierarchical and charismatic . . ."[20] Similarly at the third dialogue of the Anglican and Roman Catholic International Commission (ARCIC) in Venice (1976), the two established churches acknowledge episcopacy as a kind of official gift from the Holy Spirit. The ordained ministers follow the apostles in teaching, pastoring the community, and consecrating the sacraments.[21] The problem remains that the institutional aspects take over the noninstitutional ones, which rely on the spontaneity of the Spirit. The church tends to be satisfied with the institutional gifts and to believe that the Holy Spirit is working in the church, when in fact, his work is restricted, and he as a person of the Godhead is far from being recognized. Congar records Karl Adam writing about his "trinity," that "the

---

15. Congar, *Lay People*, 25.

16. Rahner, *Theological Investigations Vol. 12*, 81; *Spirit in the Church*, 35; Dulles, *Models of the Church*, 35.

17. Congar, *Lay People*, 45; *Word and the Spirit*, 78.

18. Dulles, *Models of the Church*, 35, 44.

19. Rahner, *Theological Investigations Vol. 12*, 86.

20. Vatican Council II, "Lumen Gentium," 4, 17.

21. *ARCIC-I Revisited: An Evaluation and a Revision*, 23.

structure of Catholic faith may be summarised in a single sentence: I come to a living faith in the Triune God through Christ in His Church. I experience the action of the living God through Christ realising himself in His Church. So we see the certitude of the Catholic faith rests on the sacred triad: God, Christ, Church."[22] Moltmann also traces the omission of the Holy Spirit from the Trinity to the time of Ignatius of Antioch, with his role being replaced by an ecclesiastical approach which can be summarized as: one God, one Christ, one bishop, and one church.[23] His criticism is that this ecclesiology undermines the Holy Spirit and the charisms with a "monarchial episcopate" and that it is theologically wrong. Consequently, Christians do not realize the crucial nature of the existence of charisms and treat the teachings in the Bible about charisms with a historical lens, which is cessationalist.

In such a church, which has been institutionally-dominated for centuries, the advent of the charismatic renewal is highly important. The renewal interrupted this pattern within the church and its history and was perceived by the Church of England as "a protest against over-rigid ecclesiastical structures," making the church recognize its flaws through the obvious work of the Holy Spirit.[24] It reminded the church of that fundamental but forgotten truth, which is that the charisms are the source of power if it is to function as it should be as the ecclesial, as distinct from closed, "absolute monarchy or totalitarian system," which was sustained solely by human authority. It pushed the church to become more like an open system for the Holy Spirit so that he could revitalize the trunk (the church) by releasing the sap (charisms) to flow within. It lifted the church out of the sense of security gained by closely attaching to its tradition, and stretched it by the power and love of the Holy Spirit to a stage where it could grow spiritually strong and become a good tree bearing good fruits. The two emphases, charisms and the Holy Spirit, are rediscovered through the charismatic renewal.

Charisms

Hans Küng points out three characteristics of charisms, according to Paul. First, they are "everyday phenomena" which, include not only the gifts that are "exceptional, miraculous or sensational," but also all those

22. Congar, *I Believe in the Holy Spirit Vol. I*, 159.

23. Moltmann, *Church in the Power*, 305.

24. Church of England, *We Believe in the Holy Spirit*, 85.

related to the service and edification of the church, which, as he puts it, are "less striking," such as exhortation, acts of mercy (Rom 12:8), service (Rom 12:7), teaching (Rom 12:7; 1 Cor 12:28), etc.[25] Similarly, McDonnell identifies charisms as ministries and states that they are closely associated with "the normal operation of the day-to-day life of the Church."[26] By pointing out the basic nature of charisms as being a normal way of serving the church, both of them "de-mystify" charisms from being something beyond daily human life, and also de-romanticize them by removing the exclusively supernatural understanding, which otherwise gives the wrong idea about their status in the eyes of the congregation to those who exercise such gifts. Secondly, charisms are diverse rather than uniform in character, so that they can be applied to the personal needs of the individual and achieve different purposes within the church. Hence he rejects the idea of charisms being exclusively connected to the institution. Third, they are universally distributed by the Holy Spirit within the church in the sense that they are not the privilege of one group of people nor do they belong solely to the authority, but are for the entire people of God.[27] Miroslav Volf also raises this point in his discussion on charisms, and he argues that, because of this universality, there is a possibility of "shared responsibility"[28] or, in Suenens's term, "co-responsibility."[29] Every member is responsible for the growth of the church, not just the leaders, as each of them is given charisms by the Holy Spirit to contribute to the whole body.[30] Finally, he affirms that charisms are still available for the church now, in the same way as they were for the early church. Hence, for Küng, the church is intrinsically charismatic in a way "which *includes but goes far beyond the hierarchical* structure of the Church."[31] His view echoes Rahner's open system marked by its charismatic rather than its institutional nature. With its vivid and universal manifestations of charisms, the charismatic renewal demonstrates the fundamental charismatic nature of the church and provides an example of how this open system functions. The charisms universally enrich the ecclesial life

---

25. Küng, *Church*, 239–40; *On Being a Christian*, 485.

26. McDonnell, "Communion Ecclesiology and Baptism in the Spirit," 692.

27. Küng, *Church*, 241–46; *On Being a Christian*, 485.

28. Volf, "Protestant Response," 40.

29. Fountain Trust, "Looking," 7.

30. Volf, "Protestant Response," 40–41.

31. Küng, *Church*, 246.

in a diversified way, and if they disappear it "represents a real impoverishment for the communion."[32] Charisms are the prominent features of the charismatic renewal; however, charisms are actually "the manifestation of the Spirit" (1 Cor 12:7). Therefore, the ultimate purpose of the charismatic renewal is to remind the church of the indispensable role of the Holy Spirit within the ecclesiastical structure who, as a Paraclete, was sent by Jesus after the ascension.

The Holy Spirit, the Paraclete

It is essential to recognize the role of the Holy Spirit as the Paraclete in the church so that there can be a meaningful understanding of the complementarity of institution and charisms. There are plenty of metaphors for the Holy Spirit such as fire (Acts 2:3), wind (Acts 2:2), finger (Matt 12:28; Lk 11:20), cloud (1 Cor 10:1–2), water (John 4:10; 19:34; Rev 22:1–2), breath (John 20:22), and dove (Matt 3:16; John 1:32). These are objects depicting his power in different forms, but none of them refer to him as a subject with a will of his own, and with thoughts, feelings, emotions, and actions. In fact, in the farewell discourse, Jesus uses none of these metaphors for the Holy Spirit, but calls him "another Paraclete" from the Father (John 14:16) which shows his personality as a distinct hypostasis. McDonnell mentions Raymond E. Brown's suggestion that John depicts the Holy Spirit in a "clearly more personal" way than other writings in the New Testament[33] and this is why the term "Paraclete" appears in his gospel to describe the Holy Spirit. Moreover, this term can serve to understand the role of the Holy Spirit in the church better, as he himself is not its object, but a subject who guides, strengthens and encourages his people. Dongsoo Kim emphasizes that John not only refers to the Holy Spirit as the Spirit of Christ, but also as the Spirit of the church.[34] Therefore, I choose to discuss the Holy Spirit as the Paraclete who is a counselor, helper, comforter, advocate, and mediator in the Johannine discourse.[35]

John mentions that the Holy Spirit as the Paraclete abides with and accompanies the church forever (John 14:16–17). Jesus assures the disciples that the Holy Spirit has already dwelt with them and will do so

32. McDonnell, "Communion Ecclesiology," 693.

33. McDonnell, "Response," 296.

34. Kim, "Paraclete," 256, note 5.

35. Congar, *I Believe in the Holy Spirit Vol. I*, 53.

forever by saying, "but you know Him because He abides with you and will be in you." (v.17) The indwelling of the Spirit within believers and the church contains three implications which are coherent with God's indwelling among the Israelites and the tabernacle in the Old Testament. Firstly, it suggests the divine identity of God's people. The Holy Spirit only dwells in those who believe in, and therefore belong to, Jesus, "Whoever confesses that Jesus is the Son of God, God abides in him, and he in God" (1 John 4:15). Similarly, God only dwelt in Israel because it was his chosen nation. After the exodus, God commanded them to build a tabernacle "that I may dwell among them" (Exod 25:8), and he "will meet there with the sons of Israel" and "will be their God" (Exod 29:43, 45). The purpose of God's indwelling was that the Israelites would remember the exodus, which was accomplished by God, so that "they shall know that I am the Lord their God" (Exod 29:46). God acknowledges that the Israelites are his people and affirms that "My soul will not reject you" and "will walk among you" (Lev 26:11–12). Therefore, the tabernacle is a spiritual symbol of the special relationship established by God with Israel, by which he is their Lord and they are his people. Because of this relationship, God dwells among them to be with them, and the tabernacle is a physical place for this meeting. Similarly, the church in the New Testament time and nowadays is also a physical and spiritual symbol representing the special relationship between God and Christians that they belong to God and God is their Lord. The promise of the eternal indwelling of the Paraclete confirms this relationship and divine identity of Christians and the church is the place where they can meet God.

Secondly, the indwelling of the Holy Spirit in the church entails sanctification and holiness. God proclaims that after the tabernacle was built he would "consecrate the tent of meeting and the altar" (Exod 29:44), which suggests that the building and the altar also belong to him and become sacred without any profanity. Similarly, the church is and should be holy, and the same should be true for individual Christians, whom Paul identifies as "the temple of the Spirit" where he dwells (1 Cor 3:16–17; 6:19); so he says, "that is what you are" (1 Cor 3:17). This temple needs to depend on the Paraclete to reprove and purify it, to ensure its constant holiness. With the indwelling of the Spirit, Christians, and the church are the possessions of God; therefore, Paul says, they do not own themselves any more (1 Cor 6:19) and are under God's protection.

Thirdly, the church where the Spirit dwells is the place where God's glory can be found. After Moses finalized the architectural work of the tabernacle by erecting the court around the tabernacle and the altar, and hanging up the veil, the cloud covered the tent and it was filled with God's glory (Exod 40:33–35). Correspondingly, the church constituted by Christians who are the temple of God should also reflect God's glory, so Paul urges the Corinthians to glorify God with their bodies (1 Cor 6:20). Since the church is dwelt by the Paraclete forever, which affirms its special identity of being the possession of God with his holiness and glory, he can work within the church by his teaching and empowering with charisms.

Besides abiding in the church, John notes that the Paraclete is a teacher of truth, a revealer of the hidden future, and the one who reminds them of Jesus' teachings. These functions are reflected in Paul's understanding of charisms. Jesus says to the disciples that this Paraclete is "the Spirit of truth" (John 14:17; 16:13) who "will teach you all things, and bring to your remembrance all that I said to you" (John 14:26) and will also "disclose to you what is to come" (John 16:13–14). Paul also identifies the Spirit as a teacher who gives words and thoughts to the preacher (1 Cor 2:13). Since the Paraclete is identical with Jesus who is "full of truth" (John 1:14) and he himself is "the truth" (John 14:6), his messages to the church will be in accordance with the truth so that it will "continue in the truth." [36] Although John does not mention charisms, his understandings of the functions of the Paraclete are coherent with Paul's teachings on charisms. Prophecy, words of wisdom and knowledge, tongues, interpretation of mysteries convey the teaching of the Spirit, and revelation of the future and hidden knowledge. He also gives fresh enthusiasm in reading the Bible so that the church is kept renewed and revitalized by Jesus' teachings. Therefore, the church can be built up on the truth that Jesus gave in the past, which is brought into present through the endowment of charisms by the Paraclete.

Finally, John implies that this Paraclete is the giver of life to the church, which grows through evangelization with the Spirit. Jesus states that the Holy Spirit is to "testify about Me" (John 15:26) and he empowered the disciples to perform signs and wonders, or in Paul's terminology, charisms, so that people "may believe that Jesus is the Christ, the Son of God; and that believing you may have life in His name" (John 20:

---

36. Stefan, "Paraclete and Prophecy," 283.

31). After Pentecost when the Spirit gave birth to the church by baptizing the disciples and equipping them with charisms, the church grew dramatically, and "the Lord was adding to their number day by day those who were being saved" (Acts 2:47). There is an intimate link between the existence of the church and the Holy Spirit. As Kim puts it "where there is no Paraclete, there is no Christian community. As the disciples without Jesus are unthinkable, so the church without the Paraclete, for John, is unimaginable."[37] What defines a church as charismatic is its openness to the Spirit, the Paraclete, who gives life and charisms.[38] The open system, in Rahner's thinking, is something that is ever growing and active. However, it is not an abstract entity; rather, as Suenens argues, it is something that needs a physical structure. In this structure, the Paraclete should be given the priority to work. As Suenens says, "If God is to be free to act, we need Spirit and life first; then we give it order. Life precedes order." Because of the indwelling of the Paraclete, the church is not purely a sociological institution; rather it is a spiritual temple where human beings can meet God, receive and be reminded of his teachings. The church as an institution needs the breath of the Spirit to revitalize it, and the Spirit needs a physical body within which to work. In this sense, the Paraclete and institution are complementary.

The charismatic renewal brings about what has been lacking and lost in the church throughout history. The lively exercise of charisms and the spontaneous move of the Holy Spirit reappear in many sectors of the church such as liturgy, ministry, sacraments, and mission. However, the charismatic renewal did not aim to abolish the institutional church but to complement it with the restoration of charisms and emphasis of the Holy Spirit. As Suenens says, "The charismatic renewal is not against the institution; it is the life of the institution."[39] It aimed at breathing into the dry bones that they "may come to life" with new sinews, flesh, and skin so that they become "an exceedingly great army" (Ezek 37:5–6, 10). If the breath is the Holy Spirit and the bones are the institution, then Ezekiel's prophecy suggests the complementarity of institution and the Spirit with his charisms. The breath needs a body to be blown into and the body needs the breath to bring it to life. Similarly, the Holy Spirit needs the institution to minister within and the institution needs the

37. Kim, "Paraclete," 269.

38. Sullivan, *Baptised into Hope*, 176.

39. Fountain Trust, "Looking," 9–10.

Spirit to prolong its life. The charismatic renewal is a catalyst for this breathing to take place within the physical structure of the church.

In addition, the charismatic renewal aims to balance tradition and experience, the past and the present. E. Haenchen provides a reason why John uses two distinct verbs, "remind" and "teach" to refer to the function of the Paraclete rather than just one. "Remind" implies an avoidance of stress on the experience in the Spirit in the present and forgetting past tradition, while the word "teach" means the opposite.[40] In the Gospel of John, both tradition and experience are indispensable for the life of the church, and so, the institution which consists of tradition and history and the charisms which denote the current experiences in the Spirit should not be mutually exclusive; rather, the church needs the Spirit to remind and teach so as to keep both in balance. The charismatic renewal demonstrates that "the dynamism of the Spirit does not conflict with the incarnate and the historical"[41] but enriches the past by adding new experience of charisms into the church. If the charismatic renewal restores the complementarity of institution and charisms for the church, it also brings the same emphasis to church unity.

Ecumenism

Ecumenically, institution and charisms are indispensable for churches if there is to be a united church. They are both the means and end. Looking at the wonder of the unprecedented ecumenical developments during the charismatic renewal, charismatics tended to jump to the conclusion that the institutional effort is a waste of time, arguing that it involves a massive concentration on pursuing doctrinal agreement rather than focusing on experience, relying on human effort rather than the Holy Spirit. For example, at the seminar on ecumenical issues at Westminster 1977, Richard Hare claimed, "I believe that basis of unity to be not doctrinal agreement but unity in the Spirit." He was also skeptical about the "agreed statements" as he thought that they were "achieved by the use of subtle ambiguity" and churches would implement them in their own way.[42] Rex Davies, as a staff member of the WCC during the 1970s, also suggests that the charismatic renewal was able to cross boundaries

40. Haenchen, *Commentary on the Gospel of John II*, 128.

41. Suenens, *Ecumenism and Charismatic Renewal*, 33.

42. Fountain Trust, *Ecumenical Issues II*.

because of its emphasis on experiences, gifts, and the Holy Spirit while the ecclesiastical structures hinder ecumenical progress.[43] However, the ecumenical function of the institution should not be underestimated. It is as vital as the experiential aspect found in grassroots unity. The founder of the WCC, W. A. Visser't Hooft, insists that it will be "surely impracticable" to abandon the institution and preserve only the experience and gifts of the Spirit, because the united church cannot "manage without rules and agreed arrangements for its common life."[44] The statement, "Gospel and the Spirit," produced by the Fountain Trust and some Anglican evangelicals in the 1970s, affirms that besides experience, doctrine is also an essential element of unity according to the New Testament; without that, there would be ongoing dangers.[45]

In the mainstream ecumenical discussions, the complementarity of institution and charisms in a united church was also a matter of concern. The first Faith and Order World Conference in Lausanne (1927) recognized that episcopal, presbyterian, and congregational systems each had their place in the structure of the united church. But the members of the Conference did not forget the significant role of spiritual gifts in the united church which they enumerated as teaching, preaching, and spiritual counsel.[46] Lukas Vischer comments that this vision at Lausanne of a united church combined "personal, collegial, charismatic and congregational elements."[47] The following Faith and Order World Conference in Edinburgh (1937) inherited this vision and reasserted that "Our unity is of heart and spirit" based on the common faith of the church as the body of Christ. This spiritual unity is the foundation of the unity expressed by institution and cooperation.[48] Ecumenists such as Carl Braaten also share this vision, which is that besides the institutional aspects, ecumenism should also take into account the pneumatological realm where the Spirit works across ecclesiastical boundaries to bring unity.[49] G. Evans sees the danger of losing the balance between institution and charisms in the united church, and says, "Too much order rigidifies and

---

43. Davis, *Locusts and Wild Honey*, 87.

44. Visser't Hooft, *Has the Ecumenical Movement a Future?*, 34.

45. Fountain Trust, *Gospel and Spirit*, 8.

46. Bate, *Faith and Order*, 469–70.

47. Vischer, "Visible Unity," 28.

48. Hodgson, *Second World Conference*, 259.

49. Braaten, *Mother Church*, 8–9.

creates oppression. Too much spontaneity can produce chaos."[50] The complementarity of institution and charisms for the unity of the church is made visible in the charismatic renewal, and the definition of visible unity, which has been the goal for the mainstream ecumenical movement, is widened by the visible expression of charisms.

Visible unity is based on the dichotomy of spiritual/institutional unity. Visible unity relates to something institutional while invisible unity relates to something spiritual. Based on John 17:21 "that they may all be one . . . so that the world may believe," ecumenists believe that although unity is a spiritual essence, it should be physically expressed by way of shared ecclesial structures, doctrines, and practicing of sacraments and mutually recognized ministry so that the world will believe in Christ. The *Toronto Statement* in 1950 affirms the visible and invisible aspects of churches and asserted that both should be considered necessary for unity.[51] This affirmation of visible unity was developed in detail at the New Delhi Assembly (1961) and the statement has become the central idea and definition of visible unity adopted by ecumenists.

> We believe that the unity which is both God's will and his gift to his Church is being made visible as all in each place who are baptised into Jesus Christ and confess him as Lord and Saviour are brought by the Holy Spirit into one fully committed fellowship, holding the one apostolic faith, preaching the one Gospel, breaking the one bread, joining in common prayer, and having a corporate life reaching out in witness and service to all and who at the same time are united with the whole Christian fellowship in all places and all ages in such wise that ministry and members are accepted by all, and that all can act and speak together as occasion require for the tasks to which God calls his people.[52]

For the Roman Catholic Church there are two symbols of the visible unity. Firstly, they believe that visible unity implies one, holy, catholic, and apostolic Church involved "in the common celebration of the

---

50. Evans, *Church and Churches*, 138.

51. The statement affirms that the WCC "does not 'imagine a church which one cannot see or touch, which would be only spiritual, in which numerous Christian bodies, though divided in matters of faith, would nevertheless be united through an invisible link.' It does, however, include churches which believe that the Church is essentially invisible as well we those which hold that visible unity is essential." (World Council of Churches, "Toronto Statement.")

52. Visser't Hooft, *New Delhi Report*, 116.

Eucharist" which is "the highest sacramental manifestation." Secondly, Vatican II confirms that the Pope is the symbol of the visible unity of the Church, including the unity of bishops and believers. He is the "perpetual and visible source and foundation" of church unity. In his encyclical letter promulgated in 1995, John Paul II identified the Bishop of Rome as "the servant of unity" who "must ensure the communion of all the Churches."[53] Although these two symbols are not universally accepted by non-Roman Catholic churches and they may well be obstacles to the kind of visible unity which they have envisaged, the Roman Catholic Church has opened itself up for dialogue with other churches since Vatican II and it has "*irrevocably*" committed to the ecumenical movement with "the ultimate goal" of "full visible unity."[54]

Ecumenists dichotomize visible and invisible unity by defining them from both the institutional and spiritual perspectives. However, the grassroots unity demonstrated in the charismatic renewal reveals that the boundary between visible and invisible unity is blurred and any clear-cut definition becomes questionable. Visible is about an object being seen, discovered or perceived, and "exposed to view."[55] Indeed, the five international conferences contained a degree of institutional visible unity which could be seen in such things as the concelebration of the Eucharist by ministers from both episcopal and non-episcopal churches and the joint participation of Christians from various traditions. This sharing of the Eucharist was a huge ecumenical advance as it implied a mutual recognition of ministry and membership of the body of Christ.

Moreover, there was also spiritual unity that was visible during the conferences. The practice of charisms such as healing, exorcism, speaking and singing in tongues, interpretation, and prophecy are visually and aurally manifest in the congregation and contribute to unity by reciprocal ministry. The inner love and caring for one another are outwardly demonstrated by the use of gifts with the added physical expression of such things as laying on of hands. This confirms what Christopher Hill notes, "as human beings the spiritual is communicated with and through our physical bodies."[56] The spiritual aspect of unity, which has been regarded

53. John Paul II, "Ut Unum Sint," para. 94, 78, 97; Vatican Council II, "Lumen Gentium," 23, 44.

54. John Paul II, "Ut Unum Sint," 3, 77.

55. *Merriam-Webster's Collegiate Dictionary.* (Electronic Dictionary)

56. Hill, "Route-Planning," 205.

as invisible, is given visual expression with the use of charisms. The semantic spectrum of visible unity is no longer limited to the institutional and sacramental realm, as the WCC and the Roman Catholic Church define it, but is expanded to the spiritual in the charismatic renewal. In this sense, the charismatic renewal strengthens the complementarity between institution and charisms by making both of them visible, and hence there can be institutional visible unity and spiritual visible unity.

Conciliar fellowship[57] is a model which can further develop the complementarities of institution and charisms and connect the official and grassroots level of a visible united church in a charismatic context. It was a concept constructed by the Faith and Order Commission during the meetings in Bristol (1967), Louvain (1971), and Salamanca (1973),[58] which refer to the united church "as a conciliar fellowship of the local churches which are themselves truly united." Each local church shares the catholicity of this united church and in communion with others. Hence, according to the New Delhi statement, sacramentally they celebrate the Eucharist together and receive the same baptism. They mutually recognize one another's members and ministries. The oneness of the church represented in this conciliar fellowship is aimed at fulfilling the shared calling of witnessing the gospel together.[59] The WCC regarded itself as a "transitional opportunity" for the conciliarity of the united church at Uppsala Assembly (1968)[60] and confirmed the definition made in Salamanca at the Nairobi Assembly (1975).[61]

However, this concept has not been developed or implemented any further by the WCC from the 1980s until now. Nonetheless, some ecumenists still insist on its significance. Lukas Vischer, the harbinger of

---

57. In English, "conciliar" is derived from the word "council" which carries two meanings. It can mean the council of a united church attended by representatives of churches or the informal and preliminary meeting of divided churches. Other languages make distinction between these two concepts, such as French (*concile/conseil*), Spanish (*concilio/consejo*), German (*Konzil/Rat*), Latin (concilium/consilium), Greek (synodos/symboulion), and Russian (sobornost/sowjet). Obviously the meaning that ecumenists refer to is the council of a united church. The process where churches are approaching to this goal is called "pre-conciliar." (Keshishian, *Conciliar Fellowship*, 1–2; Vischer, "Unity," 190, note 5; "Conciliar Fellowship and Councils," 503).

58. Keshishian, *Conciliar Fellowship*, 2.

59. World Council of Churches, "Concepts ," 121.

60. Goodall, *Uppsala 68 Report*, 17.

61. Keshishian, *Conciliar Fellowship*, 2.

this concept in 1967, still talked about "churches on their way to a universal council" in an article written in 1989.[62] An Orthodox Archbishop in Lebanon, Catholicos Aram I Kechishian, claimed in 1996 that conciliar fellowship was "the most challenging and promising model for a common vision of unity." In the foreword to Kechishian's book, Mary Tanner expressed her regret that the ecumenical movement had moved conciliar fellowship from the ecumenical agenda.[63] I also believe that conciliar fellowship is a preferable model for visible unity, particularly in the charismatic context. Since it contains both the elements of "council" and "fellowship," it suggests that the united church consists of a central institution which is responsible for the order and doctrines of the church and of the fraternal relationship of member churches at the local level. It is a model that opens up many kinds of complementarity that can be developed, particularly in the charismatic context, as the following three points will indicate.

Uniformity-Diversity

Conciliar fellowship in the charismatic context can develop a complementarity between uniformity and diversity in the church. Ecumenists tend to draw a contrast between uniformity and unity and give negative appraisals to the former and positive ones to the latter. However if a united church is so diversified, how can it be recognized as a truly united church? Without a certain degree of uniformity, the united church will have a lack of order. The council of the conciliar fellowship can settle issues of ecclesiological order, structure, and doctrines and reach agreements which member churches are required to follow. Moreover, facing the social, political, and environmental challenges, the council provides an arena for member churches to find common ground for joint action.[64] Nevertheless, diversity is to be encouraged for maintaining local cultures and the using of charisms. This is because it demonstrates that the work of the Holy Spirit differs from place to place in the variety of gifts and the customs of local churches. It can also maintain the unique aspects of the life of a particular local church. Hence the diverse charismatic elements of the united church can be preserved, but at the same time the church

---

62. Vischer, "Conciliar Fellowship," 501–14.

63. Keshishian, *Conciliar Fellowship*, iv, xi.

64. Vischer, "Conciliar Fellowship," 508.

can be disciplined by the agreed doctrine and order, protecting it both from going astray and from recurring division.

The Council-Churches at Grassroots Level

This kind of complementarity can be interpreted in two ways. Firstly, it holds together the relationship between truth and experience. The council is responsible for identifying and discerning truths, which will then be tested in the experience of churches at the grassroots level. The churches' reactions and responses to what the council has identified will provide a point of reference for future thinking. This upward and downward relationship between the council and churches can be summarized by Vischer's comment, that "the truth of a council becomes evident as the truth when it is tested in the life of the church over a long period of time. A council is deemed to have really spoken for the church and acted for the church when the truth of what it has said is demonstrated in the "reception" of the church."[65] The role of the council is vital in discerning whether the charismatic experiences are from the Holy Spirit and whether they are of the truth, and so avoiding confusion. As Lesslie Newbigin rightly notes, conciliar fellowship can serve to provide for "the imperfect discipleship of each local congregation both the correction and the support of the wider fellowship."[66]

Secondly, conciliar fellowship can bring ecumenical cooperation between church leaders and laity at the grassroots level. The council gathers leaders of local churches to discuss issues, and then they implement them in their local churches with lay people. On the one hand, it avoids the hegemony of ecumenical consensus, which is achieved mainly at the official level and then imposed on the grassroots level; and on the other hand, it avoids the over-spontaneous ecumenical impulse which bursts out at the grassroots level and produces a spark of sentimental and experiential unity, but cannot be sustained without the foundation of faith and order. As the charismatic renewal restores the lay involvement in church ministry through charisms, the cooperation between the official and grassroots level will increase. The conciliar agreements on doctrine and order can also strengthen the grassroots unity nurtured by experience and affection.

---

65. Ibid., 509.
66. Newbigin, "Truly United?," 163.

Holy Spirit-Human Beings

Conciliar fellowship will be a sustainable model of the united church only if the Holy Spirit is allowed to work within it according to his will, as is envisioned in Rahner's open system. This means that the Holy Spirit can act as the Paraclete who abides and accompanies the church, a gathering of Christians with the divine identity of God's chosen people, and reflects the holiness and glory of God. Moreover, this Paraclete should also be allowed to be the teacher of truth, the revealer of the future and hidden facts, and the one who reminds the church of truth in all circumstances. Most important, the Spirit must be allowed to be the constant giver of life so that the church can grow potently in spiritual strength and physical size. As was recorded at Edinburgh in 1937, ". . . the visible unity of the Body of Christ can issue only from the Living God through the work of the life-giving Spirit."[67] The charismatic renewal vibrantly displays the Holy Spirit as the Paraclete through charisms which are essential for the vitality of the church. This can be an example for the conciliar fellowship of the united church both in its council and local churches. The council, if it is to be "genuine," should be a "'Spirit-provoked' event," as Vischer quotes from an Orthodox theologian. He also suggests that the council should invoke the Holy Spirit to work through the council in its search for truth.[68] Hence, although human beings are explicitly present at the council and local churches, they are vessels of the guardian, the Holy Spirit, who is implicitly working through them. This complementariness enables the two kinds of complementarities mentioned above to be maintained and become beneficial to the church and the world. This is because the Holy Spirit himself embodies this complementarity, being the Spirit of both truth and experience, of discipline and spontaneity.

Conciliar fellowship develops three kinds of complementarity within the united church by combining the institution and charisms. It allows room for charisms to be used at the grassroots level while the council monitors and observes them. It also enables for the widened definition of visible unity, both spiritual and institutional, to operate within the united church.

---

67. Hodgson, *Second World Conference*, 252.

68. Vischer, "Conciliar Fellowship," 506, 508–9.

Conclusion

This section explains why institution and charisms should be complementary both in ecclesiology and ecumenism. Although the manifestation of charisms is the main feature, the charismatic renewal does not suggest a replacement of the institution with charisms in churches but promotes the complementarity between the two. It redefines visible unity such that spiritual elements can also become visible when charisms are used and unity is nurtured. To realize this complementarity of institution and charisms visibly in the church united, conciliar fellowship is believed to be the preferable model as it allows other kinds of complementarity to develop. It can also maintain the connection between unity at the grassroots and the official level.

CHRISTOLOGY AND PNEUMATOLOGY[69]

Institution and charisms are respectively christological and pneumatological elements. As a Roman Catholic theologian, Bradford Hinze, points out, "offices founded by Christ and charisms bequeathed by the Spirit" are indispensable for the church.[70] Orthodox theologian John Zizioulas also makes this distinction by defining the church "*in-stituted*" by Christ and "*con-stituted*" by the Spirit. The institution is a "fact" or "*fait-accompli*" while constitution is shaped by human participation.[71] Just as there should be a complementarity between the institution and the charisms for the church and its unity, so also there should be a complementarity between Christology and Pneumatology which form them both. This is so especially because the ecumenism constructed by the WCC and Vatican II has been justified and has sustained itself by Christology, while the charismatic renewal which has an ecumenical character, is understood in terms of Pneumatology, it is necessary to discuss how the two theologies can complement each other ecumenically. In this section, I will firstly review the Christologies of the WCC and the Vatican II and, secondly, discuss the complementarity of these two theologies both ecclesiologically and ecumenically.

---

69. Some parts of this section have been published in Au, "In Search of Complementarity," 9–37.

70. Hinze, "Releasing," 368.

71. Zizioulas, *Being As Communion*, 140.

A Review of WCC's Christologies

Ecumenists admit that Christology dominates the theology of the move-ment and its practices. Since 1910 a "Christocentric Universalism" has gradually developed. Visser't Hooft claims emphatically that "'The World Council of Churches is either a Christocentric movement or it is nothing at all.'" Raiser regards this paradigm as "deliberate"[72] and José Míguez Bonino sees that the center of movement is understood christological-ly.[73] This was particularly so when the church faced new challenges from society, such as Nazism during the second world war, communism, and capitalism on either side of the iron curtain after the war, and then also the growing religious syncretism. The Council was determined not only to safeguard its christological emphasis to counteract these ideologies, but also to apply it universally to all human beings and to the church.[74] This Christocentric Universalism penetrated every sphere of the movement: from the practical side such as mission represented by the International Missionary Council (IMC) and the social service of churches cooperating with one another represented by the Life and Work Movement (L&W), to the building up of theological frameworks by the Faith and Order Movement (F&O).

Initially, the concept of Christocentric Universalism did not occur in the IMC and it deliberately avoided any discussion of faith and order as it claimed that it was "interdenominational" and that its work did not "involve the idea of organic and ecclesiastical union." Instead, its mem-bers were "entirely dependent on the gift from God of the spirit of fel-lowship, mutual understanding, and desire to co-operate."[75] This policy was brought to an end at the Tambaram meeting in 1938 as delegates realized the necessity of searching for theological common ground. They agreed that global evangelization should be based on "the com-mon affirmation of the centrality of Christ and a common conception of the nature and task of the Church."[76] This declaration paved the way for the IMC to converge with the ecumenical movement and from 1948 to become one of the components of the WCC.

---

72. Visser't Hooft, "Calling," 224.

73. Bonino, "Concern," 166.

74. Raiser, "Confessing," 188.

75. Quoted in Visser't Hooft, *No Other Name*, 104.

76. Ibid., 105.

The L&W movement was initiated by Archbishop Söderblom in Stockholm in 1925 in response to the aftermath of the First World War. It aimed "to proclaim the lordship of Christ in all realms of life" through practical work in society.[77] Similar to the IMC, it also avoided considering any doctrinal problems, and the slogan "doctrine divides, but service unites" was used as a justification for this intention. Nevertheless, Christocentric Universalism implicitly dominated the movement. As was stated at a conference, "The nearer we draw to the Crucified, the nearer we come to one another . . . In the Crucified and Risen Lord alone lies the world's hope."[78] Again, this affirmation enabled the movement to cooperate with the IMC and F&O and subsequently became part of the WCC.

The F&O movement played a significant role in constructing Christologies for the ecumenical movement in the early stages and the WCC. The movement's confession of "Lord Jesus Christ as God and Saviour" built a foundation for the ecumenical movement and subsequently became part of the constitution of the WCC. This clearly demonstrates the Christocentric Universalism of the ecumenical movement. Despite the one confession, there were five Christologies emerging between the 1927 conference at Lausanne and the 1968 Uppsala Assembly. Firstly, Christology was discussed in terms of a personal relationship with Christ. At the first and second F&O conferences at Lausanne (1927) and Edinburgh (1937), Christology was an "ice-breaking" topic for delegates who did not know each other, coming as they did from churches around the world, and they compared their points of view regarding Jesus.[79] Apart from touching on such doctrines as Jesus as the second person of the Trinity and the head of the church, they aimed at showing the relationship of Jesus as a Savior to their personal lives especially at Lausanne.[80] At Edinburgh, this topic was only one of the sections on

77. Ibid., 108.

78. Quoted in Visser't Hooft, *No Other Name*, 109.

79. Simonson, *Christology*, vii, 47, 175.

80 The report of Lausanne states, "Through His life and teaching, His call to repentance, His proclamation of the coming of the Kingdom of God and of judgment, His suffering and death, His resurrection and exaltation to the right hand of the Father, and by the mission of the Holy Spirit, He has brought to us forgiveness of sins, and has revealed the fullness of the living God, and His boundless love towards us. By the appeal of that love, shown in its completeness on the Cross, He summons us to the new life of faith, self-sacrifice, and devotion to His service and the service of men." (Bate, *Faith and Order*, 462).

the general topic of the church which included "the church: our common faith," "the church: agreements and differences," "the church and the kingdom of God," "the function of the church," "'Una Santa' and our divisions," ministry and sacraments.[81] In other words, the church was the focus rather than Christ.

Secondly, at Lund (1952), members of F&O began to look into the ecclesiological traditions that shaped Christology.[82] Through the influence of Karl Barth, the F&O movement put the stress on the intimate relationship between the church and Christ, who is the head of the church, and on whom the church relies.[83] A christological ecclesiology was shaped at Lund, and hence Conrad Simonson regards this conference as highly significant in terms of F&O's Christology as it stretched the discussion from the level of considering Christ purely in terms of personal experience to the wider context of ecclesiology.[84]

Thirdly, a cosmic Christology emerged at the New Delhi assembly in 1961. It was proposed by Joseph Sittler[85] to counteract the "angelic Christology" which filters out the physical elements of human beings and their connection with nature regarding redemption.[86] Based on Col 1:15–20, he claimed that redemption is for the whole of nature and human history, which means "all things."[87] He widened the spectrum of redemption from being only for human beings to the whole creation and cosmos,[88] and believed that cosmic Christology could lead to *the possibility for genuine unity.*[89] However, delegates of the Assembly had

81. Hodgson, *Second World Conference*, 231–35, 239–49.

82. Simonson, *Christology*, vii.

83. As the report of Lund states, "'Christ lives in his Church and the Church lives in Christ, Christ is never without his Church; the Church is never without Christ." (Simonson, *Christology*, 72).

84. Simonson, *Christology*, 76.

85. He was a Lutheran professor of the University of Chicago Divinity School.

86. Simonson, *Christology*, 94, 96.

87. Visser't Hooft, *New Delhi Report*, 15.

88. At the assembly, he stated, "A doctrine of redemption is meaningful only when it swings within the larger orbit of a doctrine of creation. For God's creation of earth cannot be redeemed in any intelligible sense of the word apart from a doctrine of the cosmos which is man's home, his definite place, the theatre of his selfhood under God, in co-operation with his neighbor, and in caring-relationship with nature." (Visser't Hooft, *New Delhi Report*, 15).

89. Simonson, *Christology*, 97.

doubts about it because the concept was "too broad." They still adhered to the redemption of humanity without embracing the whole of nature.[90] Two years after the Assembly, cosmic Christology had still not gained much support from ecumenists.[91] For both Barthian theologians, whose approach had been mainly adopted in F&O since 1927, and the Bultmannians, who gained increasing attention in the 1960s, cosmic Christology was regarded as "poetry or nonsense."[92]

Fourthly, in contrast to the breadth of cosmic theology, existential Christology emerged at the Montreal conference (1963). Following on from Bultmann's existentialist approach, theologians such as Ernst Käsemann claimed at the conference that "Christian doctrine is not to be regarded as a statement about reality *as such*, but about reality *for me now*."[93] They focused on the here-and-now reality and the individual who is in that reality. The voice of the existentialists balanced F&O's Christology with a concern about "the inner world of decision-making man," in contrast to the predominantly Barthian emphasis on God's authority over the world.[94]

Finally, a humanity Christology approach appeared in F&O's theology at the Uppsala Assembly in 1968. On the one hand it discussed the humanity of Christ and his salvific work, and on the other hand the creation of a "new human community" through salvation.[95] This approach seems to succeed Bultmannian existential theology since it places the main focus on humanity and the reality that human beings are facing as a result of sin. It also suggests that Christ's redemption is a resolution for the hopeless situation of humanity and leads to the emergence of a new human community.

90. Visser't Hooft, *New Delhi Report*, 16.

91. At the Montreal conference of the F&O in 1963, delegates agreed that God's power and grace could be found in "the world of man outside Church and in nonhuman creation," but they questioned whether they were saved by Jesus and therefore revealed His Lordship. Theologians made the criticism that cosmic Christology enlarged the distance between Christ and human actual life. (Simonson, *Christology*, 119).

92. Simonson, *Christology*, 120.

93. Quoted in Simonson, *Christology*, 119.

94. Ibid., 120.

95. The report reads as follows, "This unity of man is grounded for the Christian not only in his creation by the one God in his own image, but in Jesus Christ who 'for us men' became man, was crucified and who constitutes the church which is his body as a new community of new creatures." (Goodall, *Uppsala Speaks*, 18).

A confession of "Jesus Christ as God and Saviour" precisely and concisely characterizes the christological approach of the ecumenical movement, and from this simple statement the three separate streams, IMC, L&W, and F&O, were drawn together to form the WCC. This phrase was originally used by the Young Men's Christian Association but adopted by the Episcopal Conference in 1910 and appeared frequently in the F&O documents.[96] This confession was a common denominator that the early ecumenists shared, and a criterion for selecting who should be invited to participate in any meetings.[97] Moreover, this phrase also makes clear the nature of the WCC, which is "a fellowship of churches which accept our Lord Jesus Christ as God and Saviour according to the Scriptures and therefore seek to fulfill together their common calling to the glory of the one God, Father, Son and Holy Spirit."[98] As the basis of the Council's constitution, it not only acts "as a point of reference . . . , a source or ground of coherence" for its members,[99] but also an element of the visible unity which they pursued, as expressed in the New Delhi statement.

Visser't Hooft notes that Christocentric Universalism had become a clearer conception by the time of the New Delhi Assembly, and, as it is constructed on this basic confession of Jesus as God and Savior, it became the common ground for the unity and justification of mission.[100] Moreover, by this confession, the WCC was partially able to clear away the suspicion within the Roman Catholic Church about the ecumenical movement. It has subsequently sent observers and representatives

96. Simonson, *Christology*, 22–23.

97. For instance, the initiator of the F&O movement, Bishop Brent, and a layman, Robert Gardiner, took this as the basis for choosing delegates. Gardiner explained at a F&O meeting in 1915 that, "Our attempt is not simply to promote kindly feeling or good fellowship, or even good works, but to reunite all Christian in the one living Body of our Lord, both God and man, incarnate, crucified, buried, risen from the dead and ascended on high, living to-day, the Head over all things to the Church which is his Body, the fullness of him that filleth all in all." In 1920, Brent declared at the pre-liminary meeting in Geneva that "we should confine our fellowship to those who had a common and deep devotion to Jesus Christ, God and Man, and that we should join with them in a conference." (Quoted in Visser't Hooft, *No Other Name*, 106; Quoted in Simonson, *Christology*, 60).

98. Visser't Hooft, *New Delhi Report*, 152; World Council of Churches, "Constitution."

99. World Council of Churches, "World Council of Churches."

100. Visser't Hooft, *No Other Name*, 113.

to the WCC assemblies and meetings such as the F&O Commission. At Vatican II, although there were still disputes over certain doctrinal issues, including those about Christ, there was an appreciation that the ecumenical movement had built its foundation on Christ. In *Unitatis Redintegratio*, a statement says, "We rejoice to see our separated brethren looking to Christ as the source and center of ecclesiastical communion." The Council even adopted this phrase in the New Delhi report to define the ecumenical movement as, "Taking part in this movement, which is called ecumenical, and those who invoke the Triune God and confess Jesus as Lord and Savior."[101] Regarding Christocentric Universalism, this phrase is particularly essential as it sustains and justifies the paradigm, the ecumenical movement and the WCC. It is a foundation for member churches to actualize unity through doctrinal discussions, social services, mission and earnest prayers for unity.

Christocentric Universalism is not just about personal confession of Jesus as God and Savior, but also aims at proclaiming the hope for humanity that Jesus is the King of the world. The early ecumenists, such as Gardiner, implanted this vision into the ecumenical movement.[102] George Bell also claimed that the purpose of a united fellowship was to "proclaim the message of the kingship of Christ, and the meaning of that kingship in action." This proclamation is based on "the sure and certain hope given by the victory of Jesus Christ." This hope is based on the kingship of Christ and it rests on an eschatological promise that this king will come back again and will reign forever.[103] The Evanston Assembly (1954)'s theme "Christ—The Hope of the World" shows that the WCC inherited this legacy of proclaiming the kingship of Christ and hope. The beginning of the report of the Advisory Commission identifies the task of the church as being to spread the message with "all humility and

---

101. Vatican Council II, "Unitatis Redintegratio," 342, note 5, 362.

102. He explained this thought in his letter written in 1919, saying, "Moreover, we believe that the only hope for the future of the world rests in that visible unity of Christians which shall manifest to the world God incarnate in the person of his Son, in Jesus Christ, manifesting himself in infinite love, that his new commandment that we should love one another even as he has loved us, may be the fundamental obligation of mankind in every relation, international, social and industrial." (Quoted in Visser't Hooft, *No Other Name*, 106).

103. Bell, *Kingship of Christ*, 12, 14, 174.

boldness" that "Jesus Christ is our hope," "the sole hope, the whole hope, the sure and certain hope of the world."[104]

This emphasis on Jesus as king and hope is one of the things that Geiko Müller-Fahrenholz describes as "Christology 'from above,'" which is found in most of the ecumenical documents. For him, Christology "from above" is marked by the "incarnational" and "cosmocrator" motifs mainly found in Anglican and Orthodox teachings while, in contrast, Christology "from below" is characterized by the "cross motif" mainly from "the primitive Christian belief." The emphasis on the Christology "from above" tends to portray a victorious Christ instead of a sufferer, a victorious church instead of a suffering church. Raiser criticizes the idea that Christology "from above" promotes a "triumphalist" sense among churches while the actual situation at the grassroots is neglected.[105] Nevertheless, the belief in the kingship of Jesus who is the hope of the world did motivate a number of churches to get involved in the ecumenical movement and to counter the ideological and political forces that were current during the first half of the twentieth century.

A Review of Vatican II's Christology

Adopting the teachings of Vatican I, Vatican II also understands the church from a christological perspective in terms of both the headship of Christ and the ecclesiastical structure.[106] The Council affirms the first of these with abundant analogies such as "the Head of the Body," "the chief corner stone," "the shepherd,"[107] "the necessary door" of the "sheepfold," "the Prince of Shepherds," "the true Vine," and "the one Mediator."[108] Christ built up his body by summoning his disciples to preach the gospel and baptize in his name. Sacramentally, baptism signifies the uniting of the believer with Christ: to suffer, die, and rise with him. It is also a uniting of the believer with other believers to build up the body of Christ. Moreover, his people constitute and share his body by celebrating the Eucharist. Through breaking the one bread, they proclaim that they belong to the same body and the same Lord whose body is for all

---

104. Visser't Hooft, *Evanston Report*, 6, 39.

105. Raiser, *Ecumenism in Transition*, 43, 72.

106. Vatican Council II, "Lumen Gentium," 37.

107. Ibid., 18, 21, 25, 31, 37; "Unitatis Redintegratio," 344.

108. Vatican Council II, "Lumen Gentium," 18–19, 22.

of them.[109] As far as the second matter of ecclesiastical structure is concerned, the documents of Vatican II repeated Vatican I's conception of the hierarchy. This reaffirms that Christ is the Head of the church and Peter was the head of the apostles as Christ promised him the keys of heaven (Matt 16:19; Mark 18:18) and summoned him to shepherd his sheep (John 21:15–17). The Pope is the successor of Peter and he is the chief bishop.[110]

Unlike the ecumenical movement and the WCC, Vatican II's ecumenism does not deal with the personal relationship with Jesus, the cosmic Christ, Christ in the existentialist framework, and Christ and humanity, but it immediately touches on the ecclesiastical nature of the church. It is undeniable that some of Vatican II's repetitions of the concept of the church established by Vatican I does not benefit the realization of visible unity, but its christological and ecclesiological approach and confession of Jesus as God and Savior do provide common ground for a dialogue with non-Catholic churches.

Vatican II's ecumenism is christological because it is based on its christological ecclesiology. As is stated in the introduction of *Unitatis Redintegratio*, "The church established by Christ the Lord is, indeed, one and unique." In the first chapter, "Catholic Principles on Ecumenism," christological elements are not lacking. One of the principles is that Christ "is the principle of the Church's unity." His salvation is to unite the whole world. He founded the church by gathering his people through the apostles "into a unity of faith, hope, and charity." He consecrated the Eucharist for an anamestic purpose and to symbolize the oneness of his body. He also invoked the Father to fulfill his desire for church unity before his death. Therefore, the Council affirms that division is a contradiction of Christ's will.[111] Because of this christologically-based ecumenism, Vatican II regards non-Catholics as "separated brethren" rather than "heretics," as in the pre-Vatican II period, and acknowledges their contribution to the Christian communities and society. It states that the Roman Catholic Church regards those who believe in Jesus and are baptized as "brothers" and "Christians" should be treated "with respect and affection" since they are also united in Christ. It further recognizes baptism as a sacrament with an ecumenical function as it connects all who

109. Ibid., 20.

110. Ibid., note 67, 37–38; "Unitatis Redintegratio," 344.

111. Vatican Council II, "Unitatis Redintegratio," 341, 343–44.

share the same faith together. Furthermore, the Council urges Roman Catholics to "joyfully acknowledge and esteem the truly Christian endowments from our common heritage which are to be found among our separated brethren." This is because Christ also works through them in the areas of evangelism, educational, medical, and psychological services for society, and world peace. Moreover, it also acknowledges that gifts of the Holy Spirit, faith, hope, charity, and conviction about "Christ's words as the source of Christian virtue," can be found among the non-Catholic brothers.[112] The christological ecumenism of Vatican II enables the Roman Catholic Church to regard non-Catholics as Christians and to discover the similarities between Catholics and non-Catholics. That becomes the point of departure for further discussions on specific issues so that more common ground can be found. Walter M. Abbott records that after the promulgation of the *Unitatis Redintegratio*, the Roman Catholic Church was willing to meet with a WCC's working group formed of eight members. Cardinal Bea who was the president of the Secretariat for Promoting Christian Unity declared that the Vatican "greets with joy and fully accepts' the World Council's invitation 'to explore together the possibilities of dialogue and cooperation." The Vatican also desired to establish contacts with churches in the West and East.[113] Hence, christological ecumenism has been a stepping-stone for the Roman Catholic Church to launch its ecumenical work and develop connections with other churches.

Justification of the Complementarity of Christology and Pneumatology

Christology has dominated both the WCC and Vatican II's ecumenism. The role of the Holy Spirit is mentioned, but he does not share the same significance as Christ. Christ seems to be the principle of church unity while the Holy Spirit is the one to realize it. There is lengthy discussion of the former while only a few remarks about the latter, given in a few sentences as supplementary details for the discussion on Christ. It is probably not a misjudgment for Amos Yong to say that the Holy Spirit has been put in "practical (if not actually theological) subordination . . . either to the Word or both Word and Father" in the making of theol-

---

112. Ibid., 345, 349, 364–65.

113. Ibid., note 77, 365.

ogy throughout history.[114] McDonnell suggests that the subordination of Pneumatology to Christology in Western theology implies a perception that sacraments and christological elements come first and then the Holy Spirit. He ironically uses the analogy that this subordination is like putting tinsel to decorate an already full grown tree.[115] This secondary consideration of the Spirit also appears in ecumenism. After observing the ecclesiology of Vatican II, John Zizioulas comments on its christo-centric emphasis and warns that if Pneumatology remains as an auxiliary to Christology and ecclesiology in Catholic theology, the huge gap between the goal and reality of church unity will remain. The internal problems of the Roman Catholic Church, such as the over-domination of institution and clergy, will also persist.[116] The charismatic renewal seems to remind the church of the hitherto inadequate attention given to the Holy Spirit. But I aver that it is not appropriate to concentrate solely on Pneumatology and neglect Christology, as that will repeat the historical problem that has arisen from the overemphasis on Christology. Rather, the complementarity between Christology and Pneumatology, which ecumenism definitely cannot avoid, should be pursued.

The Two Hands of the Father and Perichoresis

This metaphor appears in the preface to Book IV of *Against Heresies* which was written to counter the Gnosticism that Irenaeus regarded as a threat to Christian beliefs between the apostolic period and the third century.[117] Irenaeus suggests that the Son and the Holy Spirit are the right and the left hands respectively through whom the Father fulfills his work in humankind's history. He equally names the Son as Word and the Spirit as Wisdom and argues that, through them, the Father "makes everything, disposes everything, governs everything, gives existence to everything" whether it is "visible or invisible, sense-perceptible and intelligible, temporal for God's plan or eternal."[118] In *Demonstration of the Apostolic Preaching*, he explains why the Son is Word and the Spirit is Wisdom in the context of creation.

---

114. Yong, *Spirit-Word-Community*, 74.

115. McDonnell, *Other Hand of God*, 88–89.

116. Zizioulas, "Doctrine," 22; *Being As Communion*, 123.

117. Irenaeus of Lyons, "Against Heresies," 1; Yong, *Spirit-Word-Community*, 50.

118. Irenaeus of Lyons, "Against Heresies," 87.

> And as God is verbal . . . , therefore He made created things by the Word; and God is Spirit, so that He adorned all things by the Spirit, as the prophet also says, "By the Word of the Lord were the heavens established, and all their power by Holy Spirit." Thus, since the Word "establishes," that is, works bodily and confers existence . . . , while the Spirit arranges and forms the various "powers," so rightly is the Son called Word and the Spirit the Wisdom of God.[119]

He therefore concludes by stating the interdependency of the Son and the Spirit regarding the prophecy about the Son and the redemption achieved by him. As he says, "Thus, the Spirit demonstrates the Word, and, because of this, the prophets announced the Son of God, while the Word articulates the Spirit, and therefore it is He Himself who interprets the prophets and brings man to the Father."[120]

Yong suggests that the reciprocity and unity given in Irenaeus's "two hands" metaphor builds a foundation for the theology of "coinherence of the divine person" which is called *perichoresis* in Greek, *circumincession* and *circuminsession* in Latin.[121] The former Latin word was the first translation and it means "a dynamic interpenetration," and the second one refers to "a lasting and resting mutual indwelling." The verbs of *perichoresis*, *perichoreo*, and *perichoreuo* meaning "mutual resting" and "dancing around with one another." These verbs connote motion and inactivity.[122] The active and inactive connotations of *perichoresis* can be explained in terms of the immanent Trinity, which concerns God as God himself; the mutual indwelling and communication of the three persons *ad intra*; and the economic Trinity which concerns God for us, his mission within history and time, and his communication *ad extra*.

In the immanent Trinity, *perichoresis* suggests the mutuality and "*reciprocal interiority*" which creates a sense of "catholicity."[123] This catholicity enhances the distinctness and subjectivity of each person as they need to rely on the other two to build up their identity. Moltmann suggests that each person has two names depending on their relationship with each of the others. The First person is the Father when relating

---

119. Irenaeus of Lyons, "Demonstration," 43.

120. Ibid.

121. Yong, *Spirit-Word-Community*, 53.

122. Moltmann, "Trinitarian Personhood," 311–12.

123. Volf, *After Our Likeness*, 208–9.

to the Son, and he is also the producer of the Holy Spirit. The Second person is the Son when relating to the Father; and he is the Word when relating to the Holy Spirit. The Third person is the Holy Spirit when relating to the Father; and he is the Light when relating to the Son.[124] The distinctness of each of them does not just manifest that particular person but also the other two. As Jesus says "the Father is in me and I am in the Father" (John 14:11), one can see the Son through the Father and vice versa. The Father and Son also share the glory (John 17:5), truth (John 17:8), and possess the saved (John 17:9) and everything (John 17:10). The Holy Spirit accompanies, originates, "proceeds from the Father," and baptized Jesus in the river Jordan as he was being baptized by water. Hence, the mutual indwelling and resting of the Trinity does not just take place in heaven but also happened on earth when Jesus was fulfilling the Father's salvific plan.

Perichoresis can also be understood in terms of the economic Trinity, as the best translation has the active meaning of "dancing around." To fulfill the tasks for the world, the three persons become selfless. They empty themselves and cooperate with one another to a stage where they give themselves up for the world. The creation of humankind was accomplished by the God of three persons saying, "Let Us make man in Our image, according to Our likeness" (Gen 1:26). The redemption was fulfilled by the Son's willingness to obey the Father and sacrifice himself for humankind. The incarnation of the Word came about by the divine conception in Mary through the Holy Spirit. His "descending and remaining upon" Jesus during the baptism in the river Jordan (John 1:33) and his constant empowerment enabled Jesus to demonstrate the Kingdom of God. Hence people recognized that "God was with Him" and that he was "doing good and healing all who were oppressed by the devil" (Acts 10:38). At the last moment of Jesus' life, the Spirit strengthened him in Gethsemane, on the way to Golgotha and finally on the cross. Facing the suffering of the Son who was made sin, the Father also suffered as he forsook him. It gave him profound pain as he watched the death of his beloved Son. Since the subjectivity of the persons in the Trinity relies on the others to form, the fatal separation causes a drastic alteration of their identities; the Father becomes "Sonless" and the Son becomes "Fatherless."[125] Regarding the suffering of the triune God, Moltmann

124. Moltmann, "Trinitarian Personhood," 312–13.
125. Moltmann, *Experiences in Theology*, 305.

says, "If one suffers, the others suffer too" and he perceives the death of the Son as "an inner-trinitarian event" that relates to the three persons. However, the momentum of the *perichoresis* was not terminated by this separation but it has continued because the Spirit raised up the Son and accompanies the church, which is the body of Christ until the end of time. Hence, the Father's love for humankind is concretized by his Son's incarnation and sacrifice and the Son's ministry is made perceivable by the Spirit's empowerment.

Irenaeus's "two hands" motif and the concept of *perichoresis* justify the pursuit of a complementarity between Christology and Pneumatology for two reasons. Firstly, in terms of personhood, the Son and Holy Spirit are two subjects but they rely on each other to be distinct through mutual indwelling. Secondly, since the genesis, the Father has accomplished his works with both the Son and the Spirit. As Yong says, "To put it crassly, without his hand, the Father is impotent and therefore neither creator nor divine."[126] In other words, neither of them is subordinated to each other in immanent and economic Trinity. As McDonnell rightly remarks, "If the person of the Spirit is not equal to that of the Son, if the mission of the Spirit is not as important as that of the Son, then the Trinity collapses. The Trinity cannot support imbalanced, unequal persons or missions."[127] Hence, Christology and Pneumatology, as methodologies, should be used simultaneously to investigate any aspects of God's works, including the church and its unity. The charismatic renewal vividly shows the potent work of the Spirit for the church and unity. The following section will illustrate this point from the ecclesiological and ecumenical perspectives.

Ecclesiology

The charismatic events such as baptism in the Spirit and charisms reflect the fact that the church is full of *Spiriti praesens* and *Christus praesens*. The former is characterized by its tangibility, visibility, and sensibility while the latter is characterized by its connection of historicality and contemporaneity. Baptism in the Spirit brought about the genesis of the church at Pentecost and it was Jesus Christ who was the baptizer in the Spirit (John 1:33). He had both received the Spirit and given the

---

126. Yong, *Spirit-Word-Community*, 52.
127. McDonnell, *Other Hand of God*, 86.

Spirit "without measure" (John 3:34). He had been anointed by the Spirit and anointed his disciples with the Spirit. Mühlen defines the church as "the continuation of Christ's anointing of the Spirit."[128] Christ enables the church to be full of *Spiriti praesens* and formed by the Spirit who is "the subject of the church's coming-to-be."[129] Although Christ is not physically present in the church, the continuous baptism in the Spirit of believers marks the continuous work of the baptiser and his continuous presence. He breathes into the church with the Spirit, and the Spirit forms the church with charisms so that it becomes "a charismatically marked community."[130] These charisms manifest the *Spiriti praesens* and *Christus praesens* simultaneously and enable the church to see and hear Jesus' words and ministries in the present.

Concerning Jesus' words, the Spirit works in the church as a Paraclete by distributing gifts such as prophecy, words of knowledge and wisdom, and tongues with interpretation; and by reminding them of Jesus' words and teaching as well as revealing the hidden facts according to the truth which is Jesus himself. Since Jesus is the Word, once his words are proclaimed and heard his presence is known in the church. Peter Hodgson, who deals with the meaning of *Christus praesens* suggests that words or language cause a person's presence. He says, ". . . personal presence occurs when recognition is evoked by means of word, including also verbal action or enacted word."[131] *Christus praesens* can be perceived to be more striking when the words that are spoken apply to the present situation of, or to challenges facing, the church.

Moreover, his words are also seen to be effective because what he promised in the past comes into reality. The charismatic renewal shows that Jesus' promises are not just spoken for the disciples alone but also for his church in the ancient past, the present and the future. For example, before his ascension he promised, "but you will receive power when the Holy Spirit has come upon you" (Acts 1:8). This happened at Pentecost (Acts 2) and is still happening nowadays. Through this experience, *Christus praesens* takes place personally in individuals' lives and is witnessed by the church collectively. Hence the baptism in the Spirit

128. Quoted in Volf and Lee, "Spirit and Church," 390.

129. Ibid., 393.

130. Del Colle, "Spirit-Christology," 108.

131. Hodgson, *Jesus-Word and Presence*, 267, quoted in Del Colle, *Christ and the Spirit*, 171.

and the charisms, which immediately bring about the *Spiriti praesens*, simultaneously usher in *Christus praesens* through the proclamation and fulfillment of his words.

Concerning Jesus' ministry, the charisms also plays a vital role in manifesting the *Spiriti praesens* and *Christus praesens*. Miracles, such as physical and psychological healings and exorcism, are surprising but also familiar. They are surprising as they happen in the present day when "supernatural" things seem rare and science is believed to be sufficient to solve daily problems and to improve the standard of living. But they also seem familiar because similar things can be found in the Bible, which records what Jesus and the apostles did in the past. So charisms function as an anamnesis of Jesus who was determined to "work the works of Him (the Father)" (John 9:4) on the one hand, and enables us to continue his ministry "on his behalf and accompanied by him" on the other hand.[132] Hence the Holy Spirit, through charisms, "reflects in us what has already been initiated, originated and brought to fullness and perfection in Christ."[133] The charisms given by the Holy Spirit not only bring about the presence of the giver tangibly, visibly, and sensibly but also the presence of the Spirit anointer who worked on earth in human history and is still working nowadays. The historical and contemporary Jesus is connected by charisms and they are both manifested in the church at the same time.

The charismatic renewal, displayed by its vivid performances of charisms, leads to the vivid presence of the "two hands." Through charisms, the Paraclete brings Jesus' words and ministries into the present, bringing them to mind and making them a reality and so revealing the *Christus praesens*. The church is reassured that the God of Emmanuel is still accompanying it. He, as Smail describes, "is not two thousand years away in the past, remote and retired in heaven, or reserved for an apocalyptic future, but lives to keep his promises to all who turn in expectant faith towards him."[134] The *Christus praesens* mediated by charisms reveals God as a real being and hence the church no longer focuses on the gifts and the giver of gifts, but perceives God himself as God. The experience of God is not just about gaining and exercising the gifts, but about experiencing God himself as the one to

132. Volf and Lee, "Spirit and Church," 391.

133. Smail, "In Tune 2," 3.

134. Smail, *Forgotten Father*, 13.

whom we should relate. He is not only the one from whom we can ask for gifts, but the one to whom we should dedicate our lives.[135] Charisms will then no longer be exercised out of selfishness and self-centeredness, but out of a desire for God's ministry and his kingdom. Since the head of the church is present, the church's identity is confirmed; its ministry on earth, with the help and presence of the Paraclete is continued. As Ralph Del Colle says, "If the *Christus praesens* is in fact God's identity in the church, so too the Holy Spirit does not just 'make relevant' the historical-resurrected Christ but '*is* the *Christus praesens.*"[136] This perichoretic relation or "reciprocal interiority" between Christ and the Holy Spirit is made crystal clear in the charismatic renewal through the use of charisms. It therefore supports the complementarity of Christology and Pneumatology applied to the understanding of the church and its unity in the charismatic context.

Ecumenism

Since the charismatic renewal reveals the inter-relatedness of Christ and Spirit in the church through charisms and baptism in the Spirit, it is reasonable to think that unity can also demonstrate this intimate relation of these two hands. I am going to use Aloysius Pieris' model to develop this point. Although his model is invented for interreligious "core-to-core dialogue through a *communication in sacris* (communion in ritual),"[137] it can also be adopted when discussing the grassroots unity nurtured by the charismatic renewal from the christological and pneumatological perspectives. He suggests three levels of dialogue: primordial experience, which is pneumatological; collective memory, which is christological; and interpretation, which is ecclesial. Although there was no formal ecumenical dialogue in the charismatic renewal, Christians of different traditions, particularly Protestants and Roman Catholics, experienced these three levels and thus a sense of unity ignited and grew. I will interpret these three levels with three respective commonalities which brought about unity among the charismatics.

---

135. Moltmann, *Spirit of Life*, 302.
136. Del Colle, *Christ and the Spirit*, 170.
137. Ibid., 211.

Primordial Experience: Common Experience in the Spirit

Baptism in the Holy Spirit was widely acknowledged as the fundamental and primary experience among charismatics and it led to mutual recognition of one another as members of the body of Christ; hence, a sense of unity was nourished at the grassroots level. The astonishing point for charismatics was that the Spirit was not only poured out on the "born-again" or "true" Christians, but also those who had been regarded as "heretics." Chapters 2 and 3 have provided testimonies of both Protestants and Roman Catholics about their perceptions of each other before and after this common experience in the Spirit. This common experience was a point of departure for their common confession and common life in worship and ministry in the body of Christ.

Collective Memory: Common Confession of Christ as God and Savior

The baptism in the Spirit enabled charismatics to recognize one another as Christians because they discovered that they had a shared memory of salvation. They were prompted by the same Spirit to confess their sins and receive Christ as Savior and had actually believed in the same God. More important, through the use of charisms, they confessed Christ as God collectively, since charisms manifested *Christus praesens*. Volf suggests that "Just as every charisma is a concrete manifestation of Christ's grace, so also is every charismatic activity a concrete form of confession to him."[138] Hence the memory of their personal confession was not only retrieved and made the standpoint for their mutual recognition, but it caused a joint, living, and renewed confession to the Savior as they practiced the use of charisms.

Interpretation: "Common Responsibility" in the Ecclesia[139]

The church is a living interpretation of the love of God, *Christus praesens* and *Spiriti praesens*; and charisms enable members of the Body to make this interpretation tangibly and visibly. Each member is endowed with various charisms by the Holy Spirit for the purpose of edifying one another, instead of being simply for their personal benefit and glory; hence they bear responsibility for each others' spiritual lives rather than depending entirely on the leaders. Volf suggests that this common responsibility entails "*mutual subordination*" and "*interdependence*." Since

---

138. Volf, *After Our Likeness*, 229.
139. Ibid., 230.

there is no one who has the whole set of charisms from the Spirit, they need to be humble enough to be served by others for their physical and spiritual needs, and consequently the "fullness of gifts" can "be found in the entire (local) church."[140] This mutuality expressed by the use of charisms displays the church as a community of love, with the presence of God, and in front of the world. It also cultivates the unity implanted by the Spirit at the grassroots level from the time when the church was established.

Conclusion

These three commonalities reveal the christological and pneumatological factors of church unity, which are brought about by the charismatic renewal at the grassroots level. To conclude, the church and church unity are both established "in Spirit and in truth" or in Irenaeus's terms, in wisdom and in Word. The christologically-oriented ecumenisms of the WCC and the Vatican II have laid the foundation of the unity that the church pursues, but the charismatic renewal has restored the experiential elements in the Spirit, which are indispensable for unity. What is needed is the common confession of truth within this "one flock" of that "one shepherd" (John 10:16). Conciliar fellowship is a model of complementarity between institution and charism, and maintains the unity "in Spirit and in truth, in the eventfulness of the Spirit and in the truth incarnate in Christ"[141] as it deals with the uniformity of doctrine and the diversity of experience at the grassroots level. In other words, it can complement the christological and pneumatological elements within the community.

FINAL CONCLUSION

This chapter attempts to search for the complementarity between institution and charisms, and between Christology and Pneumatology in a charismatic context. With the vivid practice of charisms revealing the overwhelming presence of the Spirit, the charismatic renewal reminds the church of charisms as the other major component, apart from institution, and of Pneumatology as the indispensable partner working side by side with Christology. These two complementarities which are

140. Ibid., 230–31.
141. Smail, "In Tune 2," 7.

brought by the charismatic renewal are realized not only in the church, but also in church unity. From the perspective of complementarity, the definition of visible unity is widened and that includes both institutional and charismatic elements. They usher both *Christus praesens* and *Spiriti praesens* in through charisms and baptism in the Spirit at the grassroots level. They nurture unity among Christians from various traditions. Conciliar fellowship is a model for sustaining the unity with these two complementarities. The grassroots unity that flourished at the five international conferences was imperfect because it lacked the institutional elements to protect, strengthen, and sustain it. The mainstream ecumenical movement is criticized as being fruitless because it lacked the charismatic and pneumatological elements to bring it to life. Hence, when pursuing unity, the Father's two hands should be allowed to work simultaneously so that order and spontaneity, doctrines and experience, and truth and life may be found in the united church, and can be visibly demonstrated in this world.

6

Complementarity, Convergence and Continuity

THIS CHAPTER WILL DEMONSTRATE how ecumenical institutions, including the WCC and Vatican II, and the charismatic renewal, complemented each other in the twentieth century. It will also investigate the convergence of ecumenical streams and ecumenical continuity in modern ecumenical history. At last it will argue that with the legacy of hope left by the charismatic renewal, this historical continuity is extending to the future.

COMPLEMENTARITY

The WCC and the Vatican II: Complementarity of Institutions

The modern ecumenical movement commenced at the Edinburgh Conference in 1910 and subsequently gave birth to the Faith and Order (1927) and the Life and Work (1937) movements. These two movements merged into one to form the WCC in 1948 after being postponed by the two world wars. In 1961 and 1971, the Council included the International Missionary Council at the New Delhi Assembly and the World Council of Christian Education respectively. This whole movement was dominated by Protestant and Orthodox theologians and churches[1] as the Roman

---

1. Some of the Orthodox churches play an essential role in the ecumenical movement and the formation of the WCC. According to Visser't Hooft, there were four main ecumenical titans of the Orthodox churches. Archbishop Germanos, the Exarch of the Ecumenical Patriarch in Western Europe represented the Orthodox church to participate in ecumenical meetings since 1920 and was active in both Life and Work and Faith and Order movements. He bridged the relations between the Orthodox and non-Orthodox churches at the Amsterdam Assembly at which the WCC was founded (1948). Hamilcar Alivisatos of Athens was a "founding father of the ecumenical movement" and was involved in ecumenical meetings since 1920. Stephen Zankov of Bulgaria had been active in the ecumenical movement before and after the second world war.

Catholic Church refused to be involved in it, insisting on the ideology of "return." However, it is not true to say that the WCC therefore did not have any ecumenical impact on the Roman Catholic Church. Although there had not been any official connection with the Vatican after its formation,[2] the Council had had contact with individual Catholic theologians who had ecumenical concerns. In 1949, ten representatives from the WCC met with ten Catholic theologians at the Istina Centre in Paris. The WCC had the opportunity to clear up misunderstandings about the Council from the Roman Catholic side. During the 1950s, there was an important meeting between two Dutch priests, Fr. J. G. M. Willebrands and Fr. Frans Thijssen, and Visser't Hooft in Geneva. In 1960, Visser't Hooft had the first contact with the Vatican official, who was Cardinal August Bea, the president of the Secretariat for Unity in Milan. However, since this meeting was the first official attempt of the Vatican to establish relationships with the WCC, it was kept "top secret" to avoid any public opinion which might possibly hinder the process. Visser't Hooft thought that one of the main influences that the WCC had had on Vatican II was when the Council was drafting the decree on religious liberty. This draft was based on the study on the subject which the WCC and Roman Catholic theologians had done.[3] Visser 't Hooft and some Catholic theo-

However, due to the communist regime in Bulgaria, his church terminated its involvement in the ecumenical movement. Nevertheless, he still endeavored to defend the WCC in Eastern Europe. Patriarch Athenagoras of Constantinople was described by Visser't Hooft as a "farmer" of the WCC. He appointed a permanent representative of the Ecumenical Patriarchate at the World Council's headquarters in Geneva in 1955. He brought plenty of Orthodox churches to the WCC as members. The communist regime from the Union of Socialist Soviet Republics across Eastern Europe caused the Orthodox churches in Rumania, Bulgaria, Yugoslavia, and Poland to keep distance from the WCC except those in Greece and Cyprus. However, with the Council's endeavor under the leadership of Visser't Hooft and some Orthodox church leaders, these churches of the communist countries (including USSR), together with six other churches in Eastern Europe, became members since 1961. Visser't Hooft regards these Orthodox Church leaders with "deep gratitude" as they opened up new possibilities for the ecumenical movement and played a significant role in the formation of the WCC. He notes that "without the full contribution of the East we cannot be truly ecumenical." (Visser't Hooft, *Memoirs*, 254–56, 260, 270, 274–75, 312.)

2. Visser't Hooft, *Memoirs*, 326.

3. Ibid., 319–20, 323, 328, 336. In 1957, the Central Committee of the WCC decided to launch a study on religious liberty in the light of the oppression which was made against the Protestant churches by Roman Catholic churches in Spain and Colombia. The Roman Catholic Church regarded this study as an antagonism and the misunderstanding between the WCC and the Roman Catholic Church was deepened. The

logians believed that the convention of Vatican II was partly due to the effort that the WCC had made to try to build up relationships with individual Catholic theologians and Catholic officials. He said, "Had Joseph Cardinal Ritter of St Louis not been right when he said that Pope John had been divinely inspired when he called the Vatican Council and that 'some of the inspiration that came to Pope John from heaven came via the World Council of Churches?'"[4] Vatican II was a significant ecumenical milestone for the Roman Catholic Church. Since then it has opened itself to engage in dialogues with other churches, and has become the second ecumenical stream. Tillard regards the WCC and Vatican II as "the great Christian grace of our century" given by the Holy Spirit, which are in "necessary complementarity."[5]

Vatican II and the Charismatic Renewal: Institution Complemented the Charismatic Renewal

The complementarities of institution and charisms, and Pneumatology and Christology can be clearly found in the relation between Vatican II and the charismatic renewal. Without the Council, Catholic charismatic renewal would have been less likely to happen and for grassroots unity to grow. This was because the Council revolutionized the ecumenical principle of the Roman Catholic Church, changing it from an insistence on "return" to an openness to dialogue; and from regarding non-Catholics as heretics to regarding them as Christian with the term, "separated brethren."

For centuries, the Roman Catholic Church has regarded itself as the true church and maintained that non-Catholic churches should return to the mother church for visible and spiritual unity. There can be no question that Vatican II transformed the Church ecclesiologically, liturgically, sacramentally, and ecumenically, but even so the mindset of "return," which had been rooted within the church since the Reformation in 1517, could not be eliminated instantly. In the pre-Vatican II period, the announcement that the Roman Catholic Church regarded itself as

---

WCC invited Dr. Angel Carrillo de Albornoz, who had been a Spanish Jesuit but left the church, to write the decree. It was widely accepted by Roman Catholics, Protestants and Orthodox who had been dealing with the issue and eased the division which had arisen. (Visser't Hooft, *Memoirs*, 325–26.)

4. Visser't Hooft, *Memoirs*, 336.

5. Tillard, "Ecumenism," 218.

the "true church" can be found in Pius XII's 1943 Encyclical Letter on the Mystical Body of Jesus (*Mystici Corporis Christi*), in which he said,

> If we would define and describe this true Church of Jesus Christ—which is the One, Holy, Catholic, Apostolic and Roman Church—we shall find nothing more noble, more sublime, or more divine than the expression "the Mystical Body of Christ"— an expression which springs from and is, as it were, the fair flowering of the repeated teaching of the Sacred Scriptures and the Holy Fathers. [6]

Walter Abbot recorded that for many decades, the Roman Catholic Church officially prayed for church unity for eight days in January, but the prayer was based on the hope of the return of Protestants to the Roman Catholic fold and the termination of the schism with the Orthodox Church.[7] Pope Pius XI proclaimed in his encyclical *Mortalium Animos* in 1928 that

> For the union of Christians can only be promoted by promoting the return to the one true Church of Christ of those who are separated from it, for in the past they have unhappily left it. To the one true Church of Christ, we say, which is visible to all, and which is to remain, according to the will of its Author, exactly the same as He instituted it. [8]

The use of the idea of "return" has gradually decreased since the pontificate of John XXIII but the ideology has not faded completely. In 1960, the Pope invited the Archbishop of Canterbury, Geoffrey Fisher, to Rome which was an action unprecedented since the fourteenth century.[9] The Pope talked to the Archbishop about "the time when our separated brethren should return to the Mother Church." However, the Archbishop stated clearly to the Pope that the unity of the church would not happen just by waiting for the Protestants to return to the Roman Catholic Church, but it would be achieved if both the Protestants and Roman Catholics worked together for this goal.[10] Eventually, in 1962, the Pope

---

6. Pius XII, "Mystici Corporis Christi," para. 1.

7. Abbott, "Ecumenism," 336.

8. Pius XI, "Mortalium Animos," para. 10.

9. Butler, *Dying to Be One*, 121; Hastings, *History of English Christianity*, 522.

10. Adrian Hastings reconstructs this conversation in the following way, "At that point Fisher interrupted: 'Your holiness, not return.' The Pope looked puzzled and asked, 'Not return? Why not?' to which Fisher replied: 'None of us can go backwards,

launched "an Ecumenical Council for the whole Church"[11] and that was Vatican II, and he particularly sought for possible reconciliation with Protestants.[12] The Council Fathers carefully avoided the word "return" in the documents, as Archbishop Casinier Morcello of Saragossa, Spain, said, during the Council, "We know that our separated brethren completely regret the invitation to 'return.' The idea of 'return' is intolerable to them and dries up at the roots any possibility of working together."[13] Although the word "return" does not appear in "Unitatis Redintegratio," the ideology still implicitly governs the Catholic principle of ecumenism. For instance, the Council acknowledges that division is a sin shared by both the Roman Catholic Church and Protestants, and that "men of both sides were to blame,"[14] but it only believes that the "separated brethren" have lost the unity, saying,

> Nevertheless, our separated brethren, whether considered as individuals or as Communities and Churches, are not blessed with that unity which Jesus Christ wished to bestow on all those whom He has regenerated and vivified into one body and newness of life—that unity which the holy Scriptures and the revered tradition of the Church proclaim.[15]

This statement is confirmed by Cardinal Bea, the chairperson of the Secretariat of Unity which was begun by John XXIII in the 1960s.[16] This claim is based on the conviction that the Roman Catholic Church is the only church that can bring full salvation and it says in the same paragraph,

> For it is through Christ's Catholic Church alone, which is the all-embracing means of salvation, that the fullness of the means of salvation can be obtained. It was to the apostolic college alone, of which Peter is the head, that we believe our Lord entrusted

we are each now running on parallel courses; we are looking forward, until, in God's good time, our two courses approximate and meet.' The Pope paused to think about this and then said, 'You are right.'" (Hastings, *History of English Christianity*, 523.)

11. Abbott, "Ecumenism," 336.

12. Kilian McDonnell states that Vatican II was mainly concerned about the unity with Protestants rather than Orthodox. (McDonnell, "Ecumenism," 80.)

13. Quoted in Leeming, *Vatican Council*, 102 note 4.

14. Vatican Council II, "Unitatis Redintegratio," 345.

15. Ibid., 346.

16. Leeming, *Vatican Council*, 110.

all the blessings of the New Covenant, in order to establish on earth the one Body of Christ into which all those should be fully incorporated who already belong in any way to God's People.[17]

There can be no doubt that Vatican II moderated the standpoint of the Roman Catholic Church as the true church and the "Lumen Gentium" states that, "This Church, constituted and organized in the world as a society, *subsists in* the Catholic Church."[18] However, Kilian McDonnell suggests that "subsists in" conveys "ambiguity," and that the Roman Catholic Church did not absolutely negate the status of trueness. He assertively concludes that "The Roman Catholic was not, of course, thereby relinquishing its claim to be the unique historical realisation of this Church." Therefore, the Catholic principle of ecumenism has not in fact departed from the affirmation of being the true church nor from the deeply-rooted ideology of "return." Orthodox and Protestant theologians observed that "Rome-centeredness" in the Decree. They warned that if the Roman Catholic Church did not fully recognize them as true churches, there will be no future for ecumenism.[19] McDonnell noticed that the bilateral dialogues after Vatican II had "reinforced" this Rome-centeredness and that "Rome is the center, and the center has bilateral relations with other churches."[20]

Although the mindset of return was still embedded in Vatican II ecclesiology and ecumenism, the Council indirectly acted as a catalyst to the grassroots unity between Protestants and Roman Catholics in the charismatic renewal, which could be seen at the five international conferences. During the Council, there was a new openness toward the Holy Spirit, as du Plessis, an observer at the Council, recorded, "Then I began to discern and I discovered what the Holy Spirit was doing. I could literally see and hear and feel the breezes of the Spirit in St Peter's Basilica."[21] Pope John XXIII, who convened the Council, prayed that the Holy Spirit would "pour forth . . . the fullness of Thy gifts upon the Ecumenical Council" and "renew Thy wonders in this our day, as by a new Pentecost."[22] Paul VI who succeeded him in September 1963 contin-

17. Vatican Council II, "Unitatis Redintegratio," 346.

18. Vatican Council II, "Lumen Gentium," 23.

19. McDonnell, "Ecumenism," 72–73, 79; Cavert, "Response," 369.

20. Ibid., 80.

21. Du Plessis, "Renewal," 21.

22. "Prayer of Pope John XXIII," 793.

ued the ecumenical task of the Council and declared his determination to "promote that mystical unity which Christ left to his Apostles as the most precious and authentic heritage and as his supreme exhortation."[23] However, when both the Popes prepared and launched the Council, they did not anticipate the kind of renewal that they had envisioned would come just two years later and would be a greater fulfillment than they had expected. As Cardinal Suenens commented, "a retrospective view confirms our opinion that the Council acted in a prophetical way without realizing it, by expressing its faith in the charisma."[24] He identifies the renewal as "an extension of that current of graces which was and remains Vatican II" and he saw the manifestations of the renewal echoing the vision of the Council.[25] Edward O' Connor regards the Council as the *Magna Carta* of the charismatic renewal, which laid a theological foundation for the renewal and kindled a desire to pursue the ideals of a renewed church filled by the Holy Spirit.[26] Both Peter Hocken and Julia Duin argue that Vatican II prepared Roman Catholics, both clergy and laity, to receive the grace of the charismatic renewal which had originated in Protestant circles.[27] As a historian, Adrian Hastings also recognises the interrelation of Vatican II and the charismatic renewal. He sees that the Council was "a new leaven" for the renewal and the renewal was "a vast new forum" for the Council.[28] The late Pope John Paul II saw the Council as a new era for the Catholic Church and constantly related it to renewal in his addresses. He believed that the renewal was one of the results of the Council which brought new life to the church and new experiences of the Holy Spirit.[29] On 15 May 1987 at the Sixth International Leaders' Conference in Rome, he says, "The vigour and fruitfulness of the Renewal certainly attest to the powerful presence of the Holy Spirit at work in the Church in these years after the Second Vatican Council." On 14 March 1992 at the International Catholic Charismatic Renewal Organisation Council in Rome, he proclaims, "The emergence of the Renewal following the Second Vatican

23. O'Connor, *Pope Paul and the Spirit*, 112.

24. Quoted in Smeeton, "Pentecostal," 36.

25. Suenens, *Ecumenism and Charismatic Renewal*, 22.

26. O'Connor, "Hidden," 184.

27. Hocken, *Spirit of Unity*, 3; Duin, "Catholics," 25.

28. Hastings, *History of English Christianity*, 558.

29. http://www.universidadesrenovadas.com/english/renewal/html.

Council was a particular gift of the Holy Spirit to the Church." On 4 April 1998 at the National Service Committee of the Italian "Renewal in the Spirit" in Rome, he declares, "The Catholic charismatic movement is one the many fruits of the Second Vatican Council, which, like a new Pentecost, led to an extraordinary flourishing in the Church's life of groups and movements particularly sensitive to the action of the Spirit." Although the Council did not plan the charismatic renewal in order to fulfill its vision for the Roman Catholic Church, its openness and new understanding of some doctrinal issues such as ecumenism, laity, and liturgy wrought "a profound psychological change on" Roman Catholics, as Matthew F. O'Keeffe suggests. The teaching in the documents eventually became essential guidance for Catholic charismatics during the renewal,[30] particularly on charisms, laity, and liturgy.

Charisms

The Council's recognition of the importance of charisms for the church and unity is illustrated in "Lumen Gentium."[31] The charisms referred to are not only the supernatural ones, but include "the most outstanding or the more simple and widely diffused." Ecclesiologically, all of them "are exceedingly suitable and useful for the needs of the Church" and they equip members of the body to be "fit and ready to undertake the various tasks or offices advantageous for the renewal and upbuilding of the Church."[32] Ecumenically, the Council recognises that charisms enable unity to flourish as they are granted to everyone to mutually support and strengthen one another. It states, "Thus through the common sharing of gifts and through the common effort to attain fullness in unity, the whole and each of the parts receive increase." Since there is a diversity of charisms, the unity that is ushered in is not that of uniformity but of diversity.[33]

The Council's ecclesiological and ecumenical teachings on charisms paved the way for the Catholic charismatic renewal since they prepared Roman Catholics to receive charisms from the Spirit. Hocken confirms that they became realities in the life of the Roman Catholic Church

---

30. O' Keeffe, "Investigation," 30, 224.

31. "Dogmatic Constitution on the Church."

32. Vatican Council II, "Lumen Gentium," 12, note 41, 30.

33. Ibid., 13, 30–31, note 42.

during the renewal.[34] However, the scope of influence that the charismatic renewal had was actually much wider than just in one church. The mutual edification through charisms was found not only in the Roman Catholic Church, but also in congregations which included Protestants as well as Roman Catholics in some charismatic events such as the five international conferences. They gathered together to worship and mutually edify one another with charisms such as tongues, healing, prophecy, and intercession. Gradually, a sense of unity, which could be attributed to the Council's teaching on charisms, grew among the Roman Catholics and Protestants.

Laity

The Council's acknowledgement of the role of laity was also important for the grassroots unity to flourish in the charismatic renewal. For the Council, it was difficult to construct a theology on laity because the role of laymen in the church had not been seriously considered.[35] There was not much official material for reference apart from some works by a few theologians. Nevertheless, the Council persisted in the task because "the laity are the People of God. They are the Church—co-responsible with bishops, priests, and religious for Christ's ministries on earth."[36] Eventually the document, "Apostolicam Actuositatem"[37] was promulgated to assist with the teaching on laity in "Lumen Gentium." The discussion in the following paragraphs is based on these two documents.

The Council consciously avoided the negative definition of laity as a non-ordained group of people but declared that they were constituents of the "People of God" apart from ministers. This identity as God's people is determined by their baptism and participation in various ministries.[38] These baptized people share the priesthood which is empowered by the anointing of the Holy Spirit so that they can serve in the church and the world. This anointed priesthood is concretely expressed in the exercise of gifts which are granted to every member of the body of Christ. The Council affirms "the right and duty" of laymen to use the gifts for the church and the world, and it encourages them to "make use of" them

34. Hocken, "New," 130.
35. Smeeton, "Pentecostal," 41.
36. Work, "Laity," 487–88.
37. "Decree on the Apostolate of the Laity."
38. Vatican Council II, "Lumen Gentium," note 27, 25–26; note 163, 57.

but to co-ordinate with others in the church so that the sense of community will be maintained. With the empowerment of gifts, each individual can be "a witness and a living instrument of the mission of the Church herself, 'according to the measure of Christ's bestowal (Eph 4:7).'" The Council sees that the priesthood of laity, empowered by the Spirit who bestows gifts on each individual, is the continuation of Christ's priesthood so that his ministry will be carried out unceasingly.[39]

The Council's affirmation of the priesthood of the laity with the endowment of gifts was realized in the charismatic renewal and this indirectly nurtured the grassroots unity. Hocken believes that the Council provided guidance for laymen's involvement in leadership during the charismatic renewal in Catholic circles such as prayer groups and communities.[40] When Catholic charismatics gathered with Protestant charismatics, as happened at the five international conferences, they shared the same priesthood given by Christ and empowered by the Holy Spirit. This shared priesthood created a bonding, as they believed in the same high priest, Jesus Christ, to whom it referred. They rediscovered the common denominator as being members of the Body of Christ and they built up one another with charisms. They then both experienced the *Christus praesens* and *Spiriti praesens* simultaneously. The Council's acknowledgement of the essential role of the laity in the church and encouragement of the laity's involvement in ministries indirectly contributed to the grassroots unity that grew out of this shared priesthood in the charismatic renewal.

The Liturgy

The Council's reformation of the liturgy opens up the possibility of spontaneous worship and unity among worshipers. Pope Paul VI stressed that the liturgy was "in intrinsic worth and in importance for the life of the Church."[41] The Council's document, "Sacrosanctum Concilium"[42] shows clearly the significant role of the Council in dealing with liturgy. It recognises how the liturgy enhances the spiritual life, enables individuals and churches to cope with the challenges of the world, and brings unity within the church itself. Therefore, the liturgy is "the summit" and

39. Ibid., 10, 27, 33–34, 59–60; "Apostolicam Actuositatem," 3, 491–92, 494.

40. Hocken, "New," 130.

41. McNaspy, "Laity," 133.

42. "Constitution on the Sacred Liturgy."

"the fountain" whereby power is released to the church. The Council stresses that liturgical activities involve the whole church community and are about the togetherness of the People of God offering sacrifices. The Council refers to this as "the sacrament of unity." The main purpose of this emphasis is to ensure that worshipers participate in the liturgy "knowingly, actively, and fruitfully" and this is something about which ministers should be particularly concerned. As the statement goes, "Mother Church earnestly desires that all the faithful be led to that full, conscious, and active participation in liturgical celebrations which is demanded by the very nature of the liturgy." To achieve this goal, the Council enumerated a number of actions to be taken. For example, it promoted a wide and frequent use of scripture and recruited liturgical experts to revise liturgical books with some urgency.[43] But perhaps allowing the use of the vernacular for the liturgy was what most enabled the Roman Catholic Church to achieve this goal.[44] "Sacrosanctum Concilium" states that the use of mother tongues is only valid in "reading and directives, and to some of the prayers and chants," but not in the whole Mass. However, in 1967, Pope Paul VI extended the allowance to canon and so liturgical texts were translated or revised, and a huge reduction of the use of late medieval prayers occurred subsequently. After testing this out in some churches, the Council reached the conclusion that this new regulation might "frequently be of great advantage to the people" as it had "received generally enthusiastic acceptance by the faithful."[45] Hastings gives high praise to the Council for its determination to transform the liturgy with such "speed and decisiveness." Noticing the fact that the Roman Catholic Church had insisted on the Latin Mass for more than five hundred years despite strong objections from the reformers, he boldly concludes that "no Catholics in the fifties could have imagined what was about to happen. No young Catholic in the seventies could easily imagine what church worship had been like twenty years earlier."[46]

The Council's recognition of the importance of the liturgy and the significant practical transformation that followed paved the way for the grassroots unity in the charismatic renewal. The use of vernacular

43. Vatican Council II, "Sacrosanctum Concilium," 137, 142, 143 note 17, 144, 147.

44. Ibid., 150; Hastings, *History of English Christianity*, 526.

45. Vatican Council II, "Sacrosanctum Concilium," 150–51, note 4.

46. Hastings, *History of English Christianity*, 526.

language enabled worshipers to understand the content of prayers and hymns so that worshipers could express themselves freely. It hence opened the possibility for the vertical communication between God and people as well as horizontal communication of people with each other. It then fertilized the soil for unity among the laity at the grassroots level. Hence in the charismatic renewal Roman Catholics across the world could not only express themselves in their own languages, but could also enjoy spontaneous and dynamic worship "knowingly, actively, and fruitfully" in the Holy Spirit. Together with Protestants, this linguistic liberation of the liturgy enabled them to worship with one accord in the Spirit and the grassroots unity was gradually nurtured out of this freedom.

The renewed theological understandings of charisms, laity, and the liturgy in Vatican II prepared the way for Catholic charismatic renewal. They were guidance for Catholic charismatics regarding their renewal experiences, and so the Catholic charismatic renewal contained both praxis and orthodoxy. They enabled the Catholic charismatic renewal to join other streams of renewal and this led to a unity at the grassroots which was unprecedented since the Reformation. In the relationship of Vatican II and the charismatic renewal, we can see that with theological guidance, the official ecumenical institution complemented the actual experience of grassroots unity during the charismatic renewal.

The Charismatic Renewal and the WCC:
The Charismatic Renewal Complemented the Institution

David du Plessis, who attended some of the meetings and assemblies of the WCC, bore witness to the way that the flame of renewal permeated its deliberations. There were some members who were interested in the renewal and eager for the personal experience of baptism in the Spirit, for example. They were leaders who were old and young, global and local. He "was deeply stirred by the hunger in the hearts."[47] He was appreciative of the fifth assembly in Nairobi in 1975 where the charismatic renewal was taken seriously. The General Secretary, Philip Potter, called it a "charismatic fellowship." Du Plessis saw charismatic prayer meetings taking place every evening with 1,000 people attending and commented that "there was enough 'leaven' to leaven the 'WHOLE LUMP.'"[48] He

---

47. Hollenweger, "Extraordinary."
48. Quoted in Robinson, "To the End," 237.

concluded that "the largest and most effective charismatic movement is found in the fellowship of the WCC" as well as in Catholic circles.[49]

However, the WCC's actual response to the charismatic renewal was rather indifferent. They did not realize the necessity for a study on the relation between the Council and the renewal until the late 1970s. In terms of ecumenical contribution, it could be said that if the WCC contributed to the launching of Vatican II, as was suggested above, then the Vatican should also be regarded as motivating the WCC to engage in serious research into the renewal. Jerry Sandidge notes that the Roman Catholic-Pentecostal dialogue prompted the WCC to put such a study into their agenda.[50] The first meeting was held in Rostrever, Northern Ireland in 1977,[51] and this was followed by another one held by a sub-committee on Renewal and Congregational life on "Spirituality and the Charismatic Renewal" in Stony Point, US and Schloss Schwanberg, West Germany in 1978. The study was finalized in a consultation in Bossey, Switzerland in 1980.[52] One of the speakers at Schloss Schwanberg, Walter Hollenweger, openly criticized the WCC for the late recognition of the need for studying renewal, whereas the Vatican had already taken it seriously. He described it as "astonishing."[53] Robinson thinks that this late realization of the need for a study was due to the twofold nature of the WCC. First of all, it is an organization where representatives of churches discuss issues about which they are concerned and look for so-lutions, but it is not a church where people share life together. Secondly, the WCC was regarded as equivalent to the ecumenical movement it-self, and since the charismatic renewal was also seen as such, Robinson thinks that there was a "conflict of interest." Add to that the contrasting ecumenical style of both movements, and it is not surprising that they were not able to cooperate with each other and the WCC found that it was difficult to go beyond its own usual practices.[54] In addition to these reasons, I would like to add one more, which I think is the most obvious one. The official research on the subject was late in taking place because the General Secretary, Philip Potter, was late himself in discovering the

49. Du Plessis, "Renewal," 22.

50. Robinson, "To the End," 238.

51. Harper, *This Is the Day*, 48.

52. Bittlinger, "Introduction," 2.

53. Hollenweger, "Towards," 21.

54. Robinson, "To the End," 240–41.

ecumenical significance of the renewal. In his letter presented at Bossey Consultation, Potter admitted that not until the late 1970s had he noticed the huge impact of the renewal and the abundant related literature that had been published in the previous fifteen years, even though this had already filled four book shelves of the Council's library. He said, "This was quite a discovery for me."[55]

This enlightening "discovery" led him to acknowledge that the charismatic renewal "certainly confirms the goal of the ecumenical movement." This was clear from the grassroots ecumenical initiatives of praying, acting, and worshiping together. He pointed out three ways in which the charismatic renewal complemented the WCC ecumenically. First, in that the renewal had successfully linked the Roman Catholic Church, Protestant churches, and the Orthodox Church together. It to some extent smoothed the ecumenically rocky road, making it possible for the WCC to make greater progress. Secondly, Potter thought that the charismatic renewal renewed the "self understanding of the World Council of Churches." The WCC saw its authority as brought about by the "inherent truth and wisdom" of what it did. But the renewal complemented that with the pneumatological emphasis that the Holy Spirit was the ultimate authority rather than tradition and rules. Finally, the renewal assisted the WCC in carrying out programs for the unity of churches and of humanity, and in realizing the goal of unity in diversity.[56] Although Potter recognized how the charismatic renewal could complement the WCC after the Bossey Consultation in 1980, it was not until 1991 that it paid serious attention to the role of the Holy Spirit in ecumenism when it launched the seventh Assembly in Canberra, entitled "Come, Holy Spirit—Renew the Whole Creation," and started a Joint Working Group between the WCC and the Pentecostals in the following assembly in Harare in 1998.[57]

The WCC has not given as much official recognition of the charismatic renewal as the Vatican has. During the 1970s, Pope Paul VI appointed Cardinal Suenens to provide pastoral guidance for the renewal in the world and established the Catholic Charismatic Renewal International Information Office in Brussels.[58] He gave a warm address

---

55. Potter, "Paper," 75.

56. Ibid., 78–79, 85–86.

57. Robeck, "World," 1215–16.

58. Thigpen, "Catholic," 465.

at the Third International Congress of the charismatic renewal in 1975 in Rome.[59] The succeeding Popes, John Paul II and Benedict XVI, both acknowledged the significance of the charismatic renewal for the church and unity.[60] From the 1960s until now there has been relatively steady support for the renewal from the Vatican rather than from the WCC. The complementarities between the official and grassroots level, institution and charisms, as well as Pneumatology and Christology were found to be more obvious in the relationship of the charismatic renewal to Vatican II than to the WCC. If the WCC had discovered the ecumenical significance of the charismatic renewal earlier, it could have drawn its member churches' attention to it and got involved in the renewal, and then the grassroots unity between Protestants and Roman Catholics might have been stronger.

CONVERGENCE

Based on the above illustration of the complementarity of institution and the charismatic renewal, I suggest that modern ecumenical history can be interpreted as a convergence of three ecumenical streams: the WCC, Vatican II, and the charismatic renewal. Suenens poetically describes the convergence as "two branches of the same river, springing from the same source, washing the same banks and flowing down to the same sea." He notices the complementarity between them, saying that they "lend strength to one another, and that we are dealing with one and the same action, one and the same impulse of God, one and the same internal logic." [61] Rex Davis believes that the ecumenical movement and charismatic renewal aimed at the same purpose and that was "the restoration of the church to both unity and fullness of life."[62] Therefore, the charismatic renewal, and even its "ancestor," the Pentecostal movement, should be seen as part of ecumenical history, which is illustrated in the following chart.

---

59. "Pope Paul," 1.

60. http://biblia.com/christianity2/3b–charismatics.htm.

61. Suenens, *Ecumenism and Charismatic Renewal*, 4.

62. Rex Davis, *Locusts and Wild Honey*, 87.

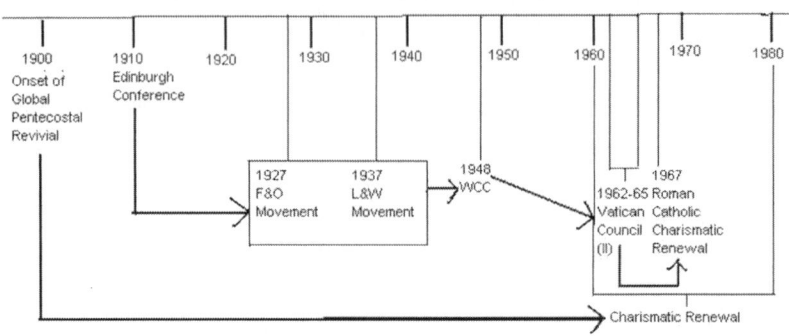

The complementarity of institution and charisms enables us to see the convergence of the three streams in modern ecumenical history and, what is more, to see the continuity.

CONTINUITY

The ecumenical flow has been moving in different streams, which appeared in different periods in the twentieth century. In the first six decades, institution played a dominant role in the ecumenical movement. Then the flow was continued in the mid 1960s to the 1970s by the charismatic renewal at the grassroots level with the functioning of charisms. This ecumenical flow has continued until now despite the current gloomy situation and the declining ecumenical influence of the charismatic renewal. But the indications are that the charismatic renewal brought about an eschatological continuity of the ecumenical movement, which connects the past, the present, and the future.

After the golden age of the ecumenical movement from the beginning of the twentieth century to the 1960s to the 1970s, when ecumenists believed that a united church could be realized in their lifetimes,[63] there has been weariness, disillusionment, and despair. The vision and influence of ecumenical institutions seem to be blurred and weakened. Outler claims that "the ecumenical glamour days are dead and gone."[64] The chairperson of the Pontifical Council for Promoting Christian Unity (PCPCU), Walter Kasper, observes that the Vatican's influence is decreasing despite the ecumenical determination that was ignited in

---

63. Evans, *Methods in Ecumenical Theology*, 1.
64. Outler, "Pneumatology," 367.

Vatican II.[65] The WCC (particularly since its General Secretary, Konrad Raiser's proposal of the necessity of an ecumenical paradigm shift in the 1990s) has been regarded as losing its way owing to its concentration on social issues and services more than on faith and order. It also claims that it is not a "primary actor" in ecumenical work, but that that is the job of the churches themselves, as is stated in the Constitution revised at the eighth assembly in 1998.[66] At the Central Committee Meeting in 2002, Raiser also declared that, "ultimately the churches themselves are the subject of the quest for visible unity and not the WCC; they have to make the doctrinal and ethical decisions and eventually proclaim consensus and cannot blame the WCC for a lack of progress in ecumenical dialogue."[67] On the other hand, the Council has been facing an internal threat from its members. The Orthodox member churches, which were once acknowledged as the main strength of the ecumenical movement, have found themselves on the periphery of the Council. They criticised the Council of making "an increasing departure from the Basis" stated in the Constitution that it "is a fellowship of churches which confess the Lord Jesus Christ as God and Saviour." They noticed a tendency to attempt to solve humanitarian problems instead of seeking for the visible unity of the divided church. And there was also a misinterpretation of Pneumatology presented at the Canberra Assembly, which contradicted the Orthodox Church's understanding, as it was not based on Christology and trinitarian doctrine. They also felt that administratively the system of quotas was unfavorable to Orthodox members within the Council. In the light of these problems, the Orthodox members asked, "*Has the time come for the Orthodox churches and other member churches to review their relations with the World Council of Churches?*"[68]

Evans explains that this general slowdown in ecumenical progress is due to fear, which brings diminishing hope and a refusal to get involved in making a commitment either to ecumenists or to non-ecumenists. The first group are disappointed by the unfulfilled promises and the latter are afraid of a denial of their tradition once they get involved in the ecumenical movement.[69] Because of the despair of the insiders and

65. Kasper, *That They May All Be One*, 14.

66. http://wccx.wcc-coe.org/wc/wjp/vilemov-02-e.html.

67. World Council of Churches, "Report," para. 28.

68. Kinnamon, *Signs of the Spirit*, 279–82.

69. Evans, *Methods in Ecumenical Theology*, 5.

the suspicion of the outsiders, together with the dwindling influence of the ecumenical institutions, the situation has been described as the "winter of ecumenism." John Murray is sceptical about the restoration of ecumenical momentum.[70] Michael Hurley quotes a French Dominican who regards the ecumenical movement as a big illusion of the century ("*l'oecuménisme aura été la grande illusion de ce siècle*").[71]

In the midst of the discouraging atmosphere, the charismatic renewal can be regarded as a sign of ecumenical hope, which brings about an eschatological continuity. "Eschatological" here does not refer to the era of *parousia*, but to human history. The miraculous manifestation of the charismatic renewal allows this word to be defined in this way because the renewal demonstrates an unshakable fact that God is with us and the Holy Spirit is our Paraclete in the present. In the midst of our weaknesses, he intervenes in hopeless situations by bestowing his power on the Church, a power which overcomes physical, spiritual, psychological, and also ecumenical problems. It also reveals the fact that we do not need to wait until the *parousia* to see the negative circumstances and distorted relationships transformed. This tells us that our hopes are not necessarily just for the *eschaton*, or only fulfilled "when the perfect comes," but they can come true in the present world, or the "pre-parousian" era.

Moltmann's concept of eschatology is coherent with this message of the charismatic renewal. He argues that eschatology becomes meaningless if it is merely concerned about the end time and the last things without relating itself to "the doctrines of the cross and resurrection, the exaltation and sovereignty of Christ." Instead, eschatology should be defined as "the doctrine of Christian hope"[72] and Christianity should be defined by eschatology, as he explains,

> From first to last, and not merely in the epilogue, Christianity is eschatology, is hope, forward looking and forward moving, and therefore also revolutionizing and transforming the present . . . Hence eschatology cannot really be only a part of Christian doctrine. Rather, the eschatological outlook is characteristic of all Christian proclamation, of every Christian existence and of the whole Church.[73]

70. Murray, "Ecumenism," 163.

71. Quoted in Hurley, *Christian Unity*, 2.

72. Moltmann, *Theology of Hope*, 15–16

73. Ibid., 16.

His concept of eschatology suggests that Christianity should not be a religion passively enduring a negative situation and waiting for transformation to come in the eschaton. Rather, with hope, it should actively bring changes to the world. The charismatic renewal is a movement concretely demonstrating this appreciation of eschatology. The miraculous works of the Holy Spirit alter the shameful or burdening past and brings living hope for future challenges. They nullify any thoughts of impossibility, conquer defeatism and despair within individuals' psyches and the church, and consequently enable Christians to reflect the glory of God until the last day. If Moltmann claims that Christianity should be eschatological because it brings hope, then the charismatic renewal, with its visible and tangible miracles, does this, bringing the kingdom of God which is actually a continuation of Jesus' ministries. It draws the present world closer to the future eschaton, shortens the distance between the present and future, and makes hopes more realistic rather than idealistic.

Therefore, in the discouraging current ecumenical situation, the charismatic renewal is a sign of hope for the present time. The charismatic renewal reminds us of the fact that even though ecumenists have become weary, the Spirit of unity is the source of power; and even though there is no human solution, the Spirit shows us the way as he is wisdom; and even though our ecumenical hope has been extinguished, the Spirit ignites a new one as he is the God of hope. Moltmann sees that the charismatic experience produces an effect "that this life, which has become old, unsuccessful and loaded with mistakes, will begin to blossom again and will therefore be young again."[74] Since the charismatic renewal suggests that divine transformations can be brought about in the present world, it is not necessary for ecumenists to wait for the far distant eschaton where perfect unity appears. Ernst Lang rightly claims, "The ecumenical movement is an anticipation of the future of Christendom." By future, he means the future within but not after human history.[75] At the Evanston Assembly, the Orthodox Church exhorts that as the Holy Spirit is still "dwelling in the Church" and "continues to breathe in the world," unity should not be perceived as a reality in the eschaton, but in the present.[76] A Methodist ecumenist, David Carter, also criticizes

74. Moltmann, "Spirit Gives Life," 35.
75. Lange, *And Yet It Move*, 25.
76. Visser't Hooft, *Evanston Report*, 94.

the view of waiting for unity to come in the eschaton as "this would be to devalue the earnest prayers of Christians from every generation" and "the urgency of the Lord's own prayer in John 17."[77] The charismatic renewal resonates to these points of view, particularly with its ecumenical achievement. But more important, the reason we can look forward to the one, holy, catholic, and apostolic church being realized again is the Holy Spirit. He fuels this hope with anamnesis and prolepsis.

The Holy Spirit: Uniting the Past, Present, and Future with Anamnesis

The charismatic renewal is a sign of an ecumenical hope as it can bring to our remembrance the unity given by the Holy Spirit. Both Moltmann and Rosato recognize that the Holy Spirit has a past that penetrates into human history. He was involved in Jesus' salvation for the world from the birth, life, death, and resurrection of Jesus. He baptized the believers at Pentecost and has accompanied the church as a Paraclete since Jesus' ascension. In the twentieth century, he wove an ecumenical history by launching the Pentecostal Movement on the one hand, and on the other hand inspiring an ecumenical vision among the Protestants and Roman Catholics resulting in the Edinburgh Conference in 1910 and Vatican II in 1962–65. Moreover, he merged the ecumenical streams within the Protestant and Roman Catholic circles in the charismatic renewal where these two parties experienced unity at the grassroots level. The Holy Spirit is actively creating an ecumenical history for the church and thus in the present, the past becomes an anamnesis for us to foresee the future with hope, because the Holy Spirit not only has a past, but also a future.[78] He not only creates history, but brings hope. Simon Chan perceives the Spirit as the one who "unites the past and future in the present" and "points the church in the direction of the future and beyond."[79] He gives anamnesis by reminding us of the history that he created in the past so that we have a renewed hope which does not disappoint. With this hope we can go through the present tribulations which bring perseverance and proven character (Rom 5:3–5).

The charismatic renewal is part of the achievement of the Holy Spirit in ecumenical history. Its influence on churches should not be

---

77. Carter, "Tradition," 154.

78. Rosato, "Called," 171, 121; Moltmann, *Church in the Power*, 34–35.

79. Chan, "Mother Church," 193.

frozen in history and merely become part of our memory. Rather, this memory should be retrieved to relate to the present situation and see into the future with hope. A refreshing and active anamnesis of what God did in the charismatic renewal can renew our hope for the future of the church despite the gloomy reality in the present.

The Holy Spirit: Uniting the Present and Future by Prolepses

The charismatic renewal reveals that the Holy Spirit is the giver of prolepses that specifically unite the present and future. *Prolepsis* is a Greek term meaning something supposed to happen in the future is imagined as happening now. Something that is "not yet" seems to have come "already." Moltmann depicts prolepsis that "hurries ahead," and is "already realizing today what is to be tomorrow."[80] It can be translated by the English word "anticipation." Pinnock identifies the Holy Spirit as a creator of hope as he connects with the future where God's will is to be fulfilled.[81] However, the charismatic renewal, characterized by miracles, connotes that the Holy Spirit is even a giver of prolepses. As James Dunn says, "*For the Spirit is the future good which has become present for the man of faith—that power of the not yet which has already begun to be realized in his present experience*" and he is "the presentness of future blessing."[82] It repeatedly shows that the impossible becomes possible by the power of the Spirit and hence it stimulates human imagination to see that events hoped for as possible in the future can be experienced in the present by anticipation. It provokes the "passion for possible," in Moltmann's phrase and casts away the anxiety of the impossible.[83]

The unity that was experienced at the five international conferences in the British charismatic renewal suggests to us that we can have a prolepsis of visible unity consisting of mutual acceptance and love within the church in the future. This historical fact showed that the kind of unity nurtured deep down in the hearts of Christians from various backgrounds has been realized in the past, and it is reasonable to believe that it can happen again, and on an even larger scale, in the future. This unity flourishing from the mutual services with gifts endowed by the Holy

80. Moltmann, *Future of Creation*, 47.

81. Pinnock, *Flame of Love*, 39, 188.

82. Dunn, *Jesus and the Spirit*, 310–11.

83. Moltmann, *Theology of Hope*, 34.

Spirit at the grassroots level justifies saying that the charismatic renewal is a sign of ecumenical hope; a hope that the unity will develop from the grassroots and will be sustained by shared faith and doctrines in a one, holy, catholic, and apostolic church. It will also be visible that the church can testify to Christ in the world. This hope could be perceived as a reality soon to come or become a prolepsis because the Spirit of unity is still accompanying the church with his power of transformation. This prolepsis creates proximity between the present and future which motivates the church to toil patiently and meanwhile wait joyfully for the anticipated unity.

The Holy Spirit: The Rejecter of the Status Quo

The Holy Spirit who inspires anamnesis brings the past to the present and strengthens us to face the future courageously with hope. The hope that he gives becomes prolepses as we anticipate the future reality which has not yet come but seems to be already there. He rescues us from being victims of the status quo who do not pursue change and better circumstances but are reconciled to the undesirable reality. His generosity in giving hope delivers us from the "sin of despair," as Moltmann puts it, which tempts people to withdraw themselves from doing good and striking for excellence.[84] His hope grants us courage to bear the trials that follow taking risks. Because of this courage, there is the possibility of improvement, of reaching perfection and of achieving the goals that God has set for us. The charismatic renewal, characterized by the miraculous works of the Holy Spirit, inspires hope among those who have tasted the grace and experienced the power. This reflects the fact that the Holy Spirit refuses to compromise with the status quo but intends to bring us a better life, personally and ecclesiologically. In the light of the gloomy ecumenical circumstances, the charismatic renewal reminds us that the Holy Spirit of hope is able to change this status quo and we can work hard for the prospect of the unity of the church with hope, for as Paul says, "the plowman ought to plow in hope, and the thresher to thresh in hope of sharing the crops" (1 Cor. 9:10). With belief in the Spirit who gives hope and power, the ecumenical continuity will not cease.

---

84. Ibid., 23.

CONCLUSION

This chapter has demonstrated how ecumenical institutions, the WCC and Vatican II, and the charismatic renewal, complemented each other. The relation between the Vatican II and the charismatic renewal shows that institution complemented the charismatic renewal while between the WCC and the renewal we see the reverse. In addition, the convention of Vatican II was partly influenced by the WCC and hence institutions also complemented each other. The complementarity happened because the whole ecumenical movement had been directed by the Holy Spirit who worked through both the institution and charisms, and who brought out the *Christus praesens* and *Spiriti praesens*. Hence we can see the convergence of these three streams and the ecumenical continuity in the modern ecumenical history. With the legacy of hope, the charismatic renewal brings about an eschatological continuity for the ecumenical movement. Although the current ecumenical situation is gloomy and the pace has slowed down, the renewal reminds ecumenists of the everlasting presence and unimaginable power of the Holy Spirit. He unites the past, present, and future with anamnesis and prolepsis so that we remember his works for church unity in the past. We can also hope for the united church to come in the future world instead of the eschaton only.

Conclusion

THE FIVE INTERNATIONAL CONFERENCES of the Fountain Trust reveal the ecumenical significance of the charismatic renewal. Apart from the Christocentric Universalism of the WCC and the christological ecumenical approach of Vatican II, the charismatic renewal reminded ecumenists of the importance of Pneumatology. Apart from the organizational ecumenical ministry, it vividly demonstrated charisms as the powerful means for mutual edification among Christians of various traditions. Apart from the official and clerical level of the ecumenical movement, it raised a new group of ecumenists from the laity who were equipped with charisms. Apart from the doctrinal discussions, it created a bonding of love through common experience at the grassroots level. The renewal did not reject the direction, refute the method, and replace the mainstream ecumenical movement for it was not *per se* an ecumenical reformation. It confirmed the ecumenical vision embraced by the forerunners in the early twentieth century, enriched their earlier ecumenical achievements, and strengthened the whole movement by bringing more ecumenical converts and pouring out the transforming power, refreshing hope, and enduring love of the Spirit.

This book tells the story of the treasure of a rediscovered unity and the sadness of this unfulfilled unity. It demonstrates the scenes of worship and Eucharist, which brought about such contradictory emotions in the five international conferences, and it provides a theological analysis using the concepts such as epiclesis, anamnesis, and *lex orandi, lex credendi*. It searches for the complementarity of institution and charisms, and Christology and Pneumatology in ecclesiology and ecumenism. It also reinterprets modern ecumenical history with the lenses of complementarity, convergence, and continuity. It discusses historically how ecumenical institutions, the WCC and Vatican II, and the charismatic renewal, complemented each other. Hence we can see a convergence of the three ecumenical streams and a historical continuity in modern ecumenical history. It carries a belief that the Spirit has worked unceasingly for the unity of the church in history through calling Christians from the Protestant, Roman Catholic, and Orthodox churches to toil for it in ecumenical institutes such as the WCC and Vatican II, and through his own direct involvement in the charismatic renewal. It also carries a hope that the same Spirit who kindled this vision for churches will sustain it until they worship the same God with one accord, remember the same Lord with the shared bread and wine in one faith and serve one another in the same Spirit before the *parousia*. This book does not over-optimistically foresee a bright and successful ecumenical future, nor pessimistically despair of such a possible prospect; but realistically conveys a message that church unity can still be worked for and proposes a complementary approach of looking at the weaknesses of both the mainstream ecumenical movement and the charismatic renewal. Although the grassroots unity in the charismatic renewal did not last, it challenges both ecumenical optimists and pessimists to believe that the almighty God can miraculously intervene in a hopeless situation; but at the same time our hopefulness should not be based merely on his miraculous works, but also on our own perseverance in reaching the goal sustained by the faith in him.

The charismatic renewal has been changed from decade to decade. The renewal of ecclesiastical structure, liturgy, spiritual life of the church and individuals, and unity emphasized in the 1970s has been replaced by power evangelism and church growth from the 1980s up to now. The power of the Holy Spirit has been utilized as a tool for the financial, numerical, and architectural expansion of the church; for the so-called "vision" of building a mega-church and the "mission" of planting such churches around the world. Contemporary charismatics still proclaim that the kingdom of God is evidently manifest "here and now" when healing, exorcism, prophecy, and other charisms are performed to save the hopeless souls, but the hidden agenda is building the kingdom of the senior pastor, who acts as the entrepreneur of the whole church business. As his kingdom expands, his ideology is spread, which tragically leads to a pathway of mono-Christian faith, mono-Christian culture, and mono-Christian discipleship.

In this version of self-governance, self-support, and self-propagation formulated in the post-missionary era, based on consumerism and capitalism and materialized with the charismatic ideology of the power of the Holy Spirit and his free gifts, which are under careful manipulation for the sake of "kingdom expansion," there is no such need of *koinonia* and *oikoumene* and no such calling for unity in diversity. Diversity becomes unfavorable for global church administration, but uniformity is highly preferable for the purposes of controllability and predictability. Since there is no need of diversity, there is no need of sharing and exchanging gifts, and eventually no need of unity. Oneness means uniformity instead of the unity constituted by diversity. The primary purposes of the charismatic renewal are completely distorted.

If this is the way that the church will progress, does that mean the story of the Fountain Trust is hardly relevant to the church nowadays and not at all prophetic for the ecumenical future? Does that mean the charismatic renewal and ecumenical movement are intrinsically discontinuous as they are moving on from decade to decade? Does that mean there is no such need of anamnesis, of remembering, and of reflection because the past only belongs to the past? If that is true, does that justify a total oblivion of the heavenly blessings, grace, and strengths, together with our seemingly avoidable weaknesses and mistakes, and henceforth, spoliation of the good and repetition of the wrong?

May the God of Spirit grant us the gift of discernment to read the signs of the time, so that we can understand what the Spirit is doing in the world; to distinguish the darnel and the wheat as they both "sprout and bear grain," so that we follow the "landowner" who sows good seeds (Matt 13:26–27); and to search our hearts, so that we will know if there is any hurtful way in us, and walk in the everlasting way (Ps 139: 23–24).

Appendix

Numbers of Non-British Attendants
of the International Conferences[1]

	Guildford 1971	Nottingham 1973	Westminster 1977	Westminster 1979
Western Europe				
Austria	0	0	6	3
Belgium	0	0	6	2
France	10	12	6	10
Germany	13	19	36	8
Holland	3	22	8	4
Ireland	4	6	7	1
Italy	0	2	1	2
Luxemburg	0	0	2	0
Malta	0	0	1	13
Spain	2	2	2	2
Switzerland	2	26	5	7
Scandinavia				
Denmark	13	6	6	13
Finland	11	4	2	0
Iceland	1	1	0	0
Norway	32	10	1	2
Sweden	10	83	12	12

North America				
Canada	2	8	12	12
USA	43	38	11	12
South America				
Argentina	0	2	0	0
Bermuda	0	1	0	0
Brazil	0	1	0	0
Australasia				
Australia	13	19	0	3
New Zealand	3	6	9	3
Africa				
Ghana	0	1	0	0
Kenya	4	0	0	0
Nigeria	0	2	1	0
Sierra Leone	0	1	0	0
South Africa	15	15	6	4
Tanzania	0	1	0	0
Tunisia	1	0	0	1
Asia				
Hong Kong	0	0	3	4
India	0	5	0	0
Japan	0	0	2	0
Nepal	0	0	1	1
Philippines	0	1	0	0
Singapore	0	0	8	0
Middle East				
Iran	1	1	0	0
Israel	0	1	0	0

ENDNOTES

1. Unfortunately it was impossible to obtain the data of Westminster 1975. The data are collected from "Guest list: Guildford"; "Guest list: Nottingham", "Guest list: Westminster '77", "Guest list: Westminster 1979."

Bibliography

PRIMARY SOURCES

Renewal

"1977 Fountain Trust Conference: Welsh Conferences." *Renewal* 67 (February–March 1977) back cover.

"And Now—Ten People Recall What Guildford '71 Meant to Them." *Renewal* 94 (August–September 1981) 32–34.

"At Last–to Wales." *Renewal* 62 (April–May 1976) 6.

"Bishop Sees Revival in Singapore." *Renewal* 54 (December 1974–January 1975) 4–5.

"Bursary Fund." *Renewal* 54 (December 1974–January 1975) 5.

"Christians at Work in the World." *Renewal* 67 (February–March 1977) 6.

"Coming Events." *Renewal* 68 (April–May 1977) 6.

"Fountain Trust Conferences in 1980." *Renewal* 85 (February–March 1980) 10–11.

"Four Conference Speakers on What I want for Nottingham—George Macleod." *Renewal* 45 (June–July 1973) 4–5.

"From Michael & Jeanne Harper." *Renewal* 59 (October–November 1975) 4.

"Guildford 1971: They Heard the Angels." *Renewal* 94 (August–September 1981) 30–32.

"History Repeated in New Zealand." *Renewal* 44 (April–May 1973) 19–20.

"Influence of Pethrus and Richards." *Renewal* 54 (December 1974–January 1975) 6.

"It's Time in Australia." *Renewal* 44 (April–May 1973) 21–22.

"Leaders Meet in Brussels." *Renewal* 62 (April–May 1976) 5.

"Looking for the Holy Spirit's Surprises." *Renewal* 46 (August–September 1973) 6–11.

"Move for Tom Smail." *Renewal* 79 (February–March 1979) 5.

"New Fountain Trust Appointment." *Renewal* 71 (October–November, 1977) 6.

"New Link Man for Healing Ministry." *Renewal* 88 (August–September 1980) 5.

"News: Work of Fountain Trust to End in December: Renewal Magazine Carries on." *Renewal* 89 (October–November 1980) 4.

"Press Comment on Massey University Conference." *Renewal* 44 (April–May 1973) 20–21.

"Prophecy given at the Westminster Conference." *Renewal* 59 (October–November 1975) 7.

Renewal 46 (August–September 1973) 21.

Renewal 71 (October–November 1977) 9.

"Spirit and Society." *Renewal* 59 (October–November 1975) 9.

"Travelling Man." *Renewal* 54 (December 1974–January 1975) 6.

"Well Met at Malines." *Renewal* 65 (October–November 1976) 4.

Westminster Splash

"Conference Aims Explained to Press and Radio." *Westminster Splash* (29 July 1975) 1.
"Daily Mass." *Westminster Splash* (29 July 1975) 2.
"Girl Car Crash Victim Healed in Four Days." *Westminster Splash* (31 July 1975) 1.
"Happier about Charismatic Movement." *Westminster Splash* (31 July 1975) 6.
"Last–minute Takeover." *Westminster Splash* (31 July 1975) 4.
"Memory Healing Work in Nottingham." *Westminster Splash* (31 July 1975) 6.
"Michael Hands over the Reins." *Westminster Splash* (28 July 1975) 1.
"Odd Job Man." *Westminster Splash* (31 July 1975) 4.
"Prayer Can Avert Ireland Disaster." *Westminster Splash* (29 July 1975) 4.
"Renewal must Result in Grass Roots Reality." *Westminster Splash* (1 August 1975) 1.
"Singapore Bishop's New Ministry." *Westminster Splash* (28 July 1975) 2–3.
"Speaker from over the World." *Westminster Splash* (28 July 1975) 2.
"What the Week Has Meant to Me." *Westminster Splash* (1 August 1975) 2.

Fountain Trust Advisory/Consultative Council Meetings

Agenda of Advisory Council Meeting (1 June 1967).
Fountain Trust Advisory Council Meeting (1 July 1967).
Fountain Trust Advisors Meeting (6 December 1968).
Fountain Trust Advisory Council Meeting (20 November 1970).
Fountain Trust Advisory Council Meeting (12 November 1971).
Fountain Trust Advisory Council Meeting (2 November 1972).
Fountain Trust Advisory Council Meeting (5 April 1973).
Fountain Trust Advisory Council Meeting (8 November 1973).
Fountain Trust Advisory Council Meeting (9 December 1976).
Fountain Trust Consultative Council Meeting (8 June 1977).
Fountain Trust Consultative Council Meeting (8 December 1977).
Fountain Trust Consultative Council Meeting (10 May 1978).
Minutes of Fountain Trust Consultative Council Meeting (6 June 1979).

Documents of the International Conferences

Guildford 1971

"Catholic Attending the International Conference on the Fellowship of the Holy Spirit."
Dallière, Emile, R. "Guildford International Conference, July 1971: A Report by Emile R. Dallière.1971."
Davison, Leslie. "Memorandum to British Council of Churches."
"Fountain Trust International Conference, 'Fellowship of the Holy Spirit' 12–17 July 1971, University of Surrey Guildford."
Guest list of the Fountain Trust International Conference, Guildford 12–17 July 1971.
Guildford University Conference, Minutes of meeting, 12 June 1970.
"International Conference on the Fellowship of the Holy Spirit."
Leaflet and Booking Form of the Conference, n. d.
Minutes: International Conference on the Fellowship of the Holy Spirit.
Notes on the Meeting of the Guildford Conference Committee, 3 July 1970.

"Press Release: International Conference."

Rough notes on the meeting of the Guildford Conference Committee, 14 October 1970.

Sullivan, Emmanuel. "Memo: Guildford Conference—July 12–17 1971."

Nottingham 1973

"Fountain Trust International Conference."

Fountain Trust International Conference, Nottingham July 1973, Detailed Programme Tuesday–Friday (Saturday to be announced).

Fountain Trust International Conference, Nottingham University 9–14 July 1973, Guest List.

Nottingham Conference 1973, "Gathered for Power." Speakers' Information.

"Nottingham University 9–14 July 1973, Gathered for Power."

International Conference, Nottingham 9–14 July 1973, Programme.

Leaflet and application form of the Nottingham Conference.

Press Release from the Fountain Trust, 2 July 1973.

Press Release: International Conference 2.

Westminster 1975

Holl, Barbara. "Glory in the Church: Fountain Trust International Charismatic Conference."

Booking Form of Westminster 1975.

Charismatic Event (July 1975).

Conference Brochure: Welcome to Westminster, Fountain Trust International Conference, 28 July–2 August 1975.

"Fountain Trust International Conference, Westminster, London, 28 July–2 August 1975."

Fountain Trust International Conference, Westminster, London, 28 July–2 August 1975, Speakers' Subjects.

"Glory in the Church: Fountain Trust International Conference, Westminster 1975."

Memorandum of an Agreement Made on the Thirtieth Day of July 1974, between the Trustees of the Central Hall and Buildings, Westminster, S.W.1 of the One Part, and Rev. Michael Harper on Behalf of Fountain Trust.

Minutes of the Working Committee for the Fountain Trust Westminster International Conference Meeting (1 October 1974).

Minutes of Westminster Conference Working Committee (31 January 1974).

Outline of the Talk of John Richards.

Press Release, January 1975.

Westminster 1977

"Fountain Trust International Conference, Westminster, Growing in the Church, 1–5 August 1977."

"Growing in the Church: An International Conference on Renewal in the Local Church, London 1–5 August 1977."

Minutes: Westminster Conference Steering Committee (21 October 1976).

Minutes: Westminster Conference Steering Committee (14 January 1977).

Minutes: Westminster Conference Steering Committee (25 February 1977).

Minutes: Westminster Conference Steering Committee (20 April 1977).
Minutes: Westminster Conference Steering Committee (6 July 1977).
Press Release: Growing in the church (April 1977).
Suggested Programme for Cardinal Suenens at Westminster Conference."
The Day at Westminster, 1–2.
Westminster '77, Growing in the Church, 1–5 August 1977, Guest List.

Westminster 1979

"Joy in the City" Westminster, 30 July–3 August 1979, Guest List.
"Joy in the City: An International Conference on Renewal and its Outreach in Society. London 30 July–3 August 1979."
"Joy in the City, London, 30 July–3 August 1979."
Speakers at Westminster 1979.

Other Document

An Invitation of the Theological Workshop from Michael Harper, n. d.
An Invitation of the Theological Workshop from Michael Harper, June 1973.
  "Gospel and Spirit: A Joint Statement." London: Fountain Trust and the Church of England Evangelical Council, April 1977.
Booking Form, n.d.
Curriculum Vitae: David MacInnes.
Curriculum Vitae: J. Rodman Williams.
Curriculum Vitae: Arnold Bittlinger.
Curriculum Vitae: Douglas Quy.
Curriculum Vitae: Loren Cunningham.
Curriculum Vitae: Athanasios Franklin Stuart Emmert.
"For the Renewal of the Church: Fountain Trust—in Christ, by the Spirit, to the Church, for the World." London: Fountain Trust, 1974.
Fountain Trust International Conference, n. d.
Memo from Bob Balkam, 13 December 1976.
Press Release of Fountain Trust: New Fountain Trust Appointment, 24 April 1972.
Theological Workshop: Address List.

Fountain Trust Audio Tapes

Fountain Trust. *Ecumenical Issues I.*1977.
———. *Ecumenical Issues II.*1977.
Ranaghan, Kevin. *The Maturity of the Body of Christ.* n. d.
Smail, Tom. *Doing: The Work of the Body.* n. d.
———. *Humanity: The Stuff of the Body.* n. d.
———. *Discipline: The Strength of the Body.* n. d.
Urquhart, Colin. *Renewal in the Local Church Fellowship.* 1975.

Correspondence

1970

Letter from David Pawson to Michael Harper, 30 April 1970.
Letter from Michael Harper to Bob Balkam, 11 May 1970.
Letter from Bob Balkam to Michael Harper, 18 May 1970.
Letter from Michael Harper to Leslie Davison, 9 July 1970.
Letter from Eric Jennings to Michael Harper, 11 July 1970.
Letter from Leslie Davison to Michael Harper, 13 July 1970.
Letter from Noel Doubleday to Michael Harper, 14 July 1970.
Letter from Michael Harper to Bob Balkam, 21 July 1970.
Letter from Eric Jennings to Michael Harper, 21 July 1970.
Letter from Harold G. Owen to Michael Harper, 28 August 1970.
Letter from Michael Pusey to Michael Harper, 16 October 1970.
Letter from Michael Harper to Michael Pusey, 29 October 1970.
Letter from Michael Harper to His Honour Judge Ruttle, 3 November 1970.
Letter from James D.G. Dunn to Michael Harper, 12 December 1970.
Letter from Michael Harper to Thurnace York, 22 December 1970.
Letter from Michael Pusey to Michael Harper, 22 December 1970.
Letter from Harold G. Owen to Michael Harper, 29 December 1970.

1971

Letter from Simon Tugwell to Michael Harper, 2 January 1971.
Letter from Michael Harper to Harold G. Owen, 2 January 1971.
Letter from Fred Pride to Michael Harper, 4 January 1971.
Letter from Michael Harper to Simon Tugwell, 5 January 1971.
Letter from Michael Harper to Bob Balkam, 5 January 1971.
Letter from Secretary to Michael Harper to Mr. E. Gwatkin, 6 January 1971.
Letter from Michael Harper to Fred Pride, 10 January 1971.
Letter from Michael Harper to David Watson, 6 April 1971.
Letter from Kevin Ranaghan to Michael Harper, 24 April 1971.
Letter from Michael Harper to Leslie Davison, 26 April 1971.
Letter from Christine Rennie to Kevin Ranaghan, 26 May 1971.
Letter from Christine Rennie to Ralph Wilkerson, 26 May 1971.
Letter from Arthur Wallis to Christine Rennie, 8 June 1971.
Letter from Michael Harper to the Archbishop of Canterbury, 6 July 1971.
Letter from Alfred Missen to Michael Harper, 13 July 1971.
Letter from Michael Harper to James Dunn, 19 July 1971.
Letter from Mr. and Mrs. Jack Evans, 19 July 1971.
Letter from David Watson to Michael Harper, 20 July 1971.
Letter from Michael Harper to Sister Gertrude, 20 July 1971.
Letter from Arthur Wallis to Michael Harper, 21 July 1971.
Letter from David Pawson to Michael Harper, 23 July 1971.
Letter from Livar Lundgren to Michael Harper, 28 July 1971.
Letter from Michael Harper to the Lord Rank, 28 July 1971.
Letter from Ivar Lungren to Michael Harper, 28 July 1971.
Letter from David Pawson to Michael Harper, 29 July 1971.

Letter from Michael Harper to David Watson, 29 July 1971.
Letter from Michael Harper to James Dunn, 29 July 1971.
Letter from F. P. Möller to Michael Harper, 29 July 1971.
Letter from Jim and Val Kincaid to Michael and Jeanne Harper, 30 July 1971.
Letter from Mr. and Mrs. James to Michael Harper, 15 August 1971.
Letter from Michael Harper to Rev. John Simons, Essex, 20 August 1971.
Letter from Simon Tugwell to Michael Harper, September 1971.
Letter from Leslie Davison to Michael Harper, 3 September 1971.
Letter from Michael Harper to Simon Tugwell, 29 September 1971.
Letter from Leslie Davison to Michael Harper, 4 October 1971.
Letter from David Pawson to Michael Harper, 4 October 1971.
Letter from Michael Harper to Brother Andrew, 4 October 1971.
Letter from Michael Harper to Dennis Bennett, 5 October 1971.
Letter from Michael Harper to Miss Nina Putman, 6 October 1971.
Letter from Colin Urquhart to Michael Harper, 8 October 1971.
Letter from Michael Harper to John Horner, 18 October 1971.
Letter from Michael Harper to Larry Christenson, 19 October 1971.
Letter from Michael Harper to Emile Dallière, 19 October 1971.
Letter from David MacInnes to Michael Harper, 29 October 1971.
Letter from Ivar Lundgren to Michael Harper, 5 November 1971.
Letter from Michael Harper to D. MacInnes, 10 November 1971.
Letter from Michael Harper to Ivar Lundgren, 12 November 1971.
Letter from Michael Harper to Ray Bringham, 22 November 1971.

1972

Letter from Michael Harper to His Royal Highness the Prince of Wales, 19 January 1972.
Letter from David Checketts to Michael Harper, 27 January 1972.
Letter from Simon Tugwell to Michael Harper, 1 May 1972.
Letter from Michael Harper to Albert de Monléon, 17 May 1972.
Letter from Michael Harper to Albert de Monléon, 6 July 1972.
Letter from Michael Harper to Simon Tugwell and John Mills, 7 July 1972.
Letter from Albert de Monléon to Michael Harper, 15 July 1972.
Letter from Michael Harper to the Bishop of Southwell, 26 July 1972.
Letter from Michael Harper to Larry Christenson, 26 July 1972.
Letter from Michael Harper to Albert de Monléon, 27 July 1972.
Letter from Michael Harper to Douglas Quy, 23 August 1972.
Letter from Ian Davidson, September 1972.
Letter from David Pawson to Michael Harper, 5 September 1972.
Letter from Douglas Quy to Michael Harper, 11 September 1972.
Letter from Albert de Monléon to Michael Harper, 20 September 1972.
Letter from Michael Harper to Albert de Monléon, 28 September 1972.
Letter from Michael Harper to William Davies, 29 September 1972.
Letter from William Davies to Michael Harper, 3 October 1972.
Letter from Michael Harper to Athanasios Emmert, 18 October 1972.
Letter from Michael Harper to David Pawson, 18 October 1972
Letter from Athanasios Emmert to Michael Harper, 1 November 1972
Letter from Derek Crumpton to Michael Harper, 2 November 1972.

Letter from William R. Davies to Michael Harper, 3 November 1972.
Letter from Michael Harper to Athanasios Emmert, 22 November 1972.
Letter from Michael Harper to Bishop Bazley, 29 November 1972.
Letter from Michael Harper to David MacInnes, 11 December 1972.
Letter from Douglas Quy to Michael Harper, 19 December 1972.
Letter from Albert de Monléon to Michael Harper, 28 December 1972.

1973

Letter from the Bishop of Southwell to Michael Harper, 1 January 1973.
Letter from Michael Harper to the Bishop of Southwell, 9 January 1973.
Letter from the Bishop of Southwell to Michael Harper, 16 January 1973.
Letter from Tom Smail to H. Walker, 17 January 1973.
Letter from J. Rodman Williams to Michael Harper, 17 January 1973.
Letter from the Secretary to John B. Leake to Michael Harper, 30 January 1973.
Letter from David Pawson to Michael Harper, 30 January 1973.
Letter from Lewis Simonfalvi to Michael Harper, 14 February 1973.
Letter from Michael Harper, 6 March 1973.
Letter from Peter Young to Michael Harper and David Watson, 28 March 1973.
Letter from Derek Crumpton to Michael Harper, 29 March 1973.
Letter from Tom Smail to James G. Matheson, 3 April 1973.
Letter from Michael Harper to J. Abraham, 4 April 1973.
Letter from Michael Harper to Rev. and Mrs. Ray Muller, 4 April 1973.
Letter from Michael Harper to J. Abraham, 4 April 1973.
Letter from Michael Harper to Rune Brännstöm, 10 April 1973.
Letter from Michael Harper to Lewis Simonfalvi, 10 April 1973.
Letter from Michael Harper to Hans Jacob Frøen, 10 April 1973.
Letter from Emmanuel Sullivan to Michael Harper, 14 April 1973.
Letter from David MacInnes to Michael Harper, 19 April 1973.
Letter from Lewis Simonfalvi to Michael Harper, 19 April 1973.
Letter from Michael Harper to Kilian McDonnell, 24 April 1973.
Letter from Tom Smail to James G. Matheson, 25 April 1973.
Letter from Alan Langstaff to Michael Harper, 25 April 1973.
Letter from Michael Harper to Lewis Simonfalvi, 1 May 1973.
Letter from Michael Harper to Bernard Palmer, 11 May 1973.
Letter from Graham Horwood to Michael Harper, 14 May 1973.
Letter from Secretary to Michael Harper to Douglas Quy, 16 May 1973.
Letter from Secretary to Michael Harper to David Pawson, 16 May 1973.
Letter from Michael Harper to William Davies, 16 May 1973.
Letter from Secretary to Michael Harper to David du Plessis, 16 May 1973.
Letter from the Secretary to Michael Harper to J. Rodman William, 16 May 1973.
Letter from Frank Lake to Sylvia Lawton, 17 May 1973.
Letter from Larry Christenson to Michael Harper, 18 May 1973.
Letter from Michael Harper to Frank Watts, 22 May 1973.
Letter from Michael Harper to Graham Horwood, 22 May 1973.
Letter from Michael Harper to Alan Langstaff, 22 May 1973.
Letter from Michael Harper to David Bartlett, 24 May 1973.
Letter from Michael Harper to Larry Christenson, 24 May 1973.
Letter from the Bishop of Grahamstown to Michael Harper, 30 May 1973.

Letter from Lewis Simonfalvi to Michael Harper, 5 June 1973.

Letter from James G. Matheson to Tom Smail, 19 June 1973.

Letter from Tom Smail to James. G. Matheson, 23 June 1973.

Letter from Michael Harper to the Bishop of Southwell, 28 June 1973.

Letter from Michael Harper to Ian Petit, 28 June 1973.

Letter from Alan Langstaff to Michael Harper, 29 June 1973.

Letter from the Secretary to Michael Harper to Frank Lake, 29 June 1973.

Letter from Tom Smail, July 1973.

Letter from the Director of Fountain Trust to the Editor of the *Church of England Newspaper*, 1 July 1973.

Letter from the Director of the Fountain Trust to Cliff Longley, 2 July 1973.

Letter from the Bishop of Southwell to Michael Harper, 3 July 1973.

Letter from Loren Cunningham to Michael Harper, 3 August 1973.

Letter from Brian Ellis to Michael Harper, 12 November 1973.

Letter from Michael Harper to Brian Ellis, 23 November 1973.

1974

Letter from Tom Smail to John Capon, 1974.

Letter from Tom Smail to Douglas A. Smith, 2 May 1974.

Letter from Michael Harper to Dr. Coggan, 17 May 1974.

Letter from Jim Brown to Tom Smail, 10 June 1974.

Letter from Francis MacNutt to Michael Harper, 8 July 1974.

Letter from Godfrey Gawkins to Michael Harper, 10 September 1974

Letter from Michael Harper to Ruth Champness, 12 September 1974.

Letter from Michael Harper to the Archbishop of Cape Town, 13 September 1974.

Letter from Michael Harper to overseas contacts, 15 October 1974.

Letter from Hans-Jacob Frøen to Michael Harper, 6 November 1974.

Letter from Michael Harper to J. Malm, 11 November 1974.

Letter form Truda Smail to G. Davies, 15 November 1974.

Letter from Michael Harper to D. White, 18 November 1974.

Letter from Chiu Ban It to Michael Harper, 30 December 1974.

1975

Letter from Mr. and Mrs. James to Michael Harper, 1975.

Letter from Michael Harper to A. D. Roake, 9 January 1975.

Letter from Tom Smail to David Popely, 10 January 1975.

Letter from Paul Lebeau to Tom Smail, 25 January 1975.

Letter from the Archbishop of Cape Town to Tom Smail, 30 January 1975.

Letter from Tom Smail to Paul Lebeau, 31 January 1975.

Letter from Sister Regina to Tom Smail, 4 February 1975.

Letter from Tom Smail to Cecil Kerr, 10 February 1975.

Letter from Ralph Bancroft to Truda Smail, 18 March 1975.

Letter from Michael Harper to Campbell McAlpine, 4 April 1975.

Letter from Michael Harper to Gavin Reid, 16 April 1975.

Letter from Michael Harper to Sundar Clarke, 21 April 1975.

Letter from Michael Harper to Chiu Ban It, 21 April 1975.

Letter from Zac Poonen to Michael Harper, 28 April 1975.

Letter from Michael Harper to Chiu Ban It, 5 May 1975.

Letter from Michael Harper to Felix Dias-Abeyesinghe, 5 May 1975.

Letter from Chiu Ban It to Michael Harper, 5 May 1975.

Letter from Michael Harper to Sundar Clarke, 8 May 1975.

Letter from Godfrey Dawkins, Kenya, to Michael Harper, 13 May 1975.

Letter from Michael Harper to David Pawson, 15 May 1975.

Letter from Sundar Clark to Michael Harper, 15 May 1975.

Letter from Michael Harper to Louis Tay, 16 May 1975.

Letter from Michael Harper to Ananda Rao Smauel, 19 May 1975.

Letter from Michael Harper to the Bishop of London, 2 June 1975.

Letter from Michael Harper to Louis Tay, 3 June 1975.

Letter from Michael Harper to the Dean of Westminster, 3 June 1975.

Letter from Michael Harper to Brenda and John Fulcher, 3 June 1975.

Letter from Zac Poonen to Michael Harper, 3 June 1975.

Letter from Michael Harper to Julius Adoyo, 3 June 1975.

Letter from Truda Smail, 6 June 1975.

Letter from Michael Harper to Neville B. Cryer, 12 June 1975.

Letter from Chiu Ban It to Michael Harper, 13 June 1975.

Letter from John F. Perry to Michael Harper, 20 June 1975.

Letter from John Horner to Michael Harper, 25 June 1975.

Letter from Gavin Reid to Michael Harper, 1 July 1975.

Letter from Julius Adoyo to Michael Harper, 3 July 1975.

Letter from the Bishop of London to Michael Harper, 4 July 1975.

Letter from Godfrey and Elizabeth Gawkins to Michael Harper, 4 July 1975.

Letter from Cecil Kerr to Michael Harper, 6 July 1975.

Letter from the Archbishop of Cape Town to Michael Harper, 7 July 1975.

Letter from the Archbishop's secretary to Michael Harper, 8 July 1975.

Letter from Robert de Maar to Michael Harper, 12 July 1975.

Letter from the Archbishop of Cape Town to Michael Harper, 15 July 1975.

Letter from Tom Smail to D. Cameron, 16 July 1975.

Letter from S. V. Winbalt Lewis to Michael Harper, 2 August 1975.

Letter from J. G. Simpson to Michael Harper, 3 August 1975.

Letter from Bill and Gladys Kuty, 4 August 1975.

Letter from John Richards to Michael Harper, 4 August 1975.

Letter from Ken to Michael Harper, 4 August 1975.

Letter from John Horner to Tom Smail, 5 August 1975.

Letter from Beryl M. Parker to the Fountain Trust, 5 August 1975.

Letter from R. A. Pyle to Michael Harper, 5 August 1975.

Letter from Beryl M. Parker to the Fountain Trust, 5 August 1975.

Letter from John Horner to Tom Smail, 5 August 1975.

Letter from Mallie Calver to Michael Harper, 8 August 1975.

Letter from Tom Smail to James Dunn, 8 August 1975.

Letter from Trevor J. Marzetti to Michael Harper, 8 August 1975.

Letter from Edwin to Michael and Jeanne Harper, 8 August 1975.

Letter from John Bedford to Michael Harper, 8 August 1975.

Letter from Michael Harper to the Bishop of London, 15 August 1975.

Letter from Mary Alison to Tom Smail, 21 August 1975.

Letter from Michael Harper to Herbert F. Stevenson, 22 August 1975.

Letter from Pamela Lucas to the Fountain Trust, 29 August 1975.
Letter from Bill and Gladys Neaty to Tom Smail, 4 September 1975.
Letter from the Bishop of Pontefract to Tom Smail, 10 September 1975.
Letter from Lorna and Ken to unknown recipient, 14 September 1975.

1976

Letter from Tom Smail to Cardinal Suenens, 14 January 1976.
Letter from Tom Smail to Tom Walker, 23 February 1976.
Letter from Tom Smail to Agnes Sanford, 23 February 1976.
Letter from Tom Smail to Paul Lebeau, 23 February 1976.
Letter from Cardinal Suenens to Tom Smail, 25 February 1976.
Letter from Tom Walker to Tom Smail, 26 February 1976.
Letter from Tom Smail to Howard Belben, 5 March 1976.
Letter from Tom Smail to Michael Harper to the author, 5 March 1976.
Letter from Tom Smail to Cardinal Suenens, 7 October 1976.
Letter from Tom Smail to Ralph Martin, 7 October 1976.
Letter from Tom Smail to Walter Hollenweger, 5 November 1976.
Letter from Tom Smail to Jack Dominian, 23 December 1976.
Letter from Tom Smail to Jan van der Veken, 23 December 1976.
Letter from Tom Smail to Paul Felton, 23 December 1976.

1977

Letter from Tom Smail to speaker, 1977.
Letter from Jack Dominian to Tom Smail, 24 January 1977.
Letter from Howard Belben to Tom Smail, 25 April 1977.
Letter from Tom Smail to Cardinal Suenens, 25 April 1977.
Letter from Agnes Sanford to Tom Smail, 2 May 1977.
Letter from Cardinal Suenens to Tom Smail, 4 May 1977.
Letter from Tom Smail to Howard Belben, 9 May 1977.
Letter from Richard Hare to Tom Smail, 19 May 1977.
Letter from Tom Smail to Briege McKenna, 27 May 1977.
Letter from Aruthur Wallis to Tom Smail, 2 June 1977.
Letter from Tom Smail to Agnes Sanford, 10 June 1977.
Letter from Tom Smail to Cardinal Suenens, 13 June 1977.
Letter from Collin McCampbell to Tom Smail, 5 August 1977.
Letter from Philip Sourbut to Tom Smail, 6 August 1977.
Letter from D. M. Adam to Tom Smail, 6 August 1977.
Letter from John Fowell to Tom Smail, 8 August 1977.
Letter from Pamela Mellyard to Tom Smail, 8 August 1977.
Letter from Peggy William to the Fountain Trust, 8 August 1977.
Letter from Ray J. Simpson to Tom Smail, 8 August 1977.
Letter from J. Pereboom to the Fountain Trust, 9 August 1977.
Letter from Pauline Ruffett to Tom Smail, 9 August 1977.
Letter from Michael Bennett to Tom Smail, 11 August 1977.
Letter from Renale Vetter to the Fountain Trust, 11 August 1977.
Letter from Gordon V. Clark to Tom Smail, 12 August 1977.
Letter from Tom Smail to Richard Hare, 12 August 1977.

Letter from Lisa Reynolds to Tom Smail, 13 August 1977.
Letter from Jack Dominian to Tom Smail, 15 August 1977.
Letter from Kath Holmes, 17 August 1977.
Letter from A. K. Pring, 18 August 1977.
Letter from Tom Smail to D. M. Adams, 19 August 1977.
Letter from Roger Hardcastle to Tom Smail, 21 August 1977.
Letter from D. Whitaker to Rev. and Mrs. Tom Smail, 21 August 1977.
Letter from Roger Hardcastle to the Fountain Trust, 21 August 1977.
Letter from J. Martin-Doyle to Tom Smail, 9 September 1977.
Letter from Hans-Dieter Gramm to the Fountain Trust, 12 September 1977.
Letter from Mr. and Mrs. Mike Carney to Tom Smail, 21 September 1977.
Letter from Tom Smail to Mr. and Mrs. M .Carney, 4 October 1977.
Letter from Tom Walker to Tom Smail, 6 October 1977.
Letter from Tom Smail to David Watson, 10 November 1977.
Letter from Tom Smail to Michael Green, 10 November 1977.
Letter from Tom Smail to Catherine Marshall LeSourd, 10 November 1977.
Letter from Tom Smail to Michael Scanlan, 10 November 1977.

1978

Letter from Tom Smail to Catherine Marshall LeSourd, 3 March 1978.
Letter from Tom Smail to Don Double, 10 March 1978.
Letter from Tom Smail to David McKee, 10 March 1978.
Letter from Tom Smail to Lesslie Newbigin, 13 March 1978.
Letter from Lesslie Newbigin to Tom Smail, 25 March 1978.
Letter from Tom Smail to David MacInnes, 31 March 1978.
Letter from Tom Smail to William McAllister, 31 March 1978.
Letter from Don Double to Tom Smail, 1 April 1978.
Letter from Tom Smail to John Bedford, 5 June 1978.
Letter from Tom Smail to David Gillett, 4 August 1978.
Letter from Tom Smail to Jim Glennon, 4 August 1978.
Letter from Jim Glennon to Tom Smail, 17 August 1978.
Letter from Tom Smail to the Archbishop Helder Pessoa Camara, 28 August 1978.
Letter from Tom Smail to Larry Christenson, 15 September 1978.
Letter from Michael Barling to Dennis J. Bennett, 18 October 1978.

1979

Letter from Michael Barling to Norma Hearth, 5 January 1979.
Letter from Michael Barling to Kent E., 22 January 1979.
Letter from Tom Smail to the Bishop of London, 6 February 1979.
Letter from Tom Smail to Tom Forrest, 6 February 1979.
Letter from Tom Smail to William Brown, 6 February 1979.
Letter from the Bishop of London to Tom Smail, 9 February 1979.
Letter from Tom Forrest to Tom Smail, 13 February 1979.
Letter from Tom Smail to the Bishop of Croydon, 23 February 1979.
Letter from William Brown to Tom Smail, 6 March 1979.
Letter from Tom Smail to David Pytches, 12 March 1979.
Letter from Michael Barling to speakers, April 1979.

Letter from David McKee to Michael Barling, 2 April 1979.
Letter from Wilfrid Brieven to Sylvia Lawton, 13 April 1979.
Letter from Tom Smail to Lesslie Newbigin, 23 April 1979.
Letter from Tom Smail to Cardinal Suenens, 23 April 1979.
Letter from Tom Smail to Michael Green, 23 April 1979.
Letter from Tom Smail to Michael Green, 2 May 1979.
Letter from Cardinal Suenens to Tom Smail, 9 May 1979.
Letter from Don Double to Michael Barling, 9 May 1979.
Letter from Michael Green to Tom Smail, 16 May 1979.
Letter from Tom Smail to Cardinal Suenens, 17 May 1979.
Letter from Michael Green to Tom Smail, 29 May 1979.
Letter from the Fountain Trust to speaker, June 1979.
Letter from the secretary to Tom Smail to Michael Green, 8 June 1979.
Letter from Tom Smail to the Bishop of London, 18 July 1979.
Letter from Tom Smail to David MacInnes, 9 August 1979.

No Date (n.d.)

Letter from Arthur Wallis to Michael Harper, n. d.
Letter from Michael Harper to Hans–Jacob Frøen, 22 November.
Letter from Ray Bringham to Michael Harper, n. d.
Letter from Robert de Maar to Michael Harper, n. d.
Letter from the Secretary to Michael Harper to Athanasios Emmert, n. d.
Letter from Tom Smail to the speakers, n. d.
Letter from the Fountain Trust to Maurice, Barnett, Simon Barrington-Ward (Church Missionary Society), Bishop of Kenington, David Bubbers, Wesley Gilpin (Elim Bible College), Kenneth Greet, Clifford Hill (Evangelical Alliance), Don Irving (Church Society), Gordon Landreth (Evangelical Alliance), R. O. Latham, James B. Lawson (St. Andrew's Garrison Church of Scotland), A. L. Macarthur, Fraser McLuskey (St. Columba's Church of Scotland), Harry O. Morton (British Council of Churches), Derek Pattinson (CoE General Synod), David S. Russell (General Secretary of Baptist Union), Harry Sutton (Evangelical Alliance), and David Taylor (Nationwide Initiative in Evangelism), n. d.

Other Materials

Awarded Certificate to Tom Smail from the Presbyter of North Belfast, Presbyterian Church in Ireland, Belfast, 27 June 1972.
"Editorial: Whiter Charismatics?". *CEN* 4144 (13 July 1973) 7.
Email from Michael Harper to the author, 5 October 2005.
Email from Michael Harper to the author, 29 June 2005.
Email from Bob Balkam to the author, 16 November 2005.
Email from Bob Balkam to the author, 18 November 2005.
Email from Bob Balkam to the author, 20 November 2005.
Michael Harper's personal note for the author, 22 July 2005.
Fax transmission from Michael Harper to John Martin, "Obituary of Archbishop Bill Burnett." 29 August, 1994.
No pages. Online: http://biblia.com/christianity2/3b-charismatics.htm.
No pages. Online: http://www.universidadesrenovadas.com/english/renewal/html.

No pages. Online: http://wccx.wcc-coe.org/wc/wjp/vilemov-02-e.html.
"Pope Paul Addresses the Charismatic Renewal".
"Reality at Westminster." *CEN* 4251 (1 August 1975) 2–16.

Interview

Interview with Michael and Jeanne Harper, 8 August 2005, Cambridge.
Interview with Michael Harper, 11 November 2005, Cambridge.
Interview with Tom Smail, 16 February 2006, Croydon.
Interview with David MacInnes, 28 June 2006, Oxford.
Telephone Interview with Tom Walker, 21 December 2006.

SECONDARY SOURCES

Abbott, Walter M. "*Ecumenism.*" In *The Documents of Vatican II: With Notes and Comments by Catholic, Protestants, and Orthodox Authorities*, edited by Walter M. Abbott. London: Geoffrey Chapman, 1966.

Ahonen, L. and Johannesson, J. E. "Sweden." In *The New International Dictionary of Pentecostal and Charismatic Movements*, edited by Stanley Burgess and Eduard M. van der Maas. Grand Rapids, MI: Zondervan, 2002.

Albrecht, Daniel E. *Rites in the Spirit: A Ritual Approach to Pentecostal/Charismatic Spirituality*. Sheffield: Sheffield Academic, 1999.

ARCIC-I Revisited: An Evaluation and a Revision. New York: Catholic Press Association, 1985.

Au, Ho Yan. "In Search of Complementarity between Christology and Pneumatology in Ecumenism in the Charismatic Renewal." *Faith Theological Review* 11/1–2 (January and June 2008) 9–37.

———."The Charismatic Renewal: A Model of Grassroots Unity." In *Ökumene der Zukunft: Hermeneutische Perspektiven und die Suche nach Identität*, edited by Stephen Lakkis et al. Frankfurt am Main: Verlag Otto Lembeck, 2008.

Balkam, Bob. "Roots in Surrey: And Now—Ten People Recall What Guildford '71 Meant to Them." *Renewal* 94 (August–September 1981) 33.

Barling, Michael. "Editorial: Farewell, but Forward." *Renewal* 91 (February–March 1981) 2–4.

———. "Editorial: Unless a Grain of Wheat Dies . . ." *Renewal* 89 (October–November 1980) 2–3.

———. *News and Prayer Letter*, 66 (December 1979).

———. *News and Prayer Letter*, 67 (May 1980).

Barrington–Ward, Simon. "Faith Active in Love?" *Renewal* 71 (October–November 1977) 7–8.

Bate, H. N. *Faith and Order: Proceedings of the World Conference, Lausanne, August 3–21, 1927*. London: Student Christian Movement, 1927.

Bebbington, D. W. *Evangelism in Modern Britain: A History from the 1730's to the 1980's*. London: Unwin Hyman, 1989.

Beckwith, R. T. "The Jewish Background to Christian Worship." In *The Study of Liturgy*, Cheslyn Jones et al. London: SPCK, 1992.

Bell, G. K. A. *The Kingship of Christ: The Story of the WCC*. Harmondsworth: Penguin, 1954.

Biddy, Wesley Scott. "Re-envisioning the Pentecostal Understanding of the Eucharist: An Ecumenical Proposal." *PNEUMA* 28/2 (Fall 2006) 228–51.

Bishop of Coventry. "A Charge to the Clergy of the Diocese of Coventry: The Great and Urgent Need for Spiritual Revival." *Renewal* 11 (October–November 1967) 4–8.

Bishop Kallistos (Ware) of Diokleia. "Communion and Intercommunion." In *Primary Readings on the Eucharist*, edited by Thomas J. Fisch. Collegeville, MN: Liturgical Press, 2004.

Bittlinger, Arnold. *Gifts and Graces*. Translated by Herbert Klassen. London: Hodder &Stoughton, 1967.

———. "Introduction." In *The Church is Charismatic: The World Council of Churches and the Charismatic Renewal*, edited by Arnold Bittlinger. Geneva: WCC, 1982.

Blatherwick, David. *Adventures in Unity: An Introduction of Ecumenical Experiment, Shared Churches and Other United Ventures in the Local Church*. London: BCC, 1974.

Bonino, José Míguez. "The Concern for a Vital and Coherent Theology." *ER* 4 1/2 (April 1989) 160–71.

Braaten, Carl E. *Mother Church: Ecclesiology and Ecumenism*. Minneapolis, MN: Augsburg Fortress, 1998.

Brown, Robert McAfee. "Ecumenism from the Grassroots." *ET* 12/6 (June 1983) 86–88.

Brox, Norbert. *A History of the Early Church*. London: SCM Press, 1994.

Buchanan, Colin. *Encountering Charismatic Worship*. Nottingham: Hassall & Lucking, 1977.

———. "Is There a Charismatic Divide?" *Renewal* 69 (June–July 1977) 21–23.

Butler, David. *Dying to Be One: English Ecumenism: History, Theology and the Future*. London: SCM, 1996.

Carter, David. "Tradition, Eschatology and Ecumenism." *OIC* 32/2 (1996) 149–61.

Chan, Simon. "Mother Church: Toward a Pentecostal Ecclesiology." *PNEUMA* 22/2 (Fall 2000) 177–208.

———. *Liturgical Theology: The Church as Worshipping Community*. Downers Grove, IL: InterVarsity, 2006.

Church of England. *The Charismatic Movement in the Church of England*. London: CIO, 1981.

———. *We Believe in the Holy Spirit: A Report by the Doctrine Commission of the General Synod of the Church of England*. London: Church House, 1991.

Cocksworth, Christopher. *Holy, Holy, Holy: Worshipping the Trinitarian God*. London: Darton, Longman & Todd, 1997.

Congar, Yves. "Amica Contestatio." In *Intercommunion: The Report of the Theological Commission Appointed by the Continuation Committee of the World Conference on Faith and Order Together with a Selection from the Material Presented to the Commission*, edited by Donald Baillie et al. London: SCM, 1952.

———. *Lay People in the Church: A Study for a Theology of Laity*. London: Geoffrey Chapman, 1959.

———. *I Believe in the Holy Spirit Vol. I: The Holy Spirit in the 'Economy'—Revelation and Experience of the Spirit*. London: Geoffrey Chapman, 1983.

———. *I Believe in the Holy Spirit Vol. II: He Is Lord and Giver of Life*. London: Geoffrey Chapman, 1983.

———. *I Believe in the Holy Spirit Vol. III: The River of the Water of Life (Rev 22:1) Flows in the East and in the West*. London: Geoffrey Chapman, 1983.

———. *The Word and the Spirit.* London: Geoffrey Chapman, 1986.

Coomes, David. "1500 'Gathered for Power.'" *CEN* 4144 (13 July 1973) 1.

———. "Nottingham: A Dynamic Freedom and Joy." *Renewal* 46 (August–September 1973) 18–19.

———. "Optimism the Key." *CEN* 4251 (1 August 1975) 1.

Cousen, Cecil. "Ten Times More: And Now—Ten People Recall What Guildford '71 Meant to Them." *Renewal* 94 (August–September 1981) 34.

Cox, Harvey. *Fire from Heaven: The Rise of Pentecostal Spirituality and the Reshaping of Religion in the Twentieth-First Century.* New York: Addison–Wesley, 1995.

Davies, J. G. *The Spirit, the Church and the Sacrament.* London: Faith Press, 1954.

Davis, Rex. *Locusts and Wild Honey: The Charismatic Renewal and the Ecumenical Movement.* Geneva: WCC, 1978.

Davison, Leslie. *Pathway to Power: The Charismatic Movement in Historical Perspective.* London: Fountain Trust, 1971.

———. *Sender and Sent: A Study of Mission.* London: Epworth, 1969.

Del Colle, Ralph. *Christ and the Spirit: Spirit-Christology in Trinitarian Perspective.* New York: Oxford University Press, 1994.

———. "Spirit-Christology: Dogmatic Foundations for Pentecostal–Charismatic Spirituality." *JPT* 3 (1993) 91–112.

"Doctrine of the Twelve Apostles." In *The Didache in Context: Essays on Its Text, History and Transmission,* edited by Clayton N. Jefford, translated by Aelred Cody. Leiden: Brill, 1995.

Duin, Julia. "Catholics on the Pentecostal Trail." *Christianity Today* 36/7 (22 June 1992) 24–27.

Dulles, Avery. *Models of the Church: A Critical Assessment of the Church in All Its Aspects.* Dublin: Gill and Macmillan, 1976.

———. "Earthen Vessels: Institution and Charism in the Church." In *Above Every Name: The Lordship of Christ and Social Systems,* edited by Thomas E. Clarks. Ramsey: Paulist, 1980.

Dunn, James D. G. *Jesus and the Spirit: A Study of the Religious and Charismatic Experience of Jesus and the First Christians as Reflected in the New Testament.* London: SCM, 1975.

Du Plessis, David. "Renewal and the WCC." *Renewal* 60 (December 1975–January 1976) 20–22.

———. *The Renewal of Christianity Must Be Both Charismatic and Ecumenical.* California: David du Plessis, n. d.

———. "Unity Breaks down Barriers." *Renewal* 34 (September 1971) 4–6.

Edwards, David L. *A Concise History of English Christianity: From Roman Britain to the Present Day.* London: Fount, 1998.

———. *The State of the Nation: A Christian Approach to Britain's Economic Crisis.* London: Church Information Office, 1976.

Evans, G. R. *Methods in Ecumenical Theology: The Lessons So Far.* Cambridge: Cambridge University Press, 1996.

———. *The Church and the Churches: Toward an Ecumenical Ecclesiology.* Cambridge: Cambridge University Press, 1994.

Farah, Charles. "Towards a Theology of Ecumenicity or Doctrinal Disagreements and Christian Fellowship." *Theological Renewal* 19 (October 1981) 21–30.

Fowke, Ruth. "Go out, Get on with the Job." *Renewal* 83 (October–November 1979) 5–6.

Fransen, Piet. "Intercommunion." In *Church Membership and Intercommunion*, edited by John Kent and Robert Murray. London: Darton, Longman and Todd, 1973.

Gelpi, Donald L. "The Theological Challenge of Charismatic Spirituality, *PNEUMA* 14/2 (Fall 1992) 185–97.

Gensichen, Hans W. *The Elements of Ecumenism*. Madras: Christian Literature Society, 1954.

Goodall, Norman. *The Uppsala 68 Report: Official Report of the Fourth Assembly of the WCC Uppsala July 4–20, 1968*. Geneva: WCC, 1968.

———. *Uppsala Speaks: Section Reports of the Fourth Assembly of the World Council of Churches Uppsala 1968*. Geneva: WCC, 1968.

Granowski, Margaret. "The Hope of Unity." *Monthly Newsletter of St. John's, Downshire Hill* 246 (August–September 1971).

Gros, Jeffrey, et al. *Growth in Agreement II: Reports and Agreed Statements of Ecumenical Conversations on a World Level, 1982–1998*. Geneva: WCC, 2000.

Grossmann, Siegfried. *Stewards of God's Grace*. Exeter: Paternoster, 1981.

Gunstone, John. *A People for His Praise: Renewal and Congregational Life*. London: Hodder & Stoughton, 1978.

———. "A Strong and Burning Light." *Renewal* 192 (May 1992) 14–17.

———. *Greater Things Than These: A Personal Account of the Charismatic Movement*. Leighton Buzzard: Faith Press, 1974.

———. "Spirit and Eucharist: Experience and Doctrine." *Renewal* 64 (August–September 1976) 11–13.

Haenchen, E. *A Commentary on the Gospel of John II*. Philadelphia: Fortress, 1984.

Harbour, Richard. "Glory in Westminster." *Renewal* 59 (October–November 1975) 4.

Harper, Michael. *A New Way of Living*. London: Hodder & Stoughton, 1973.

———. "Editorial: A Narrowing of the Divide." *Renewal* 55 (February–March 1975) 2–4.

———. "Editorial: Christian Unity—The Growing Fact." *Renewal* 30 (December 1970–January 1971) 2–5.

———. "Editorial: From Guildford to Nottingham." *Renewal* 45 (June–July 1973) 2–3.

———. "Editorial: No Cosy Marinas." *Renewal* 59 (October–November 1975) 2–3.

———. "Editorial: Ten Years Young." *Renewal* 53 (October–November 1974) 2–4.

———. "Letter of Welcome." In *Nottingham University 9–14 July 1973, Gathered for Power*.

———. "Memorandum Sent to David Pawson, Harold Owen, Fred Pride, Michael Pusey." 18 December 1970.

———. *Newsletter* 41 (February 1972).

———. *Newsletter* 43 (June 1972).

———. *Newsletter* 44 (October 1972).

———. *None Can Guess*. London: Hodder & Stoughton, 1972.

———. "Principles of Congregational Worship." *OIC* 13/1–2 (1977) 36–39.

———. "Prospects for a New Decade." *Renewal* 88 (August–September 1980) 14–15.

———. "The Coming-of-Age: Fountain Trust International Conference at Guildford 12–17 July." *Renewal* 34 (September 1971) 2–4.

———. *These Wonderful Gifts*. London: Hodder & Stoughton, 1989.

———. *This Is the Day: A Fresh Look at Christian Unity.* London: Hodder & Stoughton, 1979.

———. *Tip-toeing through the Tulips: Unity and Reconciliation, and ICCOWE's Future* (25 February 1998).

———. "30 Year of Renewal Magazine: From the London Hilton to the Toronto Vineyard." *Renewal* 236 (January 1996) 10–12.

Hastings, Adrian. *A History of English Christianity 1920–1990.* London: SCM, 1991.

Henderson, Jennifer and Anne Primavesi. "The Witness of the Holy Spirit." *ER* 41/3 (1989) 426–35.

Hill, Christopher. "Route-Planning the Future Ecumenical Journey." In *The Unity We Have and the Unity We Seek: Ecumenical Proposal for the Third Millennium,* edited by Jeremy Morris and Nicholas Sagovsky. London: T&T Clark, 2003.

Hinze, Bradford. "Releasing the Power of the Spirit in a Trinitarian Ecclesiology." In *Advents of the Spirit: An Introduction to the Current Study of Pneumatology,* edited by Bradford E. Hinze and D. Lyle Dabney. Milwaukee, WI: Marquette University Press, 2001.

Hocken, Peter. "A Survey of the Worldwide Charismatic Movement." In *The Church Is Charismatic: The WCC and the Charismatic Renewal,* edited by Arnold Bittlinger. Geneva: WCC, 1981.

———. "Charismatic Movement" and "Fountain Trust." In *International Dictionary of Pentecostal and Charismatic Movements,* edited by Stanley M. Burgess and Eduard M. van der Mass. Grand Rapids, MI: Zondervan, 2002.

———. "Charismatic Renewal the Churches and Unity." *OIC* 15/4 (1979) 310–21.

———. "New Patterns of Formation in the Roman Catholic Church and the Role of Catholic Charismatic Renewal." *AJPS* 9/1 (2006) 127–41.

———. "The Pentecostal–Charismatic Movement as Revival and Renewal." *PNEUMA* 3/1 (Spring 1981) 31–47.

———. "Revival and Renewal." *JEPTA* 18 (1998) 49–63.

———. *The Spirit of Unity: How Renewal is Breaking down Barriers between Evangelicals and Roman Catholics.* Cambridge: Grove Books, 2001.

———. *Streams of Renewal: The Origins and Early Development of the Charismatic Movement in Great Britain.* Cumbria: Paternoster, 1997.

Hodgson, Leonard. *The Second World Conference on Faith and Order Held at Edinburgh, August 3–18, 1937.* London: Student Christian Movement, 1938.

Hodgson, Peter. *Jesus-Word and Presence: An Essay in Christology.* Philadelphia, PA: Fortress, 1971.

Hollenweger, Walter J. "Towards a Church Renewed and United in the Spirit." In *The Church Is Charismatic: The WCC and the Charismatic Renewal,* edited by Arnold Bittlinger. Geneva: WCC, 1982.

———. "Two Extraordinary Pentecostal Ecumenists." *ER* 52/3 (July 2000). No pages. Online: http://www.findarticles.com/p/articles/mi_m2065/is_3_52/ai_66279090/print.

Horton, Michael S. "Can We Be Confessional & Catholic? Prospects for Christian Unity Today." *MR* 14/5 (September–October 2005). No pages. Online: http://www.modernreformation.org/mh05unity.htm.

Hurley, Michael. *Christian Unity: An Ecumenical Second Spring?* Dublin: Veritas, 1998.

Intercommunion: The Position of the Roman Catholic Church—Statement of the Ecumenical Commission for England and Wales. London: Catholic Truth Society, February 1969.

Irenaeus of Lyons. "Against Heresies: On the Detection and Refutation of the Knowledge Falsely So Called, Book 1." In *Irenaeus of Lyons*, edited by Robert M. Grant. London: Routledge, 1997.

———. "The Demonstration of the Apostolic Preaching." In *St Irenaeus of Lyons: On the Apostolic Preaching*. Translated by John Behr. New York: St Vladimir's Seminary Press, 1997.

Irvin, Dale T. "'Drawing All Together in One Bond of Love': The Ecumenical Vision of William J. Seymour and the Azusa Street Revival." *JPT* 6 (1995) 25–53.

Irwin, Kevin W. *Context and Text: Method in Liturgical Theology*. Collegeville, MN: Liturgical Press, 1994.

John Paul II. "Ut Unum Sint: On Commitment to Ecumenism." Online: http:www .vatican.va/holy_father/john_paul_ii/encyclicals/documents/hf_jp.

Jones, C. P. M. "The Eucharist: The New Testament." In *The Study of Liturgy*, edited by Cheslyn Jones et al. London: SPCK, 1992.

Kärkkäinen, Veli-Matti. *Pneumatology: The Holy Spirit in Ecumenical, International, and Contextual Perspective*. Grand Rapids, MI: Baker, 2002.

Kasper, Walter. *That They May All Be One: The Call to Unity Today*. London: Burns & Oates, 2004.

Kavanagh, Adrian. *On Liturgical Theology: The Hale Memorial Lectures of Seabury-Western Theological Seminary, 1981*. Collegeville, MN: Liturgical Press, 1984.

Kay, James F. "The *Lex orandi* in Recent Protestant Theology." In *Ecumenical Theology in Worship, Doctrine, and Life: Essays Presented to Geoffrey Wainwright on His Sixtieth Birthday*, David S. Cunningham et al. Oxford: Oxford University Press, 1999.

Kay, William K. *Apostolic Networks in Britain: New Ways of Being Church*. Milton Keynes: Paternoster, 2007.

Keshishian, Catholicos Aram I. *Conciliar Fellowship: A Common Goal*. Geneva: WCC, 1996.

Killinger, John. *Leave It to the Spirit: Commitment and Freedom in the New Liturgy*. London: SCM, 1971.

Kim, Dongsoo. "The Paraclete: The Spirit of the Church." *AJPS* 5/2 (2002) 255–70.

Kinnamon, Michael. *Signs of the Spirit: Official Report Seventh Assembly, Canberra, Australia, 7–20 August 1991*. Geneva: WCC, 1991.

Knowles, B. "New Zealand." In *The New International Dictionary of Pentecostal and Charismatic Movements*, edited by Stanley Burgess and Eduard M. van der Maas. Grand Rapids, MI: Zondervan, 2002.

Küng, Hans. *The Church*. New York: Image Books, 1976.

———. *On Being a Christian*. London: SCM, 1995.

Küng, Hans and Jürgen Moltmann. "Editorial: Towards an Ecumenical Confession of Faith." In *An Ecumenical Confession of Faith?*, edited by Hans Küng and Jürgen Moltmann New York: Crossroad, 1979.

Lange, Ernst. *And Yet It Moves: Dream and Reality of the Ecumenical Movement*. Belfast: Christian Journals, 1978.

Larere, Philippe. *The Lord's Supper: Toward an Ecumenical Understanding of the Eucharist*. Collegeville, MN: Liturgical Press, 1993.

Lathrop, Gordon. "Knowing Something a Little: On the Role of the *Lex Orandi* in the Search for Christian Unity." In *So We Believe So We Pray: Towards Koinonia in Worship*, edited by Thomas F. Best and Dagmar Heller. Geneva: WCC, 1995.

Lee, Maurice and Miroslav Volf. "The Spirit and the Church." *Advents of the Spirit: An Introduction to the Current Study of Pneumatology,* edited by Bradford E. Hinze and D. Lyle Dabney. Milwaukee, WI: Marquette University Press, 2001.

Leeming, Bernard. *The Vatican Council and Christian Unity: A Commentary on the Decree on Ecumenism of the Second Vatican Council, Together with a Translation of the Text.* London: Darton, Longman & Todd, 1966.

Machin, G. I. T. *Churches and Social Issues in Twentieth-Century Britain.* Oxford: Clarendon, 1998.

Marthaler, Bernard L. "Grassroots Ecumenism and Religious Education." *ET* 16 (April 1987) 65–68.

Mather, Anne. "The Theology of the Charismatic Movement in Britain from 1964 to the Present Day." PhD diss., University of Wales, 1983.

McCrea Cavert, Samuel. "Response." In *The Documents of Vatican II: With Notes and Comments by Catholic, Protestants, and Orthodox Authorities,* edited by Walter M. Abbott. London: Geoffrey Chapman, 1966.

McDonnell, Kilian. "A Response to Bernd Jochen Hilberath." In *Advents of the Spirit: An Introduction to the Current Study of Pneumatology,* edited by Bradford E. Hinze and D. Lyle Dabney. Milwaukee, WI: Marquette University Press, 2001.

———. "Church Reactions to the Charismatic Renewal."

———. "Communion Ecclesiology and Baptism in the Spirit: Tertullian and the Early Church." *TS* 49/4 (December 1988) 671–93.

———. "Ecumenism: Made Miserable by Success?" *Worship* 49/2, 62–84.

———. *The Other Hand of God: The Holy Spirit as the Universal Touch and Goal.* Collegeville, MN: Liturgical Press, 2003.

McNaspy, C. J. "Laity." In *The Documents of Vatican II: With Notes and Comments by Catholic, Protestants, and Orthodox Authorities,* edited by Walter M. Abbott. London: Geoffrey Chapman, 1966.

Merriam-Webster's Collegiate Dictionary. (Electronic Dictionary).

Missen, Alfred. "I Walked out: And Now—Ten People Recall What Guildford '71 Meant to Them." *Renewal* 94 (August–September 1981) 34.

Moltmann, Jürgen. *The Church in the Power of the Spirit: A Contribution to Messianic Theology.* London: SCM, 1977.

———. *Experiences in Theology: Ways and Forms of Christian Theology.* London: SCM, 2000.

———. *The Future of Creation.* London: SCM, 1979.

———. "The Spirit Gives Life: Spirituality and Vitality." In *All Together in One Place: Theological Papers from the Brighton Conference on World Evangelization,* edited by Harold D. Hunter and Peter D. Hocken. Sheffield: Sheffield Academic, 1993.

———. *The Spirit of Life: A Universal Affirmation.* London: SCM, 1993.

———. *Theology of Hope: On the Ground and the Implications of a Christian Eschatology.* London: SCM, 1967.

———. "The Trinitarian Personhood of the Holy Spirit." *Advents of the Spirit: An Introduction to the Current Study of Pneumatology,* edited by Bradford E. Hinze and D. Lyle Dabney. Milwaukee, WI: Marquette University Press, 2001.

Morton, Andrew. "Depths of Unity." *Renewal* 71 (October–November 1977) 9–10.

Mühlen, Heribert. *A Charismatic Theology: Initiation in the Spirit.* London: Burns & Oates, 1978.

————. "Charismatic and Sacramental Understanding of the Church: Dogmatic Aspects of Charismatic Renewal." *OIC* 12/4 (1976) 333–47.

Murray, John C. "Ecumenism: The Next Step." *OIC* 25/2 (April 1989) 163–68.

Newbigin, Lesslie. "What is 'A Local Church Truly United'? In *Growing Together into Unity: Texts of the Faith and Order Commission on Conciliar Fellowship*, edited by Choan Seng Song. Christian Literature Society, 1978.

Nixon, Robin. "Gospel and Spirit." *Renewal* 69 (June–July 1977) 18–21.

O'Connor, Edward. "The Hidden Roots of the Charismatic Renewal in the Catholic Church." In *Aspects of Pentecostal-Charismatic Origins*, edited by Vinson Synan. Plainfield, NJ: Logos International, 1975.

————. *The Pentecostal Movement in the Catholic Church*. Notre Dame, IN: Ave Maria Press, 1971.

————. *Pope Paul and the Spirit: Charisms and Church Renewal in the Teaching of Paul VI*. Notre Dame, IN: Ave Maria Press, 1978.

O'Keeffe, Matthew F. "An Investigation into the Charismatic Movement in So Far as It Is Related to the Nature of the Roman Catholic Church." MA diss., University of Manchester, 1980.

O'Neil, J. "Catholic Charismatic Renewal: An Investigation of the Issues". MA diss., University of Kent, 1978.

Outler, Albert C. "Pneumatology as an Ecumenical Frontier." *ER* 41/3 (1989) 363–74.

Packer, J. I. *Keep in Step with the Spirit*. Leicester: InterVarsity Press, 1984.

————. "Piety on Fire." *CT* (12 May 1989) 18–22.

Pernet, Susan, "Catholics and Communion." *Renewal* 61 (February–March 1976) 9.

Potter, Philip. "Paper: Charismatic Renewal and the WCC." In *The Church Is Charismatic: The WCC and the Charismatic Renewal*, edited by Arnold Bittlinger. Geneva: WCC, 1982.

Phypers, David. "Charismatic Renewal: Where Are We Now?" *Renewal* 83 (October–November 1979) 28–30.

"Prayer of Pope John XXIII to the Holy Spirit for the Success of the Ecumenical Council." In *The Documents of Vatican II: With Notes and Comments by Catholic, Protestants, and Orthodox Authorities*, edited by Walter M. Abbott. London: Geoffrey Chapman, 1966.

Pinnock, Clark H. *Flame of Love: A Theology of the Holy Spirit*. Downers Grove, IL: InterVarsity Press, 1996.

Pius XI. "Mortalium Animos." (1928). Online: http://www.vatican.va/holy_father/pius _xi/encyclicals/documents/hf_pxi_enc_19280106_mortalium–animos_en.html.

Pius XII, "Mystici Corporis Christi." (1943). Online: http://www.vatican.va/holy_father /pius_xii/encyclicals/documents/hf_p-xii_enc_29061943_mystici-corporis -christi_en.html.

Price, Hetley and Gordon S. Wakefield. *Unity at the Local Level*. Oxford: A. R. Mowbray, 1964.

Radano, John A. "Response: Ecumenism in the Catholic Charismatic Renewal Movement." *JES* 17/4 (Fall 1980) 657–60.

Rahner, Karl. *The Spirit in the Church*. New York: Seabury, 1979.

————. *Theological Investigations Vol. 12: Confrontation*. London: Darton, Longman & Todd, 1974.

Raiser, Konrad. "Confessing the Lord Jesus Christ as God and Saviour." *ER* 37/2 (April 1985) 182–88.

————. *Ecumenism in Transition: A Paradigm Shift in the Ecumenical Movement?* Geneva: WCC, 1991.

Ranaghan, Kevin and Dorothy. *Catholic Pentecostals.* New York: Paulist, 1969.

Richards, John. *But Deliver Us from Evil: Demonic Dimension in Pastoral Care.* London: Darton, Longman & Todd, 1974.

————. "Tears, A Gift of the Spirit?" *Renewal* 86 (April–May 1980) 31–33.

Reid, Gavin. *A New Happiness: Christ's Pattern for Living in Today's World.* Nashville: Abington, 1976.

————. *The Elaborate Funeral.* London: Hodder & Stoughton, 1972.

————. *The Gagging of God.* London: Hodder & Stoughton, 1969.

Robeck, C. M. "World Council of Churches." In *International Dictionary of Pentecostal and Charismatic Movements,* edited by Stanley M. Burgess and Eduard M. van der Mass. Grand Rapids, MI: Zondervan, 2000.

Robinson, E. B., "Youth With A Mission." In *International Dictionary of Pentecostal and Charismatic Movements,* edited by Stanley M. Burgess and Eduard M. van der Mass. Grand Rapids, MI: Zondervan, 2000.

Robinson, Martin. "The Charismatic Anglican—Historical and Contemporary: A Comparison of the Life and Work of Alexander Boddy (1854–1930) and Michael C. Harper." MLitt diss., University of Birmingham, 1976.

————. "To the End of the Earth: The Pilgrimage of an Ecumenical Pentecostal, David J. du Plessis (1905–1987)." PhD diss., University of Birmingham, 1987.

Rosato, Philip J. "Called by God, in the Holy Spirit: Pneumatological Insights into Ecumenism." *ER* 30/2 (April 1978) 110–26.

Sansom, Hugh and Teddy Saunders. *David Watson: A Biography.* London: Hodder & Stoughton, 1992.

Scotland, Nigel. *Charismatics and the New Millennium: The Impact of Charismatic Christianity from 1960 into the New Millennium.* Guildford: Eagle, 2000.

Sellgren, Eric. "God Spoke to Me: And Now—Ten People Recall What Guildford '71 Meant to Them." *Renewal* 94 (August–September 1981) 33–34.

Shadwick, Alan. "Spiritual Renewal at Guildford and Singing in Tongues." *Church Times* (23 July 1971) 14, 16.

Simonson, Conrad. *The Christology of the Faith and Order Movement.* Leiden: Brill, 1972.

Smail, Tom, "Editorial: Growth Business." *Renewal* 70 (August–September 1977) 2–4.

————. "Editorial: Lights Show Red and Amber." *Renewal* 72 (December 1977–January 1978) 2–4.

————. "Editorial: The More We Are Together." *Renewal* 71 (October–November 1977) 2–4.

————. "Editorial: Simplicity at the Centre." *Renewal* 66 (December 1976–January 1977) 2–5.

————. "Editorial: Treasure and Trash and the Need to Be Honest." *Renewal* 65 (October–November 1976) 2–3.

————. *The Forgotten Father.* Eugene, OR: Wipf & Stock, 2001.

————. "In Spirit and in Truth: Reflections on Charismatic Worship." *The Love of Power or The Power of Love: A Careful Assessment of the Problem within the Charismatic and Word-of-Faith Movements,* edited by Tom Smail et al. Minneapolis, MN: Bethany, 1994.

————. "In Tune with the Trinity 2: The Son, the Givenness of God." *Theological Renewal* 5 (1977) 2–7.

————. *Newsletter* 46 (May 1973).

————. *Newsletter* 48 (December 1973).

————. *Newsletter* 50 (September 1974).

————. *Newsletter* 51 (December 1974).

————. *Newsletter* 52 (March 1975).

————. An attached letter from Michael Harper, *Newsletter* 53 (May 1975).

————. *Newsletter* 53 (May 1975).

————. *Newsletter* 54 (August 1975).

————. *Newsletter* 56 (March 1976).

————. *Newsletter* 57 (August 1976).

————. *Newsletter* 58 (April 1977).

————. *Newsletter* 59 (April 1977).

————. *Newsletter* 61 (December 1977).

————. *Newsletter* 64 (March 1979).

————. *The Giving Gifts: The Holy Spirit in Person*. London: Hodder & Stoughton, 1988.

Smeeton, Donald Dean. "A Pentecostal Looks again at Vatican II." *PNEUMA* 5/1 (Spring 1983) 34–45.

Stackhouse, I. R. "Revivalism, Faddism and the Practice of the Church: A Theological Trajectory for Charismatic Renewal in the United Kingdom." PhD diss., University of Brunel, 2003.

Stefen, Crinisor. "The Paraclete and Prophecy in the Johannine Community." *PNEUMA* 27/2 (Fall 2005) 273–96.

Stevenson, Kenneth W. "Lex Orandi and Lex Credendi—Strange Bed-Fellows?: Some Reflections on Worship and Doctrine." *SJT* 2(1986) 225–41.

Stookey, Laurence, H. *Eucharist: Christ's Feast with the Church*. Nashville: Abington, 1993.

Suenens, Léon Joseph. *Ecumenism and Charismatic Renewal: Theological and Pastoral Orientations, Malines Document 2*. London: Darton, Longman & Todd, 1978.

————. "The Holy Spirit: Our Hope." *Worship* 49/5 (May 1975) 254–62.

————. "My Encounters with the Holy Spirit." *Renewal* 100 (August–September 1982) 27–29.

Sullivan, Emmanuel. *Baptized into Hope*. London: SPCK, 1980.

————. *Can the Pentecostal Movement Renew the Churches?* Geneva: WCC, 1972.

————. "Seeing the Whole Church Renewed." *Renewal* 46 (August–September 1973) 20–25.

Thigpen, T. P. "Catholic Charismatic Renewal." In *International Dictionary of Pentecostal and Charismatic Movements*, edited by Stanley M. Burgess and Eduard M. van der Mass. Grand Rapids, MI: Zondervan, 2000.

Till, Barry. *The Churches Search for Unity*. Harmondsworth: Penguin, 1972.

Tillard, J. M. R. "Ecumenism: The Church's Costly Hope." *OIC* 35/3 (1999) 218–27.

Torrance, T. F. "Eschatology and the Eucharist." In *Intercommunion: The Report of the Theological Commission Appointed by the Continuation Committee of the World Conference on Faith and Order Together with a Selection from the Material Presented to the Commission*, edited by Donald Baillie and John Marsh. London: SCM, 1952.

Urquhart, Colin. "My Heart Rejoiced: And Now—Ten People Recall What Guildford '71 Meant to Them." *Renewal* 94 (August–September 1981) 32.

————. *When the Spirit Comes*. London: Hodder & Stoughton, 1974.

Vatican Council II, "Apostolicam Actuositatem," "Lumen Gentium," "Sacrosanctum Concilium," "Unitatis Redintegratio." In *The Documents of Vatican II: With Notes and Comments by Catholic, Protestants, and Orthodox Authorities*, edited by Walter M. Abbott. London: Geoffrey Chapman, 1966.

Vischer, Lukas. "Conciliar Fellowship and Councils: Churches on their Way to a Universal Council." *ER* 41/4 (October 1989) 501–4.

————. "The Epiclesis: Sign of Unity and Renewal." *SL* 6 (1969) 30–39.

————. "The Unity We Seek: Origin and Meaning of the Concept 'Conciliar Fellowship.'" In *Growing Together into Unity: Texts of the Faith and Order Communion on Conciliar Fellowship*, edited by Choan Seng Song. Christian Literature Society, 1978.

————. "Visible Unity—Realistic Goal or Mirage?" *OIC* 18/1 (1982) 18–30.

Visser't Hooft, W. A. *The Evanston Report: The Second Assembly of the World Council of Churches 1954*. London: SCM, 1955.

————. "The Calling of the World Council of Churches." *ER* 14/2 (January 1962) 216–26.

————. *Has the Ecumenical Movement a Future?* Belfast: Christian Journal, 1974.

————. "The General Ecumenical Development since 1948." In *The Ecumenical Advance: A History of the Ecumenical Movement, Vol. 2, 1948–1968*, edited by Harold E. Fey. Geneva: WCC, 1970.

————. *Memoirs*. Geneva: WCC, 1973.

————. *The New Delhi Report: The Third Assembly of the World Council of Churches 1961*. London: SCM, 1962.

————. *No Other Name: The Choice between Syncretism and Christian Universalism*. London: SCM, 1963.

Volf, Miroslav, "A Protestant Response." *Concilium* 3 (1996) 37–44.

————. *After Our Likeness: The Church as the Image of the Trinity*. Grand Rapids, MI: William B. Eerdmans, 1998.

Wainwright, Geoffrey. *Doxology: The Praise of God in Worship, Doctrine and Life—A Systematic Theology*. London: Epworth, 1980.

————. *Eucharist and Eschatology*. London: Epworth, 1971.

Walker, Andrew. *Restoring the Kingdom: The Radical Christianity of the House Church Movement*. London: Hodder & Stoughton, 1985.

Walker, Tom. *Renew Us by Your Spirit*. London: Hodder & Stoughton, 1982.

Walters, Ken. "Wales and the Charismatic Renewal." *Renewal* 64 (August–September 1976) 13–15.

Whitehead, Charles, "What is the Nature of the Catholic Charismatic Renewal?" No pages. Online: http://www.ccr.org.uk/crnature.htm.

Williams, J. Rodman. "Genuine Concern for Pentecostal Theology: Fountain Trust International Conference at Guildford 12–17 July." *Renewal* 34 (September 1971) 6–9.

Work, Martin H. "Laity." In *The Documents of Vatican II: With Notes and Comments by Catholic, Protestants, and Orthodox Authorities*, edited by Walter M. Abbott. London: Geoffrey Chapman, 1966.

WCC, "A Statement of Concerns (1975)." In *Presence, Power, Praise: Documents on the Charismatic Renewal Vol. III: International   Documents, Numbers 1–11, 1973–1980*, edited by Kilian McDonnell. Collegeville, MN: Liturgical Press, 1980.

————. *Baptism, Eucharist and Ministry: Faith and Order Paper No. 111*. No pages. Online: http://wcc-coe.org/wcc/what/faith/bem3.html.

————. "Church & Ecumenical Relations: Toronto Statement." No pages. Online: http://www.wcc-coe.org/wcc/what/ecumenical/ts-e.html.

————. "Concepts of Unity and Models of Union, September 1973." In *What Kind of Unity?* Geneva: WCC, 1974.

————. "Constitution of the World Council of Churches, As Amended at the Eighth Assembly, December 1998." Online: http://wccx.wcc-coe.org/wcc/who/vilemov–02-e.html.

————. "Document No. A01: Report of the Moderator." Online: http://www.wcc-assembly.info/en/themeissues/assembly-documents/2-plenarypresentations/moderators-general-secretarys-reports/report-of-the-moderator.html.

————. "Report of the General Secretary." Online: http://www2.wcccoe.org/ccdocuments.nsf/index/gen-3-en.html.

————. "World Council of Churches." Online: http://www/wcccoe.org/wcc/who/histor-e.html.

Yong, Amos. *Spirit-Word-Community: Theological Hermeneutics in Trinitarian Perspective.* Aldershot: Ashgate, 2002.

Zizioulas, John. *Being As Communion: Studies in Personhood and the Church.* New York: St Vladimir's Seminary Press, 1985.

————. "The Doctrine of God the Trinity Today: Suggestions for an Ecumenical Study." In *The Forgotten Trinity: A Selection of Papers Presented to the BCC Study Commission on Trinitarian Doctrine Today,* edited by Alasdair I. C. Heron. London: BCC/CCBI, 1991.

————. "Eucharist and Catholicity." In *Primary Readings on the Eucharist,* edited by Thomas J. Fisch. Collegeville, MN: Liturgical Press, 2004.

Subject/Name Index

A

anamnesis, 11, 174–178, 182, 218,
242–249
Anglican evangelical, 35, 42, 196
apostolic,
apostolic authority, 167
apostolic church, 197, 242, 226, 244
apostolic college, 227
apostolic faith, 169, 197
apostolic ministry, 187
apostolic period, 213
apostolic power, 167
Apostolic Church of Mexico, 186
Apostolic Faith Mission of South
Africa, 121, 186
Assemblies of God (AG), 37–40, 45,
110, 121, 137, 186

B

Baptism in the Spirit/Spirit baptism, 12,
13, 16, 36, 37, 42, 46, 65, 74, 75,
84, 87, 100, 105, 106, 107, 121,
122, 140, 145, 216, 217, 218,
220, 222, 234
Balkam, Bob, 47, 76, 116, 118, 119, 131,
135
Barling, Michael, 37, 49, 51, 67
Barrington–Ward, Simon, 84, 112, 121
Belben, Howard, 84, 106, 121
Bennett, Dennis, 14, 40
Bennett, Michael, 109, 117
Bittlinger, Arnold, 109, 113, 121
Bradford Circle, 44
Brännström, Rune, 62
British Council of Churches, 4, 77, 133

Brown, Jim, 107
Buchanan, Colin, 35, 41, 49, 54, 93, 141
Burnett, Bill, 66, 71, 82, 87, 104, 129,
149

C

Catholic Charismatic Renewal
International Information
Office, 236
charisms, 9–13, 16, 17, 116, 140,
151–155, 162–164, 170–182,
191–203, 216–222, 230–234,
247, 248
Chiu Ban It, 64, 65, 105
Christenson, Larry, 14, 86, 109
Christian Advance Ministries, 80, 81
Christus praesens, 10, 216–222, 232, 245
Christocentric Universalism, 204, 205,
208, 209, 247
Church of England, 4, 20–22, 25, 50, 76,
121, 145, 146, 155, 189
Church of England Evangelical
Council, 42
Church of Scotland, 22, 23, 27, 48, 74,
76, 107, 121
Clark, Sundar, 63, 66
Classical Pentecostal, 33, 37, 39, 145
Classical Pentecostal Movement, 14, 26
communion,
as fellowship, 7, 17, 119, 187, 191,
194, 199, 209, 219
as eucharist, 11, 71, 104, 124, 128–
131, 165–170, 173, 176, 177
concelebration, 121, 127–129, 139, 182,
198

conciliar fellowship, 10, 199–203, 221, 222

continuity
  discontinuity, 15
  ecumenical, 244, 245
  eschatological, 8, 238, 245,
  historical continuity, 178, 223, 240, 247
  in modern ecumenical history, 8, 9, 223, 247
  of the church, 185
convergence, 8, 9, 223, 237, 238, 245, 247
Cousen, Cecil, 36, 73, 90, 111
Crumpton, Derek, 81, 82

D

Dagen, 78, 79
Dallière, Emile, 70, 83, 126
Dallière, Louis, 126
Davies, William R., 84
Davison, Leslie, 77, 84, 86, 91, 106, 131, 134
declericalization, 11, 153, 155
de Monléon, Albert, 114, 120
Demonstration of the Apostolic Preaching, 213
Denominationalism, 1
  denomination, 29, 38, 52, 55, 98, 110, 142
  denominational, 1, 5, 13, 27, 28, 38, 43, 55, 88, 96, 100, 110, 128, 137, 138, 150, 163
  diversity, 10–12, 24, 37, 98, 119, 125, 126, 146, 151, 152, 180, 190, 200, 220, 221, 230, 236, 249
Dunn, James D. G., 84, 90, 121, 243
du Plessis, David, 39, 82, 99, 113, 141, 234

E

Ecumenical Academy, 81, 109, 113, 121
ecumenical movement, 2, 4–8, 139, 146, 152, 166, 197, 198, 200,
    204, 205, 208–211, 222–224, 235–249
Elim Pentecostal Church, 37, 39
epiclesis, 11, 176–178, 182, 247
Episcopal, 14, 71, 101, 103, 196, 198, 208
Eucharist,
  and anamnesia, 174–178, 211
  and charisms, 11, 12, 172–182
  and epiclesis, 176–178
  and eschatology, 179
  and institution, 167, 175, 182, 183
  and koinonia, 177, 187
  and Roman Catholics, 170
  and the charismatic renewal, 165, 171, 181
  and the church, 168, 172, 210
  and the Holy Spirit, 11, 176–178
  and worship, 11, 98, 127, 141, 247
  as ecumenical problem, 139, 165, 172
  at the international conferences, 103, 121, 124, 128–130, 165, 170, 173, 198
  celebration of, 8, 199
  early church, 127
  unity, 81, 166–168, 171, 173, 175, 181, 182
evangelicals, 33, 36, 37, 41–43, 52, 101, 136, 138, 139
Evangelical Alliance, 53, 113, 132, 133

F

faith and order, 2, 201, 204, 239
Faith and Order/F&O, 1, 9, 166, 196, 199, 204–209, 223
Fisherfolk, 58, 69, 70, 76, 97, 156
formalism, 20, 21, 25, 186
Forrest, Tom, 86, 118
Fowke, Ruth, 111
Fox, Langton, 104, 168, 168
Full Gospel Businessmen's Fellowship International/FGBMFI, 40

G

gifts, 16, 72, 111, 114, 117, 126, 147,
149, 150, 151, 175, 178, 188,
197, 204, 230, 249
Gilpin, Wesley, 40, 121
Gospel and Spirit, 35, 42
Graham, Billy, 21, 22
Graham, Jim, 36, 108
Green, Michael, 60, 104, 125
Greene, Colin, 36
Guildford 1971, 31, 32, 38, 45, 57,
58, 61, 63, 67, 70–83, 90–111,
114, 119–126, 131, 133, 134,
137–139, 141, 143, 144, 146,
149, 155, 156, 173

H

Harbour, Richard, 115, 124, 148
Hare, Richard/Bishop of Pontefract, 71,
75, 104, 129, 170, 195
Harper, Jeanne, 48, 92, 119
Harper, Michael, 6, 8, 12, 14, 16, 21–50,
54, 55, 57, 58, 61, 62, 64, 65, 66,
68, 70, 72, 75, 76, 78– 93, 97,
105, 108, 109, 110, 112, 113, 114,
115, 119, 121–138, 146, 170
healing, 60, 95, 215, 110, 133, 147, 215
as charism, 10, 16, 60, 102, 111,
126, 140, 147, 151, 162, 181,
187, 188, 198, 231, 248
as ministry, 31, 54, 102, 105, 115,
146, 149
fellowship, 60, 102
inner, 89, 115, 118
of divisions, 101, 147, 148, 159
of relationships, 111
physical, 111, 115, 118, 146, 153,
159, 175
psychological, 111, 146
spiritual, 20, 115, 117
Holl, Barbara, 89, 124, 128, 156
Hollenweger, Walter, 77, 84, 235
Horner, John, 76, 106
house churches, 23, 33, 35–37, 43, 44,
55, 110

I

institution, 8, 9, 10, 13, 17, 182–191,
194–199, 202, 203, 221, 225,
237, 238, 245, 247, 248
intercession, 126, 149, 150, 151, 161,
162, 181, 231
intercommunion, 2, 166–169, 173, 182
International Catholic Charismatic
Renewal Organization Council,
229
International Missionary Council, 204,
223
Irenaeus of Lyons, 10, 213

J

Jones, Bryn, 43, 44

K

Kerr, Cecil, 88
Keswick movement, 40
koinonia, 149, 152, 153, 177, 249

L

laity, 4, 6, 11, 20, 55, 93, 142, 143, 154,
158, 201, 229–234, 247
Lake, Frank, 111
Langstaff, Alan, 79
Lebeau, Paul, 47, 115, 118, 128
lex orandi, lex credendi, 11, 161, 163,
164, 181, 247
Life and Work/L&W, 204, 205, 208, 223
Liturgy, 5, 93, 121, 127, 140, 144,
160–164, 176, 178, 184, 184,
230, 232, 233, 234, 248
Lord's Supper, see "Eucharist"
Lundgren, Ivar, 78

M

MacInnes, David, 8, 20
MacLeod, George, 76, 86, 107
MacNutt, Francis, 61, 115, 128, 165

Malines document, 15, 116
Mansell, David, 43
McAlpine, Campbell, 30, 52, 81, 112
McAllister, William, 89, 110
McBain, Douglas, 22, 53, 109, 171
McDonnell, Kilian, 6, 120, 122, 123,
    190, 191, 213, 216, 228
McKenna, Briege, 117
Missen, Alfred, 121, 137
Morton, Andrew, 107, 144, 146, 156
Muller, Ray, 80, 121, 134

N

National Evangelical Anglican
    Congress (NEAC), 42
National Service Committee, 26, 45, 76,
    132, 230
Neo-Pentecostalism, 14, 39
Newbigin, Lesslie, 86, 104, 201
New Delhi Assembly (1961), 197, 206,
    208, 223
Nottingham 1973, 67, 92, 124, 125, 133,
    134, 146

O

O'Brien, Veronica, 123
O'Connor, Edward, 46
Oneness Pentecostal, 41
open system, 184, 185, 189, 190, 194,
    202
Owen, Harold, 134, 135, 136

P

Packer, Jim, 26, 35, 42
Paraclete, 10, 174, 191–195, 202, 217,
    218, 219, 240, 242
parousia, 12, 177, 240, 248
Pawson, David, 36, 70, 74, 84, 108, 136
perichoresis, 10, 213–216
Pethrus, Lewi, 78
Petit, Ian, 116, 118, 122, 132, 134
Pieris, Aloysius, 10, 219
Pride, Fred, 134, 136, 138

prophecy, 10, 16, 75, 85, 89, 90, 126,
    148, 149, 151, 153, 162, 172,
    179, 181, 187, 188, 193, 194,
    198, 214, 217, 231, 248
Pulkingham, Graham, 58 80, 103
Pusey, Michael, 134, 136

Q

Quy, Douglas, 39, 40, 110, 124

R

Ranaghan, Kevin, 6, 72, 80, 114, 126,
    135, 136, 138, 139
Reid, Gavin, 35, 101, 105
restorationist, 13
Richards, Billy, 38
Richards, John, 36, 53, 84, 102, 128
Roman Catholic charismatic, 45–47,
    114, 119, 123, 138, 169, 230
Roman Catholic charismatic renewal,
    76, 114, 118, 168, 225, 230, 234
Roman Catholic-Charismatic dialogue,
    46, 99, 120
Roman Catholic-Pentecostal dialogue,
    235
Roman Catholic Renewal Committee,
    46

S

Sacraments, 167, 171, 184, 187, 188,
    194, 197, 206, 213
Smail, Tom, 6, 8, 15, 16, 28, 32, 34, 35,
    36, 39, 42, 44, 46–51, 54, 55,
    59, 60, 62, 67, 70, 71, 84, 85, 89,
    91–95, 97, 100, 102, 108, 110,
    112, 113, 116, 117, 118, 120,
    121, 129, 130, 132, 133, 145,
    149, 150, 151, 155, 166, 178, 218
speaking in tongues/tongues, 10, 36,
    38, 65, 126, 133, 143–146, 148,
    151–153, 159, 162, 172, 175,
    179, 181, 188, 193, 198, 217,
    231, 233

Spirit baptism/Baptism in the Spirit, 12, 13, 16, 36, 37, 42, 46, 65, 74, 75, 82, 84, 87, 100, 105–7, 121, 122, 140, 145, 216, 217, 219, 220, 222, 234

Spiriti praesens, 10, 216–222, 232, 245

Stott, John, 35, 41, 42, 65

Suenens, Léon Joseph, 35, 47, 69, 99, 116, 118, 124, 125, 165, 168, 170, 184–186, 194, 229, 236, 237

Sullivan, Emmanuel, 85, 95, 122–125, 139

T

Targett, Mike, 45

Temple Trust, 62, 63, 79, 80, 81

theologia prima, 161, 162, 164, 181

Theological Renewal, 34, 50, 51

Toronto Blessing, 12

Toronto Statement, 197

Tugwell, Simon, 71, 84, 114, 119

U

Uppsala Assembly, 199, 205, 207

Urquhart, Colin, 75, 103

V

Van der Veken, Jan, 107, 116

Vatican II/ the second Vatican Council, 8, 9, 16, 100, 138, 167, 176, 188, 198, 203, 209, 210– 213, 221–229, 234–239, 242, 245, 247, 248

visible unity, 10, 176, 197–203, 208–211, 222, 239, 243

Visser't Hooft, W. A., 18, 196, 204, 208, 223, 224

W

Walker, Tom, 8, 20, 35, 73, 103, 146, 149

Wallis, Arthur, 43, 81, 90, 110

Watson, David, 35, 41, 70, 101, 105, 137, 138

Watson, Merv and Merla, 70, 97

Westminster 1975, 45, 47, 51, 59, 61, 63, 65, 67, 71–76, 87–89, 93, 97, 101–108, 111–116, 124, 125, 128, 129, 133, 134, 142, 148, 149, 156, 165, 170, 173

Westminster 1977, 37, 64, 68, 69, 71–75, 94, 100–109, 111,112, 116, 120, 123, 129, 130, 132, 139, 142, 144, 146, 156, 167, 173, 195

Westminster 1979, 69, 71, 85, 89, 95, 100–104, 108, 110–112, 118, 120, 125, 130–133

Wilkerson, Ralph, 110, 113

Williams, J. Rodman, 83–85, 107, 113

World Council of Churches/WCC, 2, 3, 6, 8, 9, 105, 195–199, 203–205, 208–212, 221–225, 234–239, 245–248

Y

Youth with a Mission (YWAM), 112